THE SPANISH CIVIL WAR
AND THE BRITISH LEFT

For Lee and Pete

THE SPANISH CIVIL WAR AND THE BRITISH LEFT

Political Activism and the Popular Front

LEWIS H. MATES

Tauris Academic Studies
LONDON • NEW YORK

Published in 2007 by Tauris Academic Studies,
an imprint of I.B.Tauris & Co Ltd
6 Salem Road, London W2 4BU
175 Fifth Avenue, New York NY 10010
www.ibtauris.com

In the United States of America and Canada distributed by Palgrave Macmillan,
a division of St. Martin's Press, 175 Fifth Avenue, New York NY 10010

ISBN: 978 1 84511 298 1

A full CIP record for this book is available from the British Library
A full CIP record for this book is available from the Library of Congress

Library of Congress catalog card: available

Printed and bound in India by Thomson Press India Limited
camera-ready copy supplied by katherine@projectpublish.com

CONTENTS

ABBREVIATIONS

ACTU	Association of Catholic Trade Unionists
AEU	Amalgamated Engineering Union
AGM	Annual General Meeting
AR	Annual Report
ASW	Amalgamated Society of Woodworkers
BCC	Basque Children's Committee
BCPL	Birmingham Council for Peace and Liberty
BLPES	British Library of Political and Economic Science
BUF	British Union of Fascists
CAPR	Council of Action for Peace and Reconstruction
CCC	Churchill College, Cambridge
CLP	Constituency Labour Party
CNT	Confederación Nacional de Trabajo
CP	Communist Party (of Great Britain)
CYMS	Catholic Young Men's Society
DCFLP	Durham County Federation of Labour Parties
DMA	Durham Miners' Association
DMOR	Durham Miners' Offices, Redhill
DRO	Durham Record Office
EC	Executive Committee
GPL	Gateshead Public Library
IBDWAC	International Brigade Dependants and Wounded Aid Committee
ILP	Independent Labour Party
IWM	Imperial War Museum
LBC	Left Book Club
LHASC	Labour History Archive and Study Centre, Manchester

LLP	Local Labour Party
LNU	League of Nations Union
LP&TC	Labour Party and Trades Council
LSC	Labour Spain Committee
MFGB	Miners' Federation of Great Britain
MML	Marx Memorial Library
MP	Member of Parliament
NAC	National Administrative Council (of the ILP)
NALGO	National Association of Local Government Offices
NCL	National Council of Labour
NEC	National Executive Committee (of the Labour Party)
NEFTC	North-east Federation of Trades Councils
NJCSR	National Joint Committee for Spanish Relief
NMA	Northumberland Miners' Association
NUJ	National Union of Journalists
NUR	National Union of Railwaymen
NUWM	National Unemployed Workers' Movement
NPL	Newcastle Public Library
NRL	Newcastle Robinson Library
NRO	Northumberland Record Office
NTFLP	Northumberland and Tyneside Federation of Labour Parties
PLP	Parliamentary Labour Party
POUM	Partido Obrero de Unificación Marxista
PPC	Prospective Parliamentary Candidate
SCC	Spain Campaign Committee
SDPC	Sunderland and District Peace Council
SMAC	Spanish Medical Aid Committee
SSPL	South Shields Public Library
SWMF	South Wales Miners' Federation
TGWU	Transport and General Workers' Union
TJPC	Tyneside Joint Peace Council
TUC	Trades Union Congress
TWAS	Tyne and Wear Archives Service
UDC	Urban District Council
VIAS	Voluntary Industrial Aid for Spain
WMRC	Warwick Modern Records Centre
YCL	Young Communist League
YWCA	Young Women's Christian Association

ACKNOWLEDGEMENTS

George Orwell claimed that history ended in 1936. For myself, it actually really began then; well, then and 1990, when I first read *Homage to Catalonia*. It seemed natural to look at the north-east labour movement and the Spanish Civil War for my undergraduate dissertation in 1994, which is when this book really began its gestation. In one way or another, the subject has been with me ever since, through my Masters and PhD studies (both British Academy funded) and beyond. Researching the dissertation, and especially interviewing contemporaries, really fired my passion for historical inquiry. Sadly, many of those I interviewed then, or subsequently, have passed away including Jack Lawther (1996), Frank Graham (2006), Len Edmondson, Dave Atkinson and Walter Nunn (all in 2007). It really seemed like the end of an era and I sincerely hope that I do none of their memories an injustice. When Orwell wrote that history ended in 1936, he was referring to the deliberate manufacturing of false evidence; battles that never happened, and so forth. He had very much in mind the problems facing future historians. Clearly, this remains a highly controversial and contested area, but it seems obligatory for commentators after the event to attempt as much as possible – and with an awareness of the influences that they bring to the subject – a more independent analysis. There is no intention in any way to belittle the achievements of the left, nor to denigrate the great personal sacrifices so many made in this period in different ways. Indeed, that these sacrifices did not, in many ways, bring the desired (and also, arguably, deserved) results requires explanation. In examining political ideas and knowledge on the left, and how they influenced the thought and praxis of activists and institutions, this book tentatively considers some elements of a possible explanation.

Martin Pugh first got me started on my BA dissertation and has been my supervisor, advisor and friend ever since. It is to him that I owe the greatest debt. In terms of comments on parts of this book, I would also like to thank Gidon Cohen who has been very supportive and helped further my knowledge in many ways and Tom Buchanan, who generously commented on an early draft of chapter three. Peter Mates has offered, as usual, many useful comments on the text.

Very many have helped me in varying ways on this book. My thanks first to those who kindly offered their memories: Harry Clarke, Mrs. Gill, Joyce Hall, Graham Holtham, Tommy Kerr, Bill Reynolds, Moira Tattam, Brian Walsh and Bert Ward. Don Watson, Jim Carmody and Kevin Davies have all been extraordinarily generous with information, help and advice. Mark Annis, Craig Armstrong, Hester Barron, Mrs. J. Burns, Ray Challinor, John Charlton, Joe Conway, Douglas Davies, Dave Douglass, Ally Fisher, Andrew Flinn, Sheila Gray, Martin Green, Kath Grimshaw, H.G. Hansen, Reg Hughes, Dan Jackson, Charles Jepson, Mr. J.M. Kennedy, Rob Lee, Simon Oram, Kevin Parkes, Matt Perry, Ray Physick, Val Reynolds, Peter Rose, John Sanderson, Marlene Sidaway, Gordon Smith, John Temple, Andrew Thorpe, Nigel Todd, Natasha Vall and Steve Wilson have all offered information, advice or help.

The staff of libraries and archives were invariably friendly and helpful and I would like particularly to thank Carolyn Ball and the staff at Tyne and Wear Archives, Doris and Keith at South Shields Public Library and David Hopper who kindly allowed me access to DMA records at Redhill. The financial help and other support from the Politics Department of Durham University was gratefully received. I am also thankful to the staff at I.B.Tauris who have worked with me so patiently, Elizabeth Munns and Lester Crook, and Katherine Holmes of ProjectPublish. The interpretation and mistakes are, naturally, all my own work.

Finally, personal thanks: to those friends who have put up with my moaning; you know who you are and you're all in some way culpable. Cerys has done her very best to help by making sure I'm up and at it bright and early every morning: it is certainly a different book now she is in the world. Extra special thanks to Lucy who has consistently helped and supported (and put up with) me. To paraphrase Bill Muckle (of 1926 *Flying Scotsman* fame), she is 'one of the best' and I hope to repay the debt one day. I'd like to dedicate this book to my long-suffering parents, Lee and Pete, without whom I wouldn't be here. Thanks for everything and "Viva el gen de fracaso!"

Map of North-East England (1936)

(Constituencies marked in bold)

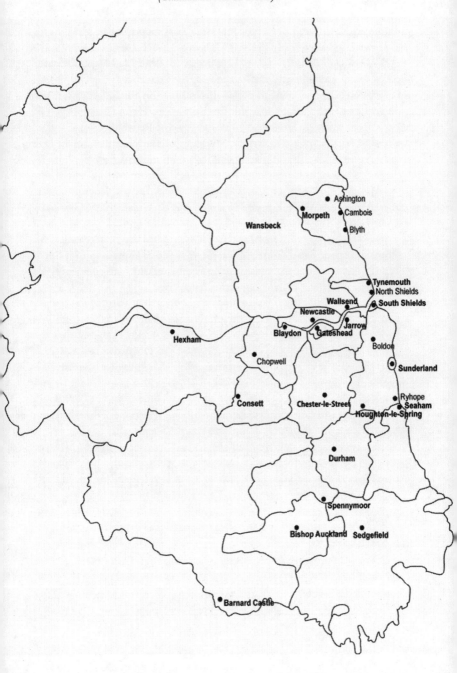

INTRODUCTION

For sections of the British left, the conflict in Spain and the debate over the necessity of a popular front at home were inseparable. It was a popular front alliance of Spanish Liberal and Socialist parties that elements of the Spanish armed forces, supported by Hitler and Mussolini, revolted against on 18 July 1936. The popular front administration had come to power only five months earlier, replacing a Catholic Conservative government that progressives feared would turn fascist. Even many members of the influential Spanish anarcho-syndicalist trade union, the CNT (Confederación Nacional de Trabajo), who had previously campaigned for abstention at elections, voted for popular front candidates in February 1936.[1]

The Spanish broad left imported the popular front from France. In February 1934, a general strike called jointly by French Socialists and Communists defeated a threatened fascist coup. The left parties reached a formal agreement in July 1934 and three months later, the French CP adopted a programme for an alliance of all progressive and democratic forces under the banner of a 'people's front' (i.e. popular front). The international Communist movement endorsed these developments when its seventh World Congress supported the 'Dimitrov resolution' in the summer of 1935.

This was the culmination of a dramatic about turn in international Communist policy. From 1928, the Communist International (Comintern) pursued the 'class against class' policy, which regarded the leaders of Social Democratic parties (such as the British Labour Party) as 'social fascists' and the greatest enemy of the Communists. However, many on the left ascribed Hitler's seizure of power in January 1933 to the fatal split in the German working-class movement between the Socialists and Communists (the German CP had been the largest in Europe) engendered by this policy.

In Britain, the CP gradually discarded 'class against class' and began renewed efforts to promote cooperation with Labour on the left and, later, to agitate for a broader alliance. Certainly, on the continent, the popular front strategy appeared to work; a popular front alliance also prevailed at the French polls in May 1936. Thus, many on the left of the labour movement, to some degree influenced by the CP, also began to support the popular front and held Spain as an example of why a progressive alliance was imperative.[2] In Spain, the battle of the era was taking place: that of democracy against fascism. Coming soon after Mussolini's aggression in Abysinnia and Hitler's more recent remilitarisation of the Rhineland, Spain was more evidence that fascism was on the march. George Orwell wrote: 'When the fighting broke out on 18 July [1936] it is probable that every anti-Fascist in Europe felt a thrill of hope. For here, at last, apparently, was democracy standing up to Fascism. For years past the so-called democratic countries had been surrendering to Fascism at every step. … It seemed – possibly it was – the turning of the tide'.[3] Thus, the Republic's struggle was a symbol of the anti-fascist fight: a theatre of war where fascism could be faced head on. As the Republic was defending itself rather than seeking imperial advantage, it forced many on the Labour left to reassess their pacifism.

For the left, the Spanish Republic had to be saved, to halt the seemingly inexorable advance of expansionist fascism. In order to do this, the British government's support for 'Non-Intervention' had to end. A policy ostensibly designed to contain the war in Spain and prevent it from escalating into a pan-European conflagration, in reality Non-Intervention denied the Spanish Republic's rights in international law to buy arms for its own defence. Nazi Germany and fascist Italy, both signatories of the pact, flouted it by supporting Franco militarily. As recent research has shown, the somewhat misnamed 'Non-Intervention' probably fatally hampered the Republic's war effort.[4]

Britain's key role in forging and maintaining the increasingly obvious sham of Non-Intervention made the British left especially significant in the Republic's struggle. However, British trade union and Labour Party leaders, guided by TUC secretary Sir Walter Citrine, initially endorsed Non-Intervention to the chagrin of the left inside and outside the party. This occurred partly as the leadership was also well aware of the possible links between the Republic and the project for a British popular front.

Support for a popular front government in Spain made it far more diffi-cult for Labour to remain opposed to a similar arrangement at home, especially as the Soviet Union began supporting the Republic.

The unwelcome spectre of cooperation with the Communist Party once again loomed. Labour had a history of opposing all CP attempts to affiliate after the latter's founding in 1920. In 1933, the party again rejected renewed Communist overtures, proscribing eleven Communist ancillary organisations. In October 1934, the TUC issued the notorious 'Black Cir-culars' in an attempt to proscribe Communists from sitting on trades councils and holding official positions within trade unions. While the pro-posal to allow the CP to affiliate to Labour in autumn 1935 received a third of the vote at Labour conference (the largest vote the party secured at any Labour conference), it was insufficient for success. Still, the party retained some powerful friends, impressed by continental popular front successes. In October 1936, Durham miner Will Lawther explained the MFGB's decision to support Communist affiliation to Labour by citing the recent French popular front victory. Lawther argued that unity, which was essential in the fight against fascism, would also bring 'that new vigour that comes from the realisation of united strength'.[5] But these arguments did not convince. In autumn 1936, the Labour leadership could still not contemplate association with a party that had condemned them as 'social fascists' until very recently.

Furthermore, there were also strong objections within the labour movement to the popular front's advocacy of cooperation with liberals. The Labour Party was relatively young in the 1930s. Established in 1900, the Labour Party only began to become a serious national political force when it adopted a new constitution and structure in 1918. It had grown at first through an electoral pact with the liberals before 1914, but in the 1920s the parties had an often difficult relationship, especially during the two Labour administrations. In the 1931 general election, liberals formed a coalition with Conservatives and some ex-Labour Party members – inclu-ding former party leader Ramsay Macdonald – standing on a 'National' ticket that smashed Labour. A distrust of liberals in what remained of the Labour Party was to be expected.

These were not the only considerations for the Labour leadership, however. As Tom Buchanan has shown, they were sceptical of the Repub-lic's claims to be regarded as a democracy and wary of many of Spain's left leaders.[6] They were also worried that a strong pro-Republic stance would alienate their own Catholic members, particularly trade unionists, some of whom were appalled by lurid press reports of attacks on the church in Republican areas. In certain areas, Labour seats depended largely on the votes of working-class Catholics.[7]

Ironically enough, the labour movement leadership, which had moved further to the right with the recent elections of Ernest Bevin and Hugh Dalton as chairs of the TUC General Council and NEC respectively, used the popular front to *defend* Non-Intervention at Labour Party annual conference in October 1936. It claimed that British Labour's opposition to Non-Intervention would place considerable political pressure on the French popular front government, which was seriously divided on the issue. When Arthur Greenwood defended Non-Intervention as the only practicable policy and 'a very bad second best', the left demurred with Stafford Cripps, Nye Bevan and Northumberland aristocrat Sir Charles Trevelyan launching devastating attacks on the leadership. Trevelyan told them: 'You are beggared of policy at this moment ... When the last great war that is looming comes and when Germany and Japan crash in to destroy Soviet Russia, I hope then the Labour Party will have some other policy to offer than sympathy, accompanied by bandages and cigarettes'.[8] In response, a 'huge cheer hit the platform' and Bevin commented 'God help the Labour movement'.[9] Yet, once again, the left's arguments did not hold sway. The leadership had used the movement's machinery, including the National Council of Labour (a committee composed of TUC and Labour Party leaders), to good effect. By the time Labour Party members had a chance to discuss the issue at the annual conference, the unions – at that time the movement's most influential institutions – had already endorsed the policy.[10]

A good deal of bitterness and confusion within the party's grassroots followed in the wake of the 1936 Labour Party conference, as, in refusing to condemn Non-Intervention, Labour apparently had abandoned 'political space' on the issue. The CP regarded this as an opportunity to capitalise on grassroots disenchantment, attempting to draw Labour activists and, indeed, liberals and others into their orbit through campaigning for the Republic. Indeed, this work began before Labour conference, when, in August 1936, Communist and Socialist doctors established the Spanish Medical Aid Committee (SMAC). This stimulated the formation of SMACs at local level.

The CP also led the British Youth Peace Assembly – composed of nearly forty political and religious youth organisations formed after the first World Youth Peace Congress in 1935 – that formed a 'Youth Foodship Committee' to organise collections throughout the country. January 1937 saw the establishment of the National Joint Committee for Spanish Relief (NJCSR), an umbrella body designed to coordinate the various campaigns that were springing up. In the north-east and Liverpool, Defence Committees emerged to support the deported north-eastern crew of the *Linaria* who staged a sit-in strike in Boston after being instructed to take a cargo of nitrates to Sevilla, a Franco held port, in February 1937.

In early May 1937, representatives from the NJCSR, Salvation Army, TUC, Quakers and the Catholic Church formed the Basque Children's Committee (BCC) to help care for 4,000 children who were refugees of the Franco offensive on Euskadi. In late 1938, the intense refugee crisis in Republican Spain engendered by the increasing loss of territory to Franco spawned the 'foodship' campaigns – twenty-nine in total – throughout Britain. The ILP, Churches and other groupings had all organised foodships before late 1938. There were specifically Christian foodships for the Basques, for example. An innovative way of providing support and in important respects quite different to those other campaigns developed in Geoffrey Pyke's 'Voluntary Industrial Aid for Spain' initiative from 1937, through which workers could donate their skills and labour in their workplaces to refurbish vehicles for use by the Republic.[11] Jim Fyrth claimed that tens of thousands in Britain were involved in efforts to support the Republic. Indeed, Fyrth went as far as to claim what he deemed the 'Aid Spain movement' became 'the most widespread and representative mass movement in Britain since the mid-nineteenth century days of Chartism and the Anti-Corn Law Leagues, and the most outstanding example of international solidarity in British history'.[12]

While the CP or party activists played roles of widely varying degrees of significance in these domestic campaigns, the main manifestation of militant solidarity with the Republic that was unequivocally the CP's own took the form of organising individuals to fight in the Republic's International Brigade. A Comintern initiative, this was organised by its western Bureau from September 1936 and around 2,500 Britons served.[13] In order to support those affected by the consequences of armed conflict, the party established the International Brigade Dependants and Wounded Aid Committee (IBDWAC) in February 1937. In spring 1937, the government re-invoked the Foreign Enlistment Act as a deterrent to potential brigaders.

In comparison, the official movement's response seemed lacklustre at best. With an official policy of support for Non-Intervention, the labour leadership encouraged the financial support of their Spanish Workers'

fund, which fed into the International Solidarity Fund (ISF). It also officially joined in the Basque Children's Committee coalition because, as Buchanan argued, it could retain political control.[14] Fundraising appeared to
placate elements of the official movement. However, other sections on
both the industrial and political wings – such as the South Wales miners
and many constituency parties – remained discontented with their movement's inactivity and sought to alter it and campaign on the issue in the
public sphere.[15] Labour MPs including Ellen Wilkinson helped to organise
an all-party 'National Emergency Conference' on Spain on 23 April 1938
at which over 1,203 separate institutions including trade unions and Labour, liberals and Communists were represented.[16]

Constituency party discontent took institutional form in the Labour
Spain Committee (LSC), which emerged from the Constituency Parties
Movement, an institution that successfully achieved stronger representation for constituencies on the party's NEC in 1937. However, this success,
claimed James Jupp, satisfied many CLPs and thus weakened the popular
front.[17] Furthermore, the Labour annual conference was moved back to
Whitsun (before the TUC conference) which unfortunately meant that
there was no Labour conference at all in the crucial year of 1938. Transport House ignored calls for a special conference on the international
situation, and especially that in Spain. By the time of the 1939 Whitsun
Labour Party conference, the Spanish Republic had been defeated and it
seemed that perhaps the government was moving away from appeasement
of its own volition.

After many months of confusing pronouncements and vacillation from
the national leadership, the autumn 1937 Labour Party conference finally
confirmed a new policy of opposition to Non-Intervention. However, the
leadership still seemed reluctant to do anything more than raise money for
humanitarian aid. Some Labour MPs asked questions on the issue in Parliament, but the National Government, which was in a strong parliamentary position, could easily afford to ignore the 'loyal' opposition. The party
created its own official Spain Campaign Committee (SCC) specifically to
campaign for the Republic, but it lapsed into inactivity after holding a
handful of big meetings in December 1937.

As the labour leadership feared, left-wing activists within the official
movement tended to endorse the CP's contention that support for the
Spanish Republic and the popular front at home were inextricably linked:
one led with inexorable logic to the other. Activists in the LSC and SCC
used the issue of Spain to pursue their popular front agenda both inside

and outside the movement. The issue played a key role in the initiatives to promote unity on the left (the 1937 Unity Campaign) and the popular front (the 1938 United Peace Alliance campaign and Cripps' 1939 Petition Campaign). While events on the international scene in 1938 – the resignation of foreign secretary Eden in February 1938 over Chamberlain's conduct of foreign policy, the annexation of Austria by Nazi Germany in March 1938 and the Munich crisis in September 1938 amongst others – all suggested the urgent need to replace Chamberlain, Spain remained central. Thus, Michael Foot was one of many to note that the primary purpose of the popular front was to save 'Spain'. When Franco marched into Madrid in March 1939, Cripps' campaign lost momentum as 'there was no longer a Spain to save'.[18] However, the popular fronters' failure to establish firmly their project before the Republic fell (as after) revealed a difficult truth. Many labour movement activists shared their view that the conflict was of fundamental importance and thought that the movement should do more. But they did not draw the conclusion that the popular front was the best way to help the Republic.

Popular fronters and most Labour activists drew from the same (dominant) discourse on Spain: that the conflict was essentially about democracy (the Republic) against fascism (Franco). However, elements of the British left adopted another significantly different understanding of the conflict and of the popular front. Most important in this context was the Independent Labour Party (ILP) that had disaffiliated from Labour in 1932 and subsequently moved to the left.[19] It aligned with a dissident anti-Stalinist Marxist party in Spain, the POUM (Partido Obrero de Unificación Marxista). This alternative discourse held that it was nascent revolution that had taken place in significant areas of Republican territory, not capitalist democracy that required defending.

This discourse also critiqued popular frontism. In order to appeal to liberals, the popular front required the jettisoning of the doctrine that fascism was the product of capitalist crisis. This held that any capitalist society was susceptible to fascism; a doctrine that was the desperate final attempt of the ruling class to retain its power in societies that appeared to be disintegrating through economic crisis. The popular front, by contrast, posited that fascism was a threat to 'democracy' and that all democratic ('progressive') forces needed to combine in order to defeat it. Crucially, it rejected the idea that fascism could not be defeated without overthrowing capitalism. Thus, as Orwell (an ILP member for a short period) wrote, the popular front had to depict fascism as 'a kind of meaningless wickedness, an aberration, "mass sadism", the sort of thing that would happen if you suddenly let loose an asylum full of homicidal maniacs'.[20] Orwell, who served in the POUM militia, was thus disdainful of the popular front: it 'is only an idea, but it has already produced the nauseous spectacle of bishops, Communists, cocoa magnates, publishers, duchesses, and Labour MPs marching arm in arm to the tune of "Rule Britannia"'.[21]

The ILP's support for the united (or workers') front was predicated on the understanding that to eliminate fascism, socialism would have to replace capitalism, and thus only socialist parties should cooperate. In contrast, Communists and many on the Labour left saw the united front of 'working-class' parties merely as a prerequisite for a successful popular front.[22] In 1936, British Communist leader Palme Dutt claimed that the united front would form the 'inner core' of a popular front coalition.[23] Disagreement over this fundamental question of political understanding and strategy bitterly divided the two left parties in Britain, and elsewhere. (The CP even abandoned this precondition when a united front began to appear unachievable in Britain). The CP's advocacy of the popular front, which necessitated 'class collaboration', permitted the ILP to criticise it from a left-wing position. The ILP itself advocated what it deemed a 'workers' front' of socialist parties, though Fenner Brockway, for one, did not dismiss out-of-hand every aspect of the popular front.[24] Bizarrely, it also allowed the Labour Party to criticise the CP for abandoning socialism. Times were strange indeed.

Given these vast differences in understanding, cooperation between the parties in the 1937 Unity Campaign was always likely to be strained. Still, there was a short history of pre-popular front cooperation between the parties that began in 1933. An important arena had been opposition to the British Union of Fascists, most famously, perhaps, in the organised disruption of the BUF Olympia Rally in June 1934. However, from the outset, both parties' involvement rested on calculations of how they could attract members of the other party. The ILP lost members who opposed cooperation with the CP in places like Lancashire. ILP criticism of the Soviet Union (such as its entry into the League of Nations in 1934) and fundamental disagreements over issues such as the Italian invasion of Abyssinia (the ILP regarded it as a conflict between imperialisms, the CP supported Abyssinia against fascist Italy) revealed deep-seated schisms. While popular fronters hoped that Spain would advance their project, the issue, paradoxically, was crucial to destroying most understanding between the CP and ILP. The Communist run Catalan police attempted to seize the CNT-controlled Barcelona telephone exchange in an effort to assert Republican government control. This provoked the 'Maydays' events: street fighting between the government forces and anarchist militants, supported by the POUM, which was subsequently scapegoated and vilified by the CP and its governmental allies.[25] Events in Spain inevitably provoked acrimony in Britain and the Unity Campaign disintegrated: aided, naturally, by the Labour leadership's proscription of the Socialist League, which responded by duly committing suicide. With failures both to promote left unity, and to make headway in the Labour Party, the emphasis altered to attempting to build a popular front without first achieving 'unity' on the left. The consequences of the association drawn between the British popular front and the Republic's cause were grave indeed.

Historical Debates

There is a tremendous volume of literature covering many aspects of the Spanish conflict from various perspectives. Indeed, there seem few better subjects to illustrate the contention that history is a battleground for ideologies. As Noam Chomsky brilliantly argued in this context, 'liberal' historians' 'objectivity' can be as problematic as the rest.[26] The first published works focussing specifically on the British International Brigaders and the solidarity campaigns in Britain were informed by authors favourable to what could be deemed a 'popular frontist' perspective. This history largely endorsed what was, broadly speaking, the CP and much of the left's attitude at that time. The term 'popular frontist' is useful in this context as it maintains continuity with a debate between Tom Buchanan and Jim Fyrth in the early 1990s and it firmly locates this perspective in the period in which it was advocated by the Communist Party and those sympathetic to it on the wider left, i.e. 1935–1939.

The popular frontist historiography sought to celebrate the achievement of the Communist inspired and run International Brigade and the so-called 'Aid Spain movement' in Britain, in which the CP supposedly played the crucial inspirational and leadership role. A salient aspect of this treatment is the acceptance, usually implicit, of the popular front as both valid and effective in informing these types of pro-Republican activism. The clearly wide-ranging involvement, in terms of social class and political perspective, of individuals in many of these campaigns prompted the claim that, in the 'Aid Spain movement', something akin to the British popular front became flesh. This perspective was clear in the first major works published on the topic. Bill Alexander, an ex-brigader himself, wrote what could be deemed the 'official' history of the British battalion in 1982.[27] Hywel Francis' book on the response to the conflict in South Wales – he published an article on the topic as early as 1970 – appeared in 1984.[28] A groundbreaking study of grassroots activities, it was the culmination of work Francis undertook through the South Wales Miners' Library, including interviewing many brigade veterans. These interviews formed the bulk of material on which the book drew and it provided a fascinating insight into brigader's attitudes and backgrounds. However, the discussion of the Spanish aid campaigns in South Wales was scant in comparison. A significant but unpublished study that adopted a more critical and detached analysis was Peter Drake's 1977 Master's thesis on the Birmingham labour movement.[29]

In 1986, the fiftieth anniversary of the outbreak of the conflict, Jim Fyrth published *The Signal Was Spain*, which considered what he (as Francis before him) deemed the British 'Aid Spain movement'. The 1986 anniversary spawned several more 'grassroots' works – in the sense of the authors, their methods and their subject material – dealing with various areas of enquiry, often written by ex-brigaders or activists and again with a popular frontist perspective.[30] All of these accounts tended to consider the major Spanish aid campaigns together, which had the effect of implying that they were of equal political significance: an initiative for a strike against Non-Intervention, for example, receiving the same treatment as one for collecting for a foodship on a humanitarian basis. This was symptomatic of a more general tendency in popular frontist accounts to depict the conflict and the solidarity stimulated by it – as many contemporaries did – as a cause that was 'black and white'.[31] The 'tragic' or 'heroic' approaches that traditionally have characterised much writing about the left, often did little to elucidate important areas of enquiry.[32]

There was also a certain irony in these popular frontist accounts. While keen to claim that many of the Spanish aid campaigns took on the appearance of popular fronts, they also tended to demote the popular front policy *itself* to something of a footnote in the history of the time. Francis, for example, claimed that the Communist Party in 1933–36 was compelled to embrace a moderate policy due to the prevailing economic circumstances, neglecting to mention the Comintern and its popular front policy, thereby implying that the party could choose its policies depending on its indigenous understanding of conditions on the ground.[33] Fyrth mentioned the popular front (or 'people's front' as he preferred) a good deal, but usually only in the context of likening it to various Spanish aid campaigns.[34]

These accounts, by omission, suggested that national Communist Parties were far freer from Comintern control to pursue their own course and political policies than in fact they were. They also neglected the real tensions, confusions and difficulties that a policy so radically different from that which went before brought the party and its activists in both theory and praxis. The implications of the application of such a policy on Republican solidarity campaigning were also neglected: there was little suggestion (particularly in Fyrth's work) that the campaigns could have been *better,* or *more effective* than they were; the tone was broadly one of celebration. Given the widespread prestige that the Soviet Union enjoyed on the British left in this period, the CP's popular front policy could not but come to define the way much of the Labour left saw the conflict, especially its revolutionary aspect. Therefore the CP, while it was not instrumental in ensuring that the Labour left *did* react to the Spanish conflict, it went a long way in determining *how* it reacted.

The 1990s brought new, more critical voices that challenged the popular frontists'. The first was Tom Buchanan, who published *The Spanish Civil War and the British Labour Movement* in 1991. An authoritative and analytical account, it concentrated on the national picture, but also drew on events at grassroots, particularly in discussing the attitudes of Catholics in the labour movement and rank-and-file initiatives. Buchanan concentrated on explaining why most of the national leaders of the British labour movement treated the issue of support of the Republic with caution or even hostility. He noted that no one had attempted to understand the conflict from the leadership's perspective, though his was not an 'apologia for labour's leaders'.[35] This contextualised their reasons for initially supporting Non-Intervention and for being reluctant to do much to oppose it later on. Rejecting the popular frontist tendency to caricature the labour leadership, Buchanan argued that their main motives were a desire to retain control over 'their' structures, and to prevent their tearing apart by the passions – primarily religious – unleashed by the conflict.

In the same year, Buchanan published a critique of the popular frontist approach to which Fyrth responded in 1993.[36] Rob Stradling also brought a new approach with works on Cardiff, aspects of the International Brigade and, most recently, Wales.[37] In 1998, James Hopkins subjected Bill Alexander's work to probing appraisal, drawing on material in the newly opened Moscow CP archives. Hopkins' book broke from the popular frontist approach, but curiously it too barely mentioned the popular front policy itself.[38] In 2004, Richard Baxell provided another perspective on the

British International Brigaders.[39] Angela Jackson published a book on the role of women in 2002, a hitherto largely unexplored area. However, she maintained much of the popular frontist discourse, again without giving its impact much direct attention.[40] The 1990s also saw the continued production of local studies, influenced to considerably varying degrees by this new, more critical approach.[41] Don Watson and John Corcoran's work on the north-east, for example, contained a balanced and sympathetic treatment of the ILP's role in the conflict, a characteristic that a contemporary activist criticised in an otherwise favourable review in the *Morning Star*.[42] All these studies, however, contain useful source material that can lend itself to other interpretations.

Notwithstanding all the published research of the last fifteen years, there is a good deal that remains broadly unexplored. One of the most significant areas in this context is the extent and nature of the solidarity expressed at grassroots level, including the effects of the experience of brigaders in Spain and their consequent impact on the issue on the home front; the nature of 'official' labour movement support for the Republic at grassroots; the extent to which Spain stimulated joint activity on the left and support for the popular front; and the nature and extent of the Spanish aid campaigns and their short and longer term effects.

Along with this there remain questions about the impact of the popular front policy itself. Left-wing activists are usually regarded as paying great attention to the ideas that inform their actions: Marxist and other theorists' ideas in general, and, for Communists of varying sorts, how these are, on a more prosaic level, interpreted in the 'party line' at any given time. Indeed, the popular front policy was particularly problematic in this respect, as it not only reversed the Communist movement's ultra-sectarian policy of the near past, it also placed the Communist Party – theoretically if not necessarily in practice – to the political right of the Labour Party. The implications of the popular front for the party were immense. But in what ways and to what extent did grassroots activists and institutions grasp and apply these implications in relation to the British left's support for the Spanish Republic, and what were their effects? Notwithstanding Tom Buchanan's work, there remains more to explore around the impact of the popular front on the rhetoric, thinking and praxis at grassroots as manifest in the various Spanish solidarity campaigns.

There clearly remains room for new approaches to this subject. Like the popular frontists, this study takes the movement's rank-and-file seriously, with all its conflicting motives, desires and fears, and maintains a healthy degree of scepticism towards the national movement leaders.[43] It thus avoids assessing these activities primarily from a national labour movement leadership perspective. Secondly, the approach places the popular front policy where it should be in this period: at the centre of discussion around the ideas and actions of those who it affected, Communists, many on the Labour left and to some degree, liberals. However, it is careful not to view the *entirety* of grassroots activities and activists through the prism of the popular front. In this, it reflects the majority outlook of the official movement rank-and-file at the time who wanted to act more vigorously on Spain (over time) but who never supported the popular front either implicitly or explicitly. It thus questions Communist claims of leadership in a mass movement.

Indeed, this study seeks, in some respects, to reinstate the somewhat maligned 'moderate' Labour Party grassroots activist in this context. Much of the work in this area implied that Labour activists were powerless or incapable of acting without the initiative of some kind of leadership, be it their own national or regional leadership or that of the Communist Party. It is clear that, while the attitudes and initiatives (or lack) of both the national and regional official movement leaderships and the CP were important in determining and defining what occurred at grassroots level, there were many Labour activists who possessed the political self-confidence and drive to act on their own initiatives – in differing ways and to varying extents – on the issue. Naturally, no grassroots activist of any party (or none) operated in a political and social vacuum and it is necessary to tease out the interplay between the prevalent discourses and their impacts on individuals' ideas and actions.

Thirdly, not only does the approach not assume that the popular front was the best – or even the only – way to aid the Republic, it is critical of a good deal of the popular frontist discourse. Indeed, it argues that the popular front acted to the detriment of a clear understanding of what was happening in Spain, why Non-Intervention had to be ended and what was needed to achieve this end. It thus rejects the claims by both national Labour leaders and popular fronters that there was nothing else to be done and suggests that other modes of action informed by another discourse could have served the Republic better.

The basis of empirical material for this – the first full length published work on British grassroots activism and activities (ostensibly in support of the Republic) outside of Wales – is a detailed case study of north-east England. Stuart Macintyre ably demonstrated that studies of particular localities are of value as they enable us 'to say much more about the dynamics of Communism and militant working-class politics than has emerged so far from national and institutional accounts'.[44] Indeed, there are many examples of regional studies that have thrown light on events of national importance.[45] The reason for choosing the north-east region is twofold and somewhat paradoxical. It is useful because of both its similarities and its differences with South Wales. On the one hand, the two regions had a good deal in common: both were traditionally reliant on coalmining and shipbuilding industries with similar sized populations of analogous social composition providing comparably strong support for Labour.[46] The two regions' coalfields, particularly, were subject to similar levels of unemployment, being among the first to feel the damaging effects of a downturn on the international markets.

On the other hand, the north-east labour movement was usually regarded as politically moderate and 'loyal' to the national leadership. This made the north-east more representative of what was occurring at grassroots level in much of Britain, in contrast to South Wales, which had a more left-wing political culture in some significant respects.[47] In some South Wales coalfield areas the Communist Party came to dominate in this period in a manner that it never managed in Britain save in parts of east London and Scotland. Still, the CP, like the ILP, Socialist League and liberals, all had an organisational presence in the north-east. Furthermore, while Labour was strong in areas of the north-east, it was far from hegemonic throughout, again making the region more representative of the country as a whole (see below). That said, no single British region could claim to represent the whole country in microcosm. Still, the existent body of work on this subject allows for insights through comparison with other localities. Indeed, Newcastle and Birmingham shared a degree of similarity as in both Labour was relatively weak in predominantly working-class cities (though there was relatively little unemployment in Birmingham by 1936 and trade unionism was also significantly weaker there).[48]

The 'North-East': Definitions, Geographies and Background

For the purposes of this study, the north-east is defined as the area broadly covered by the great northern coalfield of Durham and Northumberland. There were 23 parliamentary constituencies in this area in 1936–39, with an electorate of 1.23 million. Newcastle was the 'metropolitan centre' and regional hub of this region, which it dominated in socio-cultural terms.[49] D.J. Rowe noted that region is 'an indeterminate and fluctuating tool with which to attempt to analyse society' and there were certainly strong distinctions within the region between industrial, mining and agricultural areas, that changed over time.[50]

There was a degree of political diversity too. The Tyne was an obvious barrier in terms of north-east political culture, as people at the time were well aware.[51] In the 1935 general election, the Labour Party won one seat (Morpeth) of the nine in Northumbria. Elsewhere north of the Tyne, the 1931 election debacle heralded a period of Conservative dominance. South of the Tyne, Labour was far stronger, taking twelve of fifteen seats in 1935.[52] Margaret Gibb and Maureen Callcott argued that the 1935 general election result was probably the most accurate reflection of Labour's electoral standing in the region. The 1929 result exaggerated Labour's strength: 1931 its weakness.[53] Indeed, Cook and Stevenson pointed out that the 1931 Labour vote in many north-east constituencies was similar or higher than in 1929, the region representing 'perhaps the most interesting display of the solidarity of the Labour vote'.[54] The higher turnout, collapse of the liberal vote, the middle-classes voting Conservative, and peculiar local factors such as Macdonald in Seaham explained Labour's 1931 losses.[55]

The division of the Tyne broadly, but less clearly, defined Labour's fortunes at local level too. The party held only a third of Northumberland County Council seats in 1936. In contrast, four fifths of Durham County Council seats were Labour.[56] Indeed, in 1919, Durham was the first Labour-controlled County Council in the country; uninterrupted Labour control began in 1925.[57] In terms of municipal councils, Labour's highwater mark north of the Tyne came in the early 1930s. In 1934, Labour came within one seat of the controlling Progressives on Newcastle City Council. In 1933, Labour gained control of Wallsend for the first time, but a split brought a crushing defeat and the loss of the council in 1935. In Tynemouth, Labour was fairly moribund and never had more than four out of 36 members on the council before 1938. It had none at all on Morpeth before 1939. However, Labour was electorally dominant in Blyth municipality, the main urban area of Morpeth constituency.

Certainly the Tyne divide was not as strong in terms of municipalities. In 1935, Labour won only tenuous control of Sunderland and Jarrow south of the Tyne (for the first and second times respectively).[58] The party still did not control South Shields or Gateshead (though it was close in both) and it remained weak on Durham City council. Regarding Urban District Councils (UDC), Labour controlled several important localities in Northumberland including Ashington and Newburn. In County Durham, the party held more UDCs. It had 100 per cent representation in Stanley and Hetton-le-Hole UDCs and controlled, with differing majorities, most of the other important UDCs in the county. However, Labour remained some way from controlling the council in the mining and ironworking town of Consett.[59]

The Labour Party remained a relatively young institution and the organisation at constituency and lower levels in the north-east was still developing in this period. The 1918 party constitution introduced 'individual' members' sections, but even where the party was strong, these did not exist in every locality and some had only recently emerged. While the general trend in constituency party membership was positive, some, like Houghton-le-Spring CLP, recorded decreasing memberships in this period.[60]

Sections of the movement, including Seaham and Sedgefield CLPs, began producing their own propaganda journals in this period in a bid to counter the Conservative and liberal-biased regional press.[61] The party's youth section, the Labour League of Youth (LLY) was slowly developing but its tendency to annoy the national leadership led to its dissolution and reestablishment. This, along with defections to the Young Communist League (YCL) in places like Jarrow, left it fairly small in the region during this period, though its branches were still capable of playing a role in Spain related activities.[62] Still, a strong LLY branch in North Shields in February 1939, was, along with a Labour vote that had risen from 2,500 in 1918 to 10,000 in 1935 (the party's local councillors had risen from one to six), given as evidence by one local activist that Labour would win the next election there.[63]

As elsewhere, the trades unions were vital to explaining Labour's initial emergence, growth and vigour at local as well as national levels. The most salient example of this was the DMA, which, with around 125,000 members in 1936, was the largest union in the region. Apart from the shipbuilding and engineering areas of south Tyneside and Sunderland and small pockets of NUR membership the DMA dominated the trade union landscape in County Durham. It also had the highest percentage of members to workers of any British coalfield union in the earlier 1930s.[64] However, the miners operated in an industry that was using more machinery but remained in decline: 40 per cent fewer people worked in the Durham mines in 1934 than a decade earlier.[65]

In contrast to the miners' unions, which could only attempt to maximise their membership in a declining workforce, the general unions, strong on Tyneside and Wearside, had more potential for expansion. By

October 1936, the TGWU northern district's membership of almost 19,000 was the result of recent rapid growth attributed to the effects of rearmament.[66] By February 1938, district membership was 25,000.[67] The general unions, unlike the miners' unions, had grown in recent times from amalgamations; they were strongly centrally controlled and sought to organise, as their names suggested, in many industries: they even encroached on what the miners considered their own territory.[68] Where industries proliferated, trades councils acted as local TUCs, bringing all affiliated union branches in an area together and lending some form of coherence to joint endeavours. Like the unions that composed them, these were also recovering. Newcastle trades council, for example, had 14,882 affiliated members in 73 union branches in 1935, the largest it had been since 1926 (when it was a focal centre during the general strike).[69]

Initially resistant to the fledgling Labour Party, by the 1930s the DMA's conversion to the cause was complete. However, Beynon and Austrin claimed that this occurred 'without the development of vibrant constituency parties. The Party was very much established as the political arm of the trade union'.[70] The latter part of this claim, certainly, appeared valid. The DMA contributed the majority of members and most of the funds to Labour Parties in the county, and it regarded the constituencies that covered mining areas as its own, leading to occasionally embarrassing situations for non-miner MPs like Manny Shinwell in Seaham.[71] At local level, miners' lodges such as Seaham replicated this role, funding and subsequently controlling election candidatures and local councillors.[72] Local Conservatives attacked the DMA for dominating 'the policy of all local government in the county of Durham by placing itself in the position of paymaster and being able to bludgeon almost anyone into their way of thinking'.[73] A miner responded: 'We're not stupid. It is class warfare – and always will be – the poor help the poor'.[74]

The DMA's role in determining regional attitudes in both industrial and political matters was crucial. Beynon and Austrin deemed County Durham the 'classic case' of the dominance of a moderate labour tradition; 'the centre of moderation and respectable Labour politics in Britain ...' where '... officialdom has reigned supreme within the working-class'.[75] However, they argued that 1926 engendered a tremendous disjuncture. In its aftermath, traditional social arrangements were not re-established in the Durham coalfield: 'The "circumstances of class" had come to dominate over the politics of patronage'.[76] This was manifest in the elections of Will Lawther (in 1934) and Sam Watson (in 1935), both with left-wing reputations, as fulltime DMA officials.[77] Indeed, in the case of Watson's election, all of the three final candidates (the other two were Will Pearson of Marsden lodge and George Harvey of Follonsby) were militants.[78] Watson and Lawther remained outnumbered by more moderate DMA officials, but several militants sat for periods on the DMA's executive, allowing the left a degree of influence.

However, aspects of the traditional patterns of behaviour remained, including the strong rank-and-file loyalty to leaders, which, Shinwell claimed, ensured Ramsay Macdonald's electoral victory in Seaham in 1931.[79] The leadership's predisposition to industrial moderation also remained broadly preserved. This longer-term characteristic was evident in its apathy during the General Strike. Yet 1926 also had a deep-felt impact on former militants. Lawther, for example, was imprisoned in 1926, but promoted dialogue and conciliation with the mine owners and spoke against industrial action in the later 1930s. In August 1939, Lawther pointed out that the DMA was still paying the price of 1926: Ryhope lodge, for example, still owed £2,000 from debts incurred during the lockout. Ryhope, one of a handful of left or Communist-influenced DMA lodges, was also in debt for a 16-week dispute in 1933.[80] It and other militant lodges that took similar local industrial action against the wishes of the DMA leadership, like Follonsby, illustrated that not all Durham miners shared the DMA left-wing officials' predilection for conciliation in this period. Notwithstanding these local disputes, the DMA remained broadly in tune with the rest of the regional trade union movement in terms of industrial moderation. Thus, the north-east was the least industrially disturbed region in 1936.[81] The conflict in Spain came at a time of flux; when the complex and often contradictory effects of 1926 were still making themselves felt in the DMA and, as a consequence, in the County Durham Labour Parties and further afield.

In the Labour Party, left-wing miners or ex-miners, including Will Lawther's brothers Andy and Steve, the latter's wife Emmie, Henry Bolton and Jim Stephenson, were highly influential in Blaydon constituency. Still, their local influence was not total as Blaydon trades council, led by a Catholic, was more moderate and there were ideological clashes over the teachings at Blaydon Socialist Sunday School.[82] Two other significant regional party activists of national standing were C.P. Trevelyan and Ellen Wilkinson. Trevelyan was an aristocrat who moved to Labour from the Liberal Party through the Union of Democratic Control during the Great War. He was a well-respected Labour grandee, gained partly through service in the both Labour governments. At the Department of Education again in the second Labour administration, Trevelyan retired from Westminster politics after electoral defeat in 1931, but remained active at constituency level (Wansbeck).

A third, younger activist, also significant in this context was Arthur Blenkinsop. In April 1938, Blenkinsop, an amateur actor (in Newcastle People's Theatre) and working on a colliery's clerical staff, became Newcastle East CLP PPC aged just 26. In 1935, he had been the election agent for Newcastle North CLP and was its secretary for much of this period.[83] The Spanish Republic thus had significant advocates in the official northeast regional labour movement.

The north-east left organised within the Socialist League after ILP disaffiliation was more active on Tyneside than anywhere else outside of London.[84] Gateshead branch, run by Ruth Dodds, the most significant League member in the region, appeared to be in decline by 1935 after active anti-fascist agitation in the earlier 1930s.[85] However, the League retained a good degree of influence in the wider movement through Dodds' continued editorship of the Gateshead Labour Party newspaper in the later 1930s. It also had a notable recruit from the ILP by mid-1936 in the form of Allan Henderson, who remained active in the later 1930s.[86]

The ILP played a significant role in the establishment of the Labour Party in the north-east before 1918 and many significant left activists, like Will Lawther, had cut their political teeth in the party.[87] However, disaffiliation from Labour hit the party hard both qualitatively – it had lost several notable north-east activists by 1936 – and quantitatively. By July 1936, the region's 262 members only accounted for 7 per cent of total ILP membership, and the youth organisation was proportionately smaller again. The ILP was also electorally unsuccessful in the north-east, not winning any seats.[88] Notwithstanding this, Gateshead ILP, with over seventy active members in 1936 (a figure that the branch maintained throughout the period), retained some of its dynamism from pre-disaffiliation days and was capable of making significant interventions in local politics in the later 1930s.[89] Furthermore, the party was more attractive than the CP to some young militants. Len Edmondson, for example, who was involved in unemployed and anti-fascist activities with the CP and ILP before 1935, chose to join the latter because he thought it 'a more revolutionary party'. The crucial moment for Edmondson came with the CP's support for the popular front in 1935. He felt vindicated when the French popular front government later crushed strikes: 'I couldn't reconcile myself to that at all'.[90]

Electorally speaking, there were a handful of self-styled 'Independent Socialist' councillors who were a thorn in the flesh of Labour administrations in Sunderland, Willington and South Shields, amongst other places. These were not ILPers and they did not all share a common political position. However, individuals in Sunderland, and Charles Wilson in Willington, who ran his own 'Socialist Society' in the pit village, appeared to have a similar politics that combined a kind of populist patriotism (and in Wilson's case radical liberalism) with their 'socialist' concerns for the unemployed and poor. On the other hand, the South Shields 'independent socialist' alderman Dunlop was involved with left-wing initiatives.[91] While syndicalism and anarchism had been significant in the region before 1914 (especially in the Durham coalfield), this had faded by the late 1930s.[92] This contrasted with South Wales where anarchists were actively engaged, their politics feeding from the traditions of Spaniards living in the coalfield.[93]

The conditions in the north-east that allowed for the development of the early ILP, with its ethical socialism that eschewed class-war, were far from ideal for other parties on the left with more radical politics looking to gain a foothold.[94] The existence of a strong moderate labour tradition transposed into a Labour Party that rapidly came to dominate in some parts of the region, and concentrations of Roman Catholics and non-conformist elements that Communist atheism usually alienated, made life very tough for the CP from its birth in 1920.[95] After six years of life, the CP had made little headway in the north-east: it was 'in some ways our weakest party district amongst the great centres of British industry'.[96] However, the 1926 general strike and miners' lockout offered the CP an ideal opportunity, especially in the Durham coalfield where a timid DMA leadership allowed the party to present itself as the miners' true, militant, advocate. The recruits came flooding in and by early September 1926, the region had shown the 'highest jump of all' CP districts to 2,000 members.[97]

However, the logistical problems of coping with such rapid growth from a low base-point, combined with an employer fight back, disillusionment and high unemployment with the end of the lockout, made the new membership very difficult to consolidate.[98] By September 1927, the north-east region had just 737 members; most had gone back to Labour.[99] During the 1929 Dawdon lockout, the CP intervened to implement its 'class against class' policy, to little immediate successful effect (though the lodge's chairperson in the late 1930s was a party member).[100] Regional membership fell from 200 in December 1929 to only 89 by July 1931, rising to 200 again by 1933.[101] Still, CP district secretary George Aitken was not exaggerating when he claimed in November 1936 that the north-east had been regarded as 'one of the most backward districts of the Party for many years'.[102]

By 1936, the CP's influence within the DMA was limited largely to isolated individual activists operating in the executives of some lodges, not supported by a strong and vibrant branch life and incapable themselves of swinging any DMA lodge vote their way unaided. The CP's weak position in the DMA (and NMA) in this period contrasted strongly with its strength in the South Wales Miners Federation (SWMF), where it counted the union's president Arthur Homer, five executive members and numerous other officials amongst its active membership.[103] North-east trades councils' responses to the Black Circular suggested that the CP had made but a few abortive attempts at direct infiltration or cooperation before 1936. Newcastle trades council, for example, apparently refused several CP approaches for joint working with a small minority demurring.[104] Still, this did not prevent crypto-Communist Tom Aisbitt from occupying an important position in this period in the influential Newcastle trades council.[105] In addition, there was probable or possible Communist influence in individual branches of various unions.[106]

Electorally, the CP achieved some successes. In August 1936, the CP had five councillors in the north-east, a tenth of its national total. Of these, three came from Blyth. Bob Elliott and W.H. Breadin sat for Croft ward, a slum area populated by dockers and shipyard workers, in Blyth municipality, and Breadin also sat on Northumberland County Council. There were two further Communist councillors on Felling and Houghton-le-Spring UDCs in County Durham. In the earlier 1930s, the party fielded candidates – occasionally not as 'Communists' – in seven other municipalities, but without success. It came closest to winning in Tynemouth, where the Labour Party was relatively weak.[107] The local party contained two activists, Nell Badsey and Alex Robson, who were to become significant in relation to the Spain agitation. Badsey visited Russia early in 1936 as a delegate of the Women's Co-op Guild, and lectured frequently on the subject on her return. Robson was a seaman from 1912 who joined the CP in 1922 (aged 26), and was active within his union (NUS) in the 1930s, and in unemployed agitation.[108]

In this latter activity, Robson worked through the National Unemploy-ed Workers' Movement (NUWM). This was a Communist front organi-sation predominately led by CP activists that reached well beyond the party's parameters. It supported the unemployed at an individual level and demonstrated on the issue, drawing in and politicising many in the pro-cess. It was certainly far larger and more influential than the CP itself in the region, especially in areas associated with shipbuilding, although it, too, was weak in the Durham coalfield.[109]

It was through the NUWM that a good deal of the most militant cooperation on the left in the earlier 1930s occurred. Naturally, this cen-tred on unemployment, but anti-fascism was also a major area of activity. In North Shields in 1934, for example, Alex Robson was imprisoned for a month for his part in breaking up a British Union of Fascists (BUF) meeting in July 1934.[110] This was one engagement of many of a militant anti-fascism that was certainly strong on Tyneside in the early 1930s. The organised response culminated with the formation of the 'Anti-Fascist League' in the summer of 1934, though the main anti-fascist disturbances in Newcastle had come during two days in May 1934. Nigel Todd argued that this activity effectively ended the BUF challenge in the north-east: an attempted revival in 1935 proved abortive, and it was subsequently riven by splits. The organised anti-fascism of the left was only one element of an essentially twofold response to the BUF in the north-east. The second facet, a spontaneous revulsion or antagonism to fascism manifest in the behaviour of 'ordinary' members of the public, including children, cer-tainly boded well for the north-east Spanish aid campaigns. Elements of the regional labour movement's institutional response were also promi-sing. These included the proactive Newcastle trades council, which cont-rasted with the more cautious City Labour Party, and South Shields move-ment's active anti-fascism before 1935, personified by its secretary of Dutch Jewish decent, Albert Gompertz.[111]

Regional left politics took on a different hue after the Blackshirt threat had been swept from the streets of most north-east towns. The advance of fascism abroad came to the fore and new institutions emerged to address this. Nationally, the CP encouraged the 'Hands off Abyssinia' campaign in October 1935, which led to the formation of local peace councils. A provisional Tyneside peace council was already in existence by this time and by July 1936 there were two peace councils in the north-east: Tyneside Joint Peace Council (TJPC) and Sunderland and District Peace Council (SDPC) (and 130 in existence nationally).[112] The TJPC involved

Labour left-wingers, like its chairperson Henry Bolton, as well Communists like Nell Badsey, who was one of its secretaries by June 1937. While it contained some pacifists, this did not prevent it from positing a clear anti-Non-Intervention stance on Spain as part of a broader critique of Chamberlain's foreign policy. The TJPC agitated throughout the late 1930s, with meetings in South Shields lending a degree of credibility to its Tyneside pretensions. The shorter-lived SDPC contained more pacifists but it, too, broadly campaigned with the same basic message as its Tyneside equivalent.

The two north-east peace councils can be described accurately as popular fronts as they involved liberals, in the form of Council of Action for Peace and Reconstruction (CAPR) activists, in central roles. Lloyd George established the CAPR in the summer of 1935 to promote his 'new deal' proposals to tackle unemployment and promote peace. Local CAPR activist Frieda Bacon claimed that it was formed in response to the electorate losing faith in the country's political machinery: in the 1935 general election, eleven million voted for the National Government, ten million against it and another ten million abstained.[113] While the presence of Communists somewhat complicated the TJPC's relations with the official movement, which never wholeheartedly embraced it, it remained sufficiently influential to play a significant role in Spain solidarity work.[114] The CAPR, which, Martin Pugh pointed out, represented a 'prototype popular front in itself', also held its own occasional meetings, sometimes on Spain.[115]

Local Left Book Club (LBC) groups emerged throughout the north-east after its establishment in March 1936. The often social and political diversity of these groups gave them the appearance of popular fronts in microcosm and some groups became involved in political agitation.[116] League of Nations Union (LNU) branches were also occasionally significant in the response to Spain, though County Durham provided the lowest density of LNU members in the country (less than 0.5 per cent of the electorate).[117] The LNU nationally provided tentative support for the Spanish Republic.[118] At grassroots level, the LNU had collected information for the peace ballot in 1935, but individual branches and members differed considerably in their politics, their understanding of the international situation and the role of government foreign policy.[119] For example, in October 1936 Consett LNU held a meeting with a German speaker who 'spoke highly of Hitler's efforts to increase the wellbeing of the German people as a whole'.[120] However, Labour left-winger Henry Bolton was active in nearby Chopwell LNU and several CAPR activists – there was considerable inter-fertilisation between the two groupings – and other liberals were also involved in different branches.[121]

The Liberal Party itself was also of some significance. In aligning with Macdonald in 1931, the party had helped to deliver a severe defeat to Labour, and also ended, in the short-term at least, liberalism as an independent force in the north-east. By 1935, independent liberals only had a significant presence in Barnard Castle and Bishop Auckland in the south of County Durham, and South Shields and Tynemouth on the Tyne. The conservative nature of liberalism in the north-east was evident in the existence of anti-Labour electoral pacts with Conservatives, in effect in virtually all north-east towns by 1930. It was also evident in the relative strength of the National Liberal Party in the region.[122]

Finally there were a number of interlinking economic and social factors characterising the region that played a part in informing its response to Spain. The north-east was one of the euphemistically-named 'special areas' in the 1930s. A good deal of the regional economy found recovery from the economic slump slow and painful. Indeed, the staples of mining and shipbuilding had been in serious difficulties throughout the inter-war period. A result was high unemployment, though levels differed considerably between localities and were to varying degrees lessening in the later 1930s. Still there were 180,000 people in County Durham in receipt of poor law relief, unemployment benefit or on transitional benefit in May 1937 and there remained 50,000 unemployed in the county by November 1938.[123] Poverty was manifest in the poor health, high rates of infant mortality and low life expectancy in the region.[124]

An obvious practical effect of unemployment and poverty was that individuals would be able to afford very little in terms of donations to Spanish aid campaigns. But these conditions had wider political effects as well. Some contemporary commentary – such as a *Newcastle Journal* editorial – regarded unemployment and poverty as natural recruiting grounds for Labour.[125] Rowe claimed that the sense of solidarity induced by the depression must have contributed to Labour's rising dominance.[126] However, there was no simple relationship between appalling living conditions, Labour propaganda and consequent advancement, as the experience of Sunderland Labour Party clearly demonstrated. The Labour vote in the 1935 general election only increased by 3,000 and while it won control of the council that year, the party's efforts to build houses did not prevent it from losing municipal power again in 1938.[127]

There seemed to be little agreement as to the effect of unemployment on political (in)activity. The relative success of the NUWM revealed that the experience *could* politicise (though the CP's poor showing in the region suggested that there were limits to how far most unemployed activists were prepared to go). A Birmingham Methodist minister claimed in 1937 that the depression had helped ensure that 'north-country people are thinking more deeply than … their south-country brethren'.[128] Yet too much hardship was inimical: Shinwell, for example, 'always found people more receptive to new social concepts when they are above the borderline of poverty'.[129] Similarly, delegates at a north-east divisional ILP conference in January 1937 were 'determined to carry on despite the dire poverty and resultant apathy prevailing in the area'.[130] Some commentators on the right attributed what they perceived as the left's increasing concern with foreign affairs in the later 1930s, somewhat optimistically, to improving conditions on the home front.[131]

Other social consequences of economic conditions were relevant. The region's booming nineteenth-century economy brought immigrants into the north-east, most notably Irish Catholics. Of the English regions, only Lancashire had a higher percentage of Catholics in its population.[132] In many north-east localities, Catholics were a significant element in the unions and Labour Parties, and the situation in Spain presented a potential test of their political and religious loyalties. Immigration tailed off in the Edwardian period, and the troubled inter-war north-east economy provoked the outward migration of mostly young people, who went to London and the south-east, or even abroad to Canada or Australia, searching for work.

Rowe claimed that the north-east 'closed in' with the end of population growth after about 1910 and that outward migration from 1920 did nothing to break down the north-east's insularity.[133] Certainly, the region's geographical remoteness posed a problem for activists like Blenkinsop attempting to organise nationally.[134] But it did not prevent some regional institutions from sending delegates to events on Spain and related issues in London whether they were officially organised or not. Indeed, the north-east's response to the Spanish civil war does not support Rowe's claim. Outward migration had taken many working-class people to other parts of the country or abroad, widening their outlooks. Furthermore, elements of the remaining industry in the region could also foster an open and internationalist outlook. Chuter Ede, MP for South Shields, claimed that wherever there was trouble in the world, his constituents were sure to be involved.[135] In fact, the sizeable Muslim presence in South Shields – a result of the town's seafaring traditions – helped to inform internationalism and anti-fascism before 1936.[136] South Shields' ethnically diverse population was somewhat exceptional, but many north-east seafarers played some part in the conflict, from the special case of the *Linaria* in early 1937, to running the Franco blockade with food and supplies in ships like the *Alice Marie* and *Backworth* or attempting to maintain normal trade relations, like the ships of the Consett Iron Company. Indeed, of the nine British ships evacuating the Basque refugees in spring 1937, one was north-east based and seven had Wearsiders in their crews.[137] Their eyewitness accounts of, say, the starvation in Bilbao, often received extensive press coverage, providing human links between the region and the conflict in Spain.[138] Those who fought in Spain also performed this role and again the regional press was often ready to supply column inches. Conversely, Spanish sailors visiting the region could also intervene, for example, by supporting the Basque refugees in North Shields.[139] Life for many in the region remained very difficult, and the north-east in some respects an isolated and neglected region. But this did not necessarily preclude a varied and sometimes energetic and popular response to the conflict in Spain.

Definitions and Synopsis

For the left in the 1930s the dominant paradigm was, in the words of Labour MP William Whiteley, that the conflict in Spain was 'neither a civil war, nor a religious war, but a foreign invasion'.[140] In this respect, it was legitimate for pro-Republicans to call their activities 'Spanish aid campaigns' as, in their paradigm, 'Spain' was synonymous with the Republic: in Fyrth's words; that a 'democratic and progressive government, indeed the whole Spanish people' was under attack by Franco.[141] Some pro-Republicans conceded that Spaniards were fighting on both sides, but for the majority 'fascism' was the foreign invader, and 'Spain', the 'Spanish people' and 'democracy' were all synonymous. Indeed, Rob Stradling pointed out that International Brigaders were told that they were fighting Italians or Germans, to promote the idea that democratic Spain had been invaded by fascists.[142] This discourse was a product of – and dovetailed with – the popular front concept that all classes should unite to defeat foreign and expansionist fascism and reaction. This study thus employs the term 'Spain' to mean 'Republican Spain' when discussing the reaction of the British labour movement to the conflict. As argued in chapter two, the vast majority of labour movement institutions and activists understood that the Spanish aid campaigns would support the Republic in some form (though there were occasional significant exceptions).

Clearly, the 'foreign invasion' and 'democracy against fascism' paradigms did scant justice to the complexity of the conflict, which was very many things: a foreign invasion, a civil war and a revolution (or several) amongst others. The extent to which the 'Nationalists' were foreign and fascist and the Republic democratic were, and remain, like most aspects of this conflict, highly contentious.[143] The key here is that the majority of the contemporaneous British left saw fascism on the march in Spain and an opportunity to fight it. Indeed, notwithstanding the nature of their own regime, the Nationalists were receiving strong support from two fascist states, which was evidence enough for this particular claim.

However, as chapters five and six discuss, the involvement of activists from outside of the labour movement brought a new dimension to the campaigns and it is likely that many *did not* understand that these campaigns were *not* giving succour impartially to both sides, as some claimed they would. In this second context, 'Spanish aid campaigns' and 'Spain' are useful terms precisely because they communicate the ambiguity surrounding the motives for involvement of those who did not already subscribe to some form of left discourse. That Franco's supporters often campaigned in much the same way (but with far less support and success), by using the same language merely amplified this ambiguity.

Then there are the terms 'official' and 'unofficial'. The 'official' labour movement refers to the trade unions organised within the TUC and the Labour Party. It is defined from the 'unofficial' movement of left parties and organisations proscribed by, or not affiliated to, the Labour Party or TUC, namely, the Communist Party, the ILP, the NUWM and a whole 'solar system' of other CP-inspired organisations like the LBC. A degree of ambiguity arose at the individual level as some institutions officially or unofficially allowed overt Communists to operate in them to the extent of taking leadership positions. Other Communists involved kept their party affiliation hidden. This study explores the far more blurred distinctions between 'official' and 'unofficial' Spanish aid campaigns.

The choice of 'British left' in the title was to embrace labour movement institutions and activists and those outside it: the popular fronters' 'progressive' milieu that could stretch from liberals and even progressive Conservatives through to Communists. It is also broad enough to include those whose religious beliefs led them to certain kinds of progressive causes but who defied simple categorisation on the political spectrum. In this context, the support for the popular front from sections of the Labour left and the CP complicated political categorisation further as their programmes' appeal to liberals placed them, theoretically speaking, to the political right of the Labour Party. The ILP and anarchists remained clearly to the left of Labour, though again there was a good deal of disagreement over many issues in this period within the ILP, which also did not always clearly lend itself to simple definitions of left and right. Thus, use of the term 'popular fronter' for those who supported the policy seems of more utility in this somewhat confused period.

This book is divided into three main parts, reflecting broad types of activity grassroots individuals engaged in to support, ostensibly, the Spanish Republic. This division to some extent reflects the level of political commitment and political understanding demanded of individual activists and the potential political impact of the action taken. They reflect a division made by James Klugmann, who identified a 'highest' level of solidarity action, fighting in the International Brigade. There was an intermediate level of political action against Non-Intervention and a third level of 'extraordinarily broad' support manifest in collecting for foodships and medical supplies.[144] Thus, chapter one considers the impact of those who fought in the International Brigade or who served in the Republic's medical services (though not all of these individuals were politically motivated and there were other ways that individuals could risk their lives to support the Republic).[145] The following three chapters consider aspects of the official movement's response and the final two chapters deal with the Spanish aid campaigns. Naturally, there were overlaps between all three types of activism manifest in the activities of both institutions and individuals: a central theme of this book is to explore the interconnectedness and separations in these broad forms of solidarity action.

1

INTERNATIONAL BRIGADERS' IMPACT ON THE HOME FRONT

Recent research has provided a clearer picture of the composition of the British International Brigade contingent, building on the studies of Wales. However, there has been little attempt to assess the impact of brigaders' decisions to fight on politics on the home front, especially in areas with moderate Labour traditions like the north-east of England where the CP found it more difficult to gain a foothold. Yet brigaders, as activists who were risking their lives in a foreign land in the struggle against Franco and fascism, were potentially of great significance for political battles on the home front. This chapter will consider the complex and varied effects of the experience of fighting in Spain both on the politics and activities of individual brigaders and their families, and consequently on wider grass-roots politics in the north-east.

Effect on Brigaders: Political Inspiration?

Most north-eastern brigaders were drawn from the Communist milieu; a small proportion from the party itself, but many more from the unemployed action organisation, the NUWM.[1] While it was consequently likely that a desire to fight fascism characterised the motives, to a greater or lesser degree, of the vast majority of north-eastern brigaders, it did not follow that their experiences in Spain would necessarily invigorate, deepen and temper their politics. However, in letters home, it was clear that many brigaders' initial experiences had a profound positive effect on them; they were, like Communist Wilf Jobling, conscious of playing a part in the 'greatest event of the era'.[2] Indeed, Jobling regarded himself and his comrades as ambassadors of the British left, telling his father: 'were it not for the brigade and for the British battalion, an Englishman could not bare to hold up his head in Spain thanks to the foul Non-Intervention Policy'.[3]

Another inspirational aspect of the experience for many was the international camaraderie. Shortly after arriving in Spain in January 1937, William Johnson 'pulled up with a nice bunch of French and British soldiers'.[4] For non-Communists, too, this aspect was highly significant. Clifford Lawther told brother Will in February 1937: 'It is wonderful to think that there are many besides myself who are leaving nearest and dearest to fight against the greatest danger that international working class solidarity has had to face ...'.[5] On Christmas Eve 1936, Bart Thewles, another non-Communist, had 'not the slightest regret at the step he took ... it is quite right to be spending Christmas sharing the common joys and vicissitudes of the International Column'.[6]

The slaughter of the British battalion, and the north-east contingent, at Jarama in February 1937 and subsequent battles did not appear to alter the tone of many letters home, albeit often penned by different activists. In June 1937, Dick Hearn, a 27 year-old tinplate worker from Gateshead, reported that the troops had their own bulletin called *Our Fight* and that 'we are still going great guns' [sic.].[7] Bob Elliott was well and 'never happier in his life ... The spirit of the brigade is wonderful he says'.[8] Likewise, Stephen Codling was 'glad to be here with such a fine bunch of comrades. ... "The spirit of the different nationals is wonderful, all friendly and out for the one ideal"'.[9] Codling was pleased that 'Everybody is conscious of his duty, and the discipline could not be better in the imperial army'.[10] His South Shields NUWM comrade Sam Thompson was 'having a swell time ... away up the front and ready for anything'.[11] Writing jointly in February 1938, they were in 'fine spirit' and had formed 'many sincere friendships'.[12] On leave in May 1938, John Wilson wanted 'to return as soon as I can, for my experiences there have made me all the keener to give what little support I can to the Spanish Government'.[13] Arthur Teasdale, too, had 'never seen anything like the comradeship and morale of the troops. They would share their last cigarette. We live, fight, work and die among each other ... the feeling is wonderful'.[14] Teasdale, like many other brigaders, had formed 'fictive kinships' based on social and experiential bonds rather than blood ties or marriage.[15] The spirit of the Spaniards also deeply impressed Teasdale: 'I have seen an old father, with his family killed, grip a rifle and leave for the front line – they are so determined. ... It is wonderful the way in which the civilian population are making sacrifices on behalf of the soldiers in the front line'.[16] John Henderson also praised the 'heroic people of Spain' who were doing everything to ensure that the frontline fighters got the best conditions possible.[17] Nurse Winifred Wilson agreed that 'the Spanish youths are little short of heroes'.[18] Many other brigaders, too, commented favourably on the indigenous fighting spirit.[19]

Clearly, the brigaders writing letters directly to the regional press were cognisant of their propaganda value and were therefore unlikely to have mentioned negative experiences. It would be interesting to know, for example, how Elliott's experience as a British observer at the 20-minute trial and execution of a French commander on spying charges in January 1937 impacted on how he regarded the solidarity of the brigade.[20] Naturally, the language of these more propagandist communications was usually standard in terms of contemporary Communist discourse, and usually written by CP members. Nevertheless, this did not mean that their authors were not expressing genuine experiences, albeit in somewhat prescribed language. Letters released to the press by friends or relatives were a slightly different matter, often containing a greater degree of honesty. Still, brigaders could not always be truthful about all aspects of life in the front line for fear of upsetting their relatives (though they occasionally were: see below). Furthermore, of course, they could not be too specific about military aspects of the war. Bob Elliott for example, told his sister somewhat cryptically that 'Big things are taking place in this struggle, which we hope will lead to very definite steps being taken on our side that will make Franco sit up and take notice'.[21] Brigaders' letters were also subject to censorship.

After returning home in late 1938, the words of several brigaders' again suggested a profound experience. Three South Shields brigaders, Johns Blair, Richardson and Corby, 'left Spain with mixed feelings, happy to be going home but sorry that the government forces should lose their services'.[22] Fellow South Shields denizen Teasdale was invalided home by August 1938. Having fought in several battles, Teasdale had 'lived a life I shall never forget'.[23] In late December 1938, Teasdale again reflected on his experiences in a letter to the press: 'I wish that I could find words to describe to the people of South Shields the comradeship and the deeds of self-sacrifice among all Internationals who have fought alongside our Spanish brothers'.[24]

The evident experience of comradeship between men at the front lines did not necessarily challenge all facets of contemporary life. Some brigaders had fought with, or come across, women at the front.[25] However, talking of his experiences in the immediate aftermath of the conflict, John

Halliwell mentioned that he had never seen a woman on the front.[26] He had heard that militia women had fought and had 'probably helped' in the first months of the conflict, but that he 'doubted that women would make good soldiers'. Women were, he added, 'admired as nurses'.[27] Similarly, other brigaders, like Codling, were impressed with the work of the women, but only in their capacity as medical staff in Republican hospitals.[28]

Furthermore, not all north-east brigaders found the experience to their liking. After a visit to the front, north-east journalist John Brown claimed in June 1937, that there were a 'good number' of British brigaders disillusioned with what passed for 'democracy' in the Republic, but that pride compelled them to remain. This was, according to Brown, especially true of the non-Communists.[29] Indeed, there was some hint of this from returning brigaders. James Pearson, a Blyth shipyard worker who returned from Spain certified unfit in mid-March 1937, did not paint a glowing picture of conditions. He discussed (indeed, overstated) the casualties at Jarama, claiming that only eighty had survived from 650. Apparently 'reluctant to talk of his experiences', Pearson noted that 'the Madrid defenders were "pretty low"' when he left the front, and he also mentioned the 'trouble' in Barcelona he saw on his way home where 'Civilians were shooting at each other in the streets'.[30] Pearson was probably not a Communist, which perhaps explained his frank comments.[31] Likewise, probable non-Communists Richard and Rosamund Smith of South Shields, who had served as medics in Spain, returned home in May 1938 as they had 'had enough'.[32] (Although Rosamund Smith also said: 'if they send for us again, well I think we shall go').[33]

Others were more overtly disenchanted. Thomas Genther, for example, who appeared to have joined at least in part for political (anti-fascist) reasons: 'When I went to Spain I thought that the Communist Party, or the Government were in the right'.[34] However, Genther claimed that for six weeks service he was paid only 55 pesetas when he was promised 15 pesetas per day.[35] There was also, apparently, 'no food to be bought' and 'conditions at Bilbao were very bad. … I made a complaint about the bad conditions in general, and later I heard that on account of that the military had threatened to have me shot'.[36] Genther deserted, and claimed that he knocked out a government agent following him as he was making for the docks at Bilbao. Stowing away on a Newcastle steamer, Genther worked his passage home.

While Genther did serve in Spain, the accuracy of his account is impossible to determine; a good deal certainly sounds fanciful. Genther appeared to fit Alexander's pattern for some 'adventurers' who joined for an 'easy life' and soon deserted. On return to Britain, some 'went to the press to justify their actions with horror stories about causalities, the chaos, and "Communist repression"'.[37] Nevertheless, if taken at face value, then a considerable element of Genther's motivation was political and the disenchantment with what he found was genuine. The only north-east brigader to desert back home and go to the press, Genther was not simply an apolitical adventurer.

There was another aspect to Genther's case. In September 1937, he received a six-month sentence for stealing from Sunderland Corporation after five months working as a seasonal bus conductor. Genther claimed to have spent all the money he stole in Newcastle, his excuse being domestic trouble with his wife. The prosecutor claimed that 'everybody has been very kind' to Genther since he got back from Spain 'particularly the manager of the transport undertaking. I do not think he has shown any gratitude in doing this'.[38] Genther's criminal past – this was his fifth court appearance for theft – allowed those sympathetic to the brigade to claim that Genther was simply a malingerer. In this vein, John H. Wilson, a regular left-wing correspondent to the *Sunderland Echo*, dismissed Genther's 'extremely fantastic' account of fighting in Spain and wanted to correct the mistaken impression given by the court superintendent that the CP supported brigaders' dependants financially.[39] However, again, an individual's criminal record for offences like theft did not necessarily indicate a lack of political motive.

An experience as intense and fiercely personal (as well as collective) as serving in Spain clearly had complex, varied and often conflicting effects on individuals over time. In April 1937, Nurse Winifred Wilson, for example, thought it 'marvellous to see the spirit with which these lads and men have come here to swell the ranks and help their brother men to quell fascism'.[40] Yet, by the end of that year, the physical exhaustion brought about by extremely demanding conditions, along with Wilson's inability to work harmoniously with her colleagues, saw her return home.[41] Wilson claimed that she had fallen out of favour with the authorities as she refused to present herself as 'a strong Communist' and that she was not taken back to Spain when she volunteered again in spring 1938 on political grounds.[42]

Physical and Psychological Effects?

Balanced against the many inspirational experiences of probably the majority of brigaders must be the inevitable physical and psychological damage that any human being sustains in as extreme conditions as a war zone. Frank Graham, for example, saw two close friends from Sunderland killed at Jarama.[43] One of them, Dolan, was under his command at the time. Others, like Tommy Kerr, made new friends only to see them killed.[44] In mid-August 1938 Woods claimed that almost half the north-east brigaders returning home were wounded or of ill health.[45] Many were seriously wounded: former general labourer John Mitchison, for example, was partially paralysed by a spinal wound.[46] There were often long-term consequences of wounds and a usually poor diet (in POW camps or at the frontline).[47] John Blair, who spent most of 1938 in Spain and was wounded, had been 'living on beans, lentils and mule meat' and had become 'very run down'.[48] However, not all brigaders suffered at the front. Three weeks before news of his death, Bob Elliott was 'enjoying the best of health at the moment, thanks to the effects of glorious and continuous sunshine in Spain, and leading an out-of-doors and simple life'.[49] This was after having been in the firing line continuously for five months.

The experience of prisoners of war (POW) was, for most, a brutalising one, undergone by around a tenth of north-east brigaders. Many experienced together what most later described as cramped, filthy, living conditions, poor food under a regime of severe corporal punishment. A wounded George O'Neill, for example, received a five-minute beating by prison guards with big sticks: 'I did not complain. I did not show any sign of suffering. I was determined to let them see what a Britisher could stand'.[50] Transferral for most north-easterners to an Italian-run prison camp brought more humane treatment, though degradation remained. Some brigaders tried to organise resistance within the prison camps, and there were some small victories.[51] However, individuals like Sam Thompson claimed that there was no use protesting. A few days before his release, for example, 'we were told that if we did not stop talking the machine gunners would be sent to silence us'.[52]

Naturally, these experiences cannot fail to have damaged those who survived, regardless of the feeling of the justness of their cause and the support received. As Orwell commented: 'The essential horror of army life … is barely affected by the nature of the war you happen to be fighting in'.[53] As with any war, the experience must have psychologically scarred as well as tempered and inspired, to varying degrees, those who came through it. Frank Graham, for example, was invalided out of the brigade with 'shattered nerves' after being severely wounded (he was also suffering from typhoid).[54] Six South Shields brigaders bore 'the marks, either physical, mental or both, of the terrible dangers and hardships they faced on the battlefronts'.[55] Yet many were remarkably sanguine and resilient. While living in damp trenches left William Norris with a 'legacy of rheumatism', for example, he remained 'cheerful'.[56] Bobby Qualie, wounded for a second time by a dumdum bullet at Brunete in July 1937 and invalided home, soon resumed his weight training and remained a weightlifter.[57]

Effects on Brigaders' Families

As in South Wales, the majority of north-east brigaders were from large families, often poverty-stricken, and where a strong family unit was important. As an element of complex family networks, brigaders' actions and fate clearly had many significant effects on their loved ones. Indeed, the very act of joining up often involved brigaders deceiving their families. Some, like William Dean, claimed to be looking for work in the south, only to end up in Spain.[58] Other brigaders told only select family members (Tommy Kerr told his Communist uncle) they were joining the brigade or were, like Joseph McQuade, deliberately vague about where they were going.[59] Many feared the upset and difficulties that too much openness would bring: Thomas Dolan's mother 'begged and prayed' him not to go.[60] Harry Reynolds waited until the last moment to announce he was leaving for Spain, but a 'freak accident' meant he chose an unusual night when his parents were out. They never heard from him again.[61] After the re-invocation of the Foreign Enlistment Act, most deemed a high level of secrecy a necessity.[62] When Charlie Woods interviewed prospective brigaders with 'their womenfolk if they were married', sometimes an argument ensued.[63]

Many brigaders' families experienced harrowing times, the victims of complex and confused circumstances in Spain. Military and logistical issues combined with organisational and bureaucratic problems to make the identification and certification of those killed in Spain a longwinded and often flawed process.[64] William Dean's relatives, for example, had a torrid time. They received a letter from their son saying that he was alive in good health and fighting on the Madrid front two days after the CP told them that he had been killed in action.[65] In the Tattam household, 'the fear was always with us' for the safety of Bill and Edward.[66] There was heartache for many other families who waited sometimes months for letters that never came or for reports of 'missing' to become confirmations that a loved one had been killed. The deaths of several north-easterners at Jarama in February, for example, were not confirmed until late-July 1937.[67] However, for other relatives, there was a happier ending, as initial reports of 'missing' or 'killed in action' were updated to 'wounded' or 'captured'.[68] Still, like Charles Walton's uncle, these relatives had undergone the pain of mourning.[69] As prisoners of war, however, it was even more difficult for brigaders to maintain communication with their worried families. And, when they could communicate, POWs like Sam Thompson gave a very different impression of conditions in the camp he was in compared to after his release.[70]

In total, around 30 north-east brigaders did not come back from Spain.[71] A 'considerable number' had dependants.[72] For many married women like Eleanor Smith, the death of husbands in Spain brought considerable and long-term hardship.[73] Some wives suffered from survivor guilt, jealousy or resentment.[74] The wounds of some returning brigaders meant that they were no longer capable of earning a wage and, like the unmarried John Mitchison, they became a burden of care on their families.[75] Others, like the 25 year-old Arthur Teasdale found that their injuries severely curtailed their earning possibilities. He returned home in July 1938 with a 'shattered hand' (an aerial bomb exploding near him during retreat from Belchite left only two fingers on his right hand).[76] A former bricklayer who had been working in Ealing, Teasdale's injury prevented him from doing manual labour and he was still out of work seven months later.[77] John Henderson, on the other hand, got his old job back and got married as planned, quickly adjusting to the debilitating effect of his arm wound.[78]

The families' understandings of their relatives' motives in going to Spain varied considerably. However, often through communication with the brigaders directly, some came to understand their decisions and to feel a degree of pride. Bob Elliott's sister recognised that he 'lived every minute' from the time of his going out to Spain.[79] Eleanor Smith told a tearful public meeting in September 1937 that she was proud to be the wife of a man who had sacrificed his life.[80] However, Charlie Woods, who often had the 'unpleasant job' of informing relatives of the deaths of their loved ones, was sure that Wilf Jobling's father, for one, 'didn't understand'.[81]

Were some brigaders' relatives to some extent politicised by the experience of losing a loved one in the conflict?[82] A handful of bereaved relatives, like those of Stephen Codling, did become involved, to the extent of supporting or speaking at Spanish aid meetings.[83] The partners of some brigaders were often more likely to have a shared political understanding than were their parents or siblings. Some brigaders' partners, like Will Tattam's Communist wife, were politically affiliated beforehand.[84] Others were likely to have shared their (Communist) partner's politics in broader terms. For example, Robert Mackie's widow, who left a moving tribute to her dead husband, certainly sounded politically motivated.[85] Another example was Eleanor Smith who told a CP-organised meeting in Blaydon (to protest at the bombing of British seamen) that 'both she and her husband realised from the commencement of the war in Spain that the interests of British people were involved'.[86] Smith's political commitment appeared to sharpen after her husband's death, as she addressed meetings from September 1937 (including one in London), remained active in 1938 and even joined the CP. However, Smith's domestic situation – she had to work while her mother looked after her daughter – curtailed these activities.[87] In contrast, the wives of two probable non-Communists killed, Frank Airlie and Ernest Lower, did not appear to have become involved in any pro-Republic activity. No one in Communist Harry Reynold's Labour-supporting family became involved in the Spanish aid campaigns either. His brother Bill remembered: 'we were all trying to make some sort of a living'. Still, they were all 'very inspired by it' and, when the Second World War broke out, the brothers who signed up thought of Harry 'preceding us in the battle against fascism'.[88]

The effect of the Tattam brother's deaths in Spain was complex on an already politicised 'socialist family'; their father had lost his job on the railways in the north-east before the Great War due to his active trade unionist convictions. He remained a strong Labour man and became a Dawdon lodge official after returning from the war. Likewise, their mother was a leading member of the women's section of the local Labour Party and co-opted onto the Board of Guardians. Sister Margaret was a 17-year-old college student and secretary of the local LLY. Bill, the second oldest sibling, was the first to join the CP in the family and he convinced brother Harry that it promulgated the correct way to socialism. In many ways, the brothers' service in Spain had an energising impact. Their mother joined the CP and worked for Spanish aid and their father, too, 'did everything he could for Spain and the International Brigade, we all did'. For younger sister Moira Tattam 'it was a catalyst and I joined the CP and remain a Communist to this day'. Alun, the youngest brother, also joined the CP. Another brother, Jack, died when his ship was torpedoed in the merchant navy during the Second World War. He was 'determined to help defeat fascism and all it stood for ... he felt a link with his elder brothers'. Still, the loss of two sons in the conflict inflicted terrible suffering. Moira Tattam was not sure how her parents 'coped with their grief', but they 'did their utmost not to distress the younger members of the family'. She was sure that her father, who died of cancer in 1947, 'would not have become so ill if he had not internalised his grief at losing his sons'. Furthermore, the circumstances of Bill's death – he requested and needed leave after having fought at Jarama and becoming ill but was told he could not be spared before the battle of Brunete – 'is a bitter pill to swallow even now'. This 'broke my mother's heart, because Bill was killed going up the line in the dark'. Almost seven months of fighting without a break 'was too much for any man to endure, and the thought of it lives with me as it did with the rest of my family'. Moira Tattam felt 'I am carrying on with the memory of every one of my brothers and wondering exactly where and how Edward was killed and lost to us ...'.[89] The impacts of other brigaders' decisions to fight in Spain on their families were not always so great, but could be felt many years later. For example, Brian Walsh, while on the left anyway, 'always had the feeling that Sam [his uncle] was a hero'; the impact of Sam's example was felt more after Brian retired.[90]

One definite example of specific politicisation occurring between siblings through Spain came when Sam Walsh converted his brother Johnny to Communism and 'the true class struggle for socialism' the night before Sam left for Spain.[91] Sam Walsh's death at Brunete in July 1937 appeared to cement his brother's newfound political faith. However, other Communists, like Harry Reynolds, remained politically exceptional in their families.[92] Furthermore, the experience *could* work the other way. John Woodcock's wife and family were completely alienated from Communism after he went to Spain. She summoned him to court for failing to maintain her, where her father claimed Woodcock 'was perfectly happy a fortnight before he left [for Spain]. Communism has turned his brain'.[93]

The confusion over those missing at the front was also potentially problematic in this respect, generating anger towards the CP amongst relatives. Frank Graham claimed that his visits to the relatives of all the dead, wounded and missing in the region on a propaganda tour home in spring 1937 'certainly removed a good deal of discontent which undoubtedly existed'.[94] One angry individual in this respect was Thomas Dolan's mother who complained to the press 'We cannot get to know anything of how he died'.[95] She attributed his decision to join not to political beliefs – he was an NUWM activist – but to desperation induced by unemployment and lamented her inability to dissuade him.[96] Yet she later became politically active to the extent of appearing on public platforms and joining a deputation to the NMA in April 1938.[97] Her case appears somewhat exceptional, however. While news of Harry Reynold's death was never reported to his family, there was no anger at the CP for the lack of information: 'We understood that no one was to blame ... we were proud of Harry in a way for standing up for his political views'.[98]

Involvements and Effects on Campaigns at Home

While at the Spanish front, there were several ways in which brigaders could also attempt to aid the Republic at home. One was to appeal for the support of powerful influential contacts. A good example of this was Clifford Lawther who asked his brother Will (a Durham miners' official) in February 1937 to 'give all your influence, insight, push or anything you have to get aid for Spain'.[99] David George, from Quaking Houses in County Durham, described the Franco bombing of civilians in a letter to David Adams, Labour MP for Consett, concluding, somewhat undemandingly, 'we are going to win the struggle if you help us with everything possible, even if it is only a thought'.[100] Others made wider appeals, which often appeared in the local press.[101] Stephen Codling, for example, made a general appeal for support in his hometown through his brother in July 1937. Two months later came a specific appeal to the South Shields labour movement to support 'Spanish democracy'.[102] At William Dean's suggestion, a personal letter he sent to a comrade in Felling in June 1937 that contained an appeal to the 'people of Felling to give willing in the way of money and foodstuffs', duly appeared in the local press.[103] Others, like Bart Thewles, wrote directly to the *Shields Gazette* from Albacete, discussing his experiences and thoughts.[104] Those working for the medical side, like Winifred Wilson, also sent appeals for food and medical supplies directly to the regional press.[105]

Brigade political commissars, aware of the interest, encouraged brigaders to write to their local newspapers.[106] At first, many north-east brigaders' letters appeared in the press through their recipient's actions. However, more brigaders began writing directly to the press as time drew on. Communist Party members among the north-east brigaders, and Graham in particular, were overrepresented in terms of press coverage, but several non-Communists also featured. As well as garnering support for the Republic these letters allowed for strong propagandising against Franco in a way that otherwise did not regularly occur in the mainstream press. In

May 1937, for example, Billy Bamborough wrote: 'The way they have been blowing men, women and children to smithereens is terrible. These Fascists are nothing else but baby killers ...[107] Several other brigaders commented in a similar vein.[108] Brigaders' also intervened on more specific situations. Stephen Codling, for example, in relation to negative stories about the Basque refugee children in Britain, pointed out that they had gone through terrible experiences and that Spanish children were not, in any case, bad tempered.[109]

Brigaders back at home for various reasons often commanded prime 'guest speaker' billing at meetings on the subject. From mid-April to mid-May 1937, Frank Graham was back agitating in the region as one of four representatives from Spain sent to 'answer lies about the [Spanish] war in the English gutter press'.[110] George Aitken and other brigaders also propagandised from public platforms on the issue during visits home. On one occasion, Aitken received flattering treatment from the press, being described as a 'quiet, dark haired fellow ... a gentle, courteous man full of sincere argument'.[111] The local press interviewed others returning home, such as medic couple Richard and Rosamund Smith from South Shields. This gave them a platform to propagandise, and they spoke, for example, of having to obscure the red crosses on ambulances because Franco aircraft used them for target practice.[112]

As soon as confirmation of the deaths in action of (certain) brigaders came, the CP began engineering a process of memorialising and 'martyring' the dead. There were, for example, memorial meetings for Thomas Dolan and Wilf Jobling in April 1937.[113] Elliott, too had a CP-organised memorial meeting in mid-July 1937. Probably due to his status as a Communist local councillor, Elliott was the most memorialised of the northeast brigaders at the time. There was extensive coverage of Elliott tributes in the *Blyth News*. By late July, a committee was being formed to arrange a second Elliott memorial meeting, which came in mid-September 1937. Before this, Blyth councillors made their own round of tributes. There were also suggestions for creating a more permanent memorial. Communist William Allan requested copies of all personal letters from Elliott at the front, presumably for a commemorative publication.[114] Communist sympathiser 'Janus' argued that 'Such heroism should be recorded in the annals of time ...', and suggested a fund to buy 'working-class literature' for a 'Robert Swinney Elliott collection' in Blyth public library.[115] The September 1937 memorial meeting raised funds to place a 'memorial photograph' in a 'suitable place' in Blyth.

Before the brigaders' repatriation in October 1938, all the memorial meetings held in the region had been for Communists killed in Spain. After this time, memorials and 'welcome home' meetings were combined functions and did not usually single out Communists. They were held for contingents from localities like South Shields, Gateshead, Sunderland and Newcastle, for individual brigaders like 'Ginger' George (in a reception at West Stanley Co-op hall) and, on 15 January 1939, for the whole north-east region (in Newcastle City Hall). These certainly gave the brigade a relatively high public and media profile in late 1938 and early 1939.[116]

The City Hall memorial meeting, attended by 2,000, was a grand ceremonial event cleverly constructed to engender a strong emotional response from the audience. Two massive rolls of honour bearing the names, in large script, of north-east brigaders killed in Spain hung from the hall's ceiling above the platform. The surviving brigaders marched into the meeting to the tune of the Spanish Republican anthem 'Hymno de Riego' carrying their flags. As they entered, the audience stood in their honour. The audience then sang 'Jerusalem' and the speeches were interspersed by an organ recital and a sung solo.[117] As in South Wales, returning brigaders were lionised to a degree.[118] Indeed, even the local press deemed South Shields ex-brigaders 'heroes ... quiet-spoken and modest, they are facing the future with courage and determination'.[119]

These meetings also had the more practical task of raising money for the brigaders' dependant's aid (IBDWAC), which was another way in which brigaders influenced Spain campaigns on the home front (by becoming the object of one of them). The north-east memorial meeting did particularly well for a single public meeting, raising £142 13s. 6d.[120] In late January 1939, an 'International Brigade convoy' of two buses, 22 brigaders and two nurses touring the country to raise money for IBDWAC and support for the Republic visited the region. It organised a meeting and dinner in Gateshead, a meeting in North Shields and then a rally in Newcastle's Eldon Square to lay a wreath at the war memorial for those killed in Spain.[121] Finally, there was a 'Debt of Honour Week' for the dependants 16–23 July 1939, which began and ended with meetings in Newcastle's Bigg Market.[122]

There were also examples of localised campaigns to support individual brigaders at the front. Elliott, who was 'fathering' 100 men, inaugurated a campaign to send out boxes of woodbines, 'a very welcome guest out here'. He appealed in the *Blyth News* for cigarettes on 'an extended scale' and Blyth Communists organised the effort in the town.[123] Similarly,

friends of Codling and Thompson sent them hampers of cigarettes, cho-
colates, tea and soap at Christmas 1937.[124]

What were the effects of the brigaders' interventions and example?
Frank Graham claimed that the news of brigaders' deaths in battle 'did not
dry up the stream of volunteers, in fact it was an incentive'.[125] However,
this did not appear borne out by the patterns of north-east recruitment to
the brigade. The majority of north-east brigaders went to Spain in late
December 1936 and January 1937. Almost three times as many went in
January as December and these two months together saw by far the bulk
(over half) of north-east recruits entering Spain. The battle of Jarama in
February 1937 was the first (for the vast majority) and bloodiest as far as
north-easterners were concerned. After February 1937, there were only
small groups of new north-east brigader recruits, with a final small burst in
January 1938.[126] One example of an individual who signed up precisely
because of the death of a brigader in battle was Edward Tattam.[127] But the
brigader in question was his brother Bill, making this case exceptional.
Thus, while news of deaths in battle did not completely end recruitment, it
did not appear to act as much of an incentive for most either.

Did brigaders in some way induce individuals to devote greater efforts
to campaigning for the Republic at home? Francis implied that the brigaders' example brought others into Spanish aid activity and Alexander
made an explicit link between a Dundee brigaders' return home for medical treatment and city's anti-fascist movement rising to 'a new level as a
result'.[128] Indeed, for Communists, that the deaths of brigaders in Spain
had a palpable positive effect on activities at home was a way to justify
their sacrifice secondary only to the hope that their deaths would contri-
bute to a Republican victory.[129]

In practice, it is often difficult to delineate the effects of both the general and more specific appeals from brigaders at the front. In the context
of the latter, Clifford Lawther's appeal certainly had an effect on brother
Will, who quoted it often in speeches when arguing for some form of
Republican aid. Lawther was surely instrumental in the extensive support
the DMA provided the IBDWAC, and several other Spanish aid campaigns.[130] However, some of the other Lawther brothers argued that Will's
reticence on the NCL over Spain was contrary to the spirit of Clifford's
plea.[131] In terms of Codling's general appeal in South Shields, there was at
least one negative reaction. Codling's letter 'surprised and annoyed' a
correspondent, who thought that 'the unions have quite enough on their
hands without helping other countries, no matter what Radicals say'.[132]

The minutes of the local Labour Party and trades council gave no indication that Codling's direct appeal to them had any palpable effect in the short-term. David Adams was a Labour Party Catholic and, as such, in a potentially awkward position. It is conceivable that George's letter, and others like it, played a part in Adams' complex reaction to the issue.[133]

However, in late January 1937, left-wing correspondent 'Janus' expressed fears that Elliott's 'courage and faith' had not had the galvanising effect on the Blyth Labour Party that Elliott himself and many others had anticipated.[134] Certainly, intentions appeared good at Elliott's memorial meeting, where the resolution pledged everyone to 'do all they could to help the cause for which he, and others, had given their lives'.[135] Yet, there appeared to have been no greater intensity in Blyth official movement activity on Spain after July 1937 than before it. Indeed, Blyth Communist William Allan, noting in a tribute that Elliott had kept asking for more to be done at home against Non-Intervention but that 'very much is still to be done in this direction', tacitly recognised as much.[136] This apparent indifference must have been related in part to Elliott's party affiliation, which left him politically distant from most of the Blyth official labour movement, in spite of his personal friendships with Labour activists.

Elliott's situation contrasted with that of Jobling, who enjoyed good political relations with many key Labour activists in Blaydon. There, Jobling did not need to make such a sacrifice to energise the activity of the official movement on Spain, in spite of Labour councillor John Wilson's exhortation to 'salute our fallen comrades', and avenge them 'by the increased activity that we carry out in every sphere of the Working Class Movement'.[137] Indeed, Jobling had already helped to activate the local movement on the issue before going to Spain.[138] Sheffield brigader Arthur Newsum's sacrifice (he was killed in January 1937), 'left behind inspiration in the hearts and minds of his comrades of that time. For fifty years many of these have carried his memory with them'.[139] Perhaps this was the most achievable form of direct inspiration for Communist brigaders: for their own party comrades, rather than the wider labour movement. That said, the brigaders' example, and their interventions and appeals from the front, must have had *some* positive effect in energising Spanish aid activities at home. Nevertheless, the strength of this impact, no doubt lessened to a great extent by the political gulf between the CP and its milieu and the official movement, was slight considering the degree of sacrifice demanded to achieve it.

Still, their example, albeit mediated through fiction, could act to inspire and help to politicise future generations. A specific example of this was Graham Holtham. As a Jarrow pupil in the mid-1970s, he read *The Freedom Tree*, a (highly) fictional account of the adventures of a Jarrow lad who went to Spain to fight for the Republic:

> this book made a major impression on me and in many ways ignited my interest in politics (eventually leading to my continuing membership of the Labour Party). I have my tatty paperback copy still. I think I continue to be inspired by the idea of someone from my home town taking part in such a great and worthy endeavour (the fact it is fictional is neither here nor there).[140]

When They Came Home

Arguably, the most impact that brigaders could have on the issue in Britain was after they came home en masse in late 1938 (and in some cases early 1939). For Communist nurse Nan Green, returning home meant 'merely changing the front and the weapons ... The war was not yet lost...'. Food and medical supplies were 'needed more than ever' and the political struggle was 'more urgent still'.[141] Most South Wales brigaders returned home 'fired with enthusiasm', at least while the war was on.[142] However, those who had been the least politically active before they went to Spain lapsed back into inactivity on their return.[143] Alexander claimed that the majority of those returning were stronger, politically tempered and better able in struggle. Yet he, too, recognised that not all returning brigaders retained their faith in the cause.[144]

In the north-east, in addition to raising money for the IBDWAC, there were other Spanish aid campaigns in which brigaders could involve themselves. However, while the majority returning were likely to have been, at least in part, politically inspired by their time in Spain, this did not necessarily translate into activity on any aspect of the issue on the home front. Indeed, there was direct evidence of only eight north-east ex-brigaders and two medics (nurse Ramshaw and Frank Girling) campaigning for the Republic (mostly the Tyneside foodship) on their return from Spain after October 1938. Six of these were from South Shields, but this was the only locality in the region where ex-brigaders grouped and acted together to impact on local politics in a public way. For the majority of north-east ex-brigaders, the pro-Republic struggle did not appear to take on new forms on their return home. Indeed, ex-brigaders touring the country in the 'International Brigade convoy' appeared to make more of a public political impact on Spain in parts of the region than did its indigenous contingent, by supporting, for example, the Tyneside foodship campaign in North Shields.[145]

There were several likely reasons for this. The continued plight of the Republic, and its eventual defeat, must have been demoralising for some of those who had suffered considerably and lost friends in an endeavour to prevent this. There was a need to rest and recuperate, to enjoy 'the quiet and peacefulness' after Spain.[146] A sense of satisfaction at a job well done against impossible odds also possibly militated against renewed activity on the home front. Sam Thompson, for example, intended to settle in South Shields 'content that he has done his bit for democracy'.[147] Blair, too, was 'quite satisfied'.[148] The forms of Spanish aid activity, too, could hardly have contrasted more: going door-to-door asking for donations could not compare with fighting on the frontline in Spain.

There were practical considerations, too. The need to find a job and a readiness to move elsewhere to get one due to unemployment or blacklisting was time-consuming and potentially demoralising and, if successful, took some activists out of the area again. John Blair, for example, was 'elated' to get a labourer's job back in Bath in January 1939.[149] His five remaining comrades would 'go to Hong Kong for a job if need be'.[150] Similarly, John Potts had no plans, but 'will go where there is the prospect of employment'.[151] Physical problems as the result of wounds were also restrictive. A 'difficult' time in Spain may also have acted as a disincentive to activity at home. The circumstances in which nurse Wilson left Spain may well explain why she was not prominent in any Spanish aid campaigning after returning home.

However, Arthur Teasdale's case revealed that neither of the last two conditions *necessarily* prevented post-return activity on Spain. In August 1938, Teasdale was going to London for treatment on his hand, and planning to lecture and fundraise for Spain afterwards.[152] He joined five other South Shields ex-brigaders (including Thompson and Blair) on their return to further campaigning activities, emphasising their credentials as activists with first hand experience of the conflict and suffering of the people. Thompson had also lost his comrade Codling who he appeared to have been very close to in Spain, yet this did not prevent him from getting involved on his return.[153] Unemployment, too, was not necessarily a direct hindrance. After Blair got his job, the remaining five South Shields ex-brigaders continued to sustain themselves on the dole, devoting their time to the foodship campaign.[154] Graham was planning to 'recuperate and settle down to normal life', but still threw himself into Spain campaigning on several fronts.[155]

However, it was clear that the brigaders who *were* active on their return home did not alter in any palpable way the campaigning agenda or take the lead in the north-east Spanish aid campaigns. They appeared to take supporting roles in campaigns planned and run by other activists. Thus, they dutifully supported the Tyneside foodship campaign, which largely ignored the arms and Non-Intervention issues. Indeed, the language they used to support this campaign was broadly in accordance with the human-itarian message promoted by its main organisers, with only a hint of pro-Republican partisanship.[156] Even the organised South Shields group of ex-brigaders offered no alternative focus for rallying forces explicitly against Non-Intervention and for the shipment of arms to Spain. The 'Interna-tional Brigade convoy', too, simply organised for the dominant campaign of the time, the foodship. Certainly, there was no echo of an attempt by South Wales brigaders to organise a local strike in support of arms for the Republic (though this was unusual there, too).[157] This may well have been because the majority of north-east brigaders did not consider the arms question especially significant to the Republic's success; at least not until very late in the conflict.

Arms and the Republic's 'Invincibility'

Fighting on the front lines gave brigaders an appearance of being well qualified to comment on the fortunes of the protagonists and who was likely to prevail. They had the public outlets, too, to voice their thoughts. Alexander claimed that brigaders sought to 'step up the pressure on the government and on the Labour leaders' to end Non-Intervention.[158] How-ever, before April 1938, on the relatively rare occasions when north-east brigaders mentioned Non-Intervention in public forums, its effect was usually depicted as, at worst, postponing an inevitable Republican victory. The Republic's lack of arms did not seem a major concern for any north-east brigader reported in the regional press for the first 20 months of the war. The indefatigable spirit of the 'Spanish people', the determination and heroism of the Republican forces, pro-Republicans in Franco's army, the Negrín government and new 'popular' army after summer 1937 and Republican successes (as at Guadalajara in March 1937), left brigaders like Codling and Thompson 'increasingly confident that the ultimate victory in

Spain will be with the Government forces' in early 1938.[159] Six other north-east brigaders expressed similar sentiments, some on more than one occasion, in this period.[160] The pessimistic tone of teenager Billy Bamborough's warning in May 1937 that 'It looks as if it will be a long time before we get back to England, that is if we are still alive, because the fascists are getting pretty desperate', was rare in this period.[161]

Back from Spain in April 1938, George Aitken's speeches received detailed coverage. Aitken condemned Non-Intervention, mentioning that the Republic had poor armaments as a result. While he made the arms issue more central, there remained a lack of clarity as to whether he regarded the ending of Non-Intervention as *essential* to the Republic's chances of victory; or whether it remained merely a matter of *when* the Republic would inevitably win. Other brigaders, speaking from the frontline and in the region, continued to maintain that a Republican victory would come, but faster with arms, for the same reasons as in 1937.[162] With the return of brigaders from imprisonment or after their withdrawal in autumn 1938, came more voices certain of a Republican victory. Indeed, this very withdrawal convinced some of the strength of the Republican army. It suggested that 'for the first time' the Republic could contemplate the 'possibility of military victory'.[163]

In December 1938, the emphasis altered slightly as brigaders like John Blair began saying that Republican victory was contingent on it receiving arms, though 'people with courage and staying power like that can't be beaten in the long run'.[164] Sam Langley made similar comments: while the Republic could not be beaten, it needed arms (and food) to win.[165] In mid-January 1939, John Halliwell, whose politics did not appear particularly left-wing, was the first brigader in the region to warn that Franco was 'bound to' win ('He is much stronger in guns, planes and tanks'), unless the Republic secured belligerent rights (in which case the Republic 'would drive the rebels right on to the Portuguese border in three months').[166] By late January, Frank Graham was openly contemplating the possibility of a fascist victory in Spain: 'Arms for Spain' was now 'the only realistic slogan of today'.[167] Yet in early March 1939, condemning the government's possible recognition of Franco, Graham pointed out that 'the Spanish Republic is not yet defeated'.[168] North-east activists were not alone in 'their expectation that victory was just around the corner ... that a little more effort could do the trick'.[169]

As many recognised at the time, the Republic needed arms from the outset. Bill Alexander commented, 'No one knew better than they [brigaders] just what 'Non-Intervention' was achieving'.[170] Yet, for most of the war, north-east brigaders paid scant attention to propagandising explicitly against Non-Intervention, instead subscribing to an 'inevitability of Republican victory' thesis. The fear of appearing defeatist must have played a part, as must the inspirational experience of struggling together with other internationals and Spaniards in such testing circumstances against fascism. However, in some respects, too, this phenomenon was also a consequence of the mythology surrounding the popular front, one that held that the popular front was *the way* to defeat fascism definitively. Fascism, therefore, could not possibly defeat the popular front in Spain. There was another way in which the 'inevitability of Republican victory' thesis and the popular front dovetailed. The former did not bring to the fore awkward questions relating to the ways in which Britain's support for Non-Intervention could be ended and arms sent to Spain in large quantities; issues around the possible use of industrial direct action that were likely to abort any putative popular front coalition in Britain.[171] The effect was that many pro-Republican activists at home could neglect the arms issue, as, apparently, it was not especially important. This was particularly convenient for Labour leaders and MPs, who could subscribe to the 'inevitability of Republican victory' thesis and not worry about doing much against Non-Intervention.

Effect on Relations Between Labour and the CP

Ostensibly, the International Brigade appeared to facilitate improved relations between the Labour and Communist Parties in the north-east. Several Communists found that their status as brigaders made it easier for them to speak on platforms with Labour Party activists. Indeed, this was the most significant (in terms of numbers) of the very few ways in which Communists could access usually exclusive official north-east labour movement public platforms in this period. Graham often shared the platform with a variety of official movement activists in the 50 or 60 meetings he addressed while on his month long speaking tour.[172] On his return home in October 1938, Graham's ex-brigader status again gave him prominence in the main Spanish aid campaigns and allowed him access to some local Labour Party platforms.[173] In 1938, George Aitken addressed official movement Mayday meetings in Blaydon, Highfield and Blyth. Around the same time, less prominent Communist brigaders like George Coyle also spoke at official movement events.[174] Furthermore, Communist brigaders also, on at least one occasion, gained special access to regional trade union leaders. In April 1938, a deputation of wounded Communist brigaders (and bereaved relatives) met with the NMA executive to discuss its activity on the issue.[175]

The deaths in action of prominent Communist brigaders also appeared to promote cordial relations. Tributes came from local Labour publications like the *Gateshead Labour Herald*, for example, which paid a glowing tribute to Jobling and other brigaders: 'If this flame that burns within these fighters could sweep the ranks of youth, we would win the world'.[176] Some Labour activists eulogised Communist combatants. Henry Bolton, for example, paid tribute to Jobling in a session of Blaydon council, which he chaired, and Morpeth MP R.J. Taylor was one of several Labour figures to do likewise for Bob Elliott. Naturally, this also occurred at memorial meetings that brought Communists and official movement activists together on the platform.[177] The 'welcome home' and memorial meetings after autumn 1938 were further occasions for joint platforms and attracted wide official movement support.[178] The main north-east memorial meeting on 15 January 1939, in particular, received the patronage of so many significant figures in the regional official movement that the Communist brigader speaker, Frank Graham, appeared swamped.[179] Indeed, a good deal of the generous collection at this meeting came from sections of the official movement, which reflected longer-term support for the IBDWAC from the official side, most notably, but not exclusively, the heavy sponsorship of the DMA.[180] Among the audience at this meeting were four representatives of the (marginally) anti-Communist Newcastle City Labour Party, albeit using complimentary tickets.[181]

However, several considerations temper the above evidence. Firstly, many of the Labour activists sharing platforms with, or eulogising Communists killed in Spain, were left-wingers already favourable to the party. Gateshead left-winger Allan Henderson, for example, penned the *Herald* tribute.[182] The moderate official activists who occasionally joined them usually distanced themselves from Communism. Blyth Labour mayor Reilly, for example, was clear that; 'While I did not agree with his [Elliott's] politics in the main, I certainly admired the way in which he put forward his view, for which he fought and died'.[183] Indeed, every time Reilly spoke about Elliott, he was careful to state his disapproval of his friend's politics. Furthermore, Elliott's example did nothing to improve relations between the parties in Blyth; Labour even fielded an, albeit unsuccessful, candidate against the Communist when it came to electing Elliott's council replacement in October 1937.[184]

A crucial feature of Communist brigaders' appearances on Labour platforms was that, in these situations, their party affiliation invariably remained undisclosed. For example, Aitken spoke at the 1938 NMA and Morpeth CLP Mayday demonstration as a 'member of the Spanish International Brigade'.[185] The only occasions when Communist brigaders had their party affiliation mentioned came in the context of meetings organised by their own party.[186] Thus, the presence of a (Communist) brigader speaker at the 1938 South Shields Labour Party Mayday meeting, for example, was wholly consistent with the party's continued refusals to cooperate with Communists. The same stood for Blyth Labour Party. Brigaders were attractive speakers for these events as they had firsthand knowledge of the situation in Spain. It seems likely that, in most cases, the presence of a Communist brigader speaker on an official Labour platform was not especially significant. Like the presence of a Communist brigader on a Houghton-le-Spring CLP public platform, this, alone, normally did not indicate a change in the official institution's political outlook, nor did it help to provoke one.[187] Most of the official institutions and individuals who proffered extensive support to the IBDWAC did not regard this as synonymous with support for the CP. This stood for the increasing numbers of labour movement figures who shared platforms with Communist brigaders at memorial and 'welcome home' meetings after October 1938. In some respects the bravery and self-sacrifice of the brigaders was bigger than the party that facilitated this sacrifice. The sacrifice could be respected and celebrated, and those suffering as a result of it supported, without this leading in any way down the political road towards understanding and cooperation with the CP.

Certainly, the NMA brigader deputation was successful in as far as it got the NMA to act on the issue (and secured a brigader speaker at the NMA Mayday meeting).[188] However, the NMA's 'action' – attempts to get the national movement to mobilise on Spain – ultimately served to underscore the bonds of loyalty between it and the national, anti-Communist (and, in certain key respects, inactive on Spain) leadership.[189] The case of Elliott was significant. He had the respect and even friendship of some Labour councillors in Blyth yet his affiliation to the CP represented an insurmountable barrier between them, a wall which even empathy, at a fundamental political level, could not break through. All supported the Spanish Republic, and drew their understanding of the conflict from the same discourse (fascism against democracy); but Communists and Labour activists in Blyth continued to speak very different languages. If anything,

Elliott's death in Spain and all the memorialisation afterwards served to underline this. Most Labour activists could appreciate Elliott's honesty, bravery and self-sacrifice, but, at a fundamental level, they could not fully *understand* it. Indeed, mayor Reilly noted in his tribute that 'some even questioned the wisdom of his [Elliott's] last venture …'.[190] While the CP's popular front policy certainly furthered this incomprehension, coming as it did soon after an ultra-sectarian period, this was a more deep-seated and endemic problem for 'foreign' Communism in Britain. Communists could try in this popular front period, as at a pageant in Sunderland, to claim that their party was a manifestation of the British radical tradition (and employ brigaders as part of this process).[191] Nevertheless, on the whole, this did not wash with non-Communists.

Negative Effects on the CP and NUWM

The regional CP sustained a significant loss in that at least ten of the north-east brigaders killed were party members.[192] The loss of two of these, Jobling and Elliott, received most attention. At a Jobling tribute meeting, Woods claimed the CP 'considered it had lost one of the most promising of its members'.[193] But Elliott's death was also, for Woods, a 'serious loss' to the north-east CP.[194] W.H. Breadin, Elliott's comrade on Blyth council, commented similarly on an activist who had been in the party since the experience of the 1926 lockout.[195] Indeed, a critic claimed in December 1937 that Blyth CP did not have the calibre of candidates of Elliott to field at the local elections and its attempts at pursuing the united front with Labour in the polls were 'to gull the Croft ward electors into thinking that the Blyth Communist Party is still strong and healthy'.[196]

However, for the north-east CP, all activists lost were significant. Harry Reynolds, for example, who was killed at Jarama. Reynolds joined the British army in 1918, an experience that eventually made him a Communist and who, by 1936, was a party stalwart of a decade's experience and involved 'in any movement that was going'.[197] Another example was Harry Smith, who was only one day in the line before also being killed at Jarama. A strong character, his loss to the CP was significant also in that he was that rare political animal, a crypto-Communist who was also secretary of Jesmond Labour Party.[198] Other, younger Communists killed had also displayed potential. Edgar Wilkinson, for example, was only 19 when he left in the Sunderland 'advance' party. He also died on the first day of Jarama. Graham recalled that Wilkinson 'played a leading role in political work amongst the youth of this town'. The two had first met on the 1936

NUWM hunger march and Graham 'quickly came to appreciate his deep sincerity and political ability'.[199] A second Communist of the Sunderland advance party was Tom Dolan who had 'borne himself with a stoicism that was remarkable did you not realise that it arose from the deep convictions which had brought him so far from home ...'.[200] Stephen Codling had been a significant NUWM activist in South Shields as secretary of the town's branch and Hunger March contingent organiser.[201] Will Tattam, an ex-Durham miner, was the only CP member killed who had moved away, and thus already been lost to the regional party before 1936.[202]

A more complete and overt appreciation of the wider loss sustained by the north-east CP came from party activists themselves after time for reflection. In 1985, Woods still flagged up Jobling's death, but he also recognised the wider 'loss sustained by a party whose scant resources were stretched over such a wide area'.[203] Around the same time, he told Don Watson that he had 'misgivings, not regrets but misgivings, about maybe a mistake was made by the party. We sent our best comrades from this area to Spain, they were killed and we couldn't afford that to happen when we needed them here as cadres'.[204] Similarly, George Short, who had been responsible for interviewing potential brigaders on Teesside, later commented that 'We lost the flower of the party'.[205] Indeed, in the post-war years Communist Bert Ward remembered Short telling him that the worst part of this job 'was having to visit their families when they became casualties'.[206]

However, perhaps activists like Jobling brought the CP more respect by being killed in Spain than they would if they had remained alive. But did Jobling in death achieve more for the CP in the region than, for example, George Short, who joined the party around the same time and also attended the Lenin School in Russia, but who did not fight in Spain?[207] Certainly, Jobling's death seems to have allowed for his conversion into a form of cult or martyr figure in some north-east left circles. Francis claimed that for every Communist killed in Spain, 'there must have been many more recruited by the inspiration provided by the sacrifices in Spain'.[208] But, if Jobling's death *had* brought recruits to the north-east CP, it had clearly not brought very many, as party membership remained stubbornly low: far lower than when the party used militant language to attract miner activists during the 1926 lockout, and even after the disillusionment set in, in 1927. Surely Jobling, already somewhat of a 'hero' before 1936 for his dedicated involvement in unemployed struggles, could have made far more Communist recruits at home than he did by making the ultimate sacrifice in Spain, and becoming an image on a banner. As Communist organiser (and later anti-Communist) Douglas Hyde later commented, 'Dead men could make no contribution to the fight for Soviet Britain'.[209] Bill Alexander claimed that there was no evidence that the CP leadership wanted martyrs in Spain.[210] While the International Brigade and the sacrifices of individual Communists in it, some of which were well-publicised, must have boosted the credibility of the CP, the north-east showed that this in itself did not necessarily bring in substantial numbers of new recruits.[211]

Francis was well aware of this consequence in South Wales: 'the gap left by 20 miners killed in Spain also had its effect, for in such a small party the role of a few individual political activists can be decisive'.[212] Each individual loss dealt 'body blows' to the CP.[213] This was even more true of the north-east, given the relative and absolute weakness of the CP in the region. Those killed in Spain were only 2 per cent of the total north-east district membership. However, they were often important activists, and the north-east CP could ill afford to loose them. Several were young, just starting out on their political lives and showing potential. Their activism was as, or even more, vital to the party than the involvement of its new-found middle-class supporters. This is not, of course, to argue that the CP would have grown sufficiently to supplant the Labour Party in the region, nor that the loss of several key activists was the only aspect of the party's behaviour in the period that hampered it.[214] Still, on balance, the north-east party lost far more than it gained from the deaths of some of its main activists in Spain.

Furthermore, the party also suffered from the short-term loss of activists who eventually came back. While, as detailed above, several Communists attempted as much as practicable to intervene on the home front from Spain, this could never replace their day-to-day involvement before their departures. A graphic illustration of the obvious negative effect on a trade union branch's politics (as far as the CP was concerned) when an individual Communist is removed can be observed clearly in the Gateshead 1st ASW branch minutes. It seemed radical in the early 1930s, under John Henderson's guidance, but was inactive on Spain and other left issues after his departure for the Lenin School in the Soviet Union.[215]

The effect on the NUWM, which sent more north-east activists, was probably far worse. Several of the Communists killed in Spain, were as important to the functioning of the NUWM than they were to the CP. These included Jobling and Elliott, who were leaders at national, as well as regional and local levels.[216] The NUWM organised three anti-Means Test demonstrations in the region in early 1937, but after this, there were only a handful of sporadic, localised examples of NUWM agitation.[217] By December 1937, Communist William Allan reported 'almost complete deadness' in unemployed agitation in the north-east, despite the NUWM retaining many members in the region.[218] This was part of a national decline after the 1936 Hunger March, as mass action gave way to small scale campaigning 'stunts'. Richard Croucher attributed this development to the CP ascribing less importance to unemployed struggles, more NUWM activists securing work, and the NUWM's increasingly centralised organisation alienating activists. Croucher also noted that the NUWM 'had much to lose' when its activists went to Spain and this factor was surely crucial in explaining the decline in activity in the north-east.[219] Furthermore, as well as removing vital activists, the NUWM brigaders might well have been those more favourably disposed towards the CP, as, by late 1937, the NUWM district was 'dominated by people against the party'.[220]

A more specific and unintended possible effect came in Blyth NUWM, one of few north-east branches to remain obviously active (on unemployment and Spain) after January 1937. An exchange of letters in the local press in August 1937 aired a disagreement between two NUWM branch activists over support for the Elliott cigarette fund.[221] 'Trouble' in Blyth NUWM branch resulted in its dissolution, with a 'number' of members expelled, by mid-November 1937. It was unclear if this was a result of the 'cigarette fund' controversy, but it certainly provided an issue around which division could coalesce and in that sense contributed to the branch's momentary demise (it was running again by October 1938).[222]

What the Communists Who Came Back Did Next: Short-Term and Long-Term

The Communists who returned reacted in very different ways to their experiences in Spain in both the short and longer terms. In this context, Arthur Teasdale's case deserves closer examination. A CP branch secretary at home, Teasdale was often in trouble and had a tumultuous relationship in Spain with the CP and the International Brigade authorities who regarded him as an 'enemy of the working class'.[223] Yet Teasdale dutifully provided good propaganda for the cause from the frontline and, after returning home, remained an effective activist and propagandist on Spain with no hint of having had any kind of problem while there. Indeed, Teasdale, who had sustained disfiguring injuries, had more reasons than most to sound bitter. Yet he seemed more dedicated to the experience in Spain and the need to continue agitating on the home front than many of his regional party comrades. In January 1939, Teasdale was one of the South Shields brigaders who said that 'if the call came again they would go back to Spain'.[224] He remained active in the CP orbit outside of Spain too: in early February 1939, for example, he spoke at a Boldon NUWM meeting.[225] Another high profile Communist brigader, Sam Langley, spoke at a CP public meeting in North Shields to protest about alleged inaction over the *Jeanie Stewart*, a missing trawler (not connected to Spain) in January 1939, suggesting that he also remained sympathetic to the party soon after his return from Spain.[226] There was certainly no obvious disaffection in the region on the scale that provoked the formation by ex-brigaders of an 'Anti-Communist League'.[227]

For some Communists, the experiences in Spain informed the rest of the political lives within the party's sphere. Francis claimed that many were prepared to dedicate their lives to the CP, as they had been prepared to die in Spain for it.[228] Bobbie Qualie, for example, remained a lifelong Communist. His increasing depression in later life possibly led to his suicide in 1982, but there is no evidence that this was related to any experience in Spain.[229] For George Aitken, too, Spain was 'one of the great experiences of my life. Spain was something the like of which you cannot imagine today'.[230] While the experience was, and remained, highly important for Aitken, it was insufficient to keep him in the CP afterwards. A CP member from 1921, who attended the Lenin School 1926–7, Aitken left the party soon after returning from Spain.[231]

Similarly, many years later John Henderson provided Don Watson with a detailed account of his time in Spain. The international anti-fascist solidarity clearly impressed Henderson, who became the 'popular postman' on the Jarama front, but he was candid, too, about the poor kit and training provided.[232] For Henderson, 'Spain was hard, and I mean hard. How I got back alive, I'll never know. But I've never regretted it'.[233] Yet, again, this did not keep him in the CP in the longer-term, as he left it in the 1950s.[234] A third activist who had been to Lenin School aged 26 (1931–3) and fought in Spain was George Coyle. A miner, Coyle had only joined the party in 1930, but he gained a good reputation with the Communist authorities. He eventually left the CP in 1968.[235] Tommy Kerr dropped out of politics after 1945, though it remained unclear whether this was in some way related to the critique he retained of the different parties and political divisions in Spain he observed during the conflict.[236]

For Frank Graham, the experience clearly defined much of the rest of his life. Only 24 when he returned from Spain, Graham had crammed 'into the last two years more excitement than the average individual might expect in a lifetime. His story might have been culled from the pages of a schoolboy "thriller" ….[237] In the short-term he took over from Woods as the north-east IBDWAC secretary.[238] Graham subsequently maintained a commitment to preserving the party's narrative of the conflict. Indeed, as early as April 1937, Graham announced that he was 'historian of the English-speaking battalion and it will be his duty to collate the stories of the soldiers who have been fighting on the Madrid-Toledo front during the worst days of the war for a book which will be published in four languages'.[239] In late 1938, Graham stated his intention to write a book about his own experiences.[240] This did not happen until 1987 when he published *The Battle of Jarama*, which detailed some of his and other north-eastern brigaders' experiences. He followed this up in 1999 with a second volume, again published by his own company. Throughout, Graham maintained his political understanding of the war, as evident in his vituperative review of Ken Loach's film *Land and Freedom* in this latter volume.[241] Graham's similar claims in a 1994 interview largely corresponded with the 'maintenance of self-esteem' type of reminiscence, like Margot Heinemann's unchanged version of the conflict, discussed by Angela Jackson.[242] As there were possibly, according to Communist activist Nan Green, as many motives as brigaders, so there were as many reactions to the experience as there were brigaders, even from those drawn exclusively from the ranks of the CP.[243]

The Popular Front and the Brigaders: Mutual Implications

Finally, there are questions around the ways in which the popular front informed the language brigaders used to express their political visions, as well as the supposed lessons that the CP drew relating to the brigaders' struggle in Spain and the popular front that theoretically applied on the home front. John Hopkins claimed that for the most part British brigaders were not Marxist revolutionaries, rather they were 'of the left' fighting for the rights that 'every freeborn Englishman should enjoy'.[244] The majority of British brigaders wanted 'not to overthrow the traditional order but to have their rightful claims, and those of the international working-class, recognised by those who ruled or oppressed them'.[245]

In some respects, the way Communist brigaders in the north-east articulated their political visions certainly suggested this. For many, the defence of democracy in Spain was a prevalent theme. This was explicit in a letter George Aitken wrote to the *North Mail* in January 1937 in which he called on 'every British democrat' to protest as 'The triumph of Fascism in Spain will lead ... inevitably, to the destruction of democracy in our own country.[246] Many other brigaders expressed themselves similarly. Billy Bamborough, for example, was 'willing to give my life for the working-class of Spain and save the world for democracy'.[247] Frank Graham 'went to Spain to fight for the government because I believe that the struggle which is going on there concerns not only Spaniards but all democracy throughout the world. I was fit and felt I could help by joining up'.[248] And John Henderson joined partly for the 'domestic issue of here was an army general who'd attacked a duly and properly elected government, it wasn't even a socialist government, more like a Labour one'.[249]

However, there remains a problem of interpretation. It seems unlikely that Aitken, a long-term Communist activist, had abandoned the aim of achieving Communism in Britain and was now content to settle for a defence of capitalist democracy. Instead, Aitken, as a disciplined Communist leader, was merely expressing the language required at a time when his party was advocating the popular front policy. Douglas Hyde, Communist activist and later Communist critic, described the popular front as 'a temporary retreat, but justifiable in the light of Marxist thinking. The new tactic was to soft-pedal in public whilst sticking to everything as before in private... we went back on none of our fundamentals; we simply put some into cold storage and found new methods of dishing up the rest'.[250] There was no obvious reason why this would not stand for other longer-standing Communists. However, recruits to the party after its formal adoption of the popular front in 1935 *may well* have joined as a result of this policy, and because the party seemed to be the most vigorous anti-fascist force. As Hopkins claimed, these recruits may well have 'possessed a view of the world that was shaped more by Paineite radicalism and internationalism than socialist dogma ...', but to claim that this characterised the politics of the majority of Communist (as well as non-Communist) brigaders seems more difficult to sustain.[251] Indeed, with more middle-class recruits attracted by a programme aimed at appealing to the whole of the progressive left including liberals, but with anti-fascism at its core, the CP was beginning to look something like a popular front itself after 1935.

Clearly, all brigaders' contemporary pronouncements (Communist or not) cannot be comprehended outside the political context in which they were made. The popular front demanded a toning-down of revolutionary rhetoric, for fear of alienating potential liberal and Labour allies. This is not to argue that Communists really thought they were fighting for Communist revolution in Spain. But it was quite plausible that Communist brigaders could retain a desire to help bring about a Communist world in the long run, but be content to defend capitalist democracy against fascist onslaught in the short-term.[252]

This was because the popular front was based on the premise that the democracies would eventually ally with Soviet Russia against the fascist states. Communism would, it asserted, come later, after the defeat of fascism. How Communism would arrive in Britain was another moot point. An unnamed north-east Communist working at a Spanish aid exhibition in Newcastle in July 1937 openly admitted that armed insurrection would be necessary at the time of the British revolution, which was 'coming here. But the time is not yet'.[253] Indeed, Hyde claimed Communists went to Spain to learn how to fight, in order to bring about a Soviet Britain.[254] In August 1936 another Communist claimed that they would use democratic machinery as far as possible, but when this was destroyed by the capitalist class using violence, Communists would 'have to crush them with greater violence.' This was not, apparently, a belief in violence but a recognition of capitalist methods.[255] It was significant that both these north-east Communists (the former quoted in an informal capacity and perhaps not anticipating that their words would be reproduced publicly), were commenting before 1938, in a period when the CP was pursuing working-class unity as a prelude to the full-blown popular front. Still, the extent to which grassroots Communists understood the full and often paradoxical implications that the popular front brought their party varied considerably between individuals. To ignore the implications of this policy is to neglect one of the major discourses that informed the language and perspectives of many of the period's left activists.

The issue was as complex for non-Communist brigaders, who did not tend to leave much evidence of their political beliefs. However, John Richardson told his mother that he was in Spain 'to fight for democracy and the liberty of the human race from Fascism *and capitalism*'.[256] This was a revolutionary-sounding outlook and it was probably no coincidence that Richardson was not a Communist and therefore not quite so restricted by the requirements of the popular front.

Richardson's words touched upon another issue. When a brigader talked of defending democracy, they did not necessarily mean contemporary British democracy. This was evident in a Frank Graham letter to the *Sun-*

derland Echo in December 1938. Graham was responding to a critic who inferred that the CP's 'present defence of capitalist democracy against fascism is insincere'. Graham claimed that there was 'no such thing as pure democracy' and in Britain it was 'necessarily limited by capitalist society'. According to Graham, the 'progressive men and women' who won rights and liberties in Britain were 'in many cases actuated by the same ideas that influence Communists today in defending them against the reactionary powers'. The 'socialist democracy' in the Soviet Union was 'fuller' than the British, and 'the finest and highest stage of democracy that civilisation has yet attained'.[257] Graham clearly thought the rights held in capitalist democracy were worth defending from fascism but that Soviet 'socialist democracy' was the ultimate aim. What remained unclear was whether Graham imagined that capitalist democracy could evolve into socialism (perhaps through the popular front, which he publicly supported in early December 1939) or whether the transition necessitated revolution in Britain.[258] Either way, 'socialist democracy' meant far more to Graham than some form of 'rewritten and renegotiated social contract' between rulers and the working-class.[259] The same surely stood for Elliott who, 'fighting in Spain for working-class democracy', surely imagined this to be qualitatively better than what he had left behind in Britain.[260] Elliott's words suggest that he subscribed to the 'Republic of a new type' concept of the CP in Spain.[261] The actual prospects for the emergence of this 'new kind of democracy' in Republican Spain were naturally contentious.[262]

In advocating the popular front, British Communists like north-easterner Michael Walter Harrison employed the example of Spain: 'It is well known that Spanish Communists are laying down their lives along with liberals and Socialists'.[263] Ideally for the CP, the International Brigade would also look like a popular front in action: Communists, socialists, Labourites, liberals and non-aligned progressives fighting shoulder-to-shoulder against the common enemy. Indeed, Aitken told a 1938 Mayday meeting in Ashington that the brigade 'had achieved a popular front in defence of democracy and in opposition to fascist aggression, and what was possible in the field of battle should be possible in this country where a popular front could oust Chamberlain from power'.[264] However, even in the north-east, a far less Communist-tinged environment than South Wales (where Communists comprised the vast majority of brigaders), the party and its milieu in the NUWM still dominated in the brigade's contingent. This ensured at least that those fighting were likely to have been doing so for political reasons, i.e. anti-fascism. But it was also a graphic representation of what a north-east popular front meant in practice: Communists and fellow travellers, some Labour people (generally with connections to the CP milieu) and very little else. In one way, the north-east contingent's complexion foreshadowed an aspect of the grassroots pro-Republic campaigns in the region that drew little mainstream liberal support.

2

THE 'OFFICIAL' MOVEMENT'S RESPONSE AT GRASSROOTS

Responding to a questionnaire in 1985, Charlie Woods claimed that 'in Newcastle and the North-east, the Labour Party and many unions hesitated to throw their support into the Spain campaign so that unofficial committees with rather narrower aims conducted the work'.[1] In 1994, Frank Graham claimed in an interview that '90 per cent of north-east Labour sections raised money for Spain'.[2] While both men were contemporaneous members of the Communist Party, they had quite different understandings of the reaction of the official north-east labour movement to Spain. Woods' critical comments, more representative of the official Communist version of events at the time, informed subsequent popular frontist accounts.[3] The claim that the regional leadership of the official movement largely replicated the indecision and inactivity of the national movement leaders, in the face of the true 'rank-and-file' grassroots members who were desperate to act, and who generally did so outside of their institutions and almost invariably with Communists, was a common motif.[4] This and the following two chapters assess the extent to which existing evidence sustains these and associated claims at grassroots. This chapter examines the reactions of official north-east movement institutions and their activists to Spain. It discusses the extent and dynamics of pro-Republic solidarity sentiment, support and action within the official movement. What emerges is a complex picture of different types of support at the various levels of organisation that varied over time and place, between institutions and within them. Notwithstanding this complexity, some broad patterns are also evident.

Defining 'Support'

Broadly speaking, there were two different ways in which an institution could demonstrate support for Spain: 'financial' and 'campaigning'. The most obvious way for an institution to provide 'financial' support for Spain was to donate from its own funds. A second, slightly more proactive way of generating financial support was for an institution to issue an appeal to its members to donate to a particular fund. Trade union branches could go one step further and attempt to impose a levy on their members' pay packets. This would ensure that the 'Spanish issue would be debated, which could prove to be as valuable as the size of the donation the call produced'.[5] Levies and appeals were also useful if an institution did not have considerable disposable funds itself. They were also more democratic, requiring supportive votes. The third means of financial support was for branch members to collect funds from their fellow workers or party members. This activity partly overlapped with 'campaigning' for Spain.

The most basic form of 'campaigning' activity was for an institution to pass a resolution condemning or calling for a certain type of action from the government. The regional press often reproduced such resolutions, securing a degree of publicity for the views expressed. A second, more engaged way of acting was for the institution to send delegates to demonstrations or meetings on Spain. Institutions could also send delegates to longer lasting activities, such as the organising institutions of different Spanish aid campaigns. A third way to campaign was to organise demonstrations or other activities to raise awareness of the issues and galvanise support for Spain. Institutions could do this autonomously at local level, in conjunction with other union branches (at local federation level), within a trades council, or at constituency, county or regional federation levels. The fourth and arguably most important means of campaigning for Spain was internally, attempting to get the wider labour movement to act in unison on the issue. Initiatives could begin at branch level, attempting to secure support for a particular stance at constituency or regional union level that would in turn act at the national level. Thus a Durham miners' lodge, for example, could secure a vote of all DMA lodges for a proposed policy. If successful, the DMA could then take this policy to the national Miners' Federation (the MFGB) which, in turn, could bring the issue to the highest levels within the labour movement; the TUC and National Council of Labour. However, branches sometimes by-passed this process by sending their resolutions straight to the TUC or NCL. This was an easier action for a single branch to perform, but, naturally, far less effective in terms of challenging national movement policy, as each resolution carried the endorsement of only that particular branch rather than a district or national union.

Parties' and Unions' Financial Support

There were three different ways in which north-east trade unions reacted to financial appeals for Spain. Most provided financial support, though the extent of this differed greatly between and within institutions. The DMA, partly due to its size and consequent financial power, was the single most significant donor to Spain in the north-east labour movement.[6] There was, however, considerable variation in the amounts and types of financial support DMA lodges provided. The NMA donated regularly but more modestly, commensurate with its smaller membership.[7] The response of its lodges, too, was very varied. In contrast to the miners central district institutions, the TGWU regional district only acted twice: overseeing a national appeal for aid in autumn 1936 and donating to the International Solidarity Fund (ISF) in January 1939. There was a distinct lack of branch support for Spain funds from regional TGWU branches, too.[8] The Amalgamated Society of Woodworkers in the north-east was similar, making a single district level donation in October 1936.[9] However, the United Patternmakers District Committee donated on at least four occasions.[10] A second smaller group of unions (some of which were not TUC affiliated) provided no support for Spain and a third even smaller group revealed hostility to Spain causes.[11]

Most north-east Labour Parties at all levels provided a degree of financial support for Spain. However, in contrast to the trade unions, where the district level was likely to donate the most, the sub-constituency institutions (normally local Labour Parties), usually provided the greatest financial support. Newburn and District LLP, for example, was a regular donor to several funds. Indeed, per member, it was by some way the largest Labour Party institutional donor of those with existent internal records.[12] Other LLPs, like South Shields LP&TC, also provided a lesser degree of financial support.[13] Like miners' lodges, the financial response varied considerably, even among LLPs in the same constituency. Thus Newbiggin and North Seaton LLP – along with Newburn LLP, a part of Wansbeck CLP – donated only once to Spain.[14] The constituency organisations tended to donate less. Thus, Durham and Wansbeck CLPs donated once each.[15] Again there was diversity, though. Houghton-le-Spring CLP, for example, was more generous.[16] Extra-constituency organisations, too, appeared to donate less. The vast bulk of Newcastle City Party's donations came from the takings of one public meeting in January 1938.[17] The NT-FLP only donated £2 from its own coffers to Spain (the Basque fund) in 1937. But this was the only 'charity' it donated to that year.[18] Still, this was more than its County Durham counterpart, which donated nothing at least until June 1938 (though it again appeared to have few funds to spare).[19]

Most trade union donations came straight from their funds. The central DMA also issued appeals to members and imposed a one-off levy as its share of the levy on all MFGB members (as did the NMA). But this was exceptional, as was an unsuccessful attempt by Horden lodge to impose unilaterally a one-shilling levy on its members towards the NCL's Spain fund in February 1937.[20] Some other lodges, such as Boldon, initiated more active fund – and awareness – raising, but this again was unusual.[21] Likewise, in the NMA, Cambois lodge was atypical in organising colliery collections for Spain, as well as donating itself.[22] Indeed, in Spain for VIAS in early 1937, Jim Atkinson saw a Cambois 'miners' welfare bus' among the 'odd collection' of British vehicles being used as ambulances by the Republic.[23] In contrast, on at least some occasions most local Labour Parties took their financial appeals for Spain funds outside of the confines of the party.[24]

The minutes of three north-east trade union branches reveal opposition to Spain causes.[25] Eden lodge was the most significant of these given its size and, as a DMA lodge, the most intriguing. It consistently voted against DMA grants for Spain, its lodge committee's decision to support such a grant in August 1936 being revoked by the lodge's general committee. But it did donate once to a Spain fund; ten shillings to the 'Linaria Defence Fund', in May 1937. The most likely explanation is that lodge activists did not regard this as a Spain fund at all. Certainly, as far as the Eden lodge committee was concerned, the lodge had made no separate grants to any Spanish aid fund, and it was likely that Catholic opposition was a factor.[26] In January 1939, Gateshead No.1 ASW branch voted heavily against a national executive proposed levy of 2s. 6d. per member for the ISF. Buchanan claimed that the vote against the levy generally 'did not indicate hostility to the ISF so much as anger at the Executive's priorities in the use of union funds'.[27] This could account for Gateshead branch's attitude, although its vote against was more emphatic.[28] Still, the branch made no donations to external causes in the late 1930s, so Spain was not an exceptionally unpopular cause for the branch in this respect.

Trade Union Campaigning

The DMA was also the single most important north-east labour movement institution in terms of campaigning on Spain.[29] A small minority of DMA lodges whose minutes remain occasionally made low-level campaigning moves. A handful of other lodges occasionally adopted higher level campaigning. Ryhope and Boldon lodges, for example, sent protest resolutions to the government.[30] Boldon organised, along with Marsden lodge, a demonstration in South Shields of 4,000 on domestic issues and Spain in mid-October, 1936.[31] In March 1937, Marsden attempted to get the DMA to adopt a militant stance on Spain.[32] In January 1937, Horden lodge went straight to the NCL with a call for it do 'all in its power' to lift Non-Intervention.[33] The central NMA was less active in some forms of campaigning than the DMA. It campaigned against government foreign policy in March 1938 and, around the same time, sent representatives to a regional movement conference to consider ways of increasing efforts for Spain. But it only began to pass resolutions on the international situation and send delegates to external Spain organisations late in the period.[34] However, similarly to the DMA, it began to campaign inside the labour movement in spring, 1938. The NMA lodges were, to an extent, more active campaigners than the central organisation. Cambois lodge's minutes reveal that it was the most active, sending delegates to demonstrations, organising public meetings and placing pressure on the central NMA.[35] However, Ellington lodge was not far behind. It organised a public meeting for Basques and in 1938 urged TUC general secretary Walter Citrine and the NMA to act.[36] On the other hand, Pegswood and Burradon lodges acted only once in campaigning ways. The former sent delegates to a Spain meeting in January 1937, the latter drew the attention of the foreign secretary to fascism in Spain in December 1937. In both cases these actions coincided with a short-lived period of financial support.[37] Outside of the miners there were only isolated examples of north-east trade unions campaigning on Spain at either branch or district levels. For example, Newcastle No.3 was the only north-east ASW branch that attempted to further the cause of Spain through its national union structure, while Newcastle Shop Assistants' Union branch urged the TUC to campaign on Spain in January 1937.[38]

What determined the DMA's generally strongly supportive stance on Spain? It is clear that certain factors that explained the very similar institutional response of the SWMF to Spain did not apply to the same degree to the DMA.[39] According to Francis, the single most significant determinant in the SWMF was the influential Communist Party. In the DMA, the CP had far fewer, and far less important representatives. However, left-wing activists influenced to highly differing degrees by Communist politics, if not actually Communists, *were* significant in the DMA's response. Two left-wingers elected as fulltime officials 1934–5 (Will Lawther and Sam Watson) clearly swung the balance towards a more active engagement in foreign affairs. Indeed, Will Lawther's distinctive rhetoric sounded strongly in the wording of many of the foreign policy resolutions the DMA passed in the later 1930s. Other lodge activists like Will Pearson (checkweighman at Marsden) and George Harvey (checkweighman and secretary of Follonsby lodge) undoubtedly lent their weight to support for Spain when they served for periods on the executive (though they did not coincide on it). These individuals must have influenced the attitudes of lodge activists, and of course, as their recently elected representatives, must have reflected, in part at least, attitudes within the lodges. While support for a left-winger as a trade unionist did not necessarily indicate endorsement for their politics, but was rather recognition of their organising abilities, representative democracy remained in many respects far better served at local and regional level than it did in the higher echelons of the labour movement. Apart from the full-time (elected) officials, the DMA executive was replaced annually (half every six months) by lodge ballot and all lodge officials were subject to annual re-election. All lodges voted on the major issues of union policy.

Some of the most committed DMA lodges, including Boldon, Marsden, Ryhope and Horden, were also Communist or left-wing controlled or influenced.[40] Yet Chilton lodge, which was particularly important in helping to determine the DMA's reaction as it successfully suggested both the August 1936 £200 grant, and that the DMA pay a weekly sum to the IBDWAC in March 1937, was not especially left-influenced. There was evidence of both left-influenced lodges such as Dean and Chapter and more moderate lodges (like Heworth) making similar financial commitments to different Spain causes.[41] Similarly, activists from both left-wing lodges (like Dawdon and Ryhope) and more moderate lodges (West Stanley) all helped to create Spanish aid committees in their localities.[42] This was vital to understanding the DMA's reaction: the appeal of Spain clearly went far further than the 'usual suspects' of the left, both in the executive and amongst the lodges. Lodge votes showed this clearly. The lodges always voted heavily in favour of (financial) support for Spain, in proportions varying from six to one in March 1937 (732 votes to 115) to almost unanimous in April 1938 (863–4). But they voted just over five to one *against* a proposal that the DMA support officially the NUWM Hunger March in autumn 1936.[43] Thus, while it was often left to the more militant lodges to take the initiative, the response to their different proposals showed clearly where they had struck a chord. In the NMA, Cambois lodge's active involvement on Spain was attributable in part to the influence of lodge chair, the Communist Willie Allan. However, other lodge members were also clearly supportive. Furthermore, the presence of influential Communists was not in itself a guarantee of continual active support. Cambois lodge itself went through a six-month period of inactivity on Spain between November 1937 and May 1938 and North Shields NUS branch provided no real support for Spain causes, in spite of the presence of an influential Communist activist (Alex Robson). It did, however, attempt from October 1937 to get Robson's shipping federation ban lifted (for his part in the *Linaria* dispute) and it urged the NUS executive to act on the issue of the bombing of British ships in Spanish waters.[44]

The 'proletarian internationalism' that, according to Francis, developed in the SWMF after 1918, had no obvious counterpart in the DMA.[45] Naturally, the support for north-east miners provided by Soviet miners in 1926 must have helped to foster a degree of internationalist feeling. Communist Wilf Jobling implied as much when he claimed that local contributions to a Spanish foodship in December 1936 were part of the same 'proud tradition' of international working-class solidarity as the 1926 Soviet aid.[46] Both Blyth Communist T. Rumney and Will Pearson also referred to the international solidarity of 1926, the latter when arguing for the DMA's call for a united front at 1937 MFGB conference.[47] But there was little precedent for the DMA's stance on Spain. In the earlier 1930s, it practised only a modest degree of 'internationalism': occasional, normally small, grants and supportive gestures.[48] However, Spain galvanised the DMA in a way other causes did not before 1936. Emmanuel Shinwell (MP for the Seaham mining constituency, though not a miner himself) claimed that there was a 'very close kinship' between Republican Spain and County Durham that came 'from a similarity of views, and from a similarity of the traditional struggles fought by the Durham miners in the past'.[49] This seemed valid as the lodges voted 844–50 in favour of a Horden lodge and DMA executive proposal to send financial aid to Asturian miners in March 1934.[50] And in 1935, in something of a dry run in miniature for the 1938 2s. 6d. levy, the DMA paid £75 as its agreed share of a £250 MFGB grant to Spanish miners.[51]

There are several reasons for the disjuncture between the levels of support from individual miners' lodges. Most had disposable funds for matters outside the requirements of their members (such as elderly miners' homes), but there were many other demands on funds, including appeals from hospitals and other kinds of charities, and some chose to allocate money to these. It was perhaps a natural choice for lodges like Seaham to support causes that were closer to home: geographically close by; close in the sense that perhaps their own members would require the service in question (a hospital, for example) or close in terms of trade unionists' struggles.[52] The amount of money that went to these causes was in some cases considerable, in absolute terms and in comparison with donations to Spain. In 1938, Cowpen miners in Northumberland, for example, contributed £1,267 15s. 6d. to charities including £258 10s. to an ambulance fund and £358 19s. 2d. to a Blyth hospital.[53] Naturally, for many lodges, financial support for these causes and Spain was not mutually exclusive. Cowpen lodge, for example, also donated to the Tyneside foodship.[54]

These lodge activists were entitled to argue that their district union was supporting causes like Spain sufficiently. After all, the majority of DMA lodges did support grants to Spain causes from their central union. United Patternmakers branch activists, for example, could make a similar claim. Furthermore, the larger central DMA grants coincided with similar sums going to causes closer to home. The August 1936 grant, for example, came in tandem with one for the same amount to a Barnsley colliery disaster fund.[55] This 'dual' funding from the central DMA, of that near and far, must have helped to convince some of the more reluctant lodge activists to support both. There was another set of funding demands on lodges from what were often relatively speaking financially weaker – especially in the coal-fields – Labour Party organisations. In supporting local Labour Parties (often, of course, staffed and run by the selfsame activists), lodges were, albeit indirectly, helping to fund activity on Spain. Indeed, for political campaigning purposes, lodge activists could use the local Labour Parties to take to the streets. This in part explains the fairly limited culture of campaigning on Spain unilaterally through individual lodges. Similar considerations applied to many other trade union activists, too. While miners' lodges tended to have reasonable supplies of funds, other trade unions had less disposable money and what they had often went to causes closer to home. An almost constant shortage of funds did not, however, prevent Newcastle Typographical Association branch from making regular donations to the municipal election campaign funds of Newcastle, Gateshead and South Shields Labour Parties, nor from annually donating to five separate hospitals.[56]

The poverty of individual trade unionists limited some types of financial aid. Thus, Horden lodge members voted against paying a lodge levy, the majority evidently reluctant to loose a chunk of their hard-earned wages. The best course of action for lodges desirous of generating generous financial aid was to attempt to get the DMA to act. Levies at district or federation level, such as the 1938 2s. 6d. MFGB levy, were bound to be more accepted though, Will Lawther's claim that Durham contributed its share 'without any opposition whatever' from members was slightly overstating the case.[57]

The diversity of the DMA's reaction at the different levels underlines the 'institutional factor'. The miners differed from other unions in that their district organisations were self-contained entities that federated into a national organisation at this time. This left them with more freedom of expression and financial power at district level than other trade unions, though it was unhelpful to describe some districts, like the SWMF, as 'dynamic political parties'.[58] Furthermore, non-mining unions did not dominate in geographical localities in the same way as the Durham and Northumberland miners.

The DMA in turn had a federal structure that allowed for considerable freedom of movement for activists at central and lodge levels. Thus, the DMA acted on Spain on the initiative of all the different levels of the movement, from the lodges, to the DMA executive, to the MFGB and NCL. Indeed, its first action, a grant in August 1936, came at a lodge's suggestion. The democratic aspect of the union's workings meant that a handful of left-wing leaders could not have made the institution do what it did for Spain if the issue had not resonated to some degree with many rank-and-file miners. Like their South Wales counterparts, Durham miners were able to use their organisational machinery and union culture to mobilise in both financial and campaigning ways for Spain, and they did so to remarkably similar degrees.

However, unlike South Wales, there were very few Durham miners in Spain (and those who were appear not to have maintained contact with either their lodges or the executive). While Lawther himself must have been under personal and family pressure as his youngest brother had died in Spain, there was less DMA lodge pressure on the issue. There was certainly nothing like the suggestion from one SWMF lodge, for example, that its executive recruit 150 men to fight in the International Brigade.[59] In this respect, the DMA's response to the conflict in Spain, and especially its support for the International Brigade, was in some ways more spontaneous than that of the SWMF. The NMA's slightly less supportive role can be explained in part by its leadership, who were slightly more conservative than their Durham counterparts in the period.[60] Secondly, there was a difference in political culture in the union, stemming from its smaller size and consequent inability to play a major national role.

In strong contrast to the miners was the passive North-east district TGWU. It had brought the issue of fascism to the attention of the national TGWU leadership once in the earlier 1930s, an action perhaps prompted by fascists organising in the region's bus section in 1933.[61] On Spain, however, the regional TGWU behaved exactly as Bevin its leader would have wanted it to. It supported only officially sanctioned Spain funds and did not attempt to mobilise any part of the movement on the issue. As Buchanan wrote, the TGWU was a 'model of centralisation with little tolerance for local autonomies', and the north-east district organisation did nothing to suggest otherwise.[62] The 'very poor' response within the district union to its one fundraising effort – an appeal for 'Spanish workers' in late October 1936 that raised only £6 6s. 4d. – also contrasted with that of the north-east miners.[63] But the TGWU was not alone in its district organisation's campaigning inactivity on Spain: Tyne and Blyth District ASW did even less on the issue.

While national and district level inactivity in some unions did not necessarily determine the stance of individual branches, other factors militated against activity. For some workers, such as seamen, it was logistically difficult to maintain ordinary union branch life, let alone to act on Spain, as the sporadic and often poorly attended meetings of North Shields NUS branch testified.[64] Introversion also characterised the culture of some union branches, like Gateshead NALGO, which displayed no obvious interest in any political issue. Nevertheless, a branch culture of apathy or inactivity did not prevent Sunderland NUJ branch from *opposing* an internal resolution pledging support for the Republic against fascism in February 1937.[65]

Some trade union branches had specific problems with aspects of the Spanish aid campaigns. For example, the first minuted contact Newcastle Typographical Association branch had with Spain was when a delegate reported, in May 1937, on efforts the union was making to prevent a local Spanish Medical Aid Committee (SMAC, probably Gateshead) from printing its literature in a non-union office. After this, the branch minutes began to record receiving Spain appeal circulars, though it did not act on them. But the extent to which this apparent indifference on Spain was due to the non-union affair was unclear.[66]

From the perspective of individual activists, if one institution they were involved in was not active on Spain, there was normally another that was. James White, for example, was a TGWU regional officer also active in Gateshead Labour Party. His district union did little on Spain, but his party did a good deal more. It is conceivable in this and similar cases that individual activists regarded the Labour Party as the sole or primary outlet for campaigning activities. Indeed, the practice of the affiliation of trade union branches to local Labour Parties allowed delegated trade unionist activists straight into the heart of the party political process. For this reason, these individuals did not necessarily require, nor have to impel, activity on Spain within their unions.

Rather than attempt to act within the limiting structures of their own unions, it was often easier and more effective for trade unionists to act at branch level, along with likeminded activists of other unions. Indeed, activists who felt restricted or frustrated by their own unions' inactivity on Spain had, in some localities, a specific trade union outlet through which to pursue their political aims; the trades council.[67] In the Newcastle area, the trades council was the most active labour movement institution on Spain. Quick to oppose NCL policy on Spain, it established the first SMAC in the north-east and tried to promote more militant action.[68] The politically engaged trade unionism of Newcastle trades council had more in common with that of the miners than it did with most of the union branches affiliated to it (such as Newcastle Typographical Association branch, for example). Again, the influence of the left – in this case crypto-Communist Tom Aisbitt – was evident. An ASW member, Aisbitt identified the trades council, of which he was president, as the main way to enact his politics.[69] Yet, as with other institutions active on Spain, in order to be effective the issue had to be popular beyond left-wing activists. Newcastle trades council's activity was especially significant as it was by far the largest in the region. Unlike most others, its organising remit was four parliamentary constituencies and its affiliated membership was larger than the regional memberships of several of the unions involved and comprised half the total affiliated membership of the NEFTC. However, Newcastle trades council was exceptional in its activity on Spain. The majority of the other ten north-east trades councils were located in mining areas and consequently lacking in membership and influence due to the miners' aversion to them. Two others (Tynemouth and Sunderland) existed where the labour movement was weak or moribund. Furthermore, Newcastle trades council's size did not translate into dominance of the machinery of the NEFTC, as all affiliates had voting parity.[70]

Labour Party Campaigning

The reaction of the regional Labour Party at its various organisational levels divided chronologically into two periods: from July 1936 to October 1937 and from November 1937 to March 1939. During the first period, the Labour Party response was diffuse and centred predominantly around donating to, or organising collections for, Spain. The few public campaigning meetings specifically on the issue that did occur – indeed the response in general – in this period generally emerged from sub-constituency party sections.

The majority of parties that left internal records did no campaigning activity on Spain in this first period. The minority of active parties were involved in only in low-level campaigning, such as sending delegates to meetings on Spain.[71] In one respect Wansbeck CLP played a significant national role in this first period as C.P. Trevelyan was its delegate to the 1936 Labour Party conference where he launched a devastating attack on the leadership's support for Non-Intervention.[72] Trevelyan remained an important national critic of the policy on Spain.

However, several other Labour Parties were more active, in different ways, on Spain in this period. On south Tyneside, Jarrow LP&TC conducted house-to-house collections for official funds and took collections at public meetings.[73] In contrast, Gateshead LP&TC formed and exclusively staffed a SMAC. It also supported the LSC anti-Non-Intervention position and acted in other campaigning ways as an institution.[74] Blaydon Labour Party local councillors also formed a SMAC from January 1937, though they operated it with Communists. On north Tyneside, Wallsend Labour Party also created a SMAC. There was evidence of other campaigning activities, including holding public meetings, conducted by local Labour Parties, and party activists were involved in other SMACs in South Shields (Boldon LLP) and Felling, for example, though the extent to which the local party itself was an official sponsor was not always clear.[75]

Seaham CLP was unusual as it acted on both financial and campaigning levels simultaneously at constituency level in this first period. It held a 'Help Spain Week' in late August 1937 that consisted of eight public meetings supplemented by house-to-house collections. Morpeth CLP conducted another type of campaigning. In response to the bombing of Guernica, it called on the government to get the League of Nations to outlaw attacks on open towns. Morpeth LLP went further in June 1937 by issuing an urgent call to the NCL and TUC to mount a vigorous campaign against Non-Intervention. This was significant as it was one of few open expressions of dissent from north-east institutions over the national movement's policy on Spain in 1937. Also of significance was a NTFLP demonstration in Newcastle on 30 May 1937, which took Spain as one of its themes. In other parts of the region, local Labour Parties responded primarily with financial support. Blyth Labour Party, for example, donated to the NCL's Spanish relief fund in 1936. But, according to left-wingers, it held very few meetings on the issue at the time. In January 1937, the party provided a grant to form the basis of a Spain fund to which it called for donations. But its attitude to collecting was less proactive than some: those wishing to donate had to contact the party in the first instance, which would then fix a date for collection.[76]

Potentially of most significance regarding the campaign against Non-Intervention in this first period was the short-lived stance of the DCFLP. In December 1936, a county federation meeting endorsed a Houghton-le-Spring CLP resolution calling on the TUC to inaugurate a labour movement campaign 'to exercise their power to force the National Government to fall in line with France and Russia in the supply of arms to the Spanish workers'.[77] This was fairly remarkable considering the traditional loyalty which the Durham parties normally displayed. Indeed, this soon came in to play, as the next meeting, in March 1937, noted a leadership response to their resolution. While the nature of this response can only be surmised, it clearly had the desired effect as far as the national leadership was concerned: in August 1937, a Seaham CLP attempt to get the DCFLP to organise a campaign throughout the county to secure more aid to the Republic was rejected.[78]

After November 1937, and especially from spring 1938, the picture changed quite dramatically. The second period was characterised by increased 'campaigning' activity on Spain especially from the previously largely inactive constituency and extra-constituency (the Labour Party federations) levels, as well as that of sub-constituency sections. This more uniform response was manifest in two 'campaigning' areas: propagandising in the public sphere and agitating within the movement for more national action on the issue. Both activities were most intense in late spring and summer 1938. Again, not all institutions were active in both these spheres, and the degrees of activity and their precise timings still varied.

Newcastle City Party certainly intensified campaigning activities, for a few months at least, in the second period. In May 1938, it organised its first demonstration specifically on Spain. At around the same time, it attempted, with not much success, to get pro-Republic films shown in local cinemas.[79] Seaham CLP held more campaigning meetings on the issue in 1938 than before.[80] As well as continuing to collect funds, sections of Jarrow LP&TC began to issue statements against Non-Intervention in 1938. Jarrow's constituency agent organised the Spain Campaign Committee (SCC) meeting on Spain in Newcastle's City Hall on 12 December 1937.[81] In 1938, Blaydon Labour Party activists began agitating under the auspices of their party, holding several meetings throughout the year and into 1939.[82]

Many other parties that had been financially supportive only (or completely unsupportive) began to campaign in 1938. The starkest example of this was South Shields LP&TC, which revealed a new, urgent, campaigning attitude when it organised a 'Save Spain' public meeting in April 1938. The party also sent a delegate to an emergency conference on Spain on 23 April 1938 in London. South Shields party held three public demonstrations on Spain in May 1938. It maintained campaigning activities, although not at the same intensity as in April–July 1938, until the end of the conflict.[83] Some institutions did not begin to campaign until late in the period. For example, it was only in January 1939 that Newbiggin and North Seaton LLP made a somewhat belated call for 'a great effort' to end Non-Intervention.[84]

The other development from autumn 1937, and especially from spring 1938, was the momentary campaigning mobilisation of the constituency Labour Parties. Houghton-le-Spring CLP held public meetings on Spain in December 1937 and March 1938; Sunderland CLP followed suit in May 1938 and all participated in a DCFLP-organised demonstration on the issue on 4 June 1938. This was the first countywide set of demonstrations specifically on the issue and it also occasioned the first campaigning action on Spain by Durham CLP.[85] In contrast to its Northumberland counterpart, DCFLP did not organise its own meetings on Spain until after autumn 1937.[86]

However, most constituency parties ceased these campaigning activities after June 1938. Some institutions behaved more consistently throughout the course of the conflict. Wansbeck CLP, for example, did not intensify its activity in this second period, it merely continued to sponsor Trevelyan's agitation on the issue.[87] Conversely, there was continuity, too, in the sustained campaigning actions of affiliated sections of Morpeth CLP, which sent resolutions to the government attacking its policy on Spain.[88]

The public campaigning of the apparently newly energised CLPs accompanied arguably the most significant kind of activity: campaigning for concerted action within the movement. There came a chorus of calls for the labour movement to hold a national conference to discuss the situation in Spain (and the wider international situation). Thus, South Shields LP&TC, with its repeated calls on the national movement to act between May and July 1938, became one of many parties fighting on Spain on two campaigning fronts: the external and internal.[89] These calls came at constituency and federation levels too. Wansbeck, Sedgefield, Houghton-le-Spring, Seaham, Newcastle East CLPs – even the inactive Durham CLP – all supported the call for a national conference, and both north-east Labour Party federations were soon placing pressure on the national leadership on the issue.[90] The miners' unions, too, began agitating on the issue; the DMA from February 1938.[91] In March, the NMA began echoing these demands, first within the TUC, then within the MFGB and NEC as well.[92] By June 1938, the NEFTC also supported this request.[93] Apparently exceptional was Newcastle City Party executive. Having 'thoroughly discussed' the issue, it decided that 'as the question was one of major importance and a change of policy', it did not have the 'power' [sic.] to make such a demand.[94]

Timing, 'Mobilisation' and Organisational Issues

Contextualising the timing of these developments goes a long way to explaining the north-east Labour Parties' (and miners' union's) reaction to Spain. Clearly, the second period came after the official change in Labour Party policy to opposition to Non-Intervention in October 1937. This change was evident in the north-east when the newly formed Spain Campaign Committee (SCC) organised a demonstration in Newcastle in December 1937. In early January 1938, three north-east MPs, Shinwell, Whiteley and Jack Lawson, joined a delegation to Spain, and the visit served to fire their interest in the conflict, to differing degrees.[95] Shinwell, particularly, embarked on a flurry of activity in the weeks following his return, speaking at meetings locally and throughout the country on his experiences, releasing information to the press and formulating a memorandum by the end of January 1938.[96] At Easington, Shinwell described his visit as a 'thrilling experience, and he believed that if the people of this country could see what he and others had seen, such pressure would be brought to bear upon the government of this country that at long last the farce and tragedy of Non-Intervention would be abandoned and justice would be done in Spain'.[97] Whiteley and Lawson joined Trevelyan and Will Lawther in supporting the national Spain conference of April 1938 part organised by Ellen Wilkinson.[98]

A worsening on the international scene soon followed. In Spain, the apparent Republican success at Teruel became defeat and there were further losses on the Ebro in spring 1938. Ironically, events in Spain did not seem as important as Eden's resignation from the government in February 1938, or the Anschluss between Nazi Germany and Austria in March 1938. These two events prompted a widespread response in the northeast, manifest in March 1938 by the organisation of public demonstrations by constituency Labour Parties about the deteriorating international situation.[99] Indeed, Spain received specific attention from most north-east CLPs only in May and June 1938. After this, the issue again became merely one of many, as the Munich crisis and consequent Czech refugee issues came to the fore.

The final and in some respects most significant factor was that the national leadership was more willing to mobilise its membership in 1938. The Spain demonstrations in late May 1938 were part of a nationally organised campaign on the issue, as were, presumably, all the DCFLP demonstrations in early June.[100] The evidence suggests that it required a national initiative to mobilise Newcastle City Party, South Shields LP&TC, Durham CLP (and many other CLPs) to demonstrate on Spain. The dearth of further demonstrations organised by the hitherto more inactive constituency parties after May 1938 suggested that the only time they would act was when instructed to do so from above. Durham CLP, for example, did nothing else on Spain until February 1939 when it endorsed an NCL resolution protesting about the recognition of Franco.[101]

Tom Buchanan wrote that the national labour movement leadership feared 'mobilising its membership because this could undermine its own authority, yet it also feared that members would drift into "unofficial" campaigns beyond their control if their own campaign were not energetic enough. These two considerations were contradictory and the former took precedence over the latter'.[102] Yet, on occasion, the national leadership's campaigns on Spain did entail a degree of 'mobilisation'. Indeed, some sections appeared to require mobilising from above. However, the extent and form that this mobilisation took were clearly distinctly limited and occurred only when the national leadership deemed it appropriate.

Indeed, before 1938 the national leadership secured a degree of success in co-opting potentially politically problematic regional labour movement institutions into its vision of what 'action' for Spain should entail. Thus in January 1937, the DMA executive accepted the NCL's suggestion that it become the main ISF organiser in County Durham. The DMA duly and dutifully began to circularise its affiliates, requesting donations. While this was no attempt to get the regional movement to agitate on Spain, it must have acted in part as a sop to desires within the DMA and the wider regional movement for more action. Certainly, the DMA itself seemed content with its role during the crucial year of 1937, when it did not agitate within the movement for a change of policy on Spain, in spite of having broken with Non-Intervention in December 1936.[103] In fact, there was an unexpected, though short-lived role-reversal in the County Durham movement for a few months in early 1937 when the DCFLP had a more critical attitude towards the leadership's inactivity.

Many other labour movement institutions received NCL appeals for money for Spain throughout the period and this appeared to satisfy a proportion of them, too, for a time. In October 1936, for example, Wansbeck CLP did not support an 'unofficial' Spain conference as its local parties had acted recently on an NCL appeal.[104] In August 1938, Ellington lodge received an NEFTC circular asking for its campaigning support and for it to aid Spanish foodships. Lodge activists 'generally felt that these requests were being supported'.[105] It was unclear if this circular came at the instigation of the national movement. But it remained ironic that the official leaderships (at regional and/or national level) were by this time using 'unofficial' Spain campaigns in order to counter the claim from the CP that they were inactive on Spain. Still, not all were satisfied and institutions like Durham County Teachers' Labour Group could both strongly disapprove of the Labour Party's 'hesitancy' in urging the government to end Non-Intervention in October 1936 and also donate money to Spain relief funds.[106]

The lines of control were clear in the agitation between May and June 1938. When the national leadership wanted to mobilise the rank-and-file, it did so – with some success in the north-east – through the federations of Labour Parties and constituency institutions. It was clearly easier for the national leadership to communicate with and control these than the sub-constituency organisations. However, in mobilising the north-east grass-

roots, the national leadership let the genie out of the bottle. Once activated, almost the entire regional movement began to demand greater,
more concerted and better-coordinated national action. This clearly gave
the national leadership something of a headache in the short-term. But it
was also a canny move to outflank possible support for the popular front.
After May 1938, the national leadership generally gave its north-east
affiliates other less strenuous and potentially destabilising tasks to perform
for Spain, such as to send protests to Chamberlain against the recognition
of Franco. It also suggested slightly less passive tasks, such as a 'parcels
for Spain' scheme in December 1938.[107] And the regional clamour for a
national labour movement conference faded away in the summer of 1938.

A noteworthy feature of the official movement agitation on Spain was,
excepting early 1938 and some institutions, the general lack of campaigning conducted by the parties at constituency level. However, many, if
not the majority, of Labour Parties in the north-east only rarely operated
as constituency entities. This was due in part to the logistical problems of
organising at constituency level. Wansbeck and Hexham in Northumberland and Barnard Castle and Sedgefield in County Durham were geographically vast, predominantly rural constituencies that were difficult to
organise at a constituency level.[108] None left much evidence of having
organised public demonstrations at constituency level on Spain: as Sedgefield CLP demonstrated, it was easier to act internally, getting the county
federation to place pressure on the national party on the issue. The internal culture of some parties also militated against action at this level. In the
twelve months before May 1938, Morpeth CLP held only one demonstration as a constituency entity.[109] Many of the least active parties at constituency level were in predominantly mining constituencies. Bishop Auckland constituency, for example, covered a smaller geographical area, but its
CLP executive met very infrequently in the later 1930s.[110] Some of these
CLPs were to a degree victims of the mining culture, evident in Spain agitation, which often sought political action through the local lodge and central DMA, or at local Labour Party level. However, the support of constituency parties for internal pressure on the movement was useful and clearly
recognised as such, certainly in Houghton-le-Spring and Seaham CLPs. In
both, the influence of the more radical miners' lodges (such as Boldon and
Ryhope in Houghton-le-Spring) must have been brought to bear when
attempting to get the DCFLP to act on Spain.[111]

There were also problems in organising at extra-constituency level, evident in the records of Newcastle City Party. Its difficulties were both

symptoms and, often, causes of its organisational weakness. In February 1938, the national party agent sent Newcastle party affiliates a letter that 'viewed with some concern the position of the local organisation' and invited attendance at a special meeting to discuss the situation.[112] But this national effort to remedy the situation failed in the short-term and internal apathy continued to dog the City Party. The lack of finance was a significant reason why it organised so few public meetings on Spain, or, for that matter, on any other issue. Regarding its first (and last) specific Spain meeting, financial problems were evident even before it occurred, on 22 May 1938. The deficit from this expensive indoor meeting remained a headache for the party until well into 1939. The City Party's response to Spain was commensurate with its dependence on the national party for support and inspiration. Its main activists clearly lacked self-confidence, revealed by their belief that they did not have the 'power' to ask the leadership for a national conference in 1938.[113] However, perhaps, too, the City Party was not the institution to spend much time agitating on Spain in this way. With all the costs incurred by organising large meetings, the party attempted, in January 1939, to encourage the constituency parties to perform this task, arguing that they could organise two or more meetings for the expense of only one city-organised meeting.[114] The Birmingham Labour Party, also an extra-constituency institution with similar problems, performed in some regards a comparable role to Newcastle City Party.[115]

In fact, as the City Party told the Socialist League in September 1936, it was 'satisfied' that it was acting on the issue through its delegate on the local SMAC.[116] Indeed, the party remained satisfied by this stance until mid-1938. Thus, when there was activity in one part of the movement in a locality, either through an official institution or in the form of ad hoc organisations, this *could* serve as a disincentive for other institutions to act in more energetic ways. The same stood for the largely inactive Durham CLP. It may not have felt the need to act energetically on the issue as there was a predominantly DMA/Labour Party-run SMAC campaigning in Durham city, and the DMA itself was active in the coalfield proper areas of the constituency. The DMA's activity could account, indeed, for a good deal of the inactivity of many of the constituency parties in the Durham coalfield. Notwithstanding this, the logistical problems and their effects encountered by many constituency and extra-constituency Labour institutions clearly impacted on activities for Spain, or indeed, any other cause.

However, the general lack of constituency-based support for Spain, certainly as regards public agitation on the issue, was not especially significant as the LLPs usually carried out this work. They were the most intimate and often the most dynamic grassroots party institutions. Having their own funds, they could usually provide financial support. Thus, for example, Newburn LLP was able to donate much more to Spain causes than did the constituency party it affiliated to (though it did not appear to act in a campaigning way). Indeed, Wansbeck CLP explicitly left the bulk of donating primarily to its affiliated parties.[117] However, LLPs differed considerably in terms of their disposable resources and naturally, all LLPs had to raise funds for their own needs. Yet, a lack of party finance did not necessarily preclude financial support. South Shields LP&TC, for example, often supported Spain appeals by staging collections at internal party meetings.

As LLPs met most frequently, and were the easiest to be mobilised by their members, they were often the best vehicles for action. However, some sub-constituency sections, like South Shields LP&TC, did not stage public demonstrations on Spain before 1938. Like the CLPs, they also appeared to require prompting from the national level. Still, what they revealed was not so much a 'desire to be led' as an inability, in such a hierarchically structured movement, to conceive of acting on foreign policy issues without instruction from a higher authority.[118] Indeed, almost everything that the South Shields party did on Spain was at the prompting of a circular, mostly from nationally based bodies, the majority of which were sent out by the official movement leadership. This was even to the extent of trying to show Spain propaganda films in the town. The degree of political self-confidence and energy of key activists shaped the internal culture of the institutions in which they operated. A dynamic institutional culture formed by members fired by their understanding of the situation in Spain was clearly important in determining which LLPs acted and how.

Factors such as organisational weakness, internal apathy and membership decline, all of which had a potentially negative impact on Spain activity, were also evident at local Labour Party and ward level too (in Newcastle, Wansbeck and Morpeth constituencies, for example).[119] Another matter potentially inhibited action at all levels. There was considerable evidence of infighting between various elements of the official north-east labour movement including disputes between the DMA and Durham County Labour Party, divisions within many parties over the choice of election candidates, and in Jarrow, an internecine conflict provoked by recriminations after the Jarrow March's failure. Many of these conflicts developed or came to a head in 1937. Notwithstanding this, internal disputes in Blaydon and Gateshead parties did not prevent work on Spain in 1937. But the widespread nature of these divisions does suggest that a degree of insularity, or at least a tendency to prioritise the 'local', characterised the attitudes of some grassroots activists at this time.[120] Interestingly, none of these disputes were directly related to the movement's attitude to Spain. An isolated example of where action on the issue caused a degree of tension came in Newcastle. There, the City Party and trades council disagreed over how much of the financial burden for a costly Spain meeting each should carry. But, unlike in Birmingham, this did not strain relations greatly.[121]

There were two final considerations. The belief often remained, even where Labour was electorally dominant and well organised, that building the party should be the main concern of local activists. In 1937, Houghton-le-Spring constituency secretary, H. Bainbridge, for example, supported Dalton's call to build up the party 'and not dissipate our strength upon side issues …'.[122] To some important constituency activists, Spain must have seemed simply another 'side issue'. Certainly, many north-east Labour MPs seemed little concerned with Spain; some even after visiting the country. Instead, many concentrated their energies inside and outside parliament on attempts to address the problems of unemployment and poverty that blighted much of the region.

Arguments about prioritising the needs of the region over support for Spain were, on occasion, made within north-east labour movement institutions. For example, at the annual meeting of Blyth Shop Assistants branch in February 1937, a member objected to the donation of the proceeds of a branch dance to the 'workers of Spain' as there were 'deserving cases in Blyth'.[123] In this instance, the branch secretary's arguments against the objector received the backing of a majority vote. However, there was one example where this argument directly prevented the regional movement from acting on Spain. In June 1938, the secretary of Tynemouth CLP scotched a proposal discussed at an NEFTC and NTFLP conference to send a food and medical supply ship from the Tyne by pointing out that 'while the Spanish loyalists were to be pitied, an urgent problem faced them on Tyneside'.[124]

Activists on Spain and Communist Influences

Clearly, some of the most significant official movement grassroots activists agitating on Spain were, to varying degrees, left-wingers. While it was clear that they exercised degrees of influence in activating local and regional institutions on the issue, this also, naturally, depended on the predisposition to Spain of the other grassroots activists operating in these institutions. Furthermore, the effects of these activists' actions were sometimes unexpected and not necessarily desirable. The case of left-winger C.P. Trevelyan, influential in Wansbeck CLP, illustrates these points. A special meeting to hear Trevelyan's report on the 1936 Labour Party conference, where he had memorably attacked the leadership's support for Non-Intervention, was unanimous that he had put the constituency party's view.[125] Pegswood lodge's delegate was impressed, paying 'tribute to Sir Charles on the quality of his report'.[126] Wansbeck's sponsorship of Trevelyan – he was conference delegate again in 1937 – meant that he could reasonably claim to be speaking for his constituency party as well as himself on Spain. His critique of national policy clearly resonated with Seaton Valley LLP, which urged in March 1937 that the NEC mount a campaign against Non-Intervention.[127] However, Trevelyan could only occupy this position because his attitude to Spain chimed with that of much of his constituency party's rank-and-file. When he adopted an unpopular political stance, such as support for the popular front, his 'influence' rapidly evaporated. In addition, there was a somewhat self-defeating element to Trevelyan's role. His CLP appeared content to let Trevelyan do its talking for it and did not organise any specific agitation on the issue itself at any point. It seemed that Trevelyan's high profile and energetic advocacy for the Spanish Republic allowed the party itself to remain inactive on the issue, at both constituency and many sub-constituency levels.

Left-winger Arthur Blenkinsop (Newcastle East Labour PPC from April 1938) operated through the Newcastle movement. His interest in Spain was evident in involvement with the Labour Spain Committee in 1937. Perhaps the single most significant activist on the issue within Newcastle City Party, Blenkinsop was, however, unsuccessful in getting it to act on many of his initiatives. As Newcastle North CLP secretary, Blenkinsop was in a strong position to influence his constituency party. Thus, in the summer of 1937, Newcastle North CLP asked Transport House 'to make the issue of support for Spanish democracy the leading one at demonstrations throughout the country'.[128] Yet it was through a third official institution that Blenkinsop was most successful in 1937. He told Pole of the LSC that he wished 'to put as much of this work [on Spain] as possible through existing party channels, and as our local federation is prepared to tackle the question, I think they should be given the work to do'.[129] And the local federation in question, the NTFLP, duly revealed its preparedness to 'tackle the question' by holding, on 30 May 1937, an internal conference on Spain followed by a public demonstration.[130] With this event, Blenkinsop helped ensure that a significant section of the official northeast labour movement was immunised, at least momentarily, from criticism for inactivity on Spain. That Blenkinsop's initiative was taken up by the NTFLP again reinforces the contention that Spain was a cause that actuated much of the mainstream of the labour movement outside of the left, Communist-influenced or otherwise. This case illustrates that one individual could activate an institution, but there had to be support within it for their position. It also demonstrates that constituency and extra-constituency institutions did not always require mobilisation from above. Again however, like Trevelyan, when Blenkinsop adopted an unpopular stance in early 1939, he found much of his influence evaporated. The complex and fluctuating internal cultures of each institution, that changed to some degree as their personnel altered (in actual individuals involved and the way that their views of political affairs changed), helped determine which institutions did what and when.

The choices of a third left-wing activist also helped to explain the responses of an institution, in this case South Shields LP&TC. In contrast to trade unionists discussed above who acted politically through their local Labour Parties was the miner Will Pearson. Keen to work on Spain, Pearson, a Labour councillor, was one of the most important members of South Shields LP&TC. Yet Pearson made no effort to get his local party active on the issue in 1937, despite having the potential backing of the bulk of the party in the form of affiliated miners' lodges. Presumably Pearson, an experienced and committed militant, was content with, and occupied by, his activities on Spain within other elements of the official movement, most notably his lodge (Marsden), the local miners' federation, and in his union's executive (the DMA). Pearson supplemented this activity with appearances on the public platforms of unofficial and non-movement institutions including the TJPC (November 1936), South Shields SMAC (February 1937) and even the CAPR (July 1938).[131] This case – from the perspectives of both the individual activists and the institution – reaffirms the point that the activity of some institutions in any given locality on Spain (be they official or unofficial) *could* help to preclude it in other institutions operating in the same locality.

Another example of this came in Ashington, where union activists established their SMAC in part because they were dissatisfied with the apathy they identified in the local movement on Spain. They claimed that a film show by miners and the knitting of clothes for civilians were the only activities for Spain in Ashington before April 1937.[132] While evidence for Labour Party activity on the issue is scarce, it did make an unsuccessful attempt to enlist the local miners' federation support for a collection it was organising for Spanish workers in March 1937.[133] After a year of activity, the committee's secretary J.E. Charlton admitted that it had received donations from many union branches. Indeed, the records showed that local lodges favoured it over other official and unofficial funds. But Charlton still complained that the 'general attitude of these organisations has been one of preferred abstention'.[134] The problem for Charlton was that more were not actively involved in the committee itself: it was 'not at all representative of the labour stronghold Ashington is claimed to be... which emphasises the hollowness of that high-sounding phrase – "working-class solidarity"'.[135]

Other factors specific to the internal political culture of the local movement were also at work. Established on 1 July 1936, the individual member's section of Ashington LLP was only very young and had not had the time to build up a membership base or an activist culture.[136] In 1938, the local Labour MP had to hold 62 'back street' meetings in Ashington in an endeavour to put the party 'on the road to success'.[137] This seemed to work, as there was a big increase in membership, with Taylor claiming to have spoken to about 12,000 people. Moreover, those who were active in the party appeared loyal. In June 1937, the LLP asked local NMA lodges to endorse its resolution expressing support for the NEC in carrying out the decisions of the 1936 conference and congratulating the PLP for the 'splendid fight they have put up on behalf of the working-class'.[138] The resolution also protested at the 'inactivity of the League of Nations in allowing the slaughter of women and children in Spain'.[139]

One notable group of activists who were not, on the whole, of importance in activating grassroots institutions were the Labour MPs. Only one north-east MP, Ellen Wilkinson of Jarrow, was especially interested in Spain from the outset. Indeed, she visited the country in 1934. Wilkinson remained active on the issue on a variety of fronts, and must have been influential in the actions of her local party on Spain in 1937.[140] In contrast was Blaydon, another party also active in 1937. The constituency MP, William Whiteley, was active on the issue, especially after visiting Spain in January 1938. But inspiration before this time came from significant left-wingers in Blaydon party.[141] Similar observations stood for Seaham CLP's actions in 1937. Notwithstanding an appearance at a SCC meeting in Newcastle in December 1937, Shinwell did not appear greatly interested in the conflict until after he visited Spain in January 1938.[142] Of more importance as an individual in the earlier period was teacher and Labour councillor Fred Peart, who exerted influence on Spain through his local party, Thornley, and through his secretaryship of the constituency. He also became involved in Durham SMAC.[143]

To what extent did left-wingers within the official movement who were probably not actual crypto-Communists (in that they were not card-carrying party members) act under the influence of the CP? Certainly, it would be crass to attribute automatically all their actions to Communism's stimulus. Indeed, competing influences, many of which were not Communist and some of which were even hostile to aspects of Communism, formed the politics of Labour left-wingers. As recent work has shown, the Labour left adopted an increasingly complex position throughout the 1930s characterised by growing ambiguity and hostility towards the Soviet Union.[144] However, the Labour left was wider and more diverse than those attracted to the Socialist League or who later grouped around Cripps' *Tribune* newspaper. It also included many activists whose politics was so similar to that of the CP – and which altered in accordance with changes in CP policy – that they might as well have been card-carrying members. This was the case, for example, of many of the key activists in Blaydon Labour Party. Yet one Blaydon left-winger also active on Spain, Jim Stephenson, appeared to maintain political attitudes from his recent ILP heritage.[145] Of course, the political positions of human beings are invariably far more complex, fluctuating and often more contradictory than suggested by even the most detailed programmes of the political parties of which they are members.

Given this, the most satisfactory approach is on a case-by-case basis. For example, the CP appeared to exercise a good degree of influence on Trevelyan's politics in this period. He was certainly one of the most vigorous defenders of Stalin's Russia within the official movement.[146] But it would be mistaken to attribute Blenkinsop's achievements to Communist influence. Blenkinsop was clearly at this stage a left-winger who, like Lawther and Watson in the DMA, shared certain political concerns and attitudes with the CP.[147] But, unlike Trevelyan, Blenkinsop was no apologist for the Soviet Union in this period. Similarly, Ellen Wilkinson was an ex-CP member (in the 1920s), but her relationship with the party and its causes after 1936 was ambiguous and highly complex (as, indeed, was her stance on Spain).[148]

There is evidence that activists whose politics were, and remained, very close to the CP were instrumental in the pre-1938 campaigning on Spain of both Jarrow LP&TC and Blaydon LLP. However, Gateshead LP&TC, for example, also active before 1938, appeared not to share this characteristic.[149] It is clear that the actions of activists influenced by or sympathetic to the CP (if not actually party members) were important in many, but not all, of the Labour Party institutions active on Spain before the national mobilisations in 1938. It is equally clear that there was often no causal relationship between a left-winger's activity within the labour movement on Spain and Communist influence. In many cases, it would be wrong to attribute Communist influence to what was rather the fortunate coincidence of official movement activists adopting the same political positions as the CP. Labour activity on Spain in Gateshead was further evidence that the issue spoke to more than the Labour left, Communist-influenced or otherwise.

'Political Space' and Quantifying the Official North-East Response
The idea that the labour movement abandoned 'political space' on Spain was a cornerstone of Communist claims at the time and popular frontist accounts since about the grassroots reaction to the conflict. In this context, this simply meant that the movement had an opportunity to galvanise over the issue of Non-Intervention but that it failed to do so. This allowed the CP, with its critique of Non-Intervention, to occupy this 'political space' and reap the benefits for at least a crucial year after October 1936 (notwithstanding the *Daily Worker*'s short-term initial support for Non-Intervention).[150] In November 1936, George Aitken claimed that the north-east labour movement leadership had 'refused to do anything about' Spain; effectively a Communist claim that the official movement had abandoned political space on Spain, very much like Charlie Woods' claim quoted in the introduction to this chapter.[151] This was partially accurate. If, by regional leadership, Aitken meant the main constituency and extra-constituency level activists in the Labour Party and trade union district leaders, his claim was broadly accurate in November 1936, with the exception of individuals like Trevelyan. Indeed, even the DMA had fallen

momentarily into line with Transport House at this time. However, it was not true for leading activists in Newcastle trades council who were not Communists and other prominent Labour activists at lower levels who were campaigning on the issue in autumn 1936.

Secondly, Aitken's claim only (partially) stood for campaigning activities on Spain. Thus, while South Shields LP&TC, for example, abandoned political space on Spain in the sense that the town's market place did not ring to the sound of Labour denunciations of Non-Intervention before 1938, it did collect internally for Spain campaigns. Its activists, like many others, must have been to some extent satisfied that they *were* doing *something* 'about Spain' in November 1936. Thirdly, Aitken's comments came soon after the Labour Party conference had followed the unions in endorsing support for Non-Intervention after a fractious debate. This clearly engendered a good degree of confusion and disengagement on the issue at grassroots level. It also created anger, and brought abortive attempts from even the DCFLP to force a change in the national movement's stance. However, grassroots institutions could choose to ignore national policy and inactivity and instead propagandise in their local world. As it became increasingly clear that the national movement was content with raising funds and doing little else, more official labour movement institutions and their activists, especially at sub-constituency level, did become publicly active, in different ways and to differing degrees in late 1936 and 1937. Thus, in many Tyneside towns and the coalfields, the Labour Party and elements of the trade unions occupied (or joint-occupied) the political space on Spain to some degree in late 1936 and (more so) in 1937. The LLPs, especially, effectively *were* the Labour Party in their localities, and many *were* doing something on Spain, in spite of the national movement's torpor. At the NTFLP demonstration in May 1937 Trevelyan called on the labour movement rank-and-file to 'learn to make its own policy'.[152] In some respects, sections of it already had. Naturally, this is not to argue that they were doing enough, or that their activities necessarily aided the Republic as much as they could have. Finally, while Labour had abandoned a degree of political space in some localities for varying periods, there was no guarantee that the CP would be able to capitalise on this situation to the extent that it hoped.[153]

The north-east movement's reaction to Spain was highly complex, fluctuating over time, between institutions and within them at different levels and altering in intensity and form. It was subject to – and can thus only be understood in – the context of innumerable pressures and contingencies. This makes quantifying such a response very difficult. In simple terms, however, the evidence suggests, tentatively, that Graham's claim that 90 per cent of north-east Labour sections collected for Spain was not an exaggeration, if this is interpreted as Labour Parties that provided evidence of some form of financial or other support. Indeed, the percentage of parties actively campaigning on the issue on at least one occasion during the conflict was almost as high. However, fewer parties maintained a campaigning stance on the issue for any degree of time, especially not before 1938, though it is difficult to arrive at the proportion with any degree of certainty.

Within the TUC-affiliated trade unions, there was usually majority support for causes that were generally, but not always (for example Eden lodge), understood within the labour movement to be linked with the Republic's struggle against Franco and fascism. But this support did not necessarily manifest itself in grants from every level of any given institution (a branch could support the district donating, for example). Still, between 65 and 75 per cent of north-east trades unions at branch and district level provided some evidence of a supportive gesture on Spain. Furthermore, evidence of hostility to Spain causes within the unions was fairly rare, at around 10 per cent. Taken together it seems reasonable to claim that more than 75 per cent of north-east labour movement institutions showed a degree of positive support for Spain, with a good deal less than 10 per cent revealing open opposition.

Most of the explanations in this chapter for the differing ways in which north-east labour movement institutions reacted to Spain have been concerned with the nature of the individual institutions' internal cultures, that in turn informed, and were informed by, the attitudes and actions of key activists within them. Most of the occasionally considerable obstacles considered here – sometimes general, often more specific to the functioning of individual institutions – are broadly of a practical nature. However, political factors were possibly as important in determining the attitudes of activists in institutions that appeared ambivalent or that actually opposed support for Spain within the movement.

One consideration was that pacifism, strong within the labour movement in the earlier 1930s, could possibly inhibit action on Spain. It had certainly limited action elsewhere within institutions like Battersea and Sheffield Peace Councils and within the National Society of Painters.[154] Yet the evidence suggests that this was not an issue of great significance in the north-east. In August 1936 William Whiteley, for example, said that:

'All of us here without exception have no desire for war ... the majority of us, with all our pacifist views, would be delighted if we had the opportunity of walking side by side with our Spanish comrades to beat a Fascist dictatorship'.[155] Left-wingers like Trevelyan, amongst the most vehement pacifists in the earlier 1930s, did not appear to doubt the correct course of action.[156] And Labour activists such as mayor Summerbell of Sunderland remained pacifists and were active on Spain, albeit in the more 'humanitarian' campaigns.[157] Of potentially more importance were the attitudes of Catholics within the labour movement and the next chapter addresses this question.

3

DISSENSION OVER SPAIN? THE ATTITUDES OF LABOUR MOVEMENT CATHOLICS

The attacks on churches and clergy in parts of Republican Spain, especially in the early part of the war, posed a potentially serious conflict of loyalties for Catholic labour movement activists between their political and religious affiliations. Tom Buchanan, pointing to the 'considerable evidence of Catholic workers' hostility to the Spanish Republic', argued that labour movement Catholics formed a significant obstacle to grassroots Republican solidarity activities in many parts of Britain as they regarded the Republic as anti-Catholic.[1] Thus, the national movement leadership's fears that a pro-Republican stance would alienate Catholics came from an accurate understanding of the political situation on the ground. However, the north-east, with the second highest concentration of Catholics in England, and where sections of the labour movement contained many Catholic activists or relied on the working-class Catholic vote has not been examined in detail.

In theory, there should be considerable evidence of labour movement Catholic opposition to movement solidarity activities for the Republic in this region. Pauline Lynn claimed that the Catholic Church had 'enormous power' in the north-east as 'the priest would dispense political advice from the pulpit whilst his parishioners feared eternal damnation if they ignored his directive'.[2] Certainly, important north-east Catholic clergy and lay activists attempted to exert this power in relation to the conflict in Spain, as they reiterated the Vatican's viewpoint that the Republic was 'Communist' and 'anti-Catholic'.[3] This chapter will examine the extent to which their pronouncements influenced, informed and reflected north-east working-class Catholic attitudes and the effects of this on the regional labour movement's campaigning for Spain.

Public Controversies

There clearly was a degree of disquiet amongst some north-east labour movement Catholic activists over the issue of Spain. An ostensibly serious controversy in this context emerging into the public arena began at a NEFTC delegate meeting in early September 1936. Tom Aisbitt of Newcastle trades council moved a resolution opposing Non-Intervention in Spain and urging the TUC to support the Republic. Norman McCretton, a Catholic, countered by suggesting that the NEFTC endorse the official Labour policy of supporting Non-Intervention and that it ask the Spanish government to protest against the burning of churches. McCretton was a significant regional labour movement activist. Active in Gateshead Labour Party, he was a municipal councillor and chairperson of Northumberland and Tyneside Federation of Labour Parties, as well as NEFTC secretary. Edward Colgan (secretary of Blaydon trades council) seconded McCretton's amendment, but a large majority voted against it.[4]

A month later, divisions deepened when Newcastle trades council announced its 'disgust' at the Catholic press' attitude towards the Republic and called upon Catholic trade unionists 'openly to repudiate the activities of these fascist supporters under the guise of religion'.[5] McCretton again swiftly responded, saying that Catholic trade unionists took 'very strong exception to this … gratuitous impertinence. As Catholics, we have nothing to do with the political crisis in Spain, but we are deeply concerned with the attack upon our Church'. He advised Newcastle trades council 'to permit Catholics to decide individually their attitude towards the unfortunate troubles in Spain'.[6] The local Catholic Transport Guild, representing 230 Catholic trade unionists, supported McCretton's stand. Further endorsement came in a letter to the *Sunday Sun*. Its author argued that Catholics could choose their politics, and asked by what authority Newcastle trades council spoke for the working-class.[7] Aisbitt responded to McCretton in the *Sunday Sun*. Quoting Roman Catholic sources, Aisbitt argued that the church expected the faithful to put papal teachings before political principle. Newcastle trades council was not, Aisbitt claimed, 'presuming to instruct Catholics on matters of religion, but it is … opposing enemies of the movement'.[8] He challenged McCretton to a public debate on the matter. The controversy reached its apogee in late October 1936, when Newcastle trades council attempted to expel McCretton from the

NEFTC. This move failed as, after 'heated discussion', the NEFTC expressed its regret 'that questions of religious beliefs should be made a matter for trade union controversy' and agreed that 'no useful purpose can be served' by pursuing the matter further.[9] This effectively ended the Spain/Catholic controversy within the NEFTC.

A second example of publicly expressed disquiet from north-east Catholic activists came at the 1937 Union of Post Office Workers conference. A Newcastle No.1 branch delegate objected to the subscription of funds to the Republic, a cause opposed to his religion. However, he did not speak for all his regional coreligionists at the conference, as a second north-east delegate regretted that fellow Catholics were 'easily stampeded when the clergy cracked the whip'.[10] A meeting of the Catholic Young Men's Society (CYMS) in September 1936 suggested a wider degree of consternation. Held in the Durham pit village of Birtley, almost 200 delegates representing over 2,000 north-east Catholic trade unionists attended. The audience apparently greeted CYMS national president Joe Howley's claim that trade union leaders did not represent their members on Spain with 'prolonged acclamation'.[11]

Notwithstanding this, there was very little evidence of widespread public Catholic opposition to trade unions supporting the Republic in the north-east. As Catholic J.A. Campbell claimed, the regional press represented an important outlet for Catholics to air their grievances, especially as the national Catholic press's low circulation made it a relatively poor vehicle for Catholic dissent and uninfluential even amongst the faithful.[12] Indeed, the Vicar General of Hexham and Newcastle diocese, Hugh Cogan, estimated that only 15 per cent of British Catholics read a Catholic newspaper, and urged more to do so.[13] Yet very few who openly identified themselves as labour movement Catholics in the north-east appeared to have acted on Campbell's suggestion to write protest letters on the issue to the regional press. Indeed, Catholics were even reluctant to respond to attacks from non-Catholics in the labour movement. There were very few replies to Aisbitt's letters in the *Sunday Sun* attacking what he regarded as the pernicious role of Catholics in the labour movement. The vast majority of those who *did* respond and identify themselves as Catholics were either not from the north-east or not obviously trade unionists.[14] Miner William Gowland of Findon was the *only definite* north-east working-class Catholic who was clearly angered by Aisbitt's words. Gowland castigated Aisbitt's 'silly nonsense' and denounced men of his 'type' as 'the real enemies of trade unionism'.[15] Gowland claimed that there were 'many good earnest Catholics ... who must feel hurt and disgusted by the treatment inflicted on them by men of the Aisbitt type'. If this was true, not one of these individuals wrote in to say so. Furthermore, even Gowland did not refer explicitly to the labour movements' attitude to Spain as a source of grievance.

Communist George Aitken reported on a letters page controversy in a second regional newspaper, the *Evening Chronicle*, to a CP Central Committee meeting in November 1936. The debate, sparked by Newcastle trades council's anti-Catholic resolution, had perturbed Aitken, as it suggested widespread Catholic influence.[16] However, it seemed that Aitken was exaggerating. While there was debate over the conflict in the *Evening Chronicle*'s letters page from July 1936, Newcastle trades council's action had no palpable impact. The handful of letters expressing opposition to labour movement aid for the Republic from ostensible movement activists appeared *before* the Newcastle trades council controversy. Furthermore, none of these correspondents identified themselves explicitly as Catholics.[17] If they *were* Catholics, the decision not to make their religious loyalty as clear as their political affiliation was difficult to understand, as it surely weakened their case. Finally, there was also possible evidence in the *Evening Chronicle* of labour movement Catholic *support* for the Republic. 'Catholic', for example, argued that the Republican government, elected by the people, was not a 'red front'.[18] Thus, contrary to Aitken's claim, the *Evening Chronicle* 'controversy' suggested that north-east labour movement Catholic anger over the issue of Spain was negligible.

Similar observations apply to letters page debates in other regional newspapers. In the *Shields News*, four Catholics wrote supporting the Republic. 'RC Churchgoer' responded by arguing that if Franco's army did kill innocent women and children 'they at least respected the church' and did not murder priests and nuns.[19] This one exchange between people who did not state their party political affiliations was the only debate in the *Shields News*. There was more debate in the *North Mail* where the majority of correspondents were anti-intervention. However, those opposing Labour policy on Spain generally did not employ religious arguments. None of the very few correspondents who objected to the Republic on religious grounds was obviously a disgruntled Catholic Labour Party member or trade unionist.[20] In the *Newcastle Journal*, there were no letters on the Spanish situation from obviously north-east Catholics at all in the vital few months immediately after the outbreak of the conflict and the same was true of the *Sunderland Echo*. The specific issue of the Catholic Church in

Spain, and its role more generally, was frequently and keenly debated in the *Echo's* letters pages subsequently, but, once again, the voice of the obviously disgruntled labour movement Catholic remained undetectable.[21]

The *Blaydon Courier* published an 'Open Letter to Christians of Blaydon' in September 1936. The letter's author, Communist Wilf Jobling, 'earnestly' appealed 'to all religious minded people' to examine the Spanish situation 'calmly and soberly'.[22] Jobling presumably thought the letter necessary, as he perceived Catholic concern over the issue. However, the single respondent to the letter was only partly antagonistic and, in any case, not a Catholic.[23] In late August, 'Peace and Prosperity' asked if Blaydon Urban District Council's support for the Republic meant that councillors 'approve of the stripping naked of innocent priests and nuns, even burning them?'[24] But, again, it was unclear if this was the protest of a Labour voting Catholic. Buchanan claimed that working-class Catholic dissent over Labour's policy on Spain declined over time as the memory of initial atrocities against the church faded.[25] In as far as the number of letters on the conflict in general declined, this was also the case in the north-east. There were correspondingly fewer references to the war's religious aspect. Yet, as has been shown, there was very little *overt* labour movement Catholic dissent expressed in the regional newspapers even in the early months of the conflict.

If there was considerable working-class Catholic anger at the labour movement's support for the Republic, it is reasonable to expect at least some evidence of this expressed clearly in the letters pages of the regional press. Working-class Republic supporters certainly did this. Of course, newspapers' letters pages were limited in size and it cannot be assumed that editors chose a representative sample to publish. But, if anything, Catholic labour movement critics were *more likely* to have been published than excluded. All the major regional newspapers supported the liberals or Conservatives and tended to give particularly detailed coverage of splits within the labour movement. Indeed, it was as much in their interests 'to publicise cases of workers' disaffection with labour policy on Spain' as it was the Catholic press', and they sometimes did so, as illustrated below, on the flimsiest of pretexts.[26] The only rank-and-file labour movement Catholics who are identifiable are those who openly proclaimed themselves as such. So, if there were so many angry labour movement Catholics in the north-east, why did they not openly declare (pseudonym or not) both their religion and their politics and demand that Labour listen? Why did Labour's enemies not identify this 'split' within the movement and attempt to fuel difficulties by claiming, under pseudonyms, to be angry labour movement Catholics? Certainly, the editor of the *Sunderland Echo* never had occasion to claim that there were so many letters it was impossible to publish them all, which happened in the deluge of correspondence he received over the case of a mother being sent to prison with her 14-day-old child for stealing.[27] From this public evidence, it seems that the 'problem' hardly existed in the north-east. Notwithstanding a handful of isolated examples, Labour policy on the Republic seemed to have outraged few Catholics sufficiently to provoke a public protest, not even to the extent of simply writing a letter to a newspaper.

'Covert'/Internal Catholic Pressure and 'Direct Action'

It is, of course, conceivable that north-east Catholics opposing labour movement policy on Spain instead placed covert pressure on their leaders. In some parts of Britain, Catholics acted directly to inhibit pro-Republic activity. For example, Catholic miners in one Yorkshire pit struck in order to prevent part of their wages going to the Republic. Catholic trade unionists in a Birmingham constituency refused to pay their affiliation fees if Labour sympathised with the Republic. Some Catholic members of Camberwell Labour Party formed a breakaway 'Constitutional Labour Party' in protest at Labour's support for the Republic.[28] Whilst there was no direct parallel in the north-east, some evidence suggests that, away from the public eye, Catholics did attempt to impede labour movement support for the Republic.

One element of this evidence relates to apparent Catholic resistance to proposed financial donations to 'Aid Spain' campaigns within the Durham Miners' Association (DMA). In February 1937, the *Universe* reported on the 'scenes of considerable resentment', when a large majority voted against a Horden lodge proposal that its members pay a one-shilling levy for the Republic.[29] However, there was no suggestion, even in this national Catholic newspaper, that Catholics had achieved this apparent victory. This was probably because the story appeared to have been culled almost verbatim from the *Sunderland Echo*, which did not mention Catholics explicitly. Moreover, the *Universe* failed to reproduce the entire *Sunderland Echo* report which said that Horden lodge *did* decide to allocate £50 to the Spanish Workers' fund, albeit after 'a discussion lasting an hour and a half' and 'a good deal of opposition'.[30]

In June 1937, 'a Durham Miner' claimed that Catholic miners had "in some cases" made "strong protests" about the sending of money to the

Spanish "Reds" in which "rather surprisingly, some Non-Conformists have joined"'.[31] There is some documentary evidence suggesting that Catholics inhibited at least one DMA lodge on the issue. Eden lodge made only one Spain grant and this was, as argued in chapter two, not regarded as such by the lodge. This was particularly unsupportive for a DMA lodge of a reasonable size such as Eden. Furthermore, Eden lodge did support similar causes such as the £200 DMA grant to German and Austrian refugees in October 1937. There clearly seemed to be something wrong with Spain as far as Eden lodge was concerned and there were other hints that Catholics may have been a consideration. In December 1936, the lodge bought 50 copies of the Labour Party pamphlet 'Catholics and Spain', an unusual step that suggests a degree of concern about the feelings of Catholics. (That two of the main opponents of donating to Spain were the lodge financial secretary and treasurer suggests that close control of the purse strings was also a consideration).[32]

However, even 'A Durham Miner' had to recognise that this purported *combined* religious opposition had been 'unable to prevent' lodges financially supporting the Republic. Indeed, as argued in chapter two, the DMA as a central institution had an impressive record of support for the Republic in both financial and campaigning terms; lodges such as Eden were, and remained, in a very small minority. This was most clear in summer 1938, when all DMA lodges had the opportunity to vote against the proposed MFGB 2s. 6d. levy for the Republic. Writing to the *Sunderland Echo*, 'A Miner' condemned the MFGB's 'exploitation' of miners' generosity for its own political ends and commented: 'the most vital and important issue to religious and clear thinking miners is that they are called upon to support communism … every miner should attend meetings discussing the levy and ensure it is defeated'.[33] 'Another Miner' expected to see many letters condemning the levy, especially when only £1,000 went to the recent victims of a pit disaster.[34] However, like all other votes on large DMA grants for Spain in this period, there was very little opposition. If Catholicism had informed some or most of the opposition, it remained inconsiderable and appears not to have inhibited the DMA's – in many ways considerable – support for the Republic to any significant degree.

Notwithstanding this, two Communists made allegations about broader north-east Catholic opposition. In November 1936, George Aitken claimed that Catholics in the region had gone to their unions and local Labour Parties 'in great numbers … opposing activity on the Spanish question'.[35] Also Charlie Woods, a member of the CP district executive, recalled that

the 'divisive influence of Roman Catholicism' prompted opposition to
'Aid Spain' activities.[36] The documentary evidence suggests that there was
a degree of Catholic opposition to support for the Republic within South
Shields LP&TC. Certainly, when the party began to make moves to support the Republic in 1938, there were often a handful of dissenters. In
April 1938, five voted against a proposal that the party send a delegate to
an emergency conference on Spain (13 supported the proposal). A few
days later, one person attempted to reverse this decision and a single
dissenter voted against asking the TUC to organise a delegate conference
on Spain in April 1938. In mid-December 1938, the vote was 13–4, this
time in favour of supporting a Manchester borough LP&TC resolution
calling for an immediate national party conference.[37]

It is highly probable that at least an element of this opposition was for
religious (i.e. Catholic) reasons. One dissident was surely local councillor
Dick Ewart, a Catholic who, as Labour MP for Sunderland South in 1948,
advocated Marshall aid for Franco's Spain.[38] Yet this opposition remained
internal; it did not seep into the local press. Moreover, opposition to pro-
Republic initiatives was always a small minority; sometimes there was
none recorded at all. For example, the vote to endorse an LSC circular
calling on the NEC to organise an immediate conference on Spain in July
1938 was unanimous.[39]

The internal opposition became most evident in 1938, when South
Shields LP&TC was actively agitating on the issue. Catholic opposition
probably does not explain the institution's inactivity on Spain before 1938,
as it still donated to Spain funds in 1936 when tensions over the church's
fate in Republican territory were at their keenest. The institution's indifference in 1937 was unlikely to have been a belated reaction to this now declining ill feeling. There were many other possible explanations for this
inactivity including the satisfaction of miners, who comprised the 'backbone' of the institution 'numerically and monetarily', that their union was
sufficiently active on the issue and the institution's deference to the
national leadership (particularly on foreign policy questions).[40] Thirdly, the
party was also heavily involved in local municipal politics at this time,
taking control of the council. In 1937, the party appeared to have little
time for anything other than electioneering and municipal concerns.

Internal minority opposition to supportive gestures for Spain was evident in several north-east institutions to some degree, though records
often did not indicate the reasons for the opposition. However, in cases
such as the wrangling in Ashington Miners' Federation over a grant to

Tynemouth Basque hostel in June 1938, the conflict appeared simply to have been over the amount donated, rather than the principle.[41] In general, there were many reasons for internal opposition or the inactivity of institutions such as the north-east district TGWU or Durham CLP (before 1938) over Spain. Certainly, inactivity in itself did not necessarily indicate disgruntled Catholics at work.

Consequently, there are reasons to be sceptical of Aitken's claim. The only evidence Aitken himself cited in November 1936 was the apocryphal 'controversy' in the *Evening Chronicle* (discussed above). The context for Aitken's claim is significant. He was criticising the national CP leadership at a Central Committee meeting for not providing a lead on the issue of Catholic influence in the labour movement. The more serious the situation on the ground, the more weight his criticisms would carry. This was reason enough for exaggerating the severity of the Catholic opposition in his district. Aitken was new to the North-east District and presumably to some degree unfamiliar with its politics and open to the influence of more established figures. The single most influential Communist trade unionist in the region was the bitterly anti-Catholic Tom Aisbitt. If Aitken had attached importance to Aisbitt's perspective, then this, too, partly explained his comments.[42]

Finally, Aitken claimed in the same speech that north-east Catholics opposed united front activities in the region too, implying that had it not been for them, Labour would have supported united action with the CP in the district. This was simply not the case. The majority of non-Catholic north-east labour movement activists also rejected the united front. By attributing the failure of Communist initiatives in the north-east to the influence of labour movement Catholics, Aitken was indulging in wishful thinking. It is comforting to think that, were it not for an influential minority, your political viewpoint would hold sway. The reality, for north-east Communists, was far more unpalatable.[43] This final point also applied to Woods' claim; and even he conceded that some Catholics supported pro-Republic efforts in the region. Clearly, whatever the motives and truth behind Aitken and Woods' claims, they do not fit with the general picture of a distinct lack of considerable and effective north-east Catholic opposition to labour movement activity on Spain.

Furthermore, the *extensive positive evidence* of labour movement solidarity campaigning also suggests that Catholics in the region were *not* a major obstacle to the Spanish Republican cause. Jarrow, with its high proportion of working-class Catholic voters – around one third of the Jarrow population in 1932 were descendants of migrant groups – was particularly significant in this context.[44] Despite the Catholic presence, Jarrow Labour MP Ellen Wilkinson was an outspoken and energetic Republic supporter. Speaking at Hebburn in September 1936, she argued that the war was not about Catholicism fighting Communism, as 97 per cent of the Spanish population was Catholic. Instead, the conflict was about 'workers fighting to maintain the power of the vote'.[45] While she did have isolated critics in the local press during the early months of the conflict, once again, they did not identify themselves as Catholics.[46] Wilkinson continued to champion the Republic openly. At a Spain Campaign Committee meeting in New-castle in December 1937, she faced the issue head-on. She claimed to have received a letter from the 'Catholic Action Party' warning that they would be recording every word she said. Brandishing this letter, Wilkinson said 'let not the church that stood by the Irish Republicans identify itself with fascism and death'.[47] Local newspaper columnist 'Bede' claimed that this speech had 'apparently not increased her [Wilkinson's] popularity among the Catholic electors in the Jarrow division' as it had 'produced an uneasy feeling'.[48] 'Bede' thought that Wilkinson should make the contents of the letter known. But this supposed 'uneasy feeling' was manifest in one single letter to the press and even this did not attack Wilkinson's pro-Republic stance.[49] Indeed, Wilkinson probably anticipated this as she also said in her speech that the letter by no means represented all Catholics as 'in-fluential members have begged me to ignore the actions of this irre-sponsible section'.[50]

Ellen Wilkinson risked little in adopting this position because she did not arouse noticeable opposition within Jarrow CLP, despite its high pro-portion of Catholic members. A split involving Catholics did occur in Jarrow from November 1936, but this was the result of the behaviour of some Labour Party members during the Jarrow March. The division had nothing to do with Wilkinson's position on Spain.[51] The four Jarrow La-bour Party 'rebels' of the November 1936 split were rumoured to be plan-ning to found a 'Catholic Party'. However, one of the Catholic 'rebels' cla-rified the issue by saying: 'Politically I am a Socialist. I shall remain a Socialist'.[52] This statement was significant as it perhaps characterised the attitudes of a significant proportion of Jarrow Catholic labour movement activists. Indeed, another of the 'rebels', councillor D.F. Riley, announced in late December 1936 that he planned to raise an army of 10,000 to fight for the Republic. Although a Catholic, Riley explained, 'I feel that I must not shirk from fighting Catholics who are against the Spanish Government'. Riley regarded the Republic as 'based on democratic principles and not on atheism or any form of dictatorship'.[53] The highly ambitious plan came to nothing: Riley himself certainly did not fight in Spain. But it revealed that Riley, a Catholic, was clearly far from alienated by his party's policy on the issue. Indeed, he favoured a far more proactive approach than was countenanced by national Labour leaders. The most likely reason for the lack of a Jarrow SMAC was not Labour opposition, but rather that Wilkinson and Jarrow CLP were sufficiently active on the issue that neither they, nor anyone else, deemed a specific committee necessary.

Like Jarrow, Gateshead had a large Catholic Labour voting population and an important Catholic critic of Labour policy on Spain in the form of McCretton.[54] But this did not prevent the party from providing active support for the Republic from the formation of Gateshead SMAC through to the Tyneside foodship in 1939. Again, like Jarrow, there was evidence of a possible religion based schism in Gateshead Labour Party in June 1937. This was manifest in a cryptic set of press reports on an alleged 'plot' against sitting Catholic Labour councillors. However, this intrigue, had nothing to do with Spain either: the supposed 'feud' was of nearly three years standing. Indeed, the 'split' failed to develop and was conceivably a press creation.[55] Notwithstanding this, Gateshead Labour Party had divided in the past over religious issues. For example, in 1931 Catholics in Gateshead Council Labour group split over the issue of supplying birth control advice. Similar schisms occurred in Newcastle, Sunderland, Blyth and Wallsend in the late 1920s, and the issue proved divisive in the labour movement throughout Britain.[56] Clearly, domestic issues that effected religious matters appeared to be far more important to north-east labour movement Catholics than did the plight of their church abroad.[57]

Other Labour Parties based in areas with significant Catholic populations were also not obviously hampered in their Spanish aid activities. Indeed, one party particularly active at constituency level was Seaham, another area with a notable Catholic population.[58] As McCretton seemed to have failed to influence his party, so Colgan did not seem to inhibit Blaydon Labour's considerable efforts for Republican Spain (and cooperation with Communists). Sunderland was the only area with a substantial Catholic population where the Labour Party did not appear particularly active on Spain.[59] Internal Catholic opposition may have played a part in this, but there were several other likely reasons why Sunderland CLP was inactive on Spain. The party's wafer thin majority on the council demanded the preoccupation of councillors and the devotion of their attention to domestic council matters. The party was also financially weak and had to spend time raising funds to keep itself solvent. It was also divided internally, likely a part result of its own electoral weakness, especially in terms of general elections. A particularly hostile local press sought to accentuate any suggestions of internal problems in the party and again must have had an effect in precluding much political campaigning outside strict domestic remits. These problems were manifest in the on-off saga of the party's one PPC (for a two member constituency) local miner Joseph Hoy, who gained and then resigned the position of Sunderland Labour PPC twice in the late 1930s.[60]

Sunderland Labour Party's relative inactivity was unusual, which suggests that, taken as a whole, there was little Catholic opposition in the region. Pro-Republic activity was of course stronger and longer lived in some localities than others. But inactivity on Spain, or any other issue, was usually most evident in places like Tynemouth and North Shields (and Sunderland) where Labour organisation was moribund. Indeed, it is noteworthy that many of the most active localities on Spain in the region were also those with the largest Catholic populations. They also happened to be areas where Labour was organisationally strong and this, rather than the distribution of Catholics, was the key factor in explaining most elements of the movement's institutional response to Spain. Naturally, Catholic opposition to Spain in these areas could have prevented the response from being even more vigorous, but there is very little, if any, evidence of this ethereal opposition.

Indeed, not only did most Catholics within the movement not impede the activity of their local Labour Parties on Spain, some actually donated to Spain funds. Ellen Wilkinson claimed this when responding to the 'Catholic Action Party' in December 1937 and even Charlie Woods conceded that some Catholics at grassroots level supported these campaigns.[61] Corroborating evidence regarding Catholics supporting Spain campaigns apart from the church's involvement in housing Basque refugees is sparse. However, newspaper letters pages during the Tyneside foodship campaign (December 1938–March 1939) revealed that some Catholics supported not only the humanitarian campaigns, but also the Republic. For example, 'Love Thy Neighbour', who claimed to be a Catholic, refused 'to allow my faith to blind my power of reason' and condemned Franco's 'unchristian outrages on innocent women and children'.[62] 'Love Thy Neighbour', certain that the 'fascist papers' would not delude other Catholics, would support the foodship even if it aided atheists. In fact, 'Love Thy Neighbour' went further than the framers of the campaign themselves in depicting the foodship as a means of defeating Franco.

Clearly, there was some diversity in north-east labour movement Catholic attitudes, though this did not appear to stretch to overt support for Franco. Some, like Riley in Jarrow, were even prepared to fight against other Catholics in their desire to defend the Republic from fascism. These Catholics put politics before their religion, probably because they recognised that their coreligionists were fighting on both sides and that Franco's forces also contained Muslim Moors. The lengths Riley claimed to be prepared to take his support for the Republic were exceptional. However, other labour movement Catholic activists openly and actively supported the cause too. For example, councillor Mary Gunn, chairperson of Gateshead LP&TC in 1937, spoke at the public meeting that launched Newcastle SMAC.[63]

The attitude of the only north-east Catholic Labour MP, David Adams (Consett), is significant in this context. After some early doubts, Adams adopted a fairly robust pro-Republican stance. Tom Buchanan claimed that there were four different ways Catholic Labour MPs reacted to Spain: to defend the Republic openly; to condemn the Republic and defend the Catholic Church (a rare reaction); to oppose the labour movement's stance in coded terms or, the most common, quiescence.[64] Adams initially wavered between the first and final categories. He was the only Catholic Labour MP of eight approached who initially agreed to sign a letter penned by F. O'Hanlan, chairperson of Chichester CLP. Published in early 1938, the letter called upon Catholic bishops to denounce the Franco rebellion.[65] But 'after meeting his colleagues in the pious air of London [Adams] seems to have abandoned his sinful intention'.[66] He changed his mind once more and the final draft of the letter carried Adams' signature.[67] After this episode, Adams became an increasingly overt Republican supporter. By January 1939, he was sufficiently supportive to speak at the North-east International Brigade memorial meeting. Along with only three other north-east Labour MPs (Wilkinson, William Whiteley and Chuter Ede) Adams put his name to the Brigade's Memorial Fund appeal.[68]

On the other side of the spectrum were McCretton and Colgan who voiced high-level opposition to support for the Republic. Like Riley and Gunn, they, too, appeared a vocal minority. Then there were Catholics like Wilfred Edge, an important Labour councillor and trades unionist – he formed and was secretary of Durham trades council – in Durham City.

They were not obviously connected with Spanish aid campaigns but did not openly criticise their party's position either.[69] Edge's praise for the work of Neville Chamberlain shortly after Munich, expressed in his capacity as mayor from the platform of a Conservative bazaar at which Chamberlain's wife appeared, suggested that his views on foreign policy were not conducive to support for the Republic regardless of his religion.[70] But what can be said of the majority of rank-and-file north-east labour movement Catholics? Generally, they did not protest openly, nor did they leave much evidence of having attempted to impede their movement's activity on Spain. However, the proportion of those who were either indifferent to the policy or who acquiesced, as compared with those who approved of their party's stand on the issue and *actively supported* the pro-Republic campaigns is difficult to determine. Yet it seems likely that a significant number of the Catholics active in Jarrow and other parties involved themselves to some degree in this campaigning.

Attitudes of Non-Catholic Labour Movement Activists

Another significant aspect of this topic is the attitude of non-Catholics in the north-east labour movement. An important feature of the Spanish Civil War/Catholic controversies in the region was the relatively small number of protagonists involved. The most vocal and senior Catholic antagonist in the press was Tom Aisbitt, a high-profile member of Newcastle trades council and NEFTC president in 1938.[71] Aisbitt maintained a steady stream of letters about what he regarded as the pernicious role of religion, and especially Catholicism, throughout the late 1930s in the pages of the Amalgamated Society of Woodworkers journal.[72] As a Communist who had to keep his true political affiliation hidden for fear of persecution and possible expulsion, Aisbitt's behaviour was understandable. Aisbitt held an influential but tenuous (given his hidden political allegiances) position in the labour movement. By highlighting the tactics and behaviour of Catholics, Aisbitt could hope to deflect at least some interest from the activities of crypto-Communists like him. Simultaneously, he was aiming a blow at those whose religious beliefs were inimical to the growth of Communism within the wider labour movement. Still, Aisbitt's behaviour did not sit well with the popular front policy. Whether the CP permitted Aisbitt to continue his tirade or he refused to stop when instructed to do so by his political superiors remains unclear. As a 'crypto', though, perhaps he could express openly what some overt Communists wished to, but could not. However, if Aisbitt's comments *had* been repeated by many other important labour leaders and represented a commonplace attitude within the north-east labour movement, Catholics within it would have had good reason to fear that intolerance towards them was worsening in the later 1930s.

As it was, only one other prominent regional labour movement activist momentarily adopted Aisbitt's confrontational attitude. In September 1936, Labour left-winger Steve Lawther alleged that St. Joseph's Roman Catholic school near Blaydon held prayers for a Franco victory.[73] Refusing to believe the school's claim that the prayers were for both sides, Lawther argued that if educational institutions 'are going to be used for propaganda purposes to back up fascist aggression against the people of Spain, it is time as a committee we called a halt'.[74] Again, like Aisbitt's actions, this did not appear to enrage many working-class Catholics. Only one letter of protest followed, when 'Catholic Miner' wrote that Lawther 'should know a few facts. In Spain the issue is between Roman Catholic religion and Communist and Anarchist butchers'.[75] Yet, in contrast to Aisbitt, Lawther did not proffer further critical public comment on the Catholic issue.

On the other hand, some labour movement sections attempted to placate possible Catholic concerns. Boldon colliery Labour Party, for example, appealed to Christians to attend a meeting on Spain, 'in view of the falseness of atrocity stories, which are got up by political sections in order to steal the Catholic vote'.[76] Yet, like the overt antagonists, this attitude also appears to have been a minority one. 'Roman Catholic' of Sunderland alluded to the majority attitude when they pointed out in the *Sunday Sun* letters page debate that Aisbitt's vitriolic anti-Catholic letters had not produced a 'single word of approval or protest from his comrades in the Socialist movement', despite the size of this movement.[77] The same correspondent commented a month later that 'head officials of the Socialist movement' had still 'not uttered one word of "protest" to a member whose actions are detrimental to the movement. The fact of their silence conveys to me that this sort of thing is countenanced'.[78] This widespread impassivity does suggest general non-Catholic indifference to the issue, both within the regional leadership and rank-and-file. Had the situation been as potentially damaging to the labour movement as Aitken claimed in autumn 1936, it is surely likely that Aisbitt, particularly, would have been silenced, disciplined, or at least publicly rebuked for his very public stance. The NEFTC was less passive in March 1938 when it supported measures against Catholic guilds. McCretton's threat of protests from 24,000 northeast Catholics did not materialise, suggesting that the non-Catholic majority on the NEFTC had a better understanding of general Catholic trade unionist feeling in the region than he did. Again, as with the Spain controversy, neither McCretton nor Colgan resigned in protest.[79]

Tom Buchanan employed the example of the NEFTC/Spain controversy to illustrate the point that 'For many Catholics there was a feeling that the events in Spain were ushering in a new wave of religious intolerance in Britain…'.[80] Of course, the incident showed that there *was* some division over the issue. Yet its greater significance, surely, was that most of the NEFTC leadership acted successfully to minimise bitterness and divisions created by the conflict in Spain. Furthermore, non-Catholic leaders' *tolerance* was reciprocated by the vast majority of north-east labour movement Catholics who did not try to obstruct the workings of their movement.

A Catholic Voter Backlash?

Did the regional Labour Party suffer at the polls from a protest vote by working-class Catholic Labour (non-activist) voters? This certainly happened in Lancashire, where a Labour Party analysis of its loss of 17 seats in the county in 1938 blamed the 'Spanish factor'.[81] The problem was localised to areas where Catholics were numerous. Nevertheless, it remained potentially damaging as these areas, such as Glasgow, were often labour movement strongholds. Tom Buchanan noted that Catholic votes were the mainstay of Labour's electoral base in the north-east. However, he did not discuss Labour's wider electoral fortunes in the region.[82]

Evidence suggesting a link between a Labour defeat at the polls and Catholic anger over Spain came in June 1937. 'A Durham Miner' claimed that 'extremist' Steve Lawther's attack on the Blaydon Catholic school's prayers for a rebel victory led to over 2,000 votes being cast against him in the council elections a few months later. Lawther, 'who held an apparently safe seat' was consequently 'defeated by the biggest margin in the whole election'.[83] However, even 'A Durham Miner' did not *explicitly* claim that these were the votes of angry and usually Labour-voting Catholics. Similarly, no one in the regional press drew any link between Lawther's stand on the issue and his election defeat. Indeed, even the *Catholic Herald* itself did not comment on Lawther's defeat, despite considerable earlier coverage of the April 1937 election results. Instead, it discussed the defeat of Catholic Paul Gormley, the retiring 'Independent' in Blaydon ward. This surprise defeat of a non-Labour Catholic in the same council as Steve Lawther suggests that voting patterns here cannot be explained solely in terms of Catholic anger over the Labour policy on Spain.[84] The key year for the issue as a vote loser for Labour was 1936, when news of church burnings and priest killings was most fresh (despite Labour's support for Non-Intervention at the time). Yet the Tyneside edition of the *Catholic Herald* noted that the 'outstanding feature' of the autumn 1936 elections in the north-east was the 'very obvious apathy' (apparently the result of the 'return of prosperity').[85] This was not the response of a Labour voting Catholic population angry at the party's stance on Spain.

Notwithstanding this one case, the north-east was very different to Lancashire in terms of general working-class Catholic voting patterns. Ellen Wilkinson even criticised some Catholics openly in her speeches, but Jarrow Labour Party suffered no noticeable backlash at all at the municipal polls. In fact, despite a debilitating internal split, Jarrow Labour still fared well electorally. The party took a seat from the Labour 'rebels' in November 1937 and retained control of the council in the November 1938 elections. There was no election in Jarrow in November 1936 as the parties had agreed a political truce to conduct the Jarrow March. Had there been an election in 1936, it seems unlikely that Labour would have suffered from a Catholic backlash. The party fared well in the two wards with the largest concentrations of Catholic voters in 1937 and 1938 (East and Central). The only curious result came in Central ward in 1938. Labour won with a reduced majority of 107 over the Moderates, whose vote had increased by 90. The Labour vote had decreased by 150 from 1937.[86] It was most unlikely, however, that this was a delayed protest vote about Spain: the strongly pro-Republic Catholic Riley was elected in the same ward in 1937 with the larger Labour vote. Was Riley's unusually outspoken pro-Republic stance a *vote winner* among Catholics? Available evidence does not provide a clear answer, but it certainly did not seem to be a *vote loser*. As elsewhere in the region, it seems likely that local issues informed most voters' choices. As the inspiration and marshal for the Jarrow March, Riley must have built a strong local following. Indeed, it is possible that this local popularity persisted in spite of his pro-Republic stance.

Gateshead was another strongly Catholic area. There, Labour's electoral fortunes were not as good as in Jarrow but they were not disastrous. Having taken control of the council in 1935, Labour lost two seats to the Moderates in 1936, bringing the two parties level. Indeed, in the most strongly Catholic ward (North), the Labour majority decreased from 920 in 1935 (when the Catholic McCretton was elected) to 595 in 1936. While these losses coincided with a period when passions were strongest over attacks on the Spanish Catholic Church, it still seems unlikely that they were due wholly or in part to Labour's attitude on Spain.[87] The local Labour Party did not form Gateshead SMAC until December 1936, a month after the election. Moreover, there is no direct evidence in press local election reports that any of the parties even mentioned the issue, let alone that it caused problems for Labour. The Gateshead Ratepayers' Association newspaper did not mention the Labour Party's stand on Spain, and instead criticised the Labour administration for its general inactivity, especially its refusal to cooperate with the government over Air Raid Precautions measures. In fact, there was no indication of a specific appeal to the Catholic vote by any political party in Gateshead.[88] Thus local or other issues, the candidates' personality, or a lower turnout (figures for which are unavailable) may explain these Labour losses.[89] Unlike in Birmingham, Conservatives and liberals in the north-east did not recognise the Spanish Civil War as a vote winner for them, probably because, on the whole, it was not.[90] Indeed, so low did they rate their electoral chances that the 'Moderates' proposed a truce for the 1937 Durham County Council elections. Labour rejected the idea.[91]

Labour fared worse in a third Catholic area, Sunderland. Gains in 1934 and 1935 gave Labour control of Sunderland council. As at Gateshead, the Independents fought back in the November 1936 elections, winning four Labour seats. Single gains in the following two years allowed the Independents to wrest control of the council from Labour in 1938. However, there was again no evidence directly linking the Labour losses and the party's position on Spain. Instead, it seems that local issues, most notably Labour mayor Summerbell's pacifism, were the key to explaining the Labour losses. The town's main newspaper, the *Sunderland Echo*, urged electoral support for the Moderates by appealing to the electorate's patriotism. It highlighted the mayor's refusal on pacifist principles to visit *HMS Cairo* when it visited the town.[92] There was no critical mention in the *Sunderland Echo* of Labour's attitude to Spain at election time. Furthermore, as discussed above, Sunderland Labour Party was not particularly involved in much public Spanish aid work. Of course, it is possible that the mayor's high profile involvement in Sunderland SMAC was sufficient to alienate working-class Catholics, but there is no direct evidence of this. The salient feature of the November 1937 elections was apparently apathy and this in spite of the possibility that the Moderates could regain control of the council and that the local CP were supporting Labour.[93]

These three examples reveal that even within a single region Labour's electoral fortunes in localities with considerable Catholic Labour voting populations had no shared experience in this period. Jarrow had the largest working-class Labour voting Catholic population and arguably the most high profile and outspoken north-east Labour Party supporter of the Republic in the form of Ellen Wilkinson. Yet, curiously, Jarrow Labour experienced the best election results of the three areas. Labour in Sunderland provided the least public support for the Republic but suffered the most at the polls. However, there are too many other locality specific complicating factors to conclude that Labour did better in Jarrow because it was so actively pro-Republic. But it is safe to conclude that there was no uniform working-class Catholic voter reaction to Labour's policy on Spain. Given this, the issue clearly *did not* have a significant impact on Catholic Labour Party support in the north-east. Seen as a region, Labour's electoral fortunes were certainly no worse in Catholic areas than in 'non-Catholic' ones, again showing that Labour's electoral experience in Lancashire was clearly not shared by the north-east.[94] There was no corroborating evidence that the issue played a part in any local elections in the region.

Why So Little Division/Opposition?

That there was so little division in the north-east labour movement over attitudes to the Spanish Civil War can be explained by a combination of long-term and more immediate factors. In the long-term, the high degree of integration that characterised the Irish Catholic experience in the northeast was clearly instrumental. Several historians have argued that the experience of Irish immigrants in the north-east was characterised by an absence of indigenous hostility and widespread acceptance as part of the wider community.[95] The Reformation had little impact on parts of the region, particularly Northumberland, and Irish immigrants consequently found themselves entering a relatively accepting environment.[96] The subsequent development of a common 'community of occupation, interest and struggle' differentiated the region strongly from west central Scotland and north-west England, though there were, of course, some tensions.[97] A relative lack of sectarianism was also vital in facilitating the process of integration. Newcastle, the largest city in the region, had the reputation of being tolerant towards Irish due to the absence of an Orange movement and the strength of local liberalism.[98] By 1914, such was the integration of the Irish in the region that it produced the largest distinctive Catholic Irish contribution to the British war effort in the form of the Tyneside Irish Brigade.

This integration also broadly characterised Irish workers' involvement in the labour movement. Irish trade unionists in the north-east did not have the reputation of being blacklegs as they did in Wales. There was some small scale Irish blacklegging in the region but these cases were exceptional and soon forgotten. Much of the Irish immigration into the region occurred at a time when labour could be absorbed relatively easily and these workers probably did not represent competition to the indigenous labour force. In fact, Irish and indigenous workers generally cooperated well. Many Irish became involved in the DMA and were important in the development of other trade unions in the region.[99] Indeed, their very strength in the labour movement in many parts of the region was testament to this longer-term integration.

Several more immediate factors also provide part of the explanation for this phenomenon. As noted at the outset, some north-east Catholic leaders and organisations promulgated an anti-Republic perspective. Yet they were not able to drive home this viewpoint as relentlessly as they might have. The Rev. Thomas L. Cain, for example, told over 1,000 people at a CYMS rally in Shotton that the conflict in Spain was a struggle between the 'anti-god forces of communism and the Christian army under General Franco'.[100] Held on Sunday 2 May 1937, it was the first CYMS meeting in the region that year.[101]

This relative inactivity was a reflection of the lack of regional strength of Catholic organisations that were elsewhere doing a considerable amount of the propaganda work on the issue of Spain. Despite its sizeable Catholic population, only 5 per cent of the CYMS's total national membership of nearly 40,000 came from Hexham and Newcastle diocese. Only 1 per cent of Catholics residing in the region were CYMS members.[102] 'A Durham Miner' ascribed this weakness to the numbers of young people moving to the south for work. Moving seemed to 'strengthen the religion' of those Catholics, but 'Catholic activities have suffered in the north from the migration of so many young people'.[103] Catholic churches in Hexham and Newcastle diocese held prayers on 'outrages' committed in Spain. Still, it appears that the regional church authorities did not conduct as vociferous and unstinting an anti-Communist, anti-Republic crusade as their Merseyside counterparts in these years.[104]

The reasons that north-east Catholic Church leaders devoted less time to condemning Communism and the Republic remain unclear, but are perhaps bound up with the perception that Communism represented no kind of a threat in the region. The north-east district Communist Party was very weak, itself partly the consequence of Catholic numerical strength in the region. There certainly appeared to be little fear of Communism either within or outside the regional labour movement.[105] Asking 'Is Communism Coming?' in June 1937, 'A Durham Miner', who was 'living and moving among working folk', certainly did not think so, and this despite Durham miners having 'always been in the vanguard left wing advances'.[106] Moreover, the wider labour movement did respond when Catholic Church leaders attacked the Republic. For example, when a Labour meeting on Spain coincided with the Shotton CYMS rally mentioned above, DMA agent Sam Watson 'effectively replied to fascist slanders'.[107] This counter-propaganda, often from the mouths of some of the most respected regional leaders and institutions, must have enjoyed at least a degree of success.

Paradoxically, it seems likely that the behaviour of the Catholic Church hierarchy in the region actually helped to negate the anti-Republic message it attempted, albeit sporadically, to propound. As well as dominating the humanitarian assistance to Franco's side, the Catholic Church also became involved in the Basque Children's Committee. The Basque children received a lukewarm response from the church hierarchy as 'their plight was seen by many Catholics as a "red" cause', and, indeed, they were hated by more extremist Catholic elements.[108] Yet, by late June 1937, Hexham and Newcastle Diocese claimed to be caring for more Basque refugees than any other single diocese in the country. While it exaggerated the numbers cared for, concern for the refugees' plight from ordinary Catholics was clearly evident in the offers the diocese received to take 430 children to be cared for in private homes.[109] The Catholic Church's motives were hardly pure: it became involved in caring for the victims of a Franco offensive because it wished to deny a propaganda victory to the Republic and to keep the refugees out of the hands of the 'reds'. Certainly, in the confusion that ensued over the funding of separate Catholic and independent Basque children's homes, Catholic involvement appeared to have the effect of diverting some funds from the NJCSR.[110] Whether rank-and-file Catholics understood their church's motives, or that the Basque refugees were mostly the children of Catholic Republicans and the victims of their church's supposed saviour General Franco, is unclear. But the church's involvement in caring for Basque refugees must have muddied the waters and at the least blunted its theoretical anti-Republic position. Perhaps in this case the church's actions spoke louder than its words, though it framed its appeals for the refugees in humanitarian terms.

Final Remarks

Given an exceptional degree of integration, and the other shorter-term factors, it seemed natural for a considerable proportion of north-east labour movement Catholics to accept their movement's view of the Spanish Civil War (democracy versus fascism) and reject their Church's depiction of it as atheist Communism attempting to smash Christianity. As support for the Republic did not equate to pro-Communism for these Catholics, individuals such as the strongly pro-Republic Riley could 'Aid Spain' and overtly oppose Communism without fear of contradiction.[111] Alpert's claim that a 'significant proportion' of the Catholic press' 'largely working-class readership was not especially in sympathy with the cause which the press was reporting' [i.e. Franco], is certainly borne out by the experience of many north-east Catholics.[112]

It is clear that strong Catholic places in the north-east, such as Jarrow, did provide considerable support for the Republic, in contrast to similar areas in other parts of the country. The proportions of Catholics who actively supported the Republic compared with those who merely acquiesced cannot be accurately determined, however. Still, working-class Catholic hostility to Republican Spain certainly was not 'widespread and durable' in the north-east.[113] Naturally, there were some examples of Catholic clergy intervening effectively against pro-Republic activities in the region. Len Edmondson, for example, recalled that on the day of a concert for Spanish Medical Aid none of the artists appeared as they were Catholics and the local priest had ordered them to stay away.[114] Notwithstanding this, it remains clear that the divisions and problems caused by the Spanish Civil War in this strongly Catholic region were relatively insignificant.

However, it was different when the labour movement proposed policies that would have had a *direct impact* on a Catholics' own way of life. This explains the different reactions of north-east Catholics to the issues of birth control (which precipitated the split in Gateshead Labour Party in 1931) and education. Clearly, as far as the north-east was concerned, Spain was not the issue that brought the 'most traumatic', of a 'series of confrontations between the labour movement and active Catholics in its ranks'.[115] Birth control and education were, and continued to be, issues that were far more divisive. Thus, in 1943 Colgan and others in Hexham and Newcastle diocese established the Association of Catholic Trade Unionists (ACTU) in 1943 as a response to the education policy accepted by the TUC in 1942 that implied the end of state-funded Catholic schools.[116] Yet there is evidence that north-east Catholics did not necessarily follow the dictates of their religion even on the bread-and-butter issues. In June 1937 'A Durham Miner' noted that, while Catholics were 'very prominent' in the county's labour movement (holding between 10 per cent and 20 per cent of seats on most local councils), they did not always influence their party 'as much as might be expected'.[117] He cited Bishop Thorman's failure to persuade Durham County Council to revoke its decision to discontinue sending Catholic children to Catholic orphanages, in spite of the strong Catholic representation on the council and an 'organised effort' to influence the decision by Catholic organisations in the county. Indeed, there was even an allegation that some Catholics 'voted with their party and against the bishop's request', though 'A Durham Miner' doubted this.[118] The regional hierarchy were so concerned about this situation that, in August 1937, the Vicar General of Hexham and Newcastle diocese, Hugh Cogan, called on Catholics to show 'much more enthusiasm' for their coreligionists standing for election, and to take particular notice of attitudes to Catholic education.[119] This evidence suggests that Lynn overstated the power of the Catholic Church to influence the Catholic vote in the region. On the opening of a new Catholic Church in Boldon, the local priest claimed that in too many places Catholics were persecuted and that this was a reason to be 'even more loyal to our priests'.[120] Yet the northeast did not see much persecution and the relative lack of loyalty to priests was the result.

Clearly, their high degree of integration made the experience of northeast labour movement Catholics somewhat exceptional, though nonetheless significant given their numbers. Yet how exceptional was the region? Tom Buchanan detailed the problems that the conflict caused for labour movement Catholics, employing evidence relating to the north-west of England, areas of London and central Scotland. However, there are hints that the north-east experience may not have been a completely isolated phenomenon. According to Neil Riddell, working-class Catholics in heavily unionised and Labour dominated areas such as South Wales were more likely to place politics above religion. Wales was of particular significance as tremendous growth from a low base in the inter-war period brought the Welsh Catholic population to over 100,000 by 1939. Furthermore, the majority of Welsh Catholics were working-class and encouraged by some of their clergy to enter the labour movement.[121]

Andrew Flinn's work on Greater Manchester has shown that Labour leaders in Oldham and Bolton accepted that the Spain issue had augmented anger over domestic issues and was manifest in poor election results. While local Labour Parties did little on the issue, this did not preclude anger at the national movement's position. In contrast, the Catholic dominated Wigan Labour Party was active on Spain and did not suffer as a consequence. Wigan differed as the Labour Party was stronger in the town and Irish Catholics were well represented within the local movement's structures. They therefore did not harbour grievances that Spain could exacerbate. This situation invites comparison with Jarrow and underlines the high degree of diversity of Catholic responses even within small geographical areas.[122] Interestingly, a strong local labour movement may not always have been a prerequisite for minimising Catholic dissent over Spain. The Birmingham labour movement was not strong but, while there was some dissent over the issue, most local Catholic Labour Party members remained 'loyal to party rather than church'.[123] Further research into grassroots labour movement Catholic attitudes in other British regions will reveal the extent to which the north-east was an important but exceptional case.

4

LEFT OUTSIDE?
SPAIN, THE POPULAR FRONT
AND DIRECT ACTION

Another aspect of popular frontist discourse both at the time and sub-sequently is the claim that Spain almost inexorably led to increased coop-eration between activists of the official movement and the CP, as well as liberals and various others. Noreen Branson, for example, wrote that if Labour wanted to act on Spain at local level 'it meant doing so in asso-ciation with Communists who were in the forefront of local Aid-for-Spain activities'.[1] At the time, George Aitken made a similar claim.[2] Spain was apparently crucial in promoting increasingly favourable attitudes within the official movement to the CP, to cooperation with it and other forces outside of the movement, and, consequently, to the popular front project itself.

The first part of this chapter examines these claims in relation to the official north-east labour movement, considering the extent to which Spain provoked united 'action', both formal and informal, between insti-tutions and activists and the forms this took. It also examines the effects of Spain on attitudes within the official movement towards the CP, the united and popular fronts.[3] The second part of this chapter discusses the use of industrial direct action for political ends and the impact of the popular front policy on attitudes to its use.

Joint Action on Spain and the United and Popular Fronts
As the main focal centre for the region, Newcastle saw the earliest agita-tion that appeared to suggest the validity of the CP logic. This came in the form of a CP-organised meeting of 3,000 on Spain in mid-August 1936

that also attracted some Labour speakers.[4] Indeed, there was clearly a form of link in some sections of the official north-east labour movement between an active and energetic stance on Spain and support for the united and popular fronts. Newcastle trades council, which organised a second major Spain demonstration in Newcastle with speakers from both Labour and Communist parties, was the key official institution organising on Spain in the city.[5] It also supported all the other key Communist campaigns in this period, including the united and popular fronts.[6] Blaydon LLP activists' early cooperation with Communists on the issue became formalised in Blaydon SMAC from mid-January 1937. Joint demonstrations on Spain in Blaydon in 1938 began to associate it explicitly with the need for a popular front. Blaydon LLP activists thus attempted to engineer the popular front at political meetings and many lent their support to the popular front campaigns 1938–9. Like Newcastle trades council, Spain was not the only issue that impelled cooperation between Labour and Communists in Blaydon throughout this period.[7] In Jarrow, joint action on Spain was difficult, as the CP barely existed as a separate entity. However, Jarrow LP&TC, active on Spain, was also sympathetic towards the CP and the popular front.[8] Some of the most active miners' lodges on Spain, like Boldon, Ryhope (both DMA) and Cambois (NMA), were also pro-popular front.[9]

However, the supposed 'logic' of Spain had not stimulated a change in political attitudes in any of these institutions. The history of cooperation between these institutions and CP activists or ideas, manifest in organisations such as TJPC, predated activity on Spain.[10] In Blaydon, the Socialist Sunday School was another point of contact and cooperation before 1936. The Lawthers and Bolton had been involved in it for many years, and it was where a young Wilf Jobling learned the politics that led him into the CP and finally to his death at Jarama. In all these cases, Spain did not herald a new era of cooperation on the left. These institutions all contained activists in influential positions who were either actual Communists (often 'cryptos') or so favourable towards the party that they might have well been members.[11] Spain merely provided another way in which to promote the united and popular fronts in practice.

This predisposition to activity on Spain was true, too, of the limited cooperation between the Socialist League, ILP and CP. In Gateshead, the Socialist League and ILP cooperated on Spain briefly in late 1936 and early 1937.[12] But until the ILP disaffiliated from Labour in 1932, these activists had mostly been ILP members, so Spain merely allowed for cooperation between many erstwhile comrades, who continued, for the time being at least, to share premises (Westfield Hall). Likewise, the CP and ILP cooperation in 1936–7, manifest in some joint activity under the auspices of the Unity Campaign, built on joint anti-fascist activities in the early 1930s.[13]

Ironically, Spain also became the issue that divided the ILP and CP more decisively than any other in the decade. As in South Wales, controversy over the suppression of the POUM (linked with the ILP) in Spain in the summer of 1937 embittered relations between the CP and ILP and helped to end most cooperation between them in the north-east. Indeed, activists from both parties heckled their opponents' public meetings. Still, in addition to its own internal fundraising efforts, the north-east ILP had representatives on the management committee of Tynemouth Basque hostel.[14] The 'non-political' operation of the committee meant that political divisions could not taint relations within it. But there were still signs of occasional low-level friction, for example between Gateshead ILP and Labour Party over the reporting of an ILP-organised Basque's Christmas party in December 1938.[15] Furthermore, cooperation, and the dire situation in Spain, failed to prevent a serious deterioration in relations between the ILP and former Socialist Leaguer members in Gateshead over Westfield Hall. This culminated when the latter abandoned the Hall in December 1938.[16]

However, the behaviour of other institutions did not lend itself to simple linear explanations. In three Newcastle CLPs, there may have been some form of relationship between the issues. Newcastle North CLP supported CP affiliation to Labour in 1936, while Newcastle East CLP openly rejected repeated Communist offers to help in the autumn 1937 municipal elections. By spring 1938, Newcastle North supported the popular front and the NEC expected East to follow suit. Yet, in 1939, while Newcastle North still provided support, and Newcastle Central CLP, previously not pro-popular front, had come over to the idea, East CLP now *opposed* Cripps' popular front campaign.[17] If Spain *had* helped to bring Newcastle East to support the popular front in 1938, it had not maintained this support in 1939.

In contrast, Newcastle City Party was more consistent. While formally represented on the trades council sponsored SMAC that also involved Communists and liberals, the City Party remained, marginally, opposed to involvement in specific Communist initiatives relating to cooperation on Spain and other issues throughout the period, notwithstanding somewhat fanciful Communist claims to the contrary in spring 1938. The sudden more active interest taken by the City Party in Spain in May 1938 did not indicate a positive attitude towards the popular front as it coincided with an unqualified acceptance of an anti-popular front circular from head office. The City Party retained its loyalty to the NEC and its opposition to the popular front in 1939.[18]

Other institutions, which divided into four main groupings, showed that there were no inevitable links between action on Spain, an increasingly favourable attitude to the CP and growing support for the popular front. The first group, which included labour institutions in South Shields and Blyth, skipped a supposed 'link' between Spain and the popular front; that of good relations (or support for cooperation) with the CP. South Shields LP&TC rejected the internal involvement of Communists and NUWM activists before July 1936 and continued to eschew any kind of action with the CP and its offshoots after summer 1936. Notwithstanding a degree of cooperation at individual level over Spain in 1937 (a handful of left-wingers supported the town's nascent SMAC), Labour's institutional activity on the issue in 1938 actually served to worsen public relations with the CP in the town, which sought to associate itself with the newly energised Labour Party. This did not prevent the Labour Party from sending its secretary Gompertz to the all-party Spain conference in London on 23 April. Soon after the party supported a regional United Peace Alliance conference and Gompertz implied that there were clear links between Spain and the popular front.[19]

In Blyth, the relatively strong CP and NUWM failed before mid-1936 to promote united action with Labour.[20] A fractious debate in the local press, friction over NUWM activities and Labour intransigence at the municipal polls revealed nothing had changed in later 1936. Spain only served to exacerbate divisions between the Blyth official and unofficial movements 1936–7, as the NUWM attacked supposed Labour apathy and obstructing tactics over food collections. Unsurprisingly, when public Labour activity on Spain ensued, it remained firmly separate from 'unofficial' efforts. There was some evidence of limited cooperation at individual level in spring 1938. Yet Spain remained divisive as, in July 1938, Communist William Allan launched several attacks on the apparent inactivity of the official movement on the issue in Blyth and Ashington. While Blyth official labour opposed the United Peace Alliance in 1938, both the Labour Party and trades council supported Cripps in 1939. The evidence suggests that there was no strong link between this noteworthy development and Spain, which appeared to divide the CP and Labour.[21] In both these cases it was most likely that official support for a popular front came through a desire to cooperate with liberals rather than – indeed, not with – Communists. Liberalism remained relatively strong in South Shields. But there was no joint institutional activity between Labour and the liberals on Spain or any other issue in this period and Liberal PPC Raymond Jones was almost as eager to criticise Labour as the government's foreign policy.[22] In the case of South Shields, Spain seems to have led to the popular front, but not via the CP. In the case of Blyth, any possible links between Spain and the popular front seem more ill defined.

A second group of institutions did not follow the 'logic' through to its conclusion. They showed that strong advocacy of the Republic's causes and endorsement of united front initiatives did not lead inexorably to support for the popular front. Most important were the miners, and the DMA's attitude – as the most significant institutional advocate of the Republic in the county – was essential. The DMA most supported cooperation with the CP before Spain had had much impact on attitudes. In the summer of 1936, it supported Communist affiliation to Labour and formally invited Communists to attend its anti-Means Test demonstrations in mid-August. However, this proved to be the high-water mark of cooperation between the DMA as an institution and the CP. The DMA refused both to support various practical proposals on unemployed agitation that involved working with Communists in autumn 1936 and to endorse the 1937 Unity Campaign. When the summer 1937 MFGB conference rejected the DMA's resolution for a united front, its theoretical support ended too. The DMA executive was firmly against the popular front, thwarting, in June 1938, a lodge attempt to get the issue discussed at DMA council. Similarly, Cripps' campaign received no official DMA support and there was no lodge vote on the issue.[23] Lodges such as Brancepeth No.2, Chilton and Murton were supportive of Spain, to varying degrees, not obviously left controlled and did not gravitate towards the popular front. In this sense they all reflected the central DMA's behaviour. Indeed, Murton lodge's increasingly generous donations suggested a growing interest in Spain and it even let a Communist use its hall for a Spain meeting in 1937. Yet it was one of few lodges to adopt an overtly anti-popular front position.[24] The NMA behaved in a similar manner.[25]

Another institution in this bracket was Wansbeck CLP where a strong theoretical stance on Spain embodied by Trevelyan translated into (theoretical) support for cooperation on the left in 1937. Yet there was no backing for the popular front in 1938 and in March 1939 Wansbeck CLP decisively rejected Cambo LLP's (Trevelyan's party) call for support for Cripps and the popular front. A veiled call for a popular front from New-burn LLP, which had been financially supportive but inactive on Spain, suffered the same fate. Durham CLP was the only DCFLP affiliate to support CP affiliation to Labour in 1936, though it was inactive on Spain 1936–7. After its mobilisation on Spain in May 1938, Durham CLP re-jected a proposal to support the popular front at the time of Munich and it did not support Cripps.[26]

The Labour Party in Tynemouth, which appeared to miss both 'links' in its move to the popular front, was a case on its own. Tynemouth trades council was hostile to the CP, and the Labour Party did not act to any sig-nificant degree on any CP attempts to forge cooperation over a raft of issues including Spain in autumn 1936. Relations did not appear to im-prove in 1937. The Tynemouth/North Shields area saw three significant Spanish aid campaigns before 1939 but local Labour Party activists did not seem significant in any of them, perhaps because all three contained pro-minent local Communists. The party's own apparent public inactivity on Spain, may have been, in part, the result of organisational weakness. How-ever, a significant Tynemouth Labour activist actually helped to scotch a specific proposal for action on Spain by the official regional movement in the summer of 1938, suggesting a degree of hostility to the issue.[27] So it was surprising that the party went ahead with a Cripps meeting it had org-anised before Cripps launched his popular front campaign after he had been disciplined by the party, and more so that it then pronounced against Cripps' expulsion. Indeed, in this case perhaps the popular front had bro-ught the party somewhat belatedly to Spain, as the Cripps meeting collec-tion was for the Tyneside foodship.[28]

A third majority group were active on Spain in some form before 1938 but did not support any form of left cooperation. Most significant in this context were Gateshead, Seaham and Houghton-le-Spring parties, though the NTFLP and many other LLPs could also be included.[29] There was a good degree of hostility in the Gateshead official movement apart from the Socialist League towards the CP and its offshoots in 1936. A Gates-head Labour councillor shared a platform with Communists on Spain at the Newcastle meeting in mid-September 1936, but her party exclusively ran Gateshead SMAC.[30] Labour seemed no more inclined to cooperate with the ILP on Spain and attitudes did not change significantly 1937–9. Indeed, the Labour controlled Watch Committee even refused to permit an ILP street collection for 'Spanish workers' in October 1936.[31] Notwithstanding the choice of popular fronter Konni Zilliacus as PPC in 1939, there was no institutional support for the project. In Seaham, the CLP opposed CP affiliation, had poor relations with Communists where they had a presence, such as in Dawdon lodge, and did not support the popular front.[32] These parties (and federation) illustrated that activity on Spain did not necessarily indicate Communist influence, nor did it demand cooperation with Communists. It, equally, did not lead activists ineluctably into the arms of popular fronters.

Finally, there were the bulk of the region's CLPs that were hostile to the CP and largely inactive on Spain before 1938. When they did become active in 1938, this did not did not bring dividends for the popular front.[33] Notable in this context was Sedgefield CLP, which voted heavily against CP affiliation to Labour in 1936 and rejected a call by Thrislington lodge at its April 1938 AGM to support the popular front. Yet, it was instrumental in getting the DCFLP to call for a national labour movement conference around the same time. Unanimous support for the NEC in February 1939 made it an element of the institutional opposition to Cripps' plan, which included both federations of Labour Parties and far outweighed the support for the popular front in the north-east.[34] Indeed, the DCFLP unanimously endorsed an NEC anti-popular front circular of 13 April 1938.[35] Taken in its entirety, the evidence certainly gives the lie to claims of necessarily strong links between activism on Spain, cooperation on the left and support for the popular front.

The failure of the miners to lend any support to the popular front in either 1938 or 1939 was crucial to explaining the project's failure in the region. Indeed, as the supposed lessons of Spain became more apparent – according to Communists and many left-wingers the need for a left alliance – so the single most significant section of the north-east labour movement actually gravitated away from the idea of cooperation with Communists. In 1938, when the DMA began agitating energetically within the movement for more action on Spain, it remained firmly opposed to the popular front. In this respect, the DMA represented a significant minority trend in the north-east movement that saw united front cooperation peak in mid-1936 and then tail away. While the 1937 Unity Campaign failed to muster similar levels of interest to those generated by the 'united front' Spain agitation of autumn 1936, its support was greater than that which the 1938 United Peace Alliance could marshal; which, in turn, had more regional backing than Cripps' popular front campaign in 1939.[36] This is not to argue that there was an inversely proportional relationship in the DMA and wider north-east movement between levels of support for a left alliance and those for Republican Spain. Indeed, when the movement as a whole seemed most interested in Spain, in May 1938, the popular front garnered most support in the region, though this was still very little. But, overall, there was no discernable causal relationship between these three distinct political projects. Clearly, the Communist logic often simply did not resonate outside of its sphere of influence; even in institutions like the DMA that appeared favourably predisposed to the party in the summer of 1936.

Activists' Attitudes

From the perspective of important official movement activists, again, the links between Spain, support for cooperation with the CP and the popular front were by no means always clear. The example of three Newcastle East CLP activists illustrates this. Naturally, some of those most active on Spain also embraced the popular front; Arthur Blenkinsop, for example.[37] Harry Brook was a second activist in this category. He was involved in the City Party as a representative of Newcastle Shop Assistants' Union branch, which, in January 1937, asked the TUC directly to conduct a campaign on Spain. A City Party delegate in Spain campaigns, Brook was a prominent popular fronter in 1939, agitating for its support within the City Party under the auspices of his union branch. In contrast was B.A. Brennan, one of the City Party delegates to Newcastle SMAC in 1936 and involved in organising the City Party's meeting on Spain in May 1938. Brennan was fairly favourable towards some left initiatives like the TJPC, yet he also supported moves to state the Labour Party's case against the united front in March 1937. However, in his capacity as secretary of Newcastle East CLP he publicly, and somewhat forcefully, renounced association with Communists at the autumn 1937 elections. While this may have been a demand of his position rather than a reflection of his personal politics, Brennan also came out against the popular front in February 1939. Brennan's case illustrated that Labour activists could be involved heavily in activity on Spain, alongside Communists, and yet reject any type of formal ties with the party. There were several other examples of City Party activists who were associated with various Spain campaigns and initiatives but not 'unity'.[38]

Similar observations stand for activists in other institutions. In Jarrow, Ellen Wilkinson was active on Spain and supported the popular front; D.F. Riley, on the other hand, keenly agitated for the Republic but opposed working with Communists. While Bolton, Steve Lawther and others influenced Blaydon party's support for the popular front, not all party members prominently active on Spain went along with them. The most important example of this was Jim Stephenson. Heavily involved in united front agitation and the TJPC, Stephenson's name was conspicuous by its absence in Blaydon Labour Party campaigning on the popular front.[39] Blaydon MP William Whiteley, too, did not support the popular front even after having visited Spain and in spite of his constituency party supporting the idea from 1938.

In this, Whiteley had something in common with several other northeast MPs. Jack Lawson also began taking a greater interest in the conflict in early 1938 after visiting Spain with Whiteley. Both supported the unofficial Spain conference in London in April 1938 but Lawson, too, did not move towards the popular front.[40] A third MP on the delegation, Emmanuel Shinwell (Seaham), had a momentary flirtation with the popular front in autumn 1938, in response to Munich, but it is clear that his experiences in Spain in January 1938 did not significantly moderate his hostility to cooperation with other parties.[41] In the sources, it is often easier to identify those who were active on Spain and pro-united and popular fronts; individuals like C.P. Trevelyan, or important miners like Pearson, Watson and Will Lawther.[42] These individuals and others must have drawn some kind of link between Spain and the need for cooperation on the wider left. Indeed, Pearson took the opportunity of an appearance on a South Shields SMAC platform in February 1937 to both associate himself with its aims and make an appeal for the unity of working-class forces.[43] However, they were unrepresentative; neither Trevelyan nor these miner activists reflected the attitude of their institutions on the popular front question. The nameless majority supported action on Spain but usually opposed cooperation with Communists and overwhelmingly rejected the popular front; even more so in 1939 than 1938.

Grassroots Labour Activists: Compulsion and Rebellion?

With the above evidence in mind, there was the question of whether official movement activists were compelled into cooperation with the CP on Spain because their own movement could not accommodate them. Simply speaking, in most cases they were not. With the resources at their disposal, Newcastle trades council activists, for example, could have kept their organising efforts confined to activists within official circles. That Newcastle trades council *chose* to work with the CP was a political decision made, presumably, under the influence of Aisbitt. But it *was* a *choice*, rather than the institution being forced into the arms of the CP due to the labour movement's inactivity. In Blaydon, too, Labour left-wingers were not reluctantly thrust into the arms of the Communists, they embraced them affectionately, grateful of yet another excuse to work together.

As illustrated in chapter two, elsewhere in the north-east, there were examples of official labour movement institutions at grassroots providing many ways in which their members could manifest support for the Spanish Republic without *having* to go outside it. Thus Middleton's claim that 'there is ample scope within the possibilities of our own party for all our local comrades to do their share of work on this Spanish issue' had a degree of validity, although much of what was done under official auspices might have upset him.[44] That some grassroots activists chose to act with members of other parties was related to their lack of sectarianism, indeed, their rejection of the strictures of Citrine and Transport House, rather than being a reflection of the *need* to act with Communists as only they were doing anything. Indeed, this latter claim did an injustice to those thousands of trade unionists and Labour Party activists who did act within their institutions and did not later trumpet and exaggerate their achievements.

There was a linked question of the extent to which official labour movement activists acted as rebels when they organised on Spain with Communists. Branson pointed out that working with Communists could necessitate Labour activists breaking the rules as no Labour Party member was permitted to appear on public platforms with Communists.[45] Yet, as has been seen, there were several examples of Labour activists appearing on platforms with Communists in some localities. Notwithstanding this, there were no known cases of expulsions of prominent Labour activists for appearing on Communist platforms in the north-east over Spain and similar issues. Activists like Bolton and the Lawthers in Blaydon both agitated openly with Communists and appeared prominent in a list of official Labour Party credited speakers for the 1937 local elections.[46] In contrast, Bishop Auckland CLP did expel members for involvement in the Unity and later Cripps campaigns.[47]

There were several reasons for the lack of discipline over Spain agitation. Firstly, in some Spain campaigns, Newcastle SMAC meetings for example, it was outwardly unclear whether Labour Party activists appeared on a Communist platform, or vice-versa. In other cases, it seems likely that the Labour activists concerned, and the regional leaders, did not know that they shared a platform with Communists. This degree of ignorance combined with a higher level of tolerance of Communists at constituency and regional leadership level. But the lack of political strictures used against the Spain campaigns also suggested that the regional leaderships did not regard them as a political threat and, as argued in chapter six, they were not.

Clearly, as far as Transport House was concerned, these local Labour activists were 'rebellious'. But then, by the same token, so were national figures like Labour Party leader Clem Attlee who appeared on occasion on platforms with Communists and who associated himself in Spain with the Communist run International Brigade. As Buchanan pointed out, the 'actual practice of anti-Communism rarely matched the rhetoric'.[48] While Transport House may have desired to control institutions and activists – it certainly kept its eye on grassroots activities, preventing Felling trades council, in spring 1936, from organising locally with the NUWM – the limits on what it could do to maintain discipline were great.[49] In practice, Newcastle trades council, theoretically better controlled by Transport House than any other type of labour movement institution (trades unions sometimes jealously guarded their autonomy, Labour Parties were always likely to be more difficult to control) could do pretty much what they wanted with who they wanted on Spain (and other issues) with no repercussions.[50]

Spain as a Distraction from the Popular Front

There were often no links between activity on Spain and left cooperation, and the issue also brought disunity. Indeed, some leaders instigated activity on Spain precisely to thwart the possibility of left cooperation developing. This was most evident in a DCFLP circular issued in early May 1938. Explicitly anti-popular front, the circular ended with an appeal for CLP affiliates to organise demonstrations on Spain for 4 June.[51] It was clear that, far from leading County Durham CLPs towards the popular front, the regional leadership regarded alternative activity on Spain as a useful way of ensuring that this did not happen. Indeed, the wording of this circular intimated at many of the reasons the popular front was not especially popular in the north-east labour movement including the paramount importance of the 'elementary principle of loyalty', the 'salutary' lesson of the weakness of the left outside of Labour, a rejection of defeatism, and the need for 'socialism'.[52]

The DCFLP thus used Spain in order to *distract* its affiliates from the popular front. By acting on Spain, the movement could demonstrate the falsehood of popular frontist arguments that it was disinterested and apathetic. If the countywide movement adopted a more obviously active stance on Spain out of fear of the popular front securing grassroots support, then this was, in one sense, a victory of sorts for the idea. Nevertheless, the 'victory', if it was one, partially undermined the popular frontists' case that the movement was incapable of acting alone.

The strategy almost backfired in Blaydon, where Labour activists attempted, albeit apparently unsuccessfully, to subvert their DCFLP organised demonstration on Spain and to turn it into something more representative of the popular front by inviting Communists, youth peace groups, British Legions and churches of all denominations to attend.[53] However, it was far from clear that Durham Labour leaders had much to fear; certainly if a poorly attended conference to rally regional support for the United Peace Alliance in late May 1938 (probably the only such meeting in the region at that time) was anything to go by. Durham leaders' actions merely helped bring a greater degree of certainty.[54] The DCFLP circular, inspired by the national leadership, showed quite clearly that one way to trump the popular fronters was to give them what they wanted: to mobilise the movement on Spain rather than keep it immobile.

On saying that, sections of the movement were in different ways and to differing degrees already mobilised on Spain before 1938. Speaking at a public meeting at Wingate as part of 'Help Spain Week', Shinwell expressed pleasure that the Labour Party machine 'runs as smoothly as ever'. Indeed, the very platform that he was speaking from testified to this to some extent.[55] At the Seaham AGM in May 1937 which initiated the party's pro-Republic campaigning, Shinwell predicted a Labour government within three years if war could be avoided and the party did not turn either 'to the right or to the left for a solution'.[56] In Seaham, it did not need to, in order to get constituency level action on Spain. Seaham was an unusual CLP to be mobilised on Spain before 1938, but plenty of LLPs were so, and the evidence of their activity undermined the popular fronters' case that Labour would not act alone on Spain.

Spain diverted attention from the popular front in other ways and evident, for example, in the highly contrasting levels of official labour movement support lent to the Tyneside foodship and Cripps' campaigns in 1939.[57] Indeed, Spain even distracted some popular fronters. The national CP leadership recognised this was a problem at grassroots in 1937 and in

March 1939 north-east Communist Hymie Lee implied as much when commenting on the district's situation.[58] However, most popular fronters within the Labour Party appeared to be immune to the draw of the Tyneside foodship campaign in 1939, concentrating their energies on Cripps' agitation. This, and Trevelyan's decision to donate £100 to Cripps's campaign instead of to a scheme for sending raw materials to Spain, were examples of how the popular front occasionally distracted activists from Spain.[59] In terms of numbers, Spain diverted attention far more from the popular front than the other way round, though the DMA, for one, appeared more concerned with agitating for cooperation with the CP than on the issue of Spain, at least in 1937. However, as argued below, the popular front contributed to a form of intellectual diversion from tackling the issue of support for the Republic that was potentially far more damaging.

The popular front's critique did not resonate in some key respects and its proposals for action, alliance with liberals and Communists, were anathema to many committed labour movement activists. The main illustration of the popular front's abject failure to address the regional labour movement's concerns over Spain and the rest of the deteriorating international scene came in the summer of 1938. As illustrated in chapter two, Labour's move to official and more active opposition to Non-Intervention in Spain *failed to* placate unease in the regional labour movement over the national leadership's role. In fact, totally the contrary, as by mid-1938 the entire 'political' section of the north-east movement desired an emergency conference of the labour movement on Spain or the general international situation. However, the clearly widespread disaffection with the movement's national leadership led, at best, only a handful of north-east labour movement institutions into the arms of popular fronters, and many of these, like South Shields LP&TC, had been largely inactive on Spain before 1938. If the Spanish Civil War was the 'main recruiting sergeant' for the popular front, then it was not a particularly successful one.[60]

Ultimately, while a considerable section of the official movement rank-and-file identified the same or similar problems as the popular fronters, their solutions were, and remained, very different. There were many more potential remedies for the disease than the 'cure-all' popular front. The majority regional attitude considered the movement perfectly capable of dealing with the situation alone. There was no need either for the united or popular fronts, if only the national leadership would use the massive resources at their disposal more effectively. It thus seems most likely that the national leadership refused to organise a national conference in 1938 because it wished to avoid general criticism of its inactivity and attitude, rather than a debate over the popular front. The NEC was fully aware that it had the support of movements like the north-east's over the popular front question. (Indeed, NEC member and Durham miner J.E. Swan represented his region's majority position well in this respect). It knew that it would have won any possible vote on the popular front.[61]

Clearly, the national leadership did not want to mobilise their membership any more than they already had, and certainly not in ways that sections of the north-east movement were beginning to consider. The popular front was useful to leadership simply as an excuse to obscure the real reasons for its obduracy. As the popular front was a CP policy, the Labour leadership could use it as it employed anti-Communism: namely as a way of 'de-legitimating a swathe of dissenting voices inside the labour movement'.[62] Finally, the national leadership must have anticipated the potential consequences of its attitude. In this respect, it was correct, as its stubborn refusal to organise the national conference paid no dividends to popular front advocates either inside or outside the official labour movement. The ties of loyalty were, and remained, strong.

In South Wales, united front activity occurred in the campaign against the Means Test in autumn 1936, before breaking down in January 1937. The creation of the South Wales Council for Spanish Aid in mid-February 1937 certainly appeared to bode well for advocates of the united and popular fronts. The CP had called for its formation in December 1936, and it involved institutions including the SWMF and Cardiff trades council who represented over 300,000 members of political parties (including Labour) and trade unions. However, by late 1937, 'Aid Spain' had begun to reflect tensions that had already ended the Unity Campaign. In contrast to the north-east, the official movement increasingly bypassed the Council and in February 1938 its regional leaderships instructed CLPs and trades councils to break off association with Spanish aid committees.[63] Thus, even in South Wales – with a far larger and more influential CP operating in a more favourable political culture – Spain was not the obvious starting point for a left alliance that the CP hoped it might be. Indeed, popular front activity on Spain in South Wales was 'temporary, brittle and short-lived'.[64]

Elsewhere, the effects of Spain at grassroots were complex and often contradictory. In Birmingham, there was a limited degree of cooperation between the CP and Labour Party, formerly hostile to Communism, brought about by Spain. But here, too, the popular front confused the situation. Indeed, Birmingham trades council and Transport House put an end to cooperation with Communists when the City Party began to support the popular front in 1938. In this respect Spain, and its link with the popular front, was an internally divisive issue within the Birmingham labour movement.[65] Furthermore, the Birmingham CP realised that united agitation against the government would not in itself lead to full 'unity'.[66] Conversely, in Battersea, Mike Squires claimed that Spain helped to promote united action between Communists and the official movement, so that by Mayday 1939 the local movement was 'united as never before'.[67]

Attitudes to Industrial Direct Action

While the popular frontist logic often did not apply in practice, Labour left-wingers and Communists also had to make considerable sacrifices in pursuit of the enigma of left cooperation. In 1920, inspired by the dockers who blacked the *Jolly George*, the labour movement successfully threatened a general strike if the government intervened militarily to support Poland in its war with Russia. But the debacle of the 1926 general strike ended the discussion within much of the national movement leadership on the use of industrial direct action to put political pressure on the government. The Trades Disputes Act of 1927 outlawed sympathy strikes and their illegality was a key argument employed by leadership figures such as Citrine in the 1930s.[68] The same stood for national leaders with a power base in the north-east. At a DCFLP delegate conference after Munich, for example, Hugh Dalton argued that a general strike could not be used to bring the government 'to its senses' as this was not democratic.[69] However, attitudes in the rank-and-file varied. Even in regions with 'moderate' labour movement cultures such as the north-east, the possible use of the strike weapon for political ends continued to be debated in the 1930s. Moreover, with a hostile government in power after 1931 and the apparent failure, once again, of electoralism with the dispiriting demise of the disappointing Second Labour government, these discussions took on a new urgency. Indeed, north-east figures played an important role in the earlier 1930s in getting the national labour movement to support, theoretically at least, the use of industrial direct action against the threat of war. Trevelyan moved a successful resolution at 1933 Labour Party conference that committed the party to preparing for a general strike in the event of war threatening.[70] North-eastern Patternmaker J.S. Brown spoke in favour of such action at the 1935 TUC conference.[71] Less than six weeks before the outbreak of conflict in Spain, the NEFTC supported unanimously a Blyth trades council resolution calling for all TUC affiliated organisations to be requested to organise strike action in the event of war. Previously, the NEFTC had instructed Blyth trades council to remove inferences to cooperation with unofficial institutions in its resolution, which it did. The NEFTC clearly accepted the use of unconstitutional strike action in certain circumstances; it just did not want to organise with Communists.[72]

Attitudes to the use of strike action for industrial and political purposes within the DMA, vital to the possible success of any mooted action, were complex in the earlier 1930s. The defeat in 1926 clearly made the use of industrial militancy to increase wages unpopular amongst DMA officials a decade later, including the newly elected left-wingers amongst them. Responding to criticism over support for what many miners regarded as a poor deal in 1936, the DMA executive argued that their grievance was 'no justification for self-annihilation ... Our people shuddered at the idea of a stoppage similar to 1926'.[73] An improved Durham deal in May 1937 appeared to vindicate the DMA executive.[74]

Yet the DMA did successfully employ industrial direct action, or the threat of it at least, in a campaign against non-unionism in the coalfield. For example, Lambton Federation, which, consisting of eight pits employing 10,000 miners was the largest pit group in the county, conducted a campaign against 500 non-unionists between May and December 1937 that resulted in 100 per cent DMA membership. For left-wingers though, this campaign was not simply about building the strength of the union. Indeed, Sam Watson styled this partly as an anti-fascist campaign, as non-unionists were potentially easy pickings for fascism.[75] Clearly convinced of the utility of industrial action, Lambton Federation considered striking over the poor quality of house coal supplied to its members in March 1938.[76] For the *Sunderland Echo*, this illustrated that there was 'too great a desire to employ the strike weapon'.[77] There was also considerable support in the north-east for the national use of industrial direct action in relation to the dispute over the Spencer Union in Harworth pit in the Nottingham coalfield in Spring 1937. Durham lodges that did little or nothing on Spain (Seaham and Hamsteels) or were even hostile (Eden) all supported direct action on Harworth, as did the NMA, overwhelmingly.[78]

There had also been discussion within the DMA of employing industrial direct action for overtly political ends in the earlier 1930s. However, the lodges voted by margins of three to one against proposals for 48 hour strikes in protest against the Means Test in 1933 and 1935. Yet, at the same time as rejecting the latter proposal, lodges supported overwhelmingly (by 872 votes to 21) a resolution committing the DMA to obstruct war in 'every possible way' if it threatened to break out, which certainly implied the use of industrial direct action.[79] In August 1936, the DMA executive went further, advocating a one-day general strike of all trades to draw attention to the 'inhuman conditions involved in the Means Test'.[80] Accordingly, miner militants like George Harvey and moderates like DMA official Edward Moore all called for direct action against the Means Test at the DMA demonstrations of mid-August.[81] Claiming that the Commons debate showed that the government had no case, Will Lawther claimed that the strike was necessary to *help* the process of democracy, rather than undermining it. The government was ignoring the people of places like County Durham, argued Lawther, and required 'something very drastic' to 'awaken the government from their stupor'.[82] Of most significance for Spain was an appeal in November 1936 from Will Pearson, then a member of the MFGB executive, who asked 'all trade unionists to put aside all minor differences' and make it clear to the government that they would take strike action if it continued negotiations with Italy.[83]

Industrial Direct Action on Spain: Actual and Proposed

Activists could employ industrial direct action – which did not invariably involve striking as such – to support the Republic in many ways. A significant campaign for the Republic, Voluntary Industrial Aid for Spain (VIAS), can perhaps best be understood as an (albeit mild) form of Industrial direct action. Operating within some engineering workshops, VIAS received financial support from labour movement institutions – which it occasionally circularised – and practical help from other groups (like Corbridge Boys' Club in the north-east).[84] By April 1938, workers at Armstrong Whitworth factory in Scotswood, Newcastle, were making motorcycle combinations to be used by the Republic as ambulances or for distributing food, medical and other supplies. Costing £25 each to build and 'more powerful than a small car', Newcastle's was one of the 'strongest' of the 'voluntary workshops'.[85] This was very different from the other Spanish aid campaigns in that it effectively utilised workers' skills and provided reconditioned vehicles that were between a tenth and fifth of the cost of new ones. On occasion, the vehicles acted as propaganda pieces themselves: they were driven around different towns before being sent to Spain. Furthermore, this activity allowed individuals delivering the vehicles to visit Spain who might not otherwise have been able. Such an activist was Jim Atkinson of Hexham who, by January 1939, had taken eight ambulances to Spain. Having learnt Spanish from the Basque refugees in the region, these visits must have helped make Atkinson one of the most insightful commentators on the situation in Spain and at home in the period.[86]

More radical ways of supporting the Republic included, for example, blacking the printing of anti-Republic atrocity stories in the press or providing the resources and labour to ship arms illegally to Spain. Secondly, direct action could obstruct the enemy's war effort, such as by blacking British trade with Franco. But perhaps the most potentially effective, and most controversial, way of supporting the Republic was by employing mass strikes to place pressure on the government to alter its Non-Intervention policy (as the DMA advocated regarding the Means Test). In Belgium, the steelworkers of Charleroi advocated a general strike against Non-Intervention to force the Belgian government to lift the blockade.[87]

The north-east provided two examples of industrial direct action on Spain. In January 1937, Newcastle trades council supported a Scandinavian initiative to black ships destined for Franco's Spain.[88] The Norwegian union in Tyneside was successful in 'getting crews discharged'.[89] But the most significant event in this context was the ten-day sit-in strike by the north-eastern crew of the SS *Linaria* that began on 23 February 1937 in protest at being ordered to transport a cargo of nitrates from Boston (Massachusetts) to the Franco held port of Sevilla. Deported, the crew faced charges of obstructing the navigation of a vessel and several court appearances followed until final victory for the crew in April 1938.[90] Alex Robson, elected chair of the *Linaria* crew's strike committee, was a well-known Communist in North Shields. The evidence suggests that Robson was not only the figurehead but the main instigator of the action.[91]

The crew's statements to the press suggest that they had several partly contradictory motives for taking direct action on Spain. Before going to court the crew's (usually Robson's) words suggested that they struck as they did not wish to support Franco militarily; they did not want to provide resources to kill innocents and, somewhat bizarrely, that they wished to *uphold* Non-Intervention (British government foreign policy).[92] In court, the emphasis changed to a primary motive of not wanting to enter a war zone with a secondary desire not to break Non-Intervention.[93]

As the crew's main spokesperson, Robson's motives were difficult to discern from his public comments and statements in court. Shortly before the first court case in April 1937 Robson told the *Shieldsman* that: 'We were 75 days crossing the Western Ocean and were out of touch with what was going on as regards Spain. When we arrived in Boston ... we bought news-papers and read that England had decided on a Non-Intervention policy. We all agreed that this was the right course to take'.[94] While this may have applied to some of the crew, it seems unlikely that it was true of Robson himself. Notwithstanding 75 days at sea, Robson must have been aware of the attitudes to Non-Intervention of the left by late November 1936.[95] Robson's protestations about wishing to uphold Non-Intervention were false and designed presumably to ensure a favourable hearing from the authorities. It seems likely that Robson acted primarily to prevent poten-tial war material going to Franco. The rest of the crew, bar two of the 19 strikers who signed back on the ship and went to Spain, may well have had similar motives. While the crew threatened to 'perhaps try to organise a general strike', this was 'if the Board of Trade does not treat us fairly', ra-ther than over arms to Spain.[96] The contradictory messages emerging from the *Linaria* crew's action blunted its – potentially significant – political impact. Non-Intervention, certainly, was not on trial. Indeed, in some re-gards the trial reinforced its legality. Notwithstanding this, an individual Communist *was* willing to lead direct action on Spain. Furthermore, as with LLPs acting on Spain that effectively were the Labour Party in their localities, so Robson's action in some respects *was* synonymous with the CP for many of those reading the press coverage of the *Linaria* crew's exploits.

In March 1937, DMA lodges considered a motion to urge the unions to call a general strike if the government refused to supply arms to the Re-public. However, they voted five-to-one against the proposal (158–663 against).[97] When the issue of industrial direct action to support the Repub-lic surfaced again in early 1938, it came in the context of a reactivated official labour movement that was demanding that the national movement hold a conference to discuss the international situation. The wording of most of these demands gave no indication about what, specifically, re-gional institutions expected to be discussed at any national conference. However, a significant exception came in June 1938 when a combined NTFLP, Co-operative Party and NEFTC conference called for the na-tional movement to meet 'to formulate *industrial and political* action to re-move the Chamberlain government'.[98]

Buchanan rightly pointed out that activists embarking on rank-and-file initiatives for the Republic were a stratum of individuals no more repre-sentative of trade unionists than the leadership.[99] Yet this particular de-mand did not come from rank-and-file activists organised as such, but instead from the very heart of official institutions composed largely of 'moderate' trade unionists who were surely more representative of their members (they were certainly more accountable to them). Thus, at this crucial stage in the Republic's struggle, a considerable and highly significant part of the traditionally moderate north-east labour movement was contemplating industrial as well as political action in order to place pressure on the government over its foreign policy, including that on Spain. Particularly significant was the support of the NEFTC, as trades councils would presumably have formed the organisational units in urban centres to make any strike action effective, as they had in 1926.

It was also noteworthy that the same conference rejected a proposal to send a food and medical supply ship from the Tyne, suggesting that the regional movement regarded militant action to end Non-Intervention at a national level of more utility than piecemeal humanitarian efforts at grass-roots. Around the same time, Newcastle No.4 NUR branch asked its executive to 'approach the TUC General Council to present an ultimatum to the government calling upon them to allow the free passage of arms for the Spanish Government and, failing satisfaction, the Trade Union movement has to consider taking direct action'.[100]

However, a South Shields NUR delegate, in opposing the motion, assured his Newcastle comrades that the TUC was doing 'all in its power to influence public opinion so as to convince the Government to remove the embargo on the supply of arms to Spain'.[101] Furthermore, some significant institutions on the industrial side of the movement did not outwardly advocate direct action on Spain in 1938. Most conspicuous by their absence were the miners, and particularly the DMA that had supported such action over the Means Test in 1936. Durham miners played an important role in determining MFGB policy on Spain in 1938, but, in doing this they did not make a clear argument for industrial direct action to place pressure on the government. Jack Gilliland claimed at MFGB annual conference in July 1938 that the DMA would have provided money for arms for Spain, but he was as evasive on practicalities as fellow Durham miner Sam Watson was when addressing an MFGB special conference on Spain in late April 1938. It fell to Cumberland district – led by ILPer Tom Stephenson – to make an ultimately unsuccessful suggestion that the MFGB annual conference endorse the use of industrial action to support the Republic.[102]

In refusing to make arguments within the MFGB for industrial direct action in 1938, DMA officials were in one sense representing their members. Certainly, DMA lodges provided little evidence of interest in the issue of direct action on Spain in the summer of 1938. Indeed, after the defeated Marsden resolution of March 1937, no lodge brought the issue to the executive again. Indicative of a certain trend in the north-east were two NMA lodges, both acting in March 1938. Ellington wrote directly to Citrine urging 'all affiliated bodies to strike for one day to enforce the resignation of the Government'.[103] In the same month, Communist controlled Cambois lodge, in contrast, agitated within the NMA for it to conduct a political campaign against government foreign policy. While Cambois had attempted to secure NMA support for the united front in May 1937, it made no effort to get the union's support for direct action over Spain.[104]

The Popular Front and Industrial Direct Action

Tom Buchanan claimed that the CP 'did not support industrial action for Spain which would run counter to the appeal to the middle classes inherent in the Popular Front strategy'.[105] Communist or Communist influenced organised workers, such as the AEU Shop stewards, followed the 'non-confrontational Popular Front policy' while the militant London Busmen demanded a mass campaign by the TUC on Spain, but this did not include industrial direct action.[106] Clearly, this did not mean that every Communist and left-wing militant entirely rejected the use of industrial direct action on Spain from the very outset. But, while the *Linaria* affair showed that one Communist could instigate direct action on the issue, its significance was in its exceptionality. Also important was its timing, coinciding with other direct action initiatives in this earlier period. While the popular front was the Communist Party (and its milieu's) policy from 1935, in Britain the emphasis remained on the first step of achieving working-class cooperation until after the breakdown of the Unity Campaign in mid-1937. The aim of 'working-class unity' lent itself easily to the radical rhetoric of even moderate Durham miners in 1936. However, advocacy of the popular front clearly demanded a new rhetoric aimed at bringing liberals on board rather than alienating them. The process whereby Labour left popular fronters moderated their language varied between individuals. While the popular front did not completely eliminate talk of direct action, it came very close. Support for the popular front clearly demanded great compromises from its militant advocates.

One example was Will Pearson. He was the only DMA militant in 1936 publicly to suggest direct action against government foreign policy when a war situation was not necessarily imminent. It was Pearson's lodge, Marsden, which attempted to get the DMA to support direct action in March 1937. Speaking at the 1937 MFGB conference Pearson remarked that Communism and Socialism were synonymous and that with a united front 'we would make the capitalist class melt like snow in the sun'.[107] However, by spring 1938, Pearson was sharing a platform on Spain with a member of that selfsame capitalist class, a local ship owner angry because the Franco attacks on shipping were affecting his profit margins.[108]

A second example was George Harvey, a regular contributor to newspaper letters pages on Spain in the early months, who appeared to regard the Republic's salvation in terms of the popular front from the outset. In November 1936, for example, Harvey condemned the official movement's 'weak and timid attitude' on Spain, and praised the Soviet Union's support of the Republic and the CP's attitude. However, there was no mention of industrial direct action. Instead: 'There is a great progressive opinion which can be harnessed to fight fascism and save Europe and the world ... The popular front must be maintained to fight Fascism to the death'.[109] Harvey issued similar calls in later 1936 and early 1937.[110]

However, Henry Bolton and other Blaydon activists provided the most intriguing examples of the changes and contradictions brought about by the popular front. Writing in Blaydon CLP's 1936 annual report in his capacity as secretary, Bolton called for a united front including Communists to combat 'fascism, which is the executive committee of international capitalism... The international fascist gang have concentrated their forces on the constitutionally elected government of Spain'. Bolton then discussed the need to get rid of 'class society', claiming that the 'inevitability of gradualness' did not work.[111] This rhetoric certainly retained elements of pre-popular front discourse, especially regarding the necessity of destroying capitalism in order to defeat fascism.

By spring 1938, Bolton was attempting to work with liberals and church groups that might have been interested in Spain; individuals who would surely have seen little to agree with, and may well have been frightened by, his 1936 views. However, this did not mean that Blaydon CLP completely ignored the need for industrial direct action in 1938. Indeed, the 1938 Blaydon Mayday meeting called for a 'United People's Front', unanimously supported the Republic's freedom to buy arms and pledged those present 'to use *every means at our disposal* to rouse support for the Republic to help support supplies of food, anti-aircraft guns, coal and any other financial and material assistance that might be needed'. It avowed 'to support *any* political, economic and *industrial action* which may be taken in support of those objectives'.[112]

This was potentially awkward for Bolton, who was one of two speakers at the meeting (both of whom had represented Blaydon CLP at the 23 April national Spain conference). However, his speech – if the press report on the meeting was an accurate reflection – concentrated on discussing the popular front rather than the need for industrial direct action. In contrast, the second speaker, Councillor Parkinson, neglected the popular front altogether and argued instead that the labour movement alone 'had the power to decide the issue'.[113] Yet Parkinson made no comment on the means the movement could use beyond organising provincial conferences to rally support. Speaking at the Highfield (Blaydon constituency) Mayday meeting, Bolton did little more explicit than exhort his 'listeners to do all in their power to increase the assistance going to Spain from the workers of this country'.[114]

Similarly, Steve Lawther (and other Lawther brothers) privately attacked brother Will's inactivity on the NCL regarding Spain, but they did not mention industrial direct action. In fact, they all regarded the popular front as the way to save Spain and Steve could only criticise Will for not trying to get the movement to act at all (before 1938) and more vigorously (after 1938) in the accepted ways of 'democratic' political protest.[115] In the agitation on Spain in Blaydon in 1938, industrial direct action seemed a little referenced afterthought, firmly in the shadows of discussions on the popular front. Still, even this might have been enough to preclude firm evidence of a vibrant popular front type campaign with liberals in the Blaydon area.

British left-wingers with a more independent attitude often adopted a different understanding of the popular front at the time. ILPer Fenner Brockway wrote: 'By its very nature the Popular Front, because it is based on an alliance with Capitalist Parties, must be non-proletarian and non-Socialist. It represents a surrender of the class struggle and of the social revolution'.[116] And this alternative discourse was not only found in the pages of ILP publications; it was also present in the letters pages of the regional press. For example, in July 1936, 'Sentinel', responding to a Blyth Communist's letter, attacked the French CP as it supported capitalism and was therefore 'going against the advice of Lenin'. 'Sentinel' claimed that the failure of the CP to attract substantial numbers of workers lay behind recent united front advocacy: 'In short, they [the CP] are a spent force'. The party could not see that it was their popular front policy at fault and instead would 'blame everyone else'.[117] In mid-April 1938, a bitter debate between Communists and putative Trotskyists in the *Shields Gazette* again involved criticism of CP support for the popular front as well as its attitude to religion.[118]

Communist influenced militants, however, did not seem to need to reconcile support for the popular front with a toning down of rhetoric. They tended to talk as if they regarded it as a militant policy. In 1936, George Harvey, talking about action against the Means Test, said in his address: 'The time has gone by for the passing of resolutions; direct action is what is wanted, and that is why we are calling on Communists and every other working-class organisation to close their ranks in a working-class Popular Front against the Fascist National Government'.[119] Here Harvey conflated the strictly 'working-class' movement united front (Labour, the CP, and ILP) with the broader popular front alliance, thereby imbuing the latter with a more militant sounding status.

Harvey's letters to the press on Spain in late 1936 and early 1937 similarly discussed the popular front in radical language. They associated it with the use of Councils of Action, the most local units of militant organisation, which were employed in the 1920 'Hands off Russia' campaign and the 1926 miners' lockout, and which re-emerged in the early 1930s in South Wales.[120] Shortly before the Republic fell, Harvey (now of Harraton lodge) remained convinced of the popular front, which he still regarded as militant. Writing in the DMA *Monthly Journal*, Harvey attacked 'our own official movement' that accepted Non-Intervention whilst Russia 'assisted our Spanish comrades; and today our official movement accepts national service and class cooperation as against the Popular Front and the unity of anti-fascist forces'.[121] Clearly, Harvey did not regard the popular front as another form of 'class cooperation'. Similarly, speaking in support of Cripps' 1939 popular front programme, Bolton attacked the NEC for 'rejecting working-class unity while at the same time permitting Mr. Herbert Morrison and others to collaborate with the National Government'.[122] Again, it seemed as though Bolton did not recognise that Cripps' popular front envisaged unity between many more organisations than simply 'working-class' ones.

Notwithstanding these processes, the effects of the changes in rhetoric in the language of Durham miner militants induced by adoption of the popular front were plain to see within the DMA in 1938. There were no public calls or internal efforts to secure DMA support for industrial direct action for the Republic from left-wing DMA officials like Will Lawther and Sam Watson, nor from lodge leaders like George Harvey or Will Pearson. This was in strong contrast to their earlier calls for such against the Means Test or, in Pearson's case, against foreign policy. Thus, when much of the moderate regional movement wished to discuss industrial direct action in May 1938, the majority of radical voices – of those who might have been expected to be at the forefront, energetically and persuasively arguing for such action – were silent.

The situation was somewhat different in the SWMF, where the CP used its strong influence on the executive to *frustrate* lodge calls for industrial direct action. While practical and tactical reasons were likely to have informed this, the popular front strategy, too, played a major part in determining Communist behaviour in the SWMF. The SWMF did, after all, support direct action against company unionism in 1935, in the context of an increasingly militant coalfield (that experienced anti-bailiff, anti-fascist and anti-Means Test disturbances). Indeed, Francis claimed that the willingness to adopt militant direct action, which often resulted in criminal records and imprisonment, partly explained the South Wales miners' reaction to Spain.[123] However, a stoppage in both coalfields, as Rob Stradling pointed out, would have prevented the Republic from receiving their coal.[124]

The DMA remained apparently wedded to constitutional methods and supportive of the national labour movement leadership during the Munich crisis of September 1938. In November, DMA lodges supported both the executive's efforts to help the Czech homeless and its endorsement of the NCL's attitude on the crisis. Not surprisingly, the means envisaged to support the Czechs politically remained strictly within accepted democratic terms: to continue to 'rouse' the population to the threat of fascism.[125] Similarly, after Munich, Ellington lodge sent another resolution to national labour movement institutions in an attempt to get them to act, but this time the demand for industrial direct action had been dropped. Instead the lodge urged protest meetings against the government 'should be held throughout the country'.[126] The rest of the north-east labour movement's desire to discuss the use of industrial direct action for Spain faded away along with its calls for a national conference in the summer of 1938.

Buchanan has detailed how the left failed to alter labour movement policy for a crucial year and then how it was unable to make the movement more active on Spain.[127] However, this was not simply a failure of the 'left within the Labour Party', but of considerable numbers of 'moderate' grassroots activists (and their institutions) who wanted a national

conference to activate the movement in 1938.[128] Certainly as far as the
north-east was concerned, this failure suggested a lack of democracy in the
national labour movement structures. Indeed, it was ironic that the national leadership acted in this highhanded way, when it criticised industrial
direct action as an undemocratic method of political action. Ultimately,
when the national leadership ignored their calls (and those of many other
CLPs throughout the country) for a national conference, the regional labour movement had nowhere else to go. There was little to gain and much
at risk in employing unilateral action at regional level, apart from, perhaps,
to set an example to others.

While the outcome could well have been the same, the popular frontist
left missed a great opportunity to lend their experience to these calls in
1938 and thereby enhance their own standing within the regional movement. They, like the CP, were not inhibited by a 'fundamental aversion to
illegality', unlike the Labour leadership and even LSC activists.[129] The
popular front, in helping to preclude left-wingers from making a strong,
clear and unequivocal case for the use of industrial direct action to support
the Republic, clearly had a negative impact on the Republic's chances of
survival.

The left-wingers who did not have a base in the unions did not appear
to contemplate the use of even limited industrial direct action until late in
the conflict. Even then, the popular front remained the panacea. C.P. Trevelyan, a strong critic of labour movement policy from the outset, had,
like many others on the left, employed united front rhetoric in 1937,
which changed to appealing for a popular front in 1938.[130] He did not
refer to the use of direct action at all until October 1938. Speaking at a
Labour Spain Conference that month, Trevelyan argued that the labour
movement should challenge the government's moral authority by sending
anti-aircraft guns to defend the 'women and children of Spain'. Harnessing
the humanitarian discourse of many of the Spanish aid campaigns to a
move to break Non-Intervention with military hardware appeared a canny
proposal. If the government prosecuted the leaders who sanctioned this
action, Trevelyan argued, all would soon see whether there was a 'con-
science' in the country. Trevelyan was careful to point out that a 'political
gathering' like the one he addressed could only suggest this action to the
trade unions: 'what workers once did by industrial action they can do
again'.[131] However, even then Trevelyan still envisaged industrial direct
action employed in a somewhat limited way; certainly nothing like his
previously successful attempt to commit the whole movement to a general

strike at the threat of war. Furthermore, most of Trevelyan's speech, like many before (and after) it, consisted of an elaborate call for the popular front. This, and not industrial direct action, was still to be the Republic's saviour.

Unable to be present at this same conference, Blenkinsop also supported, possibly for the first time, a form of direct action. Blenkinsop told Pole of the LSC that he believed that 'the labour movement can afford to wait no longer to take every practical form of direct action to assist the Spanish Government'. It should, he implored, begin immediate discussions with the French labour movement about supplying arms. Yet Blenkinsop, too, remained wedded to the popular front at home: 'common action should be secured on the widest possible basis refusing the support of no organisation willing to help the Spanish government'.[132]

By February 1939, Trevelyan had abandoned all support for any kind of direct action. The first to sign the Cripps Petition campaign inaugural meeting in Newcastle on 5 February, Trevelyan thought that Cripps' plan 'exactly meets the situation'. His decision to fund Cripps' campaign and not a more direct Spain cause came as he thought that 'to fundamentally alter the position here and really threaten our government would be a bigger help to Spain than anything'.[133] Blenkinsop, another prominent north-east Cripps supporter, equally did not mention the tactic again. In these cases, too, activists realised that support for the popular front precluded much talk about using industrial direct action, especially the sort that demanded general strikes to place pressure on the government.

Contemplating the Republic's imminent defeat, Jim Atkinson of VIAS told an Ashington audience what he considered were the lessons of the Spanish experience:

> it was evident that they could no longer rely on popular opinion achieving anything under the present government, for it seemed that those in command of this country could shut their eyes entirely to public opinion. The situation was such that all efforts to help after a war had started were ineffective ... Parliament now appears to act as a sort of damper between popular opinion and national action ... he believed that a courageous stand and a firm threat of industrial action in the early stages of the Spanish war could have achieved more than all the appeals to humanity and decency which had been made since, for it was evidently futile to appeal to the sense of decency of the present government, because it had none.[134]

Revolution, Direct Action and Orwell

All the support or possible support from more moderate sections of the north-east labour movement for industrial direct action in aid of the Republic came in the context of the dominant paradigm on the left – and one that the popular frontists sustained as much as moderate Labour opinion – that the Republic was a democracy, just like the British one. This meant that the regional official movement's desire to discuss industrial direct action – essentially the use of undemocratic means to defend Spanish 'democracy' – was always on a weak footing; one easily undermined by the national leadership's appeals to legality and constitutionalism. (Indeed, the same kinds of arguments as, potentially, the government could have used in the event on any national strike action). It was doubtful that the possible Lawther defence of this as the need to be undemocratic in order to make democracy work properly would convince.

However, there was another paradigm that better suited industrial direct action. In *Homage to Catalonia*, George Orwell discussed the revolution that had occurred in many parts of Republican Spain, and claimed that Communists, Liberals and moderate Socialists of the Republican government had deliberately kept these events out of the international media. Instead, they presented the conflict as one between 'fascism' and 'democracy', because they sought to curry favour with the democracies. However, the consequence of this was that 'once the war had been narrowed down to a "war for democracy" it became impossible to make any large scale appeal for working-class aid abroad'. Orwell wrote:

> The way in which the working-class in the democratic countries could really have helped her Spanish comrades was by industrial action – strikes and boycotts. No such thing ever even began to happen. The Labour and Communist leaders everywhere declared that it was unthinkable; and no doubt they were right, so long as they were also shouting at the tops of their voices that 'red' Spain was not 'red'. … If, with the huge prestige of Soviet Russia behind them, they had appealed to the workers of the world in the name not of 'democratic Spain', but of 'revolutionary Spain', it is hard to believe that they would not have got a response.[135]

Orwell's was a controversial viewpoint, and the effects of the revolutionary paradigm widely held can only be speculated at. There were clearly massive obstacles to the possible success of industrial direct action applied at national level against government policy. The popular front was predicated on labour movement weakness: that it alone was not strong enough to defeat fascism. Clearly, the circumstances were far less auspicious than when the threat of industrial action succeeded in 1920. The labour movement in 1936 was smaller and less militant minded – 1926 had had a massively disempowering effect on attitudes throughout the movement – and the proposed action would be effectively to support war rather than, as in 1920, to prevent direct British involvement in a war from an already war weary country. The leaders of the popular front Spanish Republic themselves were unlikely to want to be associated with industrial direct action for their cause, given their desire for alliances with the capitalist democracies like Britain. Yet all these considerations served to make the June 1938 north-east official movement position even more remarkable.

It was clear that, as far as ending Britain's support for Non-Intervention was concerned, the lack of discussion and debate at a national level on the issue was a serious impediment. It largely removed from consideration arguably the most potent set of weapons in the labour movement's armoury. Ultimately, the popular front served as a distraction from Spain more than vice versa as its advocacy meant that most influential left-wing militants within the regional movement did not develop and sustain a revolutionary paradigm of events in Spain and coherent proposals for the kinds of direct action that could accompany it. This, combined with the evident groundswell of opinion in regions like the north-east, would at least have given the leadership a real struggle over the issues. Unfortunately for the Spanish Republic, the Soviet Union's 'huge prestige', as in Pearson's words, 'the inspiration to the international working-class' was firmly behind the popular front.[136] Still, there remained other ways in which, even within the 'democracy against fascism' paradigm, the popular front did not do for the Republic what it might, and these are discussed in the next two chapters.

5

ANATOMY OF THE SPANISH AID CAMPAIGNS

The conflict in Spain spawned a variety of campaigns and the ad hoc institutions necessary to operate them at grassroots. These Spanish aid campaigns, many of which were active to differing degrees in the north-east, corresponded broadly to Klugmann's third 'humanitarian' level of support. There was both diversity and similarity between campaigns and the individual institutions that operated within them; some had quite differing aims and remits, while there was also a striking degree of similarity in the campaigning languages of others. Though there was a degree of overlap in personnel, in other respects these campaigns had only loose links with each other and an often complex and ambiguous relationship with the Republic's cause (especially the campaign against Non-Intervention). This chapter will discuss the significant features of these campaigns as they operated at grassroots and assess some of their successes and failures.

Outline of the Main North-East Campaigns
The first group of campaigning institutions to emerge in the north-east were the Spanish Aid Committees. At least 18 formed; mostly in the larger towns and cities, with a handful scattered through the region's pit villages.[1] The first committee in the area was in Newcastle, established in September 1936. North Shields and Gateshead committees were operating by the end of 1936 and, in the first six months of 1937, between one and three new committees a month appeared. The last formed was Morpeth, in September 1937. The evidence suggests that most SMACs had disappeared by the time of the Tyneside foodship campaign in December 1938. However, Ashington and Bishop Auckland SMACs were still active then and the Durham committee was still operating in May 1939, after the

Republic's defeat.[2] Newcastle committee, while inactive, retained financial commitments to a Basque refugee into 1942.[3]

The SMACs were the only set of campaigning organisations considered here that were not defined basically by their supposed campaign remit; i.e. they did far more than merely raise money for the national SMAC. Thus, many collected for the Basque children's hostel in Tynemouth and the wider BCC.[4] Indeed, North Shields SMAC effectively became the Basque campaign in the town. Some SMACs also supported the *Linaria* crewmen, the Youth foodship, International Brigade Dependants' Aid and the Tyneside foodship.

Throughout a considerable part of the conflict's duration, several youth organisations in the region organised around the Youth Foodship Committee. By December 1936, 21 'youth' organisations in Newcastle were involved in collecting for a foodship, and there were also collections for it in towns like Blyth. While most Youth Foodship activity revolved around appeals in the press and house-to-house collections, there was a send-off meeting in Newcastle's Bigg Market on 14 December 1936 for a convoy bound for London and a ship embarking for Spain on 21 December. There were spurts of activity around subsequent foodships in January, April, June and September 1937. In February 1938, these activities were placed on a firmer footing with the creation of a branch of the British Youth Peace Assembly on Tyneside to assist the national campaign. Immediately before the separate Tyneside foodship campaign, there were further collections for the Youth foodship in South Shields.[5]

The campaign to support the *Linaria* crew began in America where the strike occurred.[6] On returning to Britain, the 17 crew stated their intention 'to arouse seamen all over Britain to demonstrate on our behalf' by speaking at the larger British ports.[7] A *Linaria* Defence Committee based in North Shields was in existence by mid-March 1937, when it held its first meeting. There was a second meeting in mid-April in North Shields and a third at Marsden Miners' Hall at the end of the month.[8] The committee also circularised labour movement institutions regionally and nationally requesting financial support, but this activity waned by June 1937.[9] From February 1937, the International Brigade Dependants' and Wounded Aid Committee (IBDWAC) at regional level issued circular appeals. It often received the collections taken at official and unofficial Spain meetings, especially where an International Brigader or next-of-kin spoke.[10]

The efforts to support the Basque refugees by both the NJCSR and the Catholic Church in the BCC from May 1937 sparked considerably more interest, activity and press coverage than had the SMACs to that point. The SDPC and other groups 'adopted' Basque children under a NJCSR scheme. More specifically, activity to support the Basque refugees at the Tynemouth hostel began in late June 1937, when the Duchess of Atholl appealed for aid at a meeting in North Shields. Despite some doubts about whether the poverty-stricken North Shields area was suitable to sustain financially a refugee children's hostel, the local SMAC, whose secretary was Nell Badsey, decided to proceed. Only a month later, 20 Basque boys and a female teacher arrived at No.40, Percy Park, Tynemouth. At least three committees dedicated specifically to raising money for the refuges formed in Sunderland, Newcastle and Gateshead. In February 1938, Badsey accompanied 106 children to Spain for repatriation (although she disagreed with it at that moment) including three from Tynemouth. Over time, more refugees returned to their families in Spain or moved to other places around Britain, and Tynemouth hostel was closed by 1940.[11]

The Tyneside foodship campaign began in early December 1938, the product of a TJPC conference on 29 October 1938.[12] Campaigners circularised 5,000 organisations and individuals in the area including Labour Parties, trade unions, Co-operative Societies, LNU branches, socialist societies, churches and others appealing for aid to fill the ship, to be chartered and paid for by the Republican government.[13] It raised £850 within four weeks and £1,700 after two months. Due to the urgent need, the campaigners decided not to wait until a ship could be found to sail from the Tyne but instead to transport the food from the Humber. They also 'assumed responsibility for a sum beyond our means' borrowing £500 more than had been raised in the hope of recouping it.[14] The SS *Frevadore*, technically the Yorkshire foodship, departed in early February 1939 carrying a total of £3,450 worth of goods (of which £3,031 had been raised in the north-east) and arrived safely in Valencia in early March. It was the fourth of the foodships of this period to sail from Britain.[15] 'Undaunted' by the fall of Catalonia to Franco, the central Tyneside committee announced its intention to send a second foodship at the end of February; there was £500 worth of food left after sending the first foodship. In mid-March, a lorry carrying three tons of food valued at £150 left Newcastle for London where it was loaded onto the SS *Stancroft*. The campaign held over a further £1,000 with the idea of financing a second ship from the Tyne or Humber. However, it seems that there was no second Tyneside foodship.[16]

The Tyneside foodship campaign was relatively short-lived, running from early December 1938 to late March 1939. However, this belied its size and intensity. With a central organising committee in Newcastle, it dwarfed the other Spanish aid campaigns in terms of the sheer numbers of localities that had organising subcommittees. The campaign boasted, at its peak in February 1939, 120 subcommittees; almost eight times the number of SMACs in the region.[17] It reached as far south as Bishop Auckland in spite of the alternative pull of the Teesside foodship.[18] The sheer amount of activity crammed into this feverish period, too, outshone anything that had gone before in the region. It appears to have been the only regional campaign to attempt to appoint a fulltime central organiser – albeit unsuccessfully, as the AEU rejected its appeals for funding.[19] Thus it, and not the Spanish Medical Aid Committees, was the most important of the unofficial responses at grassroots level in the north-east.[20] Indeed, the Tyneside campaign compared well with the other foodships in terms of size; the NJCSR noted that it was 'particularly well-run'.[21]

Political and Social Complexions

There was a considerable degree of political and social diversity in terms of those involved, which varied between campaigns and within them (in the SMACs and Tyneside foodship especially) and that differed over time and at the various organisational levels within institutions. Thus, the political complexion of the Spanish aid committees' organisers differed remarkably between committees. In other words, they were not all of the same degree of political diversity. Broadly speaking, they divided into three categories. On one side, several involved (or may have) activists from a wide diversity of political traditions. The clearest example was Newcastle SMAC, in which there was participation from many official movement activists in both the trade unions and Labour Party as well as Communists ('crypto' and not).[22]

Some liberals also became involved. At its launch, the committee claimed that representatives of 'other progressive organisations' were present and Newcastle CAPR was certainly drawn in and active by July 1937.[23] The committee also stretched further into those of no overt party allegiance, its approaches to local clergy yielding some fruit when Newcastle Presbytery agreed to issue a Spanish aid appeal to their congregations in July 1937. Equally, a Newcastle SMAC appeal of early July carried the signatures of many well-known dignitaries including the Bishop of Newcastle, the Archdeacon of Northumberland and the principal of Armstrong College.[24] By that time, Newcastle committee itself was 'composed of people of different political opinions'.[25]

Several other north-east SMACs *may* have been equally politically diverse, though the social diversity of some could be far less. Of the five speakers who addressed the meeting that formed Sunderland SMAC's organising committee, the only obvious labour movement figure was the town's mayor. However, while there may have been political heterogeneity, social diversity was not particularly great: the other four speakers were two clergymen (one Methodist, one Church of England), a teacher and a doctor.[26] Seaham SMAC was similar, as the signatories to its initial appeal were two clergymen and two teachers. None, when putting their names to the appeal, gave any indication of their party affiliation or political outlook (and the wording of the appeal itself did not help). Instead, their professions; their social status, seemed the appropriate way in which to promote their appeal.[27] North Shields committee, led by Communist Nell Badsey, also appeared to secure help from throughout the locality. Support came on a 'flag day' it organised from the British Legion, 'several religious organisations', a shop keeper and the manager and staff of a bank, but with the notable exception of the Labour Party.[28] Dawdon committee, established in May 1937, had an official labour movement basis but claimed to be 'representative of all interests in this area'.[29]

Durham SMAC perhaps should have been politically diverse, given that it emerged from a Left Book Club circle.[30] These usually politically heterogeneous institutions were an important source of SMACs nationally. In a letter to the press explaining the origins of the Durham SMAC, a member claimed that the LBC circle, and consequently the SMAC that emerged from it, were 'open to all' people of 'all shades of opinion'.[31] Yet most of its main organisers, while of different professions, appeared to share a common Labour, albeit often left-wing, background. The committee treasurer, Richard J.S. Baker BA, was resident sub-warden at Durham House Settlement. Fred Peart, subsequently co-opted onto the committee and the only member to live outside Durham, was also university educated and a teacher as well as a prominent Labour activist. The chairperson was miners' agent Sam Watson and the secretary, John Llyal Robson, was a DMA clerk and a Durham City Labour councillor from November 1938.[32]

A second group of committees appeared to have been more limited in their composition, to Labour and Communist Party activists. The main officials of Blaydon SMAC, the fourth established in the region, were all Labour Party councillors. But Communist Wilf Jobling also played a significant role until he went to Spain in January 1937.[33] Communists, NUWM activists, officials and members of miners' lodges, Labour Party activists and Independent Socialist councillors were all involved in a significant or supporting capacity in South Shields SMAC.[34] New Herrington and District SMAC, organised by Ryhope colliery Labour women's section and members of the Communist influenced Ryhope miners' lodge, may also have fallen into this category.[35]

The third group of SMACs appeared composed exclusively of official labour movement activists. The main example of this was Gateshead committee, the third established in the region. Wallsend SMAC was formed by the LLP and Felling committee, established in May 1937, also seemed to be an entirely official labour movement affair. The same stood for Ashington committee, formed in April 1937 by the local 'young men's trade union forum' (predominately miners) and notwithstanding its subsequent criticism of the lack of local labour movement support for its endeavours.[36] Stanley committee, the fifth established in the north-east, was a 'representative committee of the miners lodges in Stanley district and the local Socialist party'.[37]

However, there is evidence that those who volunteered to collect for some of these official committees were from outside the official movement. Thus, a 'willing band of workers drawn from all sections of the Felling community' aided its local officially run SMAC.[38] Ashington committee immediately attempted to broaden out its campaign by inviting the direct participation of local churches and 'political parties'.[39] It subsequently got Communists and the local Labour MP as speakers at its (separate) public meetings. The committee also attempted to get the positive input of institutions it circularised for donations: in January 1938, for example, asking local miners for 'suggestions whereby they may extend their programme'.[40] Elsewhere in the country, there were equally diverse SMACs. Sheffield SMAC formed 'almost at once' with a 'nucleus' of LBC members. It soon expanded to 'cover people with strong political convictions and those activated by religious and humanitarian beliefs ...'.[41] More confined to the left was Neath SMAC in South Wales, which had ILP, CP, trades council and Anarchist activists on it.[42]

Amongst the other campaigns, the involvement of clergymen often suggested a degree of diversity. Nationally, the YCL, LLY, Young Liberals, trades unions youth sections, Co-op Youth, the YWCA and many church denominations and Jewish youth groups were involved in the youth foodship campaigns.[43] In the north-east, there was evidence of support from the main labour movement youth institutions initially and, by September 1937, clergymen in Morpeth SMAC were also collecting for it. After February 1938, a local clergyman was signing directly regional youth foodship appeals.[44]

Again, with the *Linaria* campaign, the support quickly broadened from the Labour and unofficial left that rallied to greet them on their arrival back in the north-east in mid-March 1937.[45] The *Linaria* Defence Committee itself became more politically and socially diverse. Its president was Robert A. Anderson, an 'Independent' (Liberal) member of Tynemouth Council, social worker and a member of 'one of the strongest and most progressive' Bible classes in the borough'.[46] The treasurer was the Rev. John Patton of North Shields and Northumberland Street Mission and Communist Tom O'Byrne was another Defence Committee organiser. *Linaria* Defence Committee fundraising meetings reflected this diversity. At the mid-March meeting, Miss Zara Dupont, the relative of a family of arms manufacturers, was chief speaker. In mid-April 1937, there was a second clergyman on the platform, along with J.W. Spence, a Moderate member of Tynemouth Council. International Brigader Frank Graham was present at the late-April meeting.[47]

The Tynemouth Hostel management committee's 'kaleidoscopic social content' was certainly evident.[48] Hostel warden was the Communist Nell Badsey, and clergymen occupied two senior posts in the management committee, treasurer and chairperson. There were also two doctors on the management committee as well as, unusually, two ILP members.[49] Moderate Tynemouth councillor Fred Pierson put his name to a Christmas appeal for the hostel in December 1937.[50] Other diverse individuals offered their support for the Tynemouth hostel including Communists, the Labour Mayor and Mayoress of Sunderland and Liberal Mayors of Tynemouth.[51]

Elsewhere, individuals appealed for funds for the national committee. In Morpeth for example, the Rev. E.L. Allen persuaded the Mayor to receive donations for the Basque fund in May 1937. Allen's individual stance paved the way for a more concerted effort in July, as church dignitaries attempted to organise a house-to-house collection for the refugees and mooted the idea of retiring collections for the same cause. Others merely publicised national appeals for Basque refugees by forwarding them to the local press.[52]

The social and political diversity of the individuals on the Tynemouth Hostel management committee, or associated with its campaigns, was reflected in that of the institutions that organised fundraising events for the hostel. North-east ILP branches like that at Gateshead were 'very active' in collecting food and medical aid, holding jumble sales and other events for the hostels both at Tynemouth and the national ILP Basque hostel.[53] Some local Left Book Club branches were active. South Shields LBC group, for example, held three film shows between August and November 1937 for the refugees, under the patronage of the Labour Mayor of South Shields.[54] Some SMACs were also involved. Durham City SMAC, for example, held two concerts for Basque children in May 1939.[55] Gateshead SMAC was requested to aid the Basques by forming a special subcommittee and appealing 'to prominent local citizens for their help and active support'.[56] Labour Party members also organised fundraising events. For example, in March 1939, Jack Lawther (brother of Will et al.) promoted a Basque refugee concert in Allendale Temperance hall that raised over £12.[57] The industrial side of the labour movement also got involved, its support being a 'crucial factor' in ensuring Tynemouth's survival.[58] In June 1939, the DMA permitted a collection for the Basque children on Gala day.[59] Many miners' lodges, like Pegswood, donated and some were more proactive.[60] Ellington lodge (NMA), for example, arranged a concert at Lynemouth cinema to raise funds for a Basque hostel.[61] There were several church bodies involved in this work.[62] Some of these fundraising events naturally brought members of different political parties and none together. In June 1938, the Communist Nell Badsey spoke with Labour figures at a Houghton-le-Spring CLP organised demonstration in aid of 'Spanish relief'.[63] There was tremendous diversity evident at a Basque children's concert held in Consett, organised by a joint committee of Crookhall miners' lodge, the local women's Labour section, Women's Institute and the Women's Section of the British Legion branches.[64]

Given the sheer numbers involved in the Tyneside foodship campaign, it could not fail to be the most politically and socially diverse of the north-east Spanish aid campaigns. This did vary, however: the more intensively active and crucial to the running of the campaign, the less the diversity. Thus, the activists of the campaign's central committee were primarily drawn from sections of the left, broadly defined, who had been active on the issue for some time.

Taken as a whole, there was far more political and social diversity within the campaign's subcommittees. In addition to all the left groups and trade unions mentioned in connexion with the other campaigns, was involvement from clergymen, LNU, women's sections of the British Legion and the Towns Women's Guild. Again, though, diversity did vary considerably between subcommittees. The Jarrow foodship committee was one of the most diverse. An all-party organisation, it involved the Labour Mayor, a Labour councillor, the chairperson of Jarrow Conservative Association, C.V.H. Vincent, three clergymen of the Anglican and free churches, the chair of Jarrow and Monkton Towns Women's Guild and other individuals. The secretary and several members of Jarrow committee were 'non-party'.[65]

The list of individuals publicly supporting the appeal was even more disparate. Again, amongst the names of left activists of various political hues were Viscount Ridley (a foodship campaign president, no less), the Conservative Lord Mayor of Newcastle, a National Liberal PPC, Robert Aske MP, local businessmen, and other prominent 'non-political' regional dignitaries. Some Women's Institute groups and its Durham County federation organised fundraising events for the campaign, as did, for example, Bedlington Towns Women's Guild.[66] Contemporaneous foodship campaigns in Teesside, Yorkshire and Liverpool, for example, appeared to share this diversity of involvement.[67]

In strong contrast to the Tyneside foodship was the IBDWAC. Official labour movement institutions in the north-east often supported meetings organised by the CP (but under the auspices of IBDWAC), and donated to its appeals for funds for brigade dependants. However, there was no proliferation of local IBDWAC committees with a diverse variety of members as in the other Spanish aid campaigns.[68] The only direct evidence of any group to the right of Labour involved in fundraising activity for the IBDWAC was the CAPR.[69]

How the Campaigning Message Was Framed

The ways in which the various campaigns framed their message, significant when assessing various claims about them, differed considerably between campaigns, among their constituent parts and over time. This was very evident in one set of campaigning institutions, the SMACs. Some of the committees run by left-wingers were explicit in who the aid was for and why. Blaydon SMAC, for example, supported the 'British Medical units' that were 'doing such good work in the struggle of Spanish democracy against Fascist intervention'.[70] Similarly, in February 1937, the South Shields committee secretary appealed to all who were 'interested in the suffering of the women and children in Spain in the civil war which has been thrust upon them'.[71] This criticism of fascism was more implicit, but there was no mistaking the politics of Isabel Brown (a Communist member of the NJCSR), when she addressed a South Shields committee meeting in February 1937. Nor was there room for equivocation when a mass meeting the committee organised in April 1938 passed a resolution supporting the Republic's right to buy arms.[72]

Appeals from Durham SMAC were initially partisan, calling for assistance to the 'government defenders of Spain'.[73] Subsequently, several committee members, like secretary Robson in July 1937, emphasised a more neutral, humanitarian (occasionally 'Christian') angle: people 'irrespective of their political or religious opinions, are prepared to subscribe. ... towards our human appeal'.[74] However, partisanship remained; those active in the committee, Robson claimed, were 'only concerned in the preservation of democracy and the strengthening of the barriers against the ravages of fascism'.[75] This same combination of partisanship and humanitarianism characterised some of the committee's public meetings. In June 1937, Mrs. Alington, the Dean of Durham's wife, presided at a committee meeting and William Littlewood of Bishop Auckland, who had gone to Spain in September 1936 to work as an aircraft engineer for the Republican war effort, gave a short address.[76]

Three committees that appeared more middle-class in character, Seaham, Sunderland and Morpeth, framed the issue in humanitarian terms from the outset, taking claims of 'neutrality' to a new level. The Sunderland committee called for help 'in its work of bringing medical supplies to the wounded of both sides in Spain'.[77] Similarly, Seaham committee's appeal discussed the 'one aspect which overrides all Party considerations', which was the 'great suffering' that made it a 'matter of common humanity to try to relieve this anguish as far as possible'.[78] The appeal explained that Spanish Medical Aid worked in Republican territory, but this was where the 'sufferings of the civilian population are greatest', and 'treatment is given impartially to all who need it'.[79] Morpeth committee, with Rev. Dr. Allen as treasurer, supported the 'non-sectarian and non-party' youth foodship committee that had sent food and clothing to noncombatants in areas of Spain 'devastated by war' (i.e. not necessarily the Republican side).[80]

Perhaps surprisingly, several of the solidly labour movement organised committees also broadly emphasised humanitarianism in their appeals. Certainly, the names of two, 'Gateshead Spanish Workers' Relief and Medical Aid Committee' and 'Ashington Democratic Spanish Aid Committee', suggested a degree of partisanship. (Of course, Franco supporters often called themselves democrats as well). However, this belied much of their propaganda. For example, there was a slightly confusing front-page article in the *Gateshead Labour Herald* appealing on behalf of the committee for local support for the ISF in February 1937. A section of it was fairly unequivocal: 'Your contribution to the fund will help save the lives of men, women and children whose bravery and self-sacrifice defends the democratic peoples of the world'.[81] Yet, the article also emphasised the humanitarian aspect: 'This is not a matter of partisanship but a matter of saving and preserving humanity on a mass scale'. Thus 'All creeds, sects, denominations, political and industrial ...' were invited to support this 'humanitarian effort'.[82] And it was this latter message that G.C. Esther, the main Gateshead committee activist, and other Labour supporters, tended to emphasise subsequently.[83] For example, arguing in Gateshead council in support of a town's meeting on the issue, the left-wing Alderman Peacock said that 'no side would be taken, but all the sufferers would be given aid'.[84] Ashington committee's campaigning rhetoric was broadly the same. In May 1937, it depicted its first collection of food and money in the town as a 'humanitarian mission' for the 'people of Spain suffering hardship'.[85] Its circulars also called for 'assistance to help the Spanish women and children' or something similar.[86] Dawdon SMAC's 'humanitarian work' consisted of collecting 'for those unfortunate people who are suffering hunger and privation'.[87]

Perhaps even more remarkable was that two Communist influenced committees also depicted the struggle in predominantly humanitarian terms in their campaigning appeals. In a North Shields committee appeal in January 1937, Nell Badsey wrote that 'whatever our opinions of warfare in general and the Spanish civil war in particular', one aspect that 'evokes in us sympathy and help' was the medical and Red Cross units' work 'to succour the maimed and wounded'.[88] Similarly, in late October 1936, Newcastle committee called for medical supplies and clothes for suffering civilians; the British medical unit, it claimed, 'has done its work of humanity unflinchingly'.[89] An appeal in late November 1936 for aid 'for the victims, both soldiers and civilians, of this tragic struggle', neglected to mention which side they were on, as had Badsey in the North Shields appeal quoted above.[90] However, the Newcastle committee was not always as (apparently) impartial. In July 1937, the new (Communist) secretary Tom O'Byrne claimed that the committee was composed of people 'who were looking for ways and means of helping those who not only believe in democracy, but are prepared to make the supreme sacrifice in its defence'.[91]

Furthermore, there was, to some degree, a difference between what some of SMACs said in their broadly humanitarian appeals in the press and aspects of what they did. Newcastle committee initially embarked on fundraising jumble sales, whist drives, and workshop collections. Yet it also got the People's Theatre to give a special performance, and there were public meetings in the Bigg Market for some consecutive Sunday nights in autumn 1936.[92] The committee subsequently held film shows, public meetings and conferences that heard more partisan understandings of the conflict.[93] Meetings of the 'very active' Newcastle committee had a variety of often 'national' speakers; Communists, trade unionists, liberals and others, some of whom spoke about the conflict in partisan ways.[94] Between 11 and 18 July 1937, the committee organised a more ambitious 'Spain week' in Newcastle. Clearly a propagandist effort, 'Spain week' opened with a public meeting with Trevelyan speaking and included an exhibition and daily screenings of films on Spain.[95] Similarly, Gateshead committee also organised public meetings and film shows, though these seem to have been less frequent than in Newcastle, and participated in 'Spain week'.[96] These, too, employed the mixture of humanitarian and more partisan speakers. For example, at a Gateshead committee organised public meeting in March 1937, the Labour Mayor presided with Gordon Davidson who had 'recently returned from Spain' and Rev. Warner Warcup, the local Presbyterian Minister, speaking.[97]

Likewise, Ashington committee held at least two public meetings, with Taylor the Labour MP speaking in July 1937 and Communists Willie Allan and Fred Copeman in July 1938, all firmly partisan in their discussion of the conflict.[98] A showing of films about the International Brigade (and a Russian film) the committee organised clearly had a partisan message. After the films, a 'young man' then 'passionately harangued' the audience about the 'sins' of Franco and Chamberlain and appealed for donations for the 'distressed people' in the dwindling government zone.[99] The Seaham committee also organised a showing of a Republican propaganda film, *Defence of Madrid*. This was certainly more partisan than its public appeals suggested, although it was apparently to 'give some idea of the desolation caused by the war' and a way of 'emphasising the necessity and urgency of the appeal'.[100] Still, inviting International Brigader Frank Graham (who had helped to defend Madrid) to speak at the showing seemed inimical to impartiality.[101]

Several other major grassroots campaigns also sought to emphasise the humanitarian at the expense of propaganda. This was broadly true of the youth foodship campaigns, in spite of them being Communist inspired and lead. In the initial regional appeal, Communist Jim Smith asked for donations 'in the name of humanity, not in the name of any particular creed ...' which would show that the north-east was, as ever, 'a byword for humanity and generosity'.[102] Similar rhetoric characterised a follow-up appeal.[103] However, a second report on these collections did note that the aid was for the inhabitants of Madrid 'besieged in the Spanish civil war'.[104] Still, Smith usually did not make it clear whose side the 'sufferers in the civil war' were on.[105] In 1938, the Rev. Herbert Carter maintained this predominantly neutral emphasis, claiming that the aid was to 'help innocent children and no other purpose'.[106] The same broadly stood for an appeal for help to girl guides, boy scouts and boys' brigaders, penned by a local YCL activist in late 1938.[107]

Similarly, the *Linaria* Defence Committee's appeals eschewed partisanship. In this respect, they were in tune with many of the crew's own pronouncements; to an extent in the press and more so in court. Thus, the resolution passed at the Defence Committee's first public meeting merely highlighted the British authorities' double standards: a British court upheld the refusal of a ship's crew to take supplies from Malta to Republican territory, but the *Linaria* crew were penalised for refusing to take material to Franco territory.[108] The resolution did not pronounce in favour of the Republic. Councillor R.A. Anderson told a public meeting in mid-April 1937 that he was 'not concerned so much with the rights and wrongs of the crew...'; he merely wanted funds for their court case.[109] Anderson assured his audience that 'the committee is definitely non-political. ... This is not a Communist stunt'.[110] Here 'non-political' did not mean simply 'not party-political', but rather that the committee had no partisan position on Spain at all. A Defence Committee appeal issued to the press simultaneously implied that the *maintenance* of Non-Intervention and 'neutrality' was as salient a motive as any. It also mentioned that the crew did not want to enter a war zone.[111] Woodhorn lodge minuted a Defence Committee appeal circular merely as a request for financial assistance for the court case.[112] The *Linaria* Defence committee's meetings and written appeals thus seemed to have been largely fundraising exercises at the expense of making propaganda against Non-Intervention. This was in tune with the crew's court defence that concentrated on their rights as seamen and avoided a more partisan justification of their actions that would surely have seen their convictions stand.

Humanitarian language initially predominated in appeals for the Basque refugees in general and the Tynemouth hostel in particular. Thus, for example, Nell Badsey, at the heart of the Tynemouth Hostel organisation, told a South Shields LBC meeting in August 1937 that: 'The scheme to aid the children was non-political and was not attached to any religious movement – it was a humanitarian effort'.[113] Yet, as Don Watson pointed out, this language altered with the withdrawal of the Catholic Church from the BCC due to divisions over the repatriation of refugees in October 1937. This split 'seems to have encouraged a more politically articulate stand by the BCC, including the groups in this region'.[114]

However, one reason why there was 'some evidence too that the openly political stances did not alienate the presumably non political supporters' was surely that the issue was still being depicted in humanitarian terms as well as more partisan ones in 1938.[115] Thus, Cramlington Methodists anticipated 'in view of its humanitarian aims, irrespective of political creed or religious belief', extensive support for their concert for Basque refugees in March 1938.[116] Christian charity, in fact, played an important role in many of these appeals: several individuals involved in the Basque campaigns regarded their mission as 'Christian'.[117] At Christmas 1937, for example, councillor Pierson appealed to the 'Christian spirit' of people to help the refugees.[118] In 1938, too, this theme persisted. Thus, the Mayor of Sunderland deemed his appeal for Tynemouth hostel a 'test of our religion'.[119]

While a more partisan interpretation of the conflict clearly did penetrate into the Basque campaigns in 1938, it did not fully replace humanitarian, neutral appeals. Similarly, in South Wales, the response to the Basque refugee crisis was one of 'humanitarian internationalism'.[120] That 'Franco's side were only too aware of the propaganda dangers of the refugee children', did not mean that these dangers were fully realised by their political opponents.[121] Furthermore, while the Catholic Church was no longer involved in the BCC, it continued to look after Basque refugees, so their symbolism remained contested by supporters of both sides and none.[122]

The IBDWAC's activities were, by necessity, different from other Spanish aid campaigns. The men were fighting on the Republican side and this was difficult to obscure. Thus, Pegswood lodge, for example, received a letter from the CP in January 1937 appealing for financial help for the International Brigade 'to help the Spanish government'.[123] Still, some International Brigade appeals attempted to focus on the humanitarian aspect: that some brigaders were injured and that those killed had left behind needy families (the 'widows and maimed').[124] At the same time, there were occasional attempts to play down the role of the CP within the International Brigade. For example, brigader Fred Copeman told a meeting at Marsden Miners' Hall in July 1938, that the majority of brigaders were 'not interested' in the CP (though he admitted to being a CP member himself).[125] Whilst there was room for dispute over the precise role of the CP within the International Brigade, it remained a fighting force for the Republic against Franco, and partiality was thus unavoidable.

In contrast, the Tyneside foodship's central organisers consistently campaigned with a humanitarian message, adopting a 'neutral' stance on the conflict. In early January 1939, central campaign organiser T.T. Anderson claimed, in a strange echo of his namesake R.A. of the *Linaria* Defence Committee 21 months earlier, that the foodship organisers were 'not concerned with the rights and wrongs of the present conflict in Spain'.[126] They wished simply to relieve the suffering of innocent victims of the conflict, and asked those of all political and religious creeds for assistance. The vast majority of the campaign's subcommittees, like those at Blyth, Morpeth and Ashington, repeated this humanitarian message to a striking degree.[127] Indeed, referring to British government aid for refugees in Spain, Anderson called on the 'private citizen to confirm the action of his government by his own generosity', in effect praising government policy.[128]

The foodship campaign's activities centred around collecting; in the street, house-to-house and sending appeal circulars to institutions. The only sizeable public meeting the campaign held came in Newcastle, on 22 January 1939. Some of the speakers at this meeting undoubtedly injected an element of partiality into the campaign. The same was true of smaller public meetings in North Shields and Ashington in late January 1939.[129]

A handful of individuals, usually identifiable left-wingers, acting apparently independently of the subcommittees, acted likewise in depicting the foodship as a means of supporting the Republic against Franco, and occasionally, skilfully but overtly, linking the civilian suffering with fascist brutality.[130] Yet even ex-International Brigaders were somewhat cryptic in their call for all 'organisations and individuals' to send a 'concrete message of goodwill and sympathy' to the suffering Spanish people.[131] Some subcommittees made subtle reference to partisanship too, such as Sunderland's claim that the foodship was for 'democratic Spain'.[132] Similarly, the secretary of North Shields foodship committee, A. Ferguson, discussed 'the reign of brute force, and of tiny tots wasting away from hunger and disease ... refugees crowd the roads with the rattle of low flying planes, machine guns spreading indiscriminate death and panic'.[133] But Ferguson did not name the leaders behind the machine guns and, in any case, these were exceptions to the campaign's predominant and oft-repeated humanitarian message.

The Tyneside campaign's propaganda message served as a model to many other foodship campaigns around the country.[134] In South Wales, humanitarianism came to characterise all the Spanish aid campaigns. Thus, for example, the basis of Neath SMAC's appeal was 'always humanitarian rather than political'.[135] In fact, humanitarianism became prevalent in and outside of the coalfield.[136] It was striking that many of these appeals mirrored those from Franco supporting Catholics, such as the *Universe's* Medical Fund for Spain, which also neglected to mention which side the aid was for.[137] Indeed, a matter of weeks after this appeal appeared in the *Sunderland Echo*, one from the Sunderland SMAC replicated some of its language.[138]

Reasons for the Humanitarian Appeals

Arguably the main factor in determining how a local SMAC or other campaign committee framed its appeal was the influence exerted from the national level. Thus, in the campaign to support Basque refugees, the BCC set the agenda in terms of the humanitarian appeal. It, in turn, was responding to the wishes of the Basque government that had expressly stated its desire for 'politics' not to arise and for the campaign to be seen as a humanitarian venture. Vincent Tewson, the official labour movement representative on the BCC at national level, amongst others, stressed this. Indeed, Tewson, advised local labour movement institutions to look beyond their own memberships to raise money by, for example, requesting an entirely 'non-political' meeting under the auspices of the local Mayor. Tewson was also an organisational link to local trades councils directing the establishment of local BCCs.[139] The Basque ambassador in Britain, who also stressed the desire of the Basque government that no propaganda should be made from the children, invited the Catholic Church to participate, and it did so from the outset. Again, political partisanship could not enter the campaign if the Church was to stay involved. The effect of these national appeals was directly observable at local level. Thus, when M. Mareda P. Roberts of Bedlington made an individual appeal for support for the Basque refugees in July 1937, she phrased her own letter in identical terms to the appeal that she also reproduced in full from national organisers of the Basque relief effort; i.e. that in helping the Basque children, they were not 'taking sides in the Spanish war. We are simply helping children who need help'.[140]

Similar influences came into play with the other campaigns that received NJCSR sponsorship. As Don Watson pointed out 'the leadership of the NJCSR always chose to campaign in a "broad" way, seeking single-issue alliances regardless of any other differences ...'.[141] A good way to do this was, of course, to exclude potentially divisive 'politics'. Indeed, the NJCSR said that aid would go to where it was needed, implying neutrality.[142] The NJCSR agreed that its speakers be 'non-political' in order to retain Quaker support.[143] Quakers had already teamed up with the Save the Children Fund (another organisation involved in the NJCSR) to appeal for suffering civilians ('though we are sure that combatants themselves cannot desire it' [sic.]), reassuring potential donors that 'there is no question here of political or sectarian bias'.[144] The national Spanish Medical Aid committee, with its 'avowed humanitarian aims', had set the tone early on.[145] By the time of the foodships in late 1938, the pattern of framing these campaigns in a humanitarian manner was well established. The national informed the regional at an individual level in the form of activists like Isabel Brown, a national NJCSR organiser originally from North Shields who returned to the region regularly to speak for local Spanish aid campaigns, such as, for example, Newcastle SMAC in January 1937.[146]

However, the influence of the 'national' was not all pervading. As has been seen, some local SMACs did not use a humanitarian campaigning message, in spite of the lead of the national committee. Conversely, the idea of framing a humanitarian message for the Tyneside foodship seems to have emerged organically within that campaign (and helped to establish this method in similar foodship campaigns elsewhere in the country); this final set of campaigns appears to have owed less to national sponsorship and more to local and regional activists. Certainly they chimed with the grassroots far more than any set of campaigns before them. Yet these foodship campaigns also applied the humanitarian, 'non-political' message most consistently: even more so than in elements of the Basque campaigns. That said, the foodship employed the same arguments about the needs of the refugee population in the Republic as opposed to Franco's side that the Basque campaigners had used in 1937.[147] Still, many grassroots activists regarded the humanitarian appeal as the correct way to approach these issues.

This dominant humanitarian message was also prevalent in many Spanish aid activities conducted formally under the auspices of labour movement institutions. In Blyth, while there was no SMAC as such, the local NUWM branch undertook collecting for the 'British Medical Aid for Spain Association'.[148] Its initial campaigning message was a robust partisan one. In an appeal in mid-December 1936, NUWM activist William Mooney wrote of the 'life and death battle' in Spain in 'defence of democratic rights' and called for Blyth inhabitants to show their solidarity with their 'Spanish comrades' against fascism.[149]

However, the message thanking donors for their generosity a week later used quite different language. A second activist, H.E. Thomas, wrote that the food would 'help relieve the distress to women and children caused by the civil war'.[150] Clearly, the emphasis (like the author) had changed, and this from an organisation that did not need to temper its language; at least not in order to maintain its internal organisational unity and activity. Similarly, when Blyth Labour Party launched a public appeal in January 1937 it felt 'that without regard to political views on the matter, the urgent need of the poor people, rendered homeless and destitute will find a ready response from all warm-hearted people'.[151] Thus, the institutional form did not necessarily determine the message. This was also abundantly clear in the Tyneside foodship, sponsored by the clearly partisan (anti-appeasement, etc) TJPC.

There clearly were practical reasons that recommended such an approach. Again, the clearest case for this was the Basque refugee hostel where, as Don Watson pointed out, 'the costs of a large group of children could only be met by organisations. ... It was, too, an open ended commitment'.[152] Finances were required on a regular basis, and therefore anything that might alienate a potential donor, such as a partisan stance, was to be avoided. Given all these considerations, the Tynemouth hostel's campaigning in predominantly humanitarian terms was no aberration as far as the national Basque campaign was concerned. The Basque campaign had an especially salient reason, at least for a few months, for not wishing to alienate Catholics. However, presumably activists in other campaigns also sought to avoid offending them as well as Conservatives and others with money to spare who might not support a partisan stance on Spain, in order to maximise their income. Ashington SMAC, for example, aimed to 'appeal to the community at large' for support.[153] The *Linaria* campaign was distinct in this respect. It had other pragmatic reasons for eschewing a political position on Spain. The crew were defending themselves in court on the basis that they did not want to enter a war zone. Any 'politics' linked with their campaign might well have jeopardised their defence. Furthermore, this campaign was specifically about raising money to support the crew in court.

There was possibly a temporal dimension to these considerations. In South Wales, the effect of the arrival of Basque refugees was partly to depoliticise the activities of the SMACs; fundraising (mostly for the Basques) became the main feature of the committees' activity.[154] There was evidence for a similar effect in the north-east. Indeed, an appeal for the Basque refugees issued by Newcastle SMAC explicitly noted that 'The political ramifications of the struggle have made it difficult until recently to help to relieve the sufferings of Spanish people without showing more approval than many of us are able to give towards one side or the other'.[155] This was part of Newcastle SMAC's greater effort to involve the 'non-political' such as clergy after the arrival of Basque refugees. However, this effect appeared less marked in the north-east. As discussed above, several of the SMACs using humanitarian language for their appeals, including Newcastle, were doing so before the Basque refugee issue arose, and their campaign language was studded with differing degrees of political partiality both before and after May 1937. Indeed, paradoxically, in elements of the Basque campaign itself the tendency was to more partisanship as time passed.[156]

An associated point is that the kind of activities many of these campaigns organised helped to determine the language they used. It was a common attitude of activists, that if they needed to fundraise then they needed to de-politicise. In other words, they needed to make their appeal appear as much like a charity as possible. Indeed, many Spain campaign organisers actually used the word 'charity' to describe their efforts.[157] William Hogg of Ashington Tyneside foodship committee, for example, wrote: 'charity may being at home, but it must not end at home or it may end the home'.[158] If successful in this, then the campaign presumably had to have as wide an appeal as possible, spanning political and social divisions: breaking into the wealthy suburbs that might well have rejected a campaign with a partisan motif. The destination of much of the aid, too, had a reasonable claim to the 'humanitarian' (charity) label, in as much as the direct beneficiaries were usually civilians. Furthermore, while it was disingenuous to imply that medical aid went *equally* to both sides, the Republican medical units did *not* deny treatment to enemy wounded, though this did prove problematic on occasion.[159]

However, naturally, anything that went to civilians on one side of the conflict only had some degree of indirect effect on it. Anarchist historian José Peirats wrote, for example, that the first Russian foodship struck an 'emotional chord' in the Catalan people; he compared it to the effect of the massively attended funeral of well respected anarchist leader Buenaventura Durruti.[160] Clearly, the suffering of civilians, especially children, could be used to good effect as anti-Franco propaganda; the 'If you tolerate this' poster, for example. But, the image itself needed to be linked in some direct way with the forces that were causing the suffering. Claiming that aid would go to both sides impartially implied that the war itself was the problem, not the actions of one particular side of it. Furthermore, as some SMACs demonstrated (like Blaydon), it remained quite possible to collect humanitarian aid (such as food for civilian populations) with a partisan message.

Finally, there is the possibility that humanitarian appeals dominated on the ground because many involved in these campaigns actually saw the issue in these terms: i.e. it was solely about helping the suffering innocents of the conflict. Presumably, most of the identifiable Communist and Labour activists in these campaigns were involved because they opposed Franco and his supporters within and outside of Spain. It is clear in the campaign to support the Basque hostel that Nell Badsey had very little room for manoeuvre and probably took her partisanship in the campaign as far as she practically could. However, Badsey was practised in talking in humanitarian terms: she had done so previously in her incarnation as leading activist in North Shields SMAC; an institution that theoretically provided more potential leeway in terms of ways in which to frame campaigning appeals. Alex Robson must have fomented strike action on the *Linaria* because he was a Communist militant. The same stood for most of the Labour Party and CAPR activists involved in the Spanish aid campaigns.

However, in some SMACs in particular, the left representatives appeared to be in the minority (Sunderland and Seaham committees, for example). In these cases, it is conceivable that activists adopted a humanitarian campaign message because this was their only motive for involvement. The role of the clergy may have been important in some individual committees in this respect. In South Wales, a typical local SMAC 'was as much under the influence of the Nonconformist chapels as of the Communist Party branches'.[161] Indeed, individuals from non-political organisations far outnumbered the political parties on most SMACs.

In practice, it is often difficult to determine who within individual campaign committees decided to opt for humanitarianism and their motives; if local Church representatives and others helped to determine the language of a campaign or committee, or if they were attracted into them as a result of it. However, it is clear enough that left activists in many Spanish aid campaigns employed this humanitarian language about Spain for tactical reasons: to attract people like the clergy, and those who respected such individuals, if they were not already there. The most important example of this was the Tyneside foodship campaign. Established by the implacably anti-fascist and pro-Republican TJPC, the majority of its central organising committee also supported the Republic (although none were Labour or CP activists). In this case, the pro-Republicans clearly and deliberately chose and applied humanitarianism as a fundraising tactic. And applied it, with gusto, by individuals with very different understandings of the conflict and motives for involvement.[162]

Financial and Organisational Successes

To what extent did the Spanish aid campaigns' predominantly humanitarian message succeed in maximising their fundraising potential? Official pronouncements from many north-east Spanish aid campaign organisers suggested that the popular response was generous. Gateshead SMAC organisers were, for example, grateful for the 'splendid support' received between late 1936 and February 1937.[163] Likewise, the Sunderland BCC, and individual collectors for the Basques like schoolboy Eric Walker, testified to the generous support they received.[164] On their own terms, as Don Watson pointed out, campaigns like the Tynemouth Basque hostel were clearly as financially successful as they needed to be.[165]

The Tyneside foodship campaign exceeded its own target by some degree. Initially aimed at raising £2,000, the target rose to £3,000 and it actually raised around £4,500.[166] It is impossible to calculate how much most of the other regional campaigns raised, but an illustration of the scale of the Tyneside foodship's achievement came in Ashington. There, the small but active local SMAC raised £130 and six tons of food in 21 months of activity. The local foodship committee collected about the same amount in less than a month.[167]

It was tempting to equate the most successful campaign (in terms of money raised from the public as opposed to labour movement institutions), to the consistency and persistency of its humanitarian, neutral message. But there were other, arguably more significant factors at work. The

Tyneside foodship came at a time when the Republic was on its knees. While some on the left continued to claim that the Republic was not yet defeated, many not sympathetic to it could still donate without fearing that this would aid the Republic's resistance overly.

The press reaction, equally, was possibly with the same consideration in mind. While the earlier humanitarian campaigns had secured a degree of favourable coverage, the Tyneside foodship campaign received more extensive and uniformly highly favourable treatment from the predominantly conservative regional newspapers. The foodship campaign also benefited to some degree from the previous experience of campaigners. In Ashington, for example, the involvement of local SMAC activists was 'warmly welcomed' by the new, larger committee, who recognised that their cooperation was of 'immense value'.[168]

Timing was important in other ways for the Tyneside foodship. The campaign began just before Christmas and festive spirit must have helped. Furthermore, with the rapid Franco advance, the refugee crisis in Republican territory was the most acute it had been. The foodship campaigners repeatedly mentioned this, emphasising the extreme seriousness and urgency of the situation.[169] This helped to concentrate the minds of campaigners and donors alike in a way that the previous campaigns – apart from, to an extent, those for the Basques – had not been able to.

The second major factor in explaining this campaign's success, along with the press coverage, was its organisation. It was the only Spanish aid campaign to operate at a regional level. The central foodship committee based in an office in Newcastle's Haymarket, coordinated its subcommittees on Tyneside, south Northumberland and most of County Durham through a federal structure. This meant that the central organisers were much closer to the activity in geographical terms, equipped with good local knowledge, and further aided by short lines of communication. This allowed the central campaigners to recognise and state publicly the areas where work was not satisfactory (such as Gateshead and Durham in early January 1939). They also sent out emissaries to form subcommittees in targeted localities, such as Blyth and Ashington in early to mid-January 1939. Ashington was the last town of any consequence in the region without a foodship subcommittee. Once established, Ashington subcommittee then rapidly spawned further subcommittees in five outlying localities before the end of January 1939.[170]

Central foodship organisers tried to ensure, not always successfully, that there was no duplication of efforts, with as many areas as possible being covered by one well drilled subcommittee.[171] This organisation also allowed those in the subcommittees to feel that they were part of a larger regional effort: local as well as regional pride was at stake. While it seemed a little harsh that 'Wearside' did not usually get a mention in the campaign's title, organisers in Sunderland were proud to claim that, with £212 and one ton nine hundredweight of food collected including 1,500 tins of milk, they had made the second largest contribution towards the northeast's donation.[172] The Tyneside foodship was clearly a very convincing example of the utility of organising grassroots campaigns on a federal basis at regional level.

Clearly, the federal organisation of the Tyneside foodship campaign allowed it, in the narrow terms of fundraising, to become greater than the sum of its parts. Yet it was doubtful that the same stood for the Spanish aid campaigns as a whole. Different campaigns did work, to an extent, on separate issues, allowing individuals and groups an opportunity to act and donate on the aspects that most appealed to them. However, there were, in the various campaigns, differing degrees of work duplicated in the same localities or within the same institutions. This was most obvious, of course, in the competing demands of the official and unofficial funds circularised to institutions. Yet even within the unofficial campaigns, different local SMACs circularised the same labour movement institutions. Geographically speaking, it hardly seemed necessary to have two SMACs operating in the Seaham Harbour area, though that there was suggested a political and class division between activists. Elsewhere, local rivalries, as in the foodship campaign, may well have acted to spur activists on. It was not surprising, for example, that Gateshead SMAC followed Newcastle in its desire to send an ambulance to Spain.[173] In the case of the Basque refugees, there was considerable initial division over who should donate to which funds; those of the NJCSR or the Catholic Church, a confusing overlap that was surely inimical to support for either.[174] Indeed, there was a bewildering bombardment of appeals regarding the Basques on the local press from national and local institutions and individuals. Furthermore, the broadening of the campaigns meant that institutions such as Gateshead SMAC found themselves accepting part responsibility for the Tynemouth Basque hostel in addition to 'general relief work' and attempting to raise money to buy an ambulance. A proliferation of commitments made it far more difficult for any one to be fully supported, placing extra pressure on activists.[175]

Financial Failures, Exertion and Apathy

There were financial failures as well as successes. Lack of funds forced the closure of the short-lived (from mid-September to December 1937) Hexham Basque refugee hostel (the second independently-run hostel in the north-east).[176] The *Linaria* Defence Committee's neutral appeal circular secured at least one donation from an institution unfavourable to all other Spain appeals.[177] However, *Linaria* public meetings with essentially the same campaigning message were not as successful in fundraising. The second *Linaria* Defence Committee meeting, in mid-April 1937, raised only £3 16s. towards the target of £100 to cover the crew's Liverpool court appearances.

In truth, the takings at Spain meetings varied wildly, and naturally depended in part on the size of the audience. But even when examining only the larger public meetings held in the two major venues in Newcastle (City Hall and Palace Theatre), there appeared to be no clear correlation between the amount donated at any individual Spain meeting and the degree of the appeal's humanitarian neutrality. Thus, while the Tyneside foodship public meeting's collection of £191 in late January 1939 was the largest recorded (for unofficial and official meetings), the second greatest sum collected for an unofficial campaign (£142 13s. 6d.) came earlier in the same month at the north-east International Brigade memorial meeting.[178] In terms of officially organised meetings, the only one to come close was the £150 raised at a Spain Campaign Committee meeting in Newcastle in December 1937.[179] Two other official meetings on Spain only collected around £10 each, while two unofficial efforts each collected almost four times that amount.[180] Still, perhaps it was natural that the campaign that raised the most by collecting in the street, the Tyneside foodship, also collected the most at its public meeting.

Notwithstanding this, the public agitation held by the *Linaria* Defence Committee was remarkably anaemic, especially when contrasted with the highly novel initial strike action. The committee appeared to hold only three meetings in the region, with differing accounts of their attendances and little obvious public debate or controversy ensuing.[181] In the other Spain campaigns, evidence of engagement and apathy varied considerably. In terms of attendances, some unofficial organised events recorded high turnouts, especially in the first year of the conflict. There were 3,000 at the two Spain meetings in Newcastle in August and September 1936 and the Newcastle SMAC organised meeting at the Palace Theatre on Sunday 17 January 1937 was also well attended.[182] Both Blaydon SMAC's showing of the *Defence of Madrid* (raising £13 10s.) and the Gateshead town's meeting for Spain in spring 1937 had 'large' attendances.[183]

However, apathy began to become evident at these more overtly propagandistic events. A key example was Newcastle's 'Spain Week', which, according to James Spencer of the *Sunday Sun*, 'was weak'. In fact, it was an 'absolute failure' as 'not very many' saw the Spain exhibition and 'still fewer' saw the films.[184] Organiser Tom O'Byrne conceded that numbers attending the films and exhibitions 'did not satisfy the committee'.[185] Arthur Blenkinsop, too, noted privately that 'due to Labour apathy, it was not a rousing success as we had hoped'.[186] At the other extreme (in terms of type of appeal), for example, an Ellington lodge-organised concert for Basques in December 1938 was a 'failure owing to poor attendance'.[187]

There was also some evidence of varying success regarding attempts to organise the donkey-work. Blaydon SMAC, for example, managed to secure a 'large number of names' of volunteer sellers for a Spain flag day on 6 February 1937.[188] However, others experienced difficulties. In Morpeth, for example, Canon J.J. Davies was disappointed at the 'small attendance' at a meeting to arrange house-to-house collections for Basque refugees in July 1937.[189] There had been a similarly 'disappointing' attendance at a meeting to organise fundraising for the same cause in Sunderland a month earlier.[190] Ashington SMAC's problems were more long-term. Many of its founder members 'were not equal to the work and found ways of retiring from the committee', leaving a small hardcore to continue the demanding work.[191] Perhaps most surprising was the apathy evident in the Tyneside foodship campaign. There were an 'inadequate' number of collectors to 'comb out' Ashington's 30,000 population.[192] Similarly, in the equally late-starting North Shields, there were less than 40 at the campaign's local launch meeting and a subsequent dearth of collectors.[193]

Explaining these individual manifestations of apathy is difficult. Spencer's explanation for 'Spain Week's' failure was the 'very simple fact' that Britons did not like Communism or Fascism; 'They just want to keep their own sweet democracy'.[194] This was platitudinous, not least because many did not associate the Republic with Communism. The reasons for a poor attendance at any given Spain event could be specific to it; it may not have been well advertised, for example. Furthermore, apathy in one aspect of an event did not necessarily mean complete failure. Thus, there was some justification for O'Byrne's claim that 'the generosity shown in retiring collections cannot be described as a weak statement'.[195] (The inaugural 'Spain Week' meeting raised £36).[196] Indeed, apathy, even at the birth of a campaign, did not necessarily mean inevitable failure. The TJPC conference in October 1938 that spawned the Tyneside foodship campaign, for example, had an embarrassingly low attendance (only 20 delegates attended from approximately 1,000 institutions invited).[197]

Apathy was also a relative concept and perhaps some activists' expectations, like Gateshead SMAC's call for 500 volunteer collectors to deliver 50,000 collecting envelopes, were a little optimistic.[198] When Ashington foodship subcommittee appealed for 200 volunteers to help collect, it may not have been aware that there were only 13 initial collectors in nearby Blyth.[199] Again, as in North Shields, there was a strong contrast between the 'numerically unsatisfactory' collecting organisation in Ashington and the 'very satisfactory' results achieved by the collectors.[200] More immediate prosaic events also took their toll; like the 'severe weather' that dogged North Shields collectors' efforts. This certainly did not aid activists who operated in a locality with a weak and somewhat inactive labour movement.[201]

The numbers of collectors and the intensity and duration of their work for most campaigns remains unknown. But where turnout was low, this naturally compounded activists' problems as it threw more work onto fewer people, thereby acting as a stronger disincentive to potential collectors. And there was potentially a good deal of work demanded. House-to-house collecting, as the 'most effective' with the 'quickest results', was the preferred method. But this activity relied on good numbers of collectors.[202] It demanded a 'lot of energy', requiring two visits to every door; envelopes with appeals dropped in the first visit were collected on the second.[203] Thus there was a 'tremendous amount of work' done by Ashington activists, like those throughout the country.[204] In Sheffield, for example, collectors for Spain 'came as regularly as the rent man (but received a pleasanter welcome)'.[205]

Notwithstanding the reasons for apathy, its existence suggests a qualification of the basic popular frontist case that the unofficial Spanish aid campaigns were necessarily more vital than their official labour movement equivalents. In terms of types of activities, the unofficial campaigns did not necessarily herald a new departure for activists. Ostensibly, unofficial campaigns appeared to take activists to the streets to collect funds, whereas most of the official campaigns were contented with raising money through circulars 'in house'. In practice, it seemed false to divide qualitatively, for examples, Gateshead Labour Party activists, working under the auspices of the SMAC they created, collecting house-to-house for their own local fund, from Jarrow Labour activists performing the same activity for a nationally constituted, official fund. Conversely, unofficial campaigns also employed the less active method of circularising institutions with appeals for donations. This was a relatively easy, effective and undemanding way to fundraise. The only real difference here was that the unofficial funds circularised more often and were more inclined to send appeals to the smallest sections of the labour movement, the branches. However, in this activity, certainly, the unofficial campaigns were not tapping into a font of potential support that the official funds had failed to appreciate.

In fact, the vast majority of fundraising methods (including the more 'active' ones) that the unofficial campaigns employed were not novel. Indeed, many activists used the same methods to raise money for their own political parties and others that replicated the efforts of scores of charities. Indeed, most of their fundraising methods aped those of charities: house-to-house collections, flag days, collecting boxes in shops, jumble sales, appeals in the press and circulars. However, in employing both the language and methods of charities, the Spanish aid campaigns lost something of their novelty value. They were in direct competition with other charitable appeals (both in terms of circulars sent to institutions and collections on the streets), of which there were very many. Canon Davies recognised that a possible reason for the small turnout at a meeting to fundraise for Basque refugees in July 1937 was that 'there were a good number of appeals going on now'.[206] These campaigners had made it seem as though there was no difference between collecting for, say, a local hospital and collecting for Basque refugees and, on this occasion, had paid a price in palpable terms.

Indeed, perhaps not surprisingly, the charities closer to home often seemed to do better in terms of volunteer collectors (as they did in terms of institutional donations).[207] In Blyth, for example, an impressive list of names of preliminary volunteers to collect on a house-to-house appeal for a local hospital building fund suggested that it was far better volunteer supported than the town's foodship subcommittee.[208] Also running concurrently with the Tyneside foodship was a region wide appeal for the families of men killed in the *Jeanie Stewart*, a local fishing boat. By early February, this campaign had raised the same amount of money in the same period of time but without the massive amount of work put in by foodship volunteers.[209] To put the Ashington Spain achievements (SMAC and foodship) in perspective, the local British Legion branch complained in October 1938 about the money people 'squandered' when they could give more to the poppy appeal: £100 was apparently an unsatisfactory yield for a town of its size.[210]

By that time, the response of Ashington's labour movement to Spain had already come in for severe criticism from activists in the local SMAC and Allan of the CP. In July 1938, Allan took his condemnation wider, attacking the attitude of someone who he had overheard at the Northumberland miners' picnic who '"had enough troubles of our own without bothering about the troubles of the Spanish people"'. Then Allan turned to discuss the 'people who give their coppers and sixpences in aid of Spain [who] hand over their contributions as if they were doing a charitable thing, a meritorious action, as if they were helping some poor unfortunate person'. Allan claimed that what was being 'hammered out' in Spain concerned everyone as it was whether there was to 'be greater power for the common people or should it remain in grasp of rich and powerful'.[211] It was unlikely that very many within the north-east labour movement did not broadly share Allan's understanding of the issues at stake. However, for the minority who did not, it was perfectly understandable that, in donating to many of the Spanish aid campaigns, they should feel that they had committed a charitable act. After all, many of those collecting for the majority of Spanish aid campaigns had been repeatedly telling them this.

The levels of publicly expressed opposition to all the north-east Spain campaigns and, in the case of the Basques, to their actual presence, seem to have been fairly low throughout, regardless of the nature of the campaign. However, the humanitarian message and attempts to make these campaigns into normal charities did not preclude all opposition. A Sunderland SMAC activist was surprised at the 'most bitter rebuffs from many sides and from most unexpected quarters', which its humanitarian work had received.[212] Indeed, when humanitarianism became stronger with the Basque campaigns, there was more vocal opposition in the press. Several, including Lord Mayor of Newcastle alderman Grantham, argued that local children in need should be prioritised over the Basques, who required more per week to keep than the children of the unemployed. These arguments persisted into 1938.[213] While the greater opposition was no doubt due to the wider publicity the campaign received and the larger and more urgent financial demands being made rather than the more preponderant humanitarianism, it was clear that, even as a charity, there remained problems of presentation. Indeed, there was still opposition on the same grounds, though possibly less than in 1937, evident in the Tyneside foodship campaign; in spite of activists' best efforts to preclude it completely with humanitarianism. In the *Shields Gazette*, for example, 'CHARJR' wanted food for children here and not 'Red Spain' and John E. Main-Hall claimed that the food only went to Republican leaders, not children.[214] In other words, no matter how far activists went, they would never be able to avoid angering some, for political reasons or because their charity work was for foreigners when there were so many needy at home.

Some other commentators on the left were sceptical of the Spanish aid campaigns. George Orwell claimed that the British public donated 'less than half of what they spent in a single week going to the pictures'.[215] Of the unofficial funds, the figures only allow a calculation for what the Tyneside foodship raised; almost 1d. from every adult in the region. However, while it did raise impressive sums compared with many other north-east Spanish aid campaigns, the Tyneside foodship did so without the strong sponsorship of the main north-east labour movement institutions, most notably the DMA. The NMA, which was one of the very few institutions represented at the TJPC conference that planned the campaign in October 1938, also sent very little to the appeal itself.[216]

The only unofficial campaign receiving generous support from the central DMA was the IBDWAC. It remains unclear if this was related to its status as the only unofficial campaign that could not really frame a humanitarian appeal: many miners' lodges were, after all, strong supporters of the predominantly humanitarian Basque campaigns. Notwithstanding this, the DMA dedicated the very large sums it generated to miners' projects. On imposing the 2s.6d. levy, it raised in an instant well over three times what the Tyneside foodship gathered, and from a fraction of the number of people. Durham and Northumberland miners, symbolically at least, had to forgo a trip to the cinema that week.[217]

Class Dimensions and 'Respectability'

There was clearly a strong class dimension to the ways in which these campaigns were often organised and in the response to them. Some activists argued that 'if you could get a lady somebody in your committee, it helped a great deal'.[218] A national figure who local activists constantly referred to in this context was the Duchess of Atholl. As a Conservative MP (until late 1938) as well as an aristocrat who supported the Republic, her high level involvement in the NJCSR apparently lent their appeals more weight and 'impartiality'.[219] At grassroots, clergymen and other professionals were useful as they could also lend respectability to campaigns.

Bank managers made 'respectable' treasurers, as far as Gateshead SMAC and the later central Tyneside foodship campaign were concerned.[220]

In the earlier period, this process appeared to occur in a haphazard way, as professionals came to the fore (or not) in different localities and institutions. There were other ways to seek respectability, too. Gateshead SMAC, for example, sought legitimacy in a novel way, by getting the council to convene a town's appeal for 'the people of Spain' on 23 March 1937.[221] The first systematic use of appeals to 'prominent people' at grassroots level in the north-east appeared to be during the Basque campaigns.[222] By the time of the late 1938 foodship campaigns, securing the prominent support of professionals was an established and, indeed, central, aspect of the Tyneside foodship (and other areas) campaigners' tactics.[223] Indeed, the Tyneside foodship organisers took this to a fairly extreme degree, approaching 800 'professional people' when initiating the campaign.[224] Partly aiming to lend the campaign legitimacy and preclude possible allegations of partiality, in getting professionals to put their names to appeals there must also have been the hope that this would render the campaign one to which other professionals would be more likely to donate.

However, the evidence suggests that the north-east working-class, and often the more impoverished sections of it, invariably provided the bulk of charitable donations, irrespective of the campaign. For example, Jarrow Labour's collection for Spain funds in December 1937 raised £10, mostly from unemployed men. Ellen Wilkinson commented 'I know what that means in Jarrow'.[225] There was abundant evidence of great individual sacrifice, such as the 7lb. bag of sugar one workingman's wife gave Ashington SMAC collectors in May 1937.[226] In June 1937, Gateshead SMAC thanked the 'warm-hearted' support it received, noting that the response from 'poorer people ... merits commendation. As the wife of one unemployed man said to a collector "our bairns need help, we just cannot keep them as we should, but our bairns don't have to be targets from bombs, machine guns and the like"'.[227] The most numerous examples of the generosity of the poorest in the region came during the Tyneside foodship campaign. Initially, some had expressed doubt at the advisability of staging such a campaign on Tyneside 'but we have found that the working people, even unemployed, have only been too eager to give a little ...'.[228] The foodship received 'Many pathetic gifts ... One envelope marked "widow's note" contained 24 farthings. A little girl at South Shields brought in a bag of biscuits and miners' wives, with no money, rather than

not give anything at all have handed over food from their scanty lar-
ders'.[229] On Wearside, donors were the 'working people of Sunderland
themselves'.[230] Sometimes, a poor individual's generosity was such as to
embarrass the collector.[231]

Several contemporary activists also commented on this: Len Edmondson described the response to collecting efforts he was involved in during
the period as 'generally very good … people didn't have a lot but could
afford to give us something'.[232] Similarly, Labour Party activist Jack Lawther said that 'people generally gave as much as they could afford, or more
than they could afford, in many cases'.[233] Likewise, Jim Atkinson claimed
that three-quarters of British medical aid to Spain came from 'working
people and socialists … The place to get money for Spain is in the small
village, especially in industrial areas. These are the places where, to give
two pence, means something. It is not just a gesture'.[234]

Not every Spain activist regarded the region's populace as too poor. In
July 1937, for example, the Rev. Lewis Maclachlan thought that the 'hos-
pitable spirit' of a 'now prosperous Tyneside' could help both Basque
children and local children.[235] However, it was unusual to emphasise prosperity in appealing for support. Indeed, some activists regarded the very
poverty of the region as a positive precondition for a generous response.
As a central Tyneside foodship activist told an Ashington audience: 'men
and women in a mining community know what suffering means. Their
history is a story of recurring struggles and disputes, in which they have
experienced hardships and scarcity of food, therefore this appeal for gifts
of life to men, women and children who are suffering helplessly in as brut-
al and bitter a war as has ever been fought by human beings, should meet
with a prompt and generous response …'.[236]

Similarly, Newcastle SMAC, too, openly recognised that the working-
class were often generous donors and the reasons for this. An appeal it
issued for contributions to the local fund for Basque refugees noted that,
'all experience goes to show that those who are most sensitive to human
need at their own doors are usually people whose charity has a wider
range'.[237] The implicit obverse was that those with more money were less
likely to part with it. A *Morpeth Herald* reporter, describing an Ashington
SMAC meeting in December 1937, was more explicit. While the meeting's
speaker 'persuaded people not blessed with a generous share of this
world's goods to throw shillings and sixpences on the stage … There were
many of us in the audience who without great hardship to ourselves, could
have substantially increased that collection but we preferred to hold on to

our spare cash …. Most people … above the "subsistence wage" level of working-class existence like to hang on to the extra easements which a slightly higher wage level brings'.[238] Sheffield and Welsh activists recorded similar experiences.[239]

From the campaigning side, Jim Atkinson was similarly explicit: 'much money and effort has been wasted in trying to get money for Spain in well-to-do localities'.[240] By the time Atkinson uttered these words the Tyneside foodship campaign was well under way, suggesting that he was aware that it, too, was failing for the most part to tap the apparently hitherto largely untouched resources in the middle-class suburbs. Indeed, while the names of professionals dominated in lists of 'prominent' foodship supporters, they still totalled only about an eighth of those who the campaigners had contacted personally requesting their patronage. Furthermore, many of these professionals had supported earlier humanitarian Spain campaigns; their support for the foodship was thus not a coup.[241] Other evidence supported Atkinson's assessment. The only real successes the foodship campaign achieved in attracting new institutional support came from a handful of Women's Institutes and Towns Women's Guilds. Churches had supported the earlier funds (most notably the Basques) and the bulk of the institutional donations still came from those largely working-class ones inside and outside the labour movement that had donated on previous occasions. In Felling, for example, miners' lodges and Felling Ex-servicemen's Association donated both to Felling SMAC and to the later Felling foodship subcommittee.[242]

On the positive side, it is likely that the prominence of professionals did lend a certain 'respectability' to the campaign, thereby helping to ensure that the Tyneside foodship had better publicity than any of the previous Spanish aid campaigns in the north-east. The respectability must also have negated a degree of overt hostility to the campaign. However, the main effect of the Tyneside foodship's respectability appears to have been to allow campaigners to collect more successfully from the more conservative sections of the region's working-class. And even then, its respectable, humanitarian charity appeal had no answer to individuals like 'Labourer's Wife' who had no money, was 'fed up' with foodship collectors, and thought that 'we should help our own'.[243] This echoed earlier opposition, such as the individual who complained about the Basque campaign that 'thousands of begging envelopes are being printed and distributed among poor people who have no money to give'.[244] The vast majority of foodship campaign appeals, as with many of the earlier humanitarian appeals, made little or no attempt to engage such individuals with the wider issues at stake, to convince them that, in supporting the Republic, they *were* 'helping their own'.

For the most part, it was likely that the Labour-inclined majority of the north-east working-class, including the Catholics amongst them, did not require any Spanish aid campaign to be framed in these humanitarian-neutral ways. YCL activist Moira Tattam recalled that the vast majority in her village donated in response to a robust pro-Republican appeal for aid she delivered. The 'very, very small exception' who did not lived in two or three 'pleasant houses' that were 'almost without exception' occupied by Conservatives.[245] Indeed, as the urge for respectability demanded the removal of partisanship as much as possible from the campaigns, this was possibly a *disincentive* for some to donate, as it was not completely clear that the aid would go to the anti-Franco side. For those not inclined to donate, especially the middle-classes, an appeal in humanitarian language made little difference. In South Wales, the core of the response to Spain was 'overwhelmingly proletarian'.[246] In terms of numbers and sacrifices, it was the same in the north-east as well, but this was not the impression given in the lists of patrons' names in the press attached to the Tyneside foodship and some other Spain campaigns.

6

WHAT DO THE SPANISH AID CAMPAIGNS MEAN?

The predominant humanitarian message in Spanish aid campaigns like the Tyneside foodship appeared to forsake some major labour movement support in the ultimately largely fruitless search for donations from the more affluent. However, the humanitarian language sacrificed a good deal more than this. Before considering this, however, some other areas of debate require consideration.

'Humanitarianism', 'Politics' and 'Pro-Republicanism' Debates

Many texts have discussed the 'political' and 'humanitarian' aspects of the motives of those involved, recognising some kind of distinction between them and echoing a division noted by many contemporaries. Michael Alpert, for example, wrote that 'to help relieve Spanish suffering was a positive way of reacting, for some in political terms, others in solely humanitarian ones'.[1] However, the use of 'political' in this context is unhelpful. Indeed, almost any human thought or action could be defined as 'political'; and any viewpoint on the Spanish conflict, even a 'neutral' one, was in some senses a 'political' position. Instead, when contrasting the 'humanitarianism' in the Spanish aid campaigns, 'political' is better replaced by a more specific term; 'pro-Republican'. Put simply, this was the perspective that activists should support the Republic as it was fighting fascism. Pro-Republicanism, then, was not simply an 'anti-fascist' perspective as it did not include those who opposed fascism but who did not regard the National Government's foreign policy of supporting Non-Intervention and later developing 'appeasement' as effectively pro-fascist. Central to pro-Republicanism was the need to end Non-Intervention to help the

Republic defeat fascism in Spain. The liberal Party and the Labour Party from autumn 1937 (officially) had pro-Republican positions on Spain.

There was the connected issue of the relations between individual activists and the institutions through which they worked. Jackson accepted that there was a 'distinction between the institutions with "humanitarian" motives and those with a manifestly "political" agenda'. But, as many individuals worked through both types of institution, 'it seems inappropriate to attempt to maintain the notion of a political/ humanitarian division at the level of grassroots activity'.[2] Yet the relationship between activists and campaigns was more complex than this. In the north-east, no complete set of institutions within a campaign were *entirely* humanitarian (though some individual Spanish aid committees appear to have been). Thus, there was no *total* binary division at the institutional level. In terms of individual activists, there were clearly some, like Jim Atkinson, involved in both overtly pro-Republican and predominantly 'humanitarian' campaigns.[3] However, most of the examples of 'overlap' of individuals were those involved in multiple humanitarian Spain campaigns. Thus, for example, at least seven of the 21 individuals involved in the establishment of Sunderland SMAC in February 1937 were also prominent supporters of the Tyneside foodship in 1938–9. Miss Winifred Moul (headmistress of Bede Collegiate School) was involved in a third predominantly humanitarian campaign, Sunderland Women's Basque Refugee committee.[4] The Rev. John Patton, chairperson of the Tynemouth Basque hostel and treasurer of the *Linaria* Defence Committee beforehand, was another individual involved at high levels in two campaigns that could easily accommodate humanitarians.[5] In fact, the overlap at individual activist level between the strongly pro-Republican and humanitarian campaigns appeared numerically less than that between different humanitarian campaigns.

It is quite clear at the level of individual activists that the division between the humanitarian and pro-Republican ('political') was valid. Indeed, an understanding of this was essential to grasp much of the political significance of the Spanish aid campaigns. Two examples from the Tyneside foodship campaign illustrate this. The first was C.V.H. Vincent, chairperson of Jarrow Conservative Association and involved in the Jarrow foodship subcommittee. He clearly did not have a pro-Republican perspective. But Vincent was a rare (named) Conservative involved at the subcommittee level. More significant was Thomas Tindle Anderson (junior), the single most important activist (honorary secretary) in the campaign. A grammar school teacher by profession, Anderson was also a social worker heavily involved in charitable public work. The balance of evidence suggested that Anderson became involved in the foodship campaign for humanitarian motives informed by his Quakerism rather than from pro-Republicanism.[6] In July 1937, he helped establish a Quaker committee in South Shields to support Basque refugees and signed a Newcastle SMAC humanitarian appeal for them that explicitly rejected partisanship.[7] In fact, the only evidence of Anderson pronouncing explicitly on Spain on a public political (i.e. non-foodship) platform came when he chaired a rare CAPR organised meeting on Spain in South Shields in July 1938. However, Anderson's speech discussed solely the attacks on British shipping trading with Republican ports and gave no inkling of any kind of pro-Republicanism. Indeed, with his (late) father a ship-owner, Anderson had other possible reasons for concern on this issue.[8] Clearly, contrary to Jackson's claim, 'Broad political and humanitarian concerns' were not necessarily 'inseparable, just two sides of the same coin'.[9]

Naturally, those with a pro-Republican attitude were likely to have had humanitarian motives as well; i.e. the suffering of human beings moved them as the fascist aggression enraged them. But the reverse did not necessarily follow. Rather than another side of the same coin, humanitarianism was a base on which all could agree at some level; they could not all necessarily agree on 'anti-fascism', let alone on a pro-Republican perspective. And, in order to be involved in many of these campaigns – even at the highest levels – they did not have to.

In the cases of individual activists, the ways in which they expressed their motives demand close and individual consideration. For example, there was Joyce Hall who collected signatures in Tynemouth for a petition to allow Basque refugees to come to Britain in spring 1937. At college, she and fellow students 'had very strong ideas, that the elected government in Spain should have been supported by this country … in this country there was a sort of idea that Communism was a menace. And it seemed to us a sort of spurious excuse that our government was giving for not supporting the elected government in Spain …'. However, she described her motivation for collecting signatures for the Basque petition as 'fundamentally from the humanitarian side and also knowing what was going on in other parts of the world as well. I was very much on the side of those people who were being persecuted'.[10] While humanitarianism was thus a vital motive, it was also clear that, for the purposes of this discussion, Joyce Hall was a pro-Republican. She clearly had an unequivocal anti-Non-Intervention stance on the issue; she wanted the British government to support the Republic, and this came before her involvement in the Basque petition.

Both Jackson's and Fyrth's claims implied that in some cases the 'humanitarian' and the pro-Republican ('political') *were* occasionally separate in the minds of those taking part. So, the real discussion is about the extent to which the predominance of humanitarian language reflected a preponderance of involvement from individuals with humanitarian and not pro-Republican motives. It is likely that there were far fewer 'humanitarians' involved than the language used by the campaigns suggested and that the majority of the main organisers in most – if not all – campaigns were pro-Republican. However, it seems likely that the lower levels of involvement, such as occasionally collecting door-to-door, for example, brought in more humanitarians.

Another area of contention was the relationship between the 'pro-Republicans' and the 'humanitarians'. Regarding the Basque campaigns, Don Watson wrote that there was 'apparently productive coexistence' between the two groupings.[11] In the day-to-day terms of raising money and running the hostel, this was substantiated. However, the claim that the two elements did not cancel each other out seems less convincing.[12] It was clear that the 'pro-Republicans' did tame their language considerably in many of these campaigns, which they presumably considered necessary to maintain the integrity of the humanitarian appeal. The achievement of the Basque campaigners in the region certainly was 'noteworthy' but the extent to which it was a 'noteworthy contribution to the Republican cause' was a different matter.[13]

The pro-Republicans clearly made sacrifices to maintain the coalition with humanitarians, but why did they do this? Tom Buchanan wrote of 'beguiling simplicity' with which the Spanish Medical Aid Committee 'channelled the humanitarian impulse in a political direction'.[14] Angela Jackson took issue with this 'hint at a calculated manipulation of naive good intentions' and argued that it was 'overly simplistic to regard the members of such committees ... as little more than devious political opportunists'.[15] This was because the "political" and "humanitarian" were issues for most activists. However, this understates the degree to which there were solely humanitarians involved and, as important, donating to these appeals. In this respect it *was* manipulative of the 'pro-Republicans' to claim (false) neutrality: though individuals like T.T. Anderson *were* being truthful to themselves and prospective donors when they protested humanitarian neutrality.

Perhaps a more salient consideration was the considerable self-deception present, and on both sides. Indeed, in some regards the pro-Republicans deceived themselves as much as they manipulated the 'humanitarians'. In promoting a 'deceptive' humanitarian message, they sacrificed much political capital for their cause in pursuit of the often highly illusive wealthy humanitarian. In some regards, campaigns like the SMACs did channel humanitarian impulses in a political direction; in that some who were not pro-Republic but moved by the human suffering provided aid that went to the Republic (albeit civilians). However, these campaigns' channelling of the pro-Republican sentiments of many into humanitarian and ultimately politically almost silent (and therefore ineffective) channels more than counterbalanced this first effect.

Levels of Politicisation

The extent to which the Spanish aid campaigns were pro-Republican had important implications for the degree to which they politicised. Fyrth claimed that the 'Aid Spain' campaigns politicised to such an extent that they made a significant contribution to the 1945 Labour election victory.[16] Clearly, those who first became involved with humanitarian motives *could* have become politicised by their involvement. However, the individual high profile cases on which there is sufficient evidence suggest that politicisation was unlikely to occur. Thus, the support of some Women's Institutes in the foodship campaign was not evidence of politicisation occurring through the Spanish aid campaigns. Rather it was an indication of the success that the framers of the campaign had had in depoliticising what was a highly politically controversial issue.[17] Indeed, far from moving over time from a more humanitarian to a more pro-Republican emphasis as a process of politicisation took effect, the north-east Spanish aid campaigns, if anything, did the reverse, with the Tyneside foodship the epitome of the humanitarian model most consistently applied. The Basque campaigns were an exception to this, but the process there was not the politicisation of humanitarians but rather the circumstances of the campaign changing in a way that gave the hitherto muted pro-Republicans a little more freedom to voice their politics.

It is more difficult to comment on the processes undergone by those individuals who collected on occasion for the humanitarian campaigns but normally remained unnamed in most sources. Yet it was by no means clear that collecting for these campaigns *inevitably* involved arguments that politicised individual collectors.[18] The humanitarian campaigns employed a language, to differing degrees, that could be used by individual collectors to dodge doorstep political debate and their own inadvertent politicisation. This was evident, for example, in T.T. Anderson's stock responses to recurrent questions asked of Tyneside foodship collectors all of which carefully avoided any statement that could be construed as favouring the Republic.[19] Clearly, some 'humanitarians' must have been politicised by their involvement in the humanitarian Spanish aid campaigns. But the potential for politicisation was minimised by 'pro-Republicans' who framed most of their campaigns in such overwhelmingly humanitarian language.

Finally, there were those who donated to these campaigns. Certainly, the act of donating itself was not necessarily 'political' (i.e. pro-Republican).[20] An individual ignorant of the situation in Spain could be forgiven for thinking that their donation to a Sunderland SMAC appeal, for example, was as likely to go to the wounded on Franco's side as it was to those on the Republic: a collector (humanitarian or not) using humanitarian arguments was not going to change this perspective. Indeed, if pro-Republican collectors had followed the lead of key humanitarian campaign organisers then even those predisposed to discuss the issue in 'political' terms on the doorstep would not have done so, further diminishing the campaign's potential to politicise. Only with campaigns that expressed a clear and consistent pro-Republican message, such as Blaydon SMAC, was it reasonable to assume that the donors (and collectors) largely agreed with the analysis and therefore accurate to describe collecting and donating in these campaigns as 'political' (pro-Republican).

It seems likely, given the evidence of contemporary public opinion polls (and notwithstanding some of their methodological problems), that the majority of donors to all the Spanish aid campaigns had some kind of pro-Republican perspective.[21] But, as many of the campaigns they donated to had almost no pro-Republican element in their appeals, it seems that the vast majority of these donors must have had these views beforehand. Of course, the Spanish civil war did politicise sections of the British populace. But the role played by the predominantly humanitarian Spanish aid campaigns in this process has been exaggerated. Not only was it unlikely that many of these campaigns contributed significantly to help clarify the ideas of 'ordinary people about the world threat of fascism'.[22] The humanitarian language of these campaigns actually *militated against* a pro-Republican understanding of the conflict; politicisation (understood in this context as the gaining of a pro-Republican perspective) occurred, to an extent, in spite, rather than because of the predominantly humanitarian campaigns.

However, there was some local-specific evidence that at least one campaign had had a certain 'progressive' impact, a form of politicisation. Don Watson pointed out that the Tynemouth Basque hostel had helped to make the local climate more accepting. When German and Austrian Jewish refugee children were housed in a nearby building during the early months of the Second World War, 'there was none of the press outcry which had accompanied the Basques' arrival two years earlier'.[23] Notwithstanding this, there remains considerable doubt about claims of the wide reaching longer-term effects of many of the Spanish aid campaigns.[24] Certainly, none of the high-profile humanitarian activists within the north-east Spanish aid campaigns provided any evidence of having adopted a pro-Republican stance while active in the Spanish aid campaigns nor of endorsing a critique of Chamberlain's foreign policy after the Republic's fall.[25] Surely, if these predominantly humanitarian campaigns had had such an important impact in 1945, there would be more evidence of this before the Second World War altered fundamentally the political landscape. Furthermore, it was one thing to equip the uninitiated humanitarian with a critique of Non-Intervention, but it was quite another to mount an effective political challenge within the labour movement against the leadership's inactivity on Spain. As Buchanan observed, the Spanish aid campaigns were 'spectacularly unsuccessful in affecting the politics of either the labour movement or the government'.[26] These observations certainly call into question whether the Spanish aid campaigns can be regarded as a 'movement'.[27]

A De Facto Popular Front?

The discussion around the humanitarian and 'political' aspects of the campaigns and the probable low levels of politicisation are significant for the debate over whether the Spanish aid campaigns were akin to a popular front. Echoing the language of contemporary Communist activists like Douglas Hyde, Francis claimed that an 'informal Popular Front' emerged in South Wales from late 1936 founded on solidarity with the Republic.[28] Similarly, Fyrth claimed that 'The Aid for Spain Campaign was the nearest thing to a People's Front that came about in Britain'.[29] On the surface, there appeared a good degree of evidence that in the north-east, too, the Spanish aid campaigns constituted a de facto popular front. Taken as a whole, the social and political diversity of the main organisers and supporting activists in many of these campaigns certainly suggested this possibility. The committees that did not appear to be de facto popular fronts themselves organised meetings that often did.

However, it is necessary to go beyond appearances. The British popular front was a project based on a clear understanding of the problems in world affairs and the way to deal with them. In the context of Spain, the popular front position was unequivocally pro-Republican (though clearly far from all pro-Republicans were pro-popular front). Thus, to be regarded as a de facto popular front, evidence is required that those involved in the Spanish aid campaigns either held this pro-Republican (popular front) perspective, or that they adopted it subsequently as a result of the process of politicisation that occurs in any 'political' campaign or movement worthy of the name. In other words, there should be evidence that those of no definite political party or tradition shared – or came to share – a similar political understanding of the situation in Spain with (the majority of) those involved from the labour movement.[30] This is not to create impossible criterion for these unofficial, ad hoc institutions. Indeed, the two contemporary north-east peace councils both involved politically diverse activists from liberals (mostly in the form of CAPR activists) to Communists who campaigned on Spain with a clear pro-Republican message. Indeed, the first political statement on Spain heard in Newcastle came at a TJPC meeting in early August 1936 and the SDPC organised at least three meetings on Spain in September and October 1936. In both peace councils, a de facto popular front, albeit one with rather limited liberal involvement, was manifest and actively pro-Republican, in contrast to some of their counterparts elsewhere in the country.[31]

Clearly, the discussion above suggests that the *entirety* of the Spanish aid campaigns at all levels, from the central organisers, through to occasional collectors and even the donors did not fit the criteria for constituting a de facto popular front. However, consideration of the highest levels of organisers separately might yield more support for the popular frontist case. In the sources these were the people usually named; the secretary, chair and treasurer of an individual committee and occasionally extra committee or subcommittee (in the case of the Tyneside foodship) members. As some of the most committed activists, they were also the people arguably most likely to have or adopt pro-Republican motives. Furthermore, these diverse campaigns need to be separated into their broad categories; Spanish aid committees, Basque committees and so forth, as considering them together tends to obscure key differences between them.

Indeed, in campaigns with multiple organising committees, it is also necessary to examine, as far as possible, individual committees and subcommittees within these campaigns.

Of the Spanish aid committees, at least one appeared to be a de facto popular front. The Communist secretary of Newcastle SMAC, Tom O' Byrne, claimed that it was 'composed of people of different political opinions' who 'have always worked amicably together to find ways and means of helping those who not only believe in democracy, but are prepared to make the supreme sacrifice in its defence'.[32] If this was an accurate representation of the opinions of those on the committee, then Newcastle SMAC was quite clearly (in late July 1937 at least) a de facto popular front.

On the other hand, other SMACs certainly were not de facto popular fronts. Indeed, some did not even look like popular fronts: a handful appeared more politically narrow and thus more akin to united than popular fronts; and others were narrower still, confined to official labour movement participation. Others were diverse but, on closer inspection, did not fulfil the criteria. A prime example was Sunderland SMAC.[33] At its first public meeting in February 1937, the speeches of several key committee activists suggested that they were not simply feigning neutrality to raise more money. Rev. R.W. Stannard, for example, said that 'neither side in Spain would find much sympathy' in Britain: 'I think it is the duty of this country to keep out of any form of conflict ... any kind of military assistance ... would be bound to spread the area of conflict and do infinite damage'.[34] Winifred Moul was a little more circumspect. She said 'The people of Spain called out for sympathy ... men are hurt there and it does not matter to what political side they belong'.[35] Dr W. Grant Waugh, on the other hand, seemed primarily interested in the lack of adequate medical attention most received and the spread of tetanus.

While there is evidence that Stannard was some sort of progressive, his prayers of thanksgiving for the Munich Agreement, which included thanks for Chamberlain's 'courage' and 'desire to do right', suggested that his time in Sunderland SMAC had not led him to a pro-Republican perspective.[36] The same stood for Moul whose views on 'Moral Rearmament' in February 1939 revealed that her understanding of the situation in Spain was far divorced from that of the pro-Republicans, even at this late stage and after working in three separate Spanish aid campaigns. In support of 'Moral Rearmament', Moul wrote: 'It is not bigger guns that bring a sense of security, but the knowledge of God's guidance ... it is not political realism that will solve our fears, but spiritual idealism'.[37]

The complexity of any discussion regarding individuals' political affiliations in relation to attitudes to these questions was evident in mayor Summerbell's speech at the same meeting. Summerbell said that 'while we must not take part in the war we should, as human beings with feelings and sympathy, try to do something to relieve the suffering in Spain'.[38] An important Labour Party activist, Summerbell's pacifism sounded here as though it would have prevented him from advocating the lifting of Non-Intervention and the sale of arms to Spain (even had this been official Labour policy at the time). Thus, due to a principled rejection of war based on pacifist thought, sometimes informed by Quakerism, even some Labour Party members and others on the left did not necessarily adopt a clear pro-Republican stance.

Two other campaigns did not fit the de facto popular front criteria. The clearer examples were the Basque campaigns, at both the specific and more general levels. At the general level, as Buchanan pointed out, the very presence of the official labour movement at national level in the BCC 'represented a further step in the de-politicisation of its relief work'.[39] Secondly, as noted in chapter five, the Catholic Church was heavily involved in the campaign for some months, and even after leaving the BCC it continued to care for many children, thereby further confusing the issue and clearly militating against the possibility of the campaign being a de facto popular front.

Regarding the Basque Tynemouth hostel, Communist Charlie Woods remarked on the involvement of humanitarians and Don Watson made a similar claim for the Basque campaigns more generally, which generated a 'coalition of support [that] contained the highly political, where support for the Republic was concerned, as well as the primarily humanitarian ...'.[40] Furthermore, the involvement of two members of the anti-popular front ILP on the committee also suggested it was not a de facto popular front. The central organising Tyneside foodship committee included T.T. Anderson who did not have, nor did he adopt, a pro-Republican stance; nor did C.V.H. Vincent who was involved in one of the most politically and socially diverse subcommittees, Jarrow. While others of the subcommittees, if taken as separate entities, might have been de facto popular fronts, the campaign as a whole at committee and subcommittee level clearly was not.

The evidence for those involved in several committees of different campaigns is insufficient to draw a firm conclusion about their motives. Much of the interpretation rests on the perspectives and motives of clergymen, who were prominently involved in some of the Spanish aid committees (such as Seaham and Morpeth), the youth foodship committee, the *Linaria* Defence Committee and the Tyneside foodship. Clearly, it would be fallacious to claim that the clergy involved in these campaigns were so necessarily for humanitarian reasons: they could have been acting from a pro-Republican motive. A good example was the Rev. Lewis Maclachlan, who was chairperson of the CAPR's Northern Area Council.[41]

Certainly, some clergy sounded as though they were involved for reasons of Christian charity and were not pro-Republican. For example, the Ashington Methodist Rev. Percy Carden, supporting the Tyneside foodship from his pulpit, described the campaign's organisers as 'great humanitarians in Newcastle who are better Christians than they know'.[42] Carden, who was one of the main foodship organisers in his town, explicitly rejected the 'left' critique of Munich and defended the settlement.[43] There was no evidence that any involvement in the Spain campaigns changed his mind.

Another example was the Rev. E.L. Allen who collected for Basque refugees and then helped form Morpeth SMAC. A Christian message pervaded Allen's letter on the Basque refugees in May 1937. Allen organised around the Basque issue with other local clergy including Canon J.J. Davies and Rev. J.M. Paulin. All three were also involved in Morpeth LNU, which certainly indicated a keen interest in foreign affairs, though it did not necessarily denote pro-Republicanism. While Morpeth LNU branch supported various Spanish aid funds, it was not pro-Republican as defined here, as it did not make a strong connection between this activity and opposition to Non-Intervention. Indeed, the branch was more interested in Abyssinia than Spain and supported Eden, the architect of Non-Intervention, but also, curiously, refused to condemn outright the government over Eden's resignation.[44]

After his death in early 1938, Canon Davies' replacement in the church and as LNU branch chairperson was Canon Baker.[45] Baker, too, did not appear to be a 'pro-Republican'. In supporting a 'sale of work' for the Tyneside foodship, Baker thought that 'this internecine warfare between brother and brother ought to have stopped months ago' and was 'indignant that it has been continued by people outside the territory of Spain', suggesting that he deplored support of either side.[46] The 'various opinions' individuals had on the conflict had 'no room in our gathering this afternoon, because what brings us here is sheer humanity'.[47] As well as allowing clergy to express their Christian charity in deeds, this kind of humanitarian activity also helped them to raise the profile of their Church and to demonstrate that it was actively concerned in the world, with only the faintest possibility of offending anyone politically.

There are similar questions of interpretation regarding the involvement of clergymen and local councillors in the *Linaria* Defence Committee. Its appeal was such that it *could* have involved pro-Republicans; pacifists opposed to the selling of war materials to either side in any war; humanitarians opposed to the waging of war on civilians; those who supported the rights of seamen to refuse to enter a war zone and even those who wanted to see Non-Intervention properly enforced. The Rev. Patton's subsequent involvement in the Basque Tynemouth hostel did nothing to elucidate his motives. The case for regarding this, and some other individual Spain campaign committees, as de facto popular fronts remains unproven. But it is clear that the two largest campaigns in the region at the highest activist level, the Basque refugees and the Tyneside foodship, did not fit the criteria for being regarded as such.

This was not how some contemporaries saw things. Arthur Blenkinsop, for example, certainly drew lessons about the relevance of the popular front from the experience of the Spanish aid campaigns. In announcing his support for Cripps' popular front memorandum in 1939, Blenkinsop argued that those who had campaigned recently on the foodship and other Spanish aid campaigns 'understand how effective such cooperation can be'.[48] Trevelyan and Jim Fyrth (who was also active at the time), amongst others, made similar links.[49] However, there was no evidence that the activists who were involved but not already favourable to the popular front regarded the Spanish aid campaigns as such. Given the total lack of discipline meted out to north-east Labour activists in these campaigns, it seems highly unlikely that the regional Labour leadership regarded them as 'backdoor' popular fronts either; if they did, they (like the national leaders) certainly did not consider them much of a threat.[50]

In fact, an important consideration both militating against regarding the Spanish aid campaigns as a de facto popular front and indicating a dearth of a specific form of politicisation was the abject failure of the explicitly popular front campaigns in the region. Indeed, this failure was most stark in early 1939 when Cripps' popular front campaign was running concurrently with the Tyneside foodship campaign. As in Birmingham, ostensibly objective conditions could hardly have been better: Cripps even launched his campaign in Newcastle.[51] But Cripps' campaign gained even fewer adherents in the region than the poorly supported United Peace Alliance in May 1938.[52] Labour popular fronters tended not to be heavily involved in the foodship campaign: concentrating their energies instead on the Cripps campaign and, possibly, because they were too 'political' for the foodship. But the more significant lack of cross-fertilisation came from the other side: the clergy and other 'humanitarians' in earlier Spanish aid campaigns who did not appear explicitly linked to any popular front agitation before, during or after the Cripps campaign. The failure of Cripps to galvanise support at a time when a good deal of the regional labour movement, as well as other individuals and institutions were mobilised for the foodship surely suggested that the one had no real relevance for the other, as far as most of those involved were concerned. If the north-east was representative, very few non-aligned activists came to support the popular front through involvement in the humanitarian Spanish aid campaigns. Equally, Labour activists' involvement in these campaigns clearly had little or no impact on attitudes to the popular front in most cases.[53]

The role of liberals in this debate is also significant. As discussed in chapter five, liberals of some type were involved at the higher levels in many of the campaigns. However, this and the pro-Republican policy of the Liberal Party had no palpable impact in making liberals more favourable to a popular front pact with Labour in these crucial times.[54] The overwhelming majority of mainstream liberal opinion in the north-east continued to regard Labour as the main enemy. Only members of the tiny CAPR were clearly prominently involved in both the Spanish aid and popular front campaigns and they had worked with the Labour left and CP within the TJPC on Spain since the outbreak of the war.

As might be expected, identifiable Conservatives in these campaigns were rarer. Indeed, many contemporaries claimed that individual Conservatives were not involved in collecting.[55] Frank Graham's more circumspect statement that 'even the Conservative Party weren't hostile' to the campaigns appeared borne out, to a very limited extent, by the Tyneside foodship campaign, at least.[56] But no north-east Conservative acted like the Duchess of Atholl in making a stand against their own government's foreign policy.

In the light of this evidence, Tom Buchanan's claim that 'there is no evidence that humanitarian work for Spain on a Popular Front basis translated into effective political action' requires consideration.[57] Here 'humanitarian work for Spain' is taken to mean fundraising for medical supplies and food and 'on a Popular Front basis' is understood as politically and socially diverse. Then, of course, is the meaning of 'effective political action'. Some Spanish aid committees, as has been seen, did engage in some 'political action', in holding meetings where Non-Intervention was attacked from a pro-Republican standpoint (and collections taken for humanitarian aid). Presumably, these meetings had some effect in propagating a pro-Republican understanding in the wider public. As discussed in chapter four, precisely what constituted 'effective political action' action against Non-Intervention was highly contentious. Furthermore, the anti-Non-Intervention agitation that did occur was definitely only a small part of what occurred under the banner of 'Aid Spain' and certainly far less than Fyrth depicted. Only a minority of elements of some of these campaigns organised meetings with 'speakers from all parties supporting the Republic' and most did not make a critique of Non-Intervention their most salient campaigning activity.[58] Clearly, the northeast showed that these campaigns certainly did not lead to effective political action in terms of building a popular front 'from below', regardless of how popular frontists involved saw them.[59]

In the north-east, all the Spanish aid campaigns that looked like de facto popular fronts used a predominantly humanitarian campaigning message and eschewed a pro-Republican rallying cry. This did not mean necessarily that a pro-Republican perspective did not unite the key organisers in these campaigns, but that this was not a prerequisite for involvement. The IBDWAC campaign could not frame its campaign in largely humanitarian language, no matter how much some may have tried. The campaign to support it was consequently limited in terms of organising to the CP, with support of some from the Labour left, the labour movement more generally in terms of donations to the fund, and CAPR members. There was no evidence of involvement from 'non-political' clergy or those to the right of the labour movement (apart from the CAPR) and this was no coincidence. In general, and certainly in the Basque and Tyneside foodship campaigns, it seems clear that the *appearance* of a popular front was the direct result of the *lack* of a clear pro-Republican campaigning message. Drake made similar observations on the Basque campaign in Birmingham.[60] Francis claimed that 'Spanish Aid Committees became a "popular front" in Welsh mining towns and villages, unofficially uniting not only working-class bodies but all who were hostile to fascism'.[61] If accurate, these committees clearly constituted a de facto popular front in South Wales, but even there it did not last.[62]

Those supporting the de facto popular front interpretation argued that, as the funds raised by the Spanish aid campaigns were directed to the Republic, those involved in and donating to the campaigns were (if not actual) unconscious (or 'objective') 'pro-Republicans'. But this was not enough to make their activities part of a de facto popular front. The popular front project demanded a definite, conscious stand. Many of the main activists involved did not make such a stand. Others did have a clear political outlook, but it was not favourable to even the basic popular front case. Indeed, while the de facto popular front criteria above have demanded only evidence of a pro-Republican perspective in Spanish aid activists, this was but a starting point for building a true popular front. For the popular front not only argued for the need to end pro-fascist Non-Intervention, it posited that this could only occur with a cross-party progressive alliance. While most Labour activists in the Spanish aid campaigns were pro-Republican, they were not, and certainly did not become, pro-popular front. In this sense, it was perhaps more accurate to describe institutions like Newcastle SMAC as, at best, proto popular fronts. The forming of a vibrant 'unofficial' de facto popular front of 'progressives' over the issue of aid to the Republic was difficult (and rare) enough. But even then, this was still many stages away from the formation of an electoral alliance with an agreed programme on domestic as well as foreign affairs. Thus, even if Fyrth's claim that the Spanish aid campaigns were the 'closest thing' to a popular front in Britain was valid, then, for the majority of grassroots activists, the British popular front was not even on the horizon in the late 1930s, let alone manifest and active throughout the land.[63]

Clearly the 'de facto popular front' paradigm as applied to the *entirety* of the Spanish aid campaigns was unsuitable for the north-east. Did the collection of signatures for the LNU's 'peace ballot' constitute a de facto popular front? North-east Communists certainly implied as much, discussing in their propaganda the coalition of Labourites, trade unionists, Communists and liberals who had worked 'side-by-side on the door-to-door canvas on Tyneside'.[64] However, again, this activity merely united all who opposed war, and that in itself was not the basis for any kind of political programme. As ILP MP John McGovern told an Ashington audience, 'every political party is desirous of peace; unfortunately some of their policies lead to war'.[65] Even pro-Republicanism demanded a little more political coherence than that. However, some north-east Spanish aid committees *did* look like LNU branches. Indeed, they sometimes came from the local LNU branch (Morpeth SMAC and Consett Tyneside food-ship subcommittees for example).[66] This model was more apt: LNU branches were not de facto popular fronts because the unifying idea was nothing more definite than support for the idea of the League of Nations. This wide remit accommodated almost all political perspectives: it was not even necessarily anti-fascist, let alone anti-Non-Intervention. A perhaps less predictable but arguably equally valid comparator was the British Legion. Blyth branch, for example, prided itself on its 'non-political' and democratic basis; just like many Spanish aid committees. Reminiscent of the lists of Tyneside foodship supporters, its officials included, amongst others, Viscount Ridley, Labour councillors and local clergymen.[67] Perhaps it, like some other north-east British Legion branches, donated to a Spanish aid cause but surely, no one would argue that this was evidence of a de facto popular front in action. Finally, there were normal charities, the methods and language of which many Spanish aid campaigns employed, along with some, like both R.A. and T.T. Anderson, who were charity or social workers themselves.

CP Motives, Roles, Gains and Losses and 'Political Space'

Another group of debates relate to the role of the Communist Party in the Spanish aid campaigns, the contested 'political space' and the benefits the party accrued from its activity. In response to Jim Fyrth's work, Tom Buchanan claimed that Communists should not necessarily be credited with the 'leading historical role' in Spanish aid activities.[68] Angela Jackson pointed out that 'No single party should be seen as the brains behind the campaigns. The disparate approaches of the different groups prevented the domination of one group over the others'.[69] This section will attempt to arrive at a more nuanced understanding of the CP's role, achievements and failures in the north-east Spain campaigns.

There were several ways in which Communists could seek to influence the agitation on Spain, even in a region like the north-east where the party was relatively weak. In November 1936, Communist George Aitken, re-porting on a 'tremendous campaign' on Spain, claimed that 'once we took the initiative and demonstrated' many influential official movement acti-vists 'were only too anxious to take the platform alongside of us'.[70] Cer-tainly, the initiative did appear to have come from Communists, or Com-munist influenced institutions, which took the earliest political stands on Spain in the region. Indeed, the first institution to act on Spain in the region was South Shields NUWM branch, which held a meeting on the issue on 26 July 1936 that attracted an audience of 'several hundred'.[71] The first demonstration in Newcastle taking Spain as its main theme came in mid-August 1936 and was Communist organised.[72] The CP took the early initiative in some other localities, too. In Birmingham, action came through the peace council, on which the CP was instrumental, while early events in Battersea echoed in some respects those in Newcastle.[73]

The CP also played a role in organising the second major demonstration on Spain in Newcastle a month later (though the ILP also claimed to have cooperated in organising it) and in the creation of Newcastle SMAC that emerged from it.[74] Aitken averred that the impetus for the 'big and growing Help Spain committee' in Newcastle came from approaches the CP 'made in a painstaking way' to local Labour and trade union officials.[75] It was likely that there was some form of communication between the CP and Newcastle trades council officials, including crypto-Communist Tom Aisbitt, over the issue. Whether the trades council would have acted in a similar way without Communist intervention is of course unknowable. But, as Buchanan pointed out, 'Communist historians have been much too ready to claim the credit for developments such as the rank-and-file movements which would probably have occurred, in some form, anyway'.[76] Indeed, as Aisbitt himself wrote: 'There are thousands of revolutionary Socialists in the trade union ranks who understood Socialism and worked and sacrificed for it before the Communist Party came into existence'.[77] Notwithstanding this, the CP clearly had a right to claim that it played a part in the establishment and running of this important SMAC, though the institution vital to its functioning was, and remained, the official trades council. The former needed the latter far more than vice-versa.

However, in the months after the fraught Labour conference of October 1936, local Labour Parties began increasingly to take action and this was not necessarily on the initiative of Communists, nor did it invariably lead to activity with them.[78] Notwithstanding this, there were examples of where Communist activity appeared to shame the Labour Party into a more publicly agitational stance. In Blyth, for example, it must have been more than mere coincidence that the Labour Party announced collections for Spain immediately after receiving severe criticism from the NUWM and Communist supporting left in the local press.[79] It is conceivable that this 'negative' or indirect kind of influence also played a part in official movement activity in places like Seaham and Gateshead; that official activists' local as well as political pride could not stomach being outdone by the pioneering actions in the region of Newcastle and North Shields activists, but this cannot be demonstrated.[80] Moreover, it was fairly clear that *positive* Communist influence played little or no part in the actions of these institutions.

Another claim about Communist leadership requires attention. Charlie Woods asserted that the Left Book Club (along with the CP) provided the 'driving force' of the Spanish aid campaigns in the region.[81] Certainly, LBC groups like Ashington, which held a talk on the background of the 'Spanish struggle' from a Mr. J.W. Fowler MA (a master at Bedlington secondary school), performed a, primarily internal, educative role.[82] However, the only evidence of sustained LBC involvement in north-east Spanish aid campaigns before 1939 (some groups did collect for the Basque refugees) was Durham LBC group, which established Durham SMAC.[83] There were also one-off meetings organised at national level to promote the LBC and support a cause like Spain. For example, Gollancz spoke at a LBC meeting in Sunderland in October 1937, making an appeal for 'relief' in China and Spain.[84] The LBC was also 'very active' in the Tyneside foodship campaign, but its role was a supportive one amongst many other groups rather than a leading one.[85] Similarly, Birmingham LBC groups – there were 12 by June 1937 – played little part in the Spanish aid campaigns.[86] That said, the LBC spawned local 'Theatre Guilds', which propagandised on the issue by performing plays such as *On Guard for Spain*.[87] Dave Atkinson, a Communist activist in Newcastle remembered a performance of the play that he was involved in receiving 'good reactions from political meetings and equally good reactions from cinema crowds who wouldn't have gone anywhere near a political meeting'.[88]

While the CP failed to engineer cooperation in most north-east localities over Spain, there were clearly some places in the early period where political space had opened up to a degree. However, the party faced two contradictory problems, both of which stemmed from its essential weakness and were exacerbated by the popular front policy. Firstly, the myriad of groupings the party was involved in served in some regards to detract from its *own* party activity on the issue. Secondly, the CP in some localities could not always maintain the organisational machinery capable of fully capitalising on the vacant political space.

A clear example of the former was in South Shields where the NUWM branch was a very quick starter on Spain, linking it with unemployment issues, like their South Wales counterparts.[89] In August, the town's CP branch also began agitating on the two issues, demanding arms for the 'Spanish democratic government'.[90] A week later, it held a meeting of 300 solely on Spain and important local Communist and NUWM activists kept the issue in the letters pages of the local press in September 1936. However, the CP and NUWM then seemed to cede the political space in the town to the TJPC, which held public meetings there on Spain and other foreign policy issues in autumn 1936. In early 1937, the CP was one of the three Unity Campaign parties agitating on Spain in South Shields. Apart from that, the party seemed to vanish for the crucial year of 1937, working through the SMAC. In later 1937, another CP 'satellite', the LBC, also began organising fundraising films nights and meetings for Tynemouth Basque hostel.

It was only in early 1938 that the CP and NUWM again began receiving publicity for their meetings on Spain.[91] That this occurred when the town's Labour Party also entered this political space in spring 1938 revealed that the niche carved out July–September 1936 had not been completely sacrificed. However, while Communists were involved in the SMAC, TJPC and LBC, their activities surely did not have the same level of impact for the party as meetings organised under its own, or even NUWM, auspices. While the Birmingham equivalent of the TJPC (the Council for Peace and Liberty: BCPL) reflected more credit on the CP than Labour, this did not seem to be the case in the north-east, where Labour left-wingers and CAPR activists were as or more prominent in it than Communists.[92] This must have been in part the result of a deliberate policy because, as Battersea Communists found, some Labour speakers would not talk under CP auspices, but would speak at a meeting under the SMAC banner.[93] However, as far as public perceptions were concerned, certainly, the CP did not maintain an obvious high profile as being active on Spain in the South Shields press from autumn 1936 to early 1938. Arguably, it could have made more political capital out of a favourable situation in South Shields than it did, as a result of its own, albeit partial and unsustained policy of involvement in satellite institutions into which it deliberately attempted to disappear. It also did not criticise local Labour for its inactivity, though the desire to build links with Labour did not prevent Blyth Communists, for example, from criticising local Labour inactivity on the issue.

While Blyth NUWM waited until after the October 1936 Hunger March before acting on Spain, as regards the local press, it still made an earlier and more publicly energetic response than local Labour. Between November and December 1936, it and the CP organised a concert that had a 'large attendance', and made collections of foodstuffs door-to-door and at a stall in the market place.[94] In early 1937, Blyth Labour began jostling with the NUWM for space in the pages of the local press over Spain and the NUWM then disappeared altogether as a public active force after August 1937 as a result of its demise. While the CP had a strong electoral following in part of Blyth, it did not appear to have the organisational wherewithal to continue the NUWM's fundraising work to the same degree. Indeed, somewhat ironically, the issue of Spain itself, and particularly Bob Elliott's death in the International Brigade, had contributed to, or thrown into sharp relief, these local weaknesses.[95]

Notwithstanding this, Communists *were*, and continued to be, involved and influential in many Spanish aid campaigns. In one respect, the CP was influential in the formation of local Spanish aid committees as it had played a key part in initiating national committee that inspired them. There were detectable Communists in at least five north-east SMACs: in the cases of North Shields (the second established in the region), South Shields and Blaydon the evidence is sufficient to suggest that Communists were the main or sole instigators.[96] The SMACs with more identifiable CP influence tended to come the earliest and last the longest except where, as in the case of North Shields SMAC, the key activist (Nell Badsey) moved into another arena of Spain work. While it is impossible to be certain whether Communists were involved and at what levels in the majority of SMACs, partly due to the policy of 'invisibility', it seems unlikely that they played a direct role in every north-east Spanish aid committee. The picture was similar in South Wales, though there the CP appeared to have been swamped in the SMACs, rather than to have 'disappeared' itself voluntarily.[97]

In other campaigns, the CP in general, or individual Communists, performed central roles. The British Youth Foodship and IBDWAC campaigns were Communist initiated and controlled and examples of the former; the *Linaria* campaign and Tynemouth Basque hostel examples of the latter. The CP was also influential in workplaces like Armstrong's where most VIAS work occurred.[98] The Communist influenced TJPC initiated the Tyneside foodship campaign and some party members overtly supported it. But it was clear that Communists numerically constituted only a small part of this mass campaign (though it is likely that the party dedicated considerable resources to it). The mention of CP involvement in the Ashington foodship effort was very rare for this particular campaign, even with the extensive press coverage it received.[99]

In replying to Buchanan's critique, Fyrth claimed that Communists were not dominant in 'Aid Spain' as a whole, but they were dominant, or prominent, in some campaigning organisations and active in many.[100] Certainly, the personal dedication and commitment of some north-east Communist activists like Nell Badsey and Alex Robson was astounding. While Fyrth's latter two claims were evident for the north-east, the question of 'dominance' and, more importantly, how the CP used it, was problematic. Firstly, the CP often used its influence or dominance in many of these campaigns to help to bring about an external humanitarian, neutral campaigning message in contravention to its own strongly pro-Republican position. Thus, it sacrificed a good deal of possible external influence it might have exercised in advancing party policies. Yet the influence or dominance it exerted also had some strange internal effects. In Newcastle SMAC, for example, the party was clearly influential if not necessarily dominant. Yet, as its Communist secretary Tom O'Byrne announced in July 1937, no member of Newcastle SMAC was allowed to introduce their 'particular brand of political opinion' into the committee's workings.[101] At the least, the CP must have accepted this internal policy if it had not actually promoted or supported it. Effectively, in Newcastle SMAC, the CP had hobbled itself, or allowed itself to be hobbled. Paradoxically, presumably in the pursuit of the chimera of a popular front, the CP's influence had not been employed to ensure that it exercised internal (or external) influence. This internal model of 'no party politics' was present in the Tynemouth Basque hostel committee and, at least some, Tyneside foodship subcommittees.

Similar considerations of building united or popular fronts confused the situation elsewhere. In Battersea, for example, the 'united front strategy' meant that the CP did not 'want the [local] peace council to be dominated by one organisation'.[102] Thus, the north-east CP at grassroots seemed keener to run the Spain campaigns by not running them, as it were. However, this policy of using influence in favour of humanitarianism rather than pro-Republicanism in Spain campaigning committee appeals and of negating possibilities for exercising internal influence did not always prevail, for example within Blaydon SMAC. In this context Fyrth's claims of Communist altruism in these campaigns appear partly substantiated. Yet they were also, as Buchanan claimed, in some regards disingenuous. Clearly, the issue must have actuated Communist activists, but some, at least, must also have hoped that their activity would benefit their party directly, in spite – or perhaps even because – of the lengths the party had gone to in order to ensure that this *did not* happen.

The popular front policy appeared to demand that CP activists become involved in all Spanish aid campaigns regardless of their nature and at any political price. But it also brought another unexpected drawback. In late 1937 and early 1938, the situation looked promising for Communists, as much of the hitherto inactive element of the regional movement, especially at constituency and extra-constituency levels, began to move into essentially the same 'political space' on Spain as the CP: all agreed on the need to demonstrate against Non-Intervention. However, somewhat ironically, much of the official regional movement, with its desire to contemplate industrial direct action, then swept on to a more radical political space; one which the CP was likely to have occupied before adopting popular front policy. The north-east CP thus found itself, albeit momentarily, almost alone in its 'moderate' advocacy of the Republic. In attempting to garner support from those to the right of the labour movement, the CP sacrificed potential policies that, at this juncture, could have resonated with a substantial element of the regional organised working-class. Indeed, the party had abandoned pursuit of its 'natural' militant working-class constituency at the very point when it perhaps had the best opportunity to capitalise on regional rank-and-file official movement feeling since the end of the 1926 lockout.

As a result of these considerations, it seems unlikely that Communists gained much respectability in the public eye by working in the humanitarian campaigns as they usually remained unknown by their party label, their achievements unheralded.[103] Viewed from the 'outside', it was often not obvious that Communists *were* involved in, indeed sometimes crucial to, specific Spain campaigns. Wilf Jobling, for example, was a behind-the-scenes operator rather than a Blaydon SMAC official and his role in initiating it probably would have remained undisclosed had Steve Lawther not written a tribute to him after his death in Spain.[104] The important role the CP played in the formation and running of Newcastle SMAC was by no means clear to those on the outside. A key individual on the committee, Tom Aisbitt, kept his CP affiliation secret out of necessity, though he did appear on Communist platforms.[105] But the early Newcastle SMAC press appeals were always clear that the trades council inaugurated the committee.[106] None of the Communists who acted in the *Linaria* Defence Committee or who spoke at its functions except Robson himself, who had stood as a CP candidate locally, was stated publicly as such. Like Robson, Badsey's politics were already known by some in her locality, which explained some of the local hostility to the Basque hostel in Tynemouth.[107]

However internally too the likely result of the 'no party politics' rule was that the party affiliations of many Communists in the Spanish aid campaigns remained unknown even to those who they worked with on a regular basis who were not already Communists or party sympathisers. Some Communist activists *must* have gained a degree of 'respect' for their committed involvement in these campaigns. But this was more likely to have been accorded them as individuals and as such the party itself could not hope to benefit greatly. Indeed, it is arguable that individual Communists were likely to have achieved an apparent 'respectability' as a direct result of their party membership *not* being widely known.

That 'respect' for individual Communist activists whose party affiliations were often unknown did not bring recruits was all too obvious to Communist district leader Hymie Lee in March 1939. Commenting on the situation in the north-east, Lee complained that: 'in all the mass activity we are hiding the face of the party. Communists are working everywhere but they don't show that they are Communists'.[108] Lee then noted that: 'there is no feeling about the party growing'.[109] There was almost certainly a causal link between these two observations, the latter being borne out by the figures: the north-east CP membership decreased by 10 per cent (50 individuals) in early 1939.[110] This was a real blow, as the region already had a low membership, even by CP standards. In August 1930, just over 5 per cent of the party's membership was in the North-east District. This proportion was less than 4 per cent in August 1938 (550 members) and under 3 per cent by June 1939, and the YCL was proportionately weaker again.[111]

Similar problems dogged the party elsewhere. In Birmingham, most of the initiatives on Spain throughout the duration of the conflict came from the CP, Communist backed BCPL and later the CP and LBC. Yet all the agitation on Spain had no palpable effect on the party's electoral support.[112] Thus, while Len Edmondson's comment that the CP was adept at times for 'claiming credit for what others did' broadly stood, in the north-east Spanish aid campaigns it did not, at the time, claim the credit it was due.[113] These observations also illustrate a failure of the Spanish aid campaigns to politicise in another specific way: that of bringing recruits to the CP. The district party's inability during the Tyneside foodship campaign even to maintain its already low membership was an indictment of the policy of energetic but unseen involvement in the humanitarian, so-called popular front Spanish aid campaigns.

Labour Movement Activists, Local Parties; 'Official'/'Unofficial'

Finally, there is the discussion about the nature of the relationship between the Labour Party and its activists to the Spanish aid campaigns at grassroots. Tom Buchanan wrote that popular frontist claims that 'the institutions of labour consigned themselves to the fringes of a broad social movement' inverted the real relationship, as 'the very existence of support for organisations like Spanish Medical Aid reflected the continuing strength of labour's institutions'.[114] All authorities accept that Labour activists were driven to work with forces outside the movement and that they did so as individuals. This was obscured 'because neither the labour movement nor its rivals were willing to recognise publicly that there was no common humanitarian effort for the Spanish people and that there were, in fact, fundamental divisions between them in terms of methods of organisation and objectives'.[115]

In light of the evidence of the north-east grassroots, this perspective requires modification. Firstly, as illustrated in chapter two, Labour activists could act on Spain before the national party officially adopted the anti-Non-Intervention policy within their institutions in several different ways. Some parties even created new ad hoc institutions and it was inaccurate to describe all of these simply as 'unofficial committees'.[116] Gateshead SMAC, for example, drew inspiration from an unofficial campaign form but was most accurately described as an 'official' institution as it contained solely Labour activists whose local party sponsored it officially. Likewise, official labour movement activists in Wallsend also showed that they could create and staff 'new' structures exclusively with no need for Communist initiative or participation.

Secondly, even where official and non-movement activists worked together on Spain in ad hoc institutions, the former did not necessarily do so as *individuals* who had been *forced* into organisations and activities entirely created and defined by Communists. This was the case for official activists in Newcastle SMAC, the organisational backbone of which was the trades council. Indeed, as far as the very loyal City Labour Party was concerned, Newcastle SMAC, on which it was officially represented, was a 'subcommittee to assist the Spanish workers [that] was set up by the trades council'.[117] It was unclear whether South Shields LP&TC regarded Newcastle SMAC as official but it was striking that one of its few campaigning acts in the early part of the war was to send a delegate to a Newcastle SMAC public meeting in January 1937.[118] This also suggests that the divisions between official and unofficial institutions and campaigns at grassroots level were often vague or perhaps non-existent, even for the loyal. In all these cases, national Labour torpor had led elements of the local movement into a form of activity that involved the creation of campaigning institutions that were linked directly with their own official party institutions. In this respect, then, these activists were not forced outside their own institutions as individuals in order to act on Spain. That the more official movement SMACs did not tend to last much into the period after autumn 1937, when the national movement adopted the anti-Non-Intervention policy, suggests that they were responses to this policy in the first period and simply not deemed necessary when it altered. Instead, there then came the unenviable task of trying to get the movement to act concertedly and effectively on its policy.

But what of the campaigns that originated from clearly unofficial institutions nationally or locally? In terms of financial support, from the DMA down, the vast majority of regional labour movement institutions donated to both the official and unofficial campaigns.[119] The TGWU district was unusual in differentiating between official and unofficial campaigns in January 1939. Even then, it suggested that the Tyneside foodship and NJCSR apply to the ISF, which it was donating to, for a grant.[120] In February 1937, an attempt to get Ashington Miners' Federation to favour the official over the unofficial campaigns was defeated on a vote.[121] On the 'political' side, the only institution that donated consistently to official funds exclusively was Newcastle City Labour Party.[122] Clearly, the 'careful delineations of "official" and "unofficial" activities was largely lost on the rank-and-file', not necessarily out of ignorance but more because grassroots activists, on the whole, were not concerned by these supposed divisions; ones that local factors had blurred almost to invisibility.[123] For example, the broadly official movement Dawdon SMAC asked the Spanish ambassador in London advice as to where to send money it raised. He replied listing three possible funds and the SMAC chose the ISF; 'but why should he quibble as to which fund as long as we understand that we are relieving the stress and pain of the stricken people of Spain'.[124] Other wholly official movement SMACs, like New Herrington, sent money raised to the ISF, but Gateshead SMAC, conversely, supported unofficial funds.[125]

Indeed, the 'local' was a more significant factor in determining grass-roots labour movement support. That the destination of unofficial funds was often local rather than national in the first instance (i.e. money went to the local SMAC rather than the Labour Party's national fund; although in practice the SMAC would often merely forward the money to a national fund) made them more attractive to some potential donors. However, the 'local' was also a factor in determining which unofficial funds received donations. In Ashington, for example, official institutions like Woodhorn lodge donated to Ashington SMAC after its creation and stopped supporting its Newcastle equivalent.[126] This must have been in part because activists in these institutions knew who was operating the local campaign; at times, it would have been their own lodge members, or even themselves.

In addition, the unofficial campaigns did not invariably monopolise the 'local': when the DMA began operating as the ISF agent in January 1937, it suddenly brought this official campaign to County Durham in a more tangible way.[127] This action and the evidence of local labour movement institutions' donations suggests that the north-east, certainly, was not particularly guilty of favouring the unofficial over the official (ISF) funding, as much as they recognised this division, contrary to Citrine's claims.[128] Indeed, somewhat perversely, there was at least one instance of Citrine forwarding money sent to him by an official movement institution in the north-east that was raised at a Spain meeting it organised to the national SMAC![129]

In terms of direct involvement in institutions that did not directly originate in the local official movement, the relationships varied. Thus, in South Shields SMAC for example, some Labour activists were involved as individuals rather than as representatives of their party. In the Tyneside foodship, in contrast, it is clear that support came in many localities from the Labour Party as a *local institution* rather than from individual Labour activists. Several women's Labour sections organised collections and other fundraising events for the foodship under their own auspices. Seaham CLP went as far as to instruct its LLPs to raise funds for the foodship and at least five LLPs all duly did so. It is possible that Morpeth CLP did so too, given that at least two of its women's sections (Bedlington and Choppington) acted.[130] Even the inactive Tynemouth Labour Party donated a collection made at a Cripps public meeting to the foodship.[131]

Some parties went even further. Newcastle City Labour Party, which was so keen to donate only to official campaigns, appointed delegates to Newcastle foodship committee meetings. Just like the representatives it had on Newcastle SMAC from the outset, these delegates kept the party in detailed touch with the grassroots running of the campaign, and this despite the campaign's originator, the TJPC, being an unofficial institution with rather tenuous links with the official movement.[132] All this meant that the official/unofficial divide was blurred indeed. It also meant that Labour activists actually had many choices, not only to act on internal official funds and (more so after 1937) demonstrations and conferences; they could also support and campaign on other initiatives that did not come from within the official movement but which often involved official activists. Moreover, they could often do this as a part of their official local party activity. In this respect, all these activities were in some regards complementary. The Tyneside foodship was a prime example of a 'common humanitarian effort for the Spanish people'. Furthermore, within this campaign at least, there was *no* fundamental division between the official labour movement (grassroots institutions and activists) and others 'in terms of methods of organisation and objectives' (unless, of course, the CP aimed to form a popular front out of the campaign).[133]

The case of the north-east suggests that Buchanan's claim that 'Rank-and-file members who worked for "unofficial" organisations often did so in a spirit of rebellion, or at least alienation, from a labour movement campaign that had been devised to restrict their political expression' also requires qualification on two counts.[134] Firstly, as suggested by the discussion above, the levels of alienation cannot have been great as many regional movement activists supported their own party's or union's campaigns (as well as others). Furthermore, regardless of their national leaders' desires, local activists did have room for manoeuvre within the movement and often found means to give voice to their political expression on Spain.

Secondly, far from being liberatory for Labour activists, many of the unofficial campaigns did not provide a qualitatively different experience than that available inside the labour movement. While the unofficial campaigns did mobilise activists to a greater degree in some regards, the kind of work most ended up doing such as collecting door-to-door was more drudgery than anything else, hardly inspiring activity, and differing only in intensity from what sections of the official movement did at grassroots. This offers a reason why Labour activists and institutions at grassroots could often move between and support official and unofficial campaigns almost without noticing the differences. The reality of their praxis (as well as their personnel) meant that, in many cases, there hardly *were* any differences to notice. However, there was one potential difference: if Labour activists followed the lead of the key organisers in humanitarian campaigns like the Tyneside foodship, then their political expression was *actually restricted* as the campaign was not talked about in 'pro-Republican' terms.

As Buchanan wrote, the Labour leaders' claims that their rank-and-file did the Communists' work for them were misleading.[135] This was partly because it presupposed that the Spanish aid campaigns were somehow the property of the Communists. CP activists, too, sometimes made similar implications. Charlie Woods, for example, claimed that 'individual members of the Labour Party at grassroots level became actively associated with the ['aid Spain'] campaign'.[136] While the CP was in the forefront of *some forms* of Spanish aid activity, the relationship between what were often its initiatives and what then occurred did not entitle it to make these claims of ownership. Trevelyan described the relationship somewhat differently. In March 1939, he claimed that when Transport House backed Non-Intervention, local labour had to act alone. But this proved 'no difficulty' and there was 'almost complete cooperation' in the north-east.[137] In a speech arguing for Cripps, Trevelyan was implying that these campaigns demonstrated the utility of the popular front. However, implicit also was the image of the labour movement at grassroots acting on its own initiatives, with cooperation on Spain between it and other groupings (including Communists, whether consciously or not) emerging sporadically but organically when the national movement refused to show the way. This, rather than an emphasis on the CP making all the telling interventions, seems to provide a more accurate model for what occurred in the Spanish aid campaigns in the north-east. In this respect, Fyrth's claim that 'Aid Spain' was not apart from and in competition with the efforts of labour movement activists and their institutions at local level seems substantiated, at least as far as the majority of activists were concerned.[138]

Certainly, the 'picture of a labour movement paralysed by anti-communism needs to be modified'.[139] While many north-east local official movement institutions and activists remained to varying degrees hostile to the CP and its projects like the popular front, this did not prevent a sizeable proportion of them from cooperating with Communists on many of these campaigns whether they knew it or not (as well as occasionally creating their own non-Communist institutions). From the Labour perspective, if local official institutions wished to raise humanitarian aid for Spain they could do so in their own branch and locality and, if there was a vibrant externally organised campaign going on that seemed more effective, there was often no obvious reason not to support it financially or with active involvement. Armed with this pragmatic attitude, considerations of control did not necessarily come into play. Where there was apathy or weakness in the local labour movement, especially, then cooperation was often the obvious choice. (The generally uncooperative attitude of Tynemouth Labour seems exceptional in the north-east). It was clear that, for the most part, there was little paranoia in official north-east movement ranks about the possibility of working with Communists or other groups or individuals on the ground. It was this nonchalant attitude towards cooperation with external groups that was the true testament of the strength and adaptability of official movement institutions at grassroots level.

CONCLUSION

The consequences of the popular frontist left's view that the conflict in Spain and the popular front at home were inextricably bound, were immense. While the popular front was certainly 'an irrelevance' as far as much of the labour movement were concerned, it was very relevant to explaining a good deal of the politics – or lack thereof – of the Spanish aid campaigns and the reasons for the lack of a serious, sustained and coherent challenge to the movement's national leadership over the issue of action on Spain.[1] It is clear that in many ways, the popular front, as it applied to the thinking and praxis of the Labour left and CP, was actually inimical to providing the Spanish Republic with what it needed to fight Franco. Essentially, the Republic needed arms. As a Spanish anarchist, León Filipe, was prevented from telling a European labour movement congress on Spain in Paris in spring 1937: 'We Spaniards are greatly thankful for your charity and the lint and ointments which you send us to repair Don Quixote's wounds; but we should be much more thankful if you were to outfit him with a new lance and an up-to-date shield".[2] The best way of procuring arms was for the Republic to be able to buy them on the open market; i.e. for Non-Intervention to be lifted. As Lt. Comm. Fletcher MP said at a Seaham CLP meeting in January 1939: 'when history came to be written, if the Spanish government lost it would be said that it was not Italian and German intervention which finally turned the scale, but the economic intervention of this country, under the Non-Intervention committee'.[3] Before this time, too, this message was sometimes clear from the public platform. The resolution passed at a Unity Campaign meeting at Marsden Miners' Hall in March 1937, for example, demanded that 'immediate steps be taken to help the Spanish people to get the guns and materials to enable them to inflict a crushing defeat upon the Fascist armies now invading Spain'.[4]

Yet, in various ways, aspects of the popular front served, over time, to divert activists from this simple truth. Those who fought in Spain from the north-east certainly did not represent a popular front in terms of their social and political backgrounds: they were drawn largely from the CP's sphere in the NUWM. However, the idea of the popular front's uniquely fashioned ability to combat fascism contributed to them not agitating for the end of Non-Intervention as they might have on the home front. When, in January 1939, ex-brigader Frank Graham argued for 'Arms for Spain' and opposition to the National Government, he continued: 'If I thought that we could save Spain without introducing politics into it then I would certainly refrain from doing so'.[5] The desire to avoid introducing an audience to 'politics' from the platform of a Labour Party meeting – a party that was also opposed to Non-Intervention – was symptomatic of the kind of rhetoric that the popular front had come to demand from its left-wing advocates, and certainly in regard to much of the activity on Spain.

By this time, Graham had spent many weeks at home campaigning on the issue, much of it in the strictly humanitarian based Tyneside foodship campaign. Indeed, in this respect the issue of Spain (humanitarian aid) distracted from Spain (the campaign against Non-Intervention). There was so much humanitarian campaigning going on during the time of the foodship that there was barely anything overtly political in terms of pro-Republic, anti-Non-Intervention demonstrations. Did activists in the foodship campaign even want to change government foreign policy on Spain? Some did, but many others, especially in this, the last and in some regards most impressive campaign, did not.

In one respect, the negative influence of the popular front; i.e. the fear of it, may have yielded some limited benefits for the Republic's cause. Certainly, the County Durham demonstrations on the issue in June 1938 came in the context of a circular against the popular front. Yet, here Spain did not feed the popular front but distracted from it. But, like the national leadership, the regional leadership of the County Durham movement must have known that they had nothing to fear from the popular front.[6]

A crucial problem for popular fronters was not being able firstly to determine whether to deploy the popular front as a strategy or a tactic, and, secondly, if a strategy, what was it a strategy for? If it was a tactic as applied to many of the Spanish aid campaigns; i.e. to eliminate as much as possible any revealing signs of partisanship in order to maximise the money raised, then there was a prima facie case in its favour. However, the tactic failed in that money appeared for the most part to come from those who were likely to have been pro-Republic and have donated anyway, with those hostile, and the middle-classes in general, broadly remaining so. (This changed to a degree in the Tyneside foodship campaign, partly because it was obvious to many of its opponents by this time that the Republic could not win).

However, as a strategy for helping the Republic, the popular front was clearly counterproductive in this regard, as almost all of the politics of the Republic's struggle had been eliminated from most of the campaigns (and certainly the Tyneside foodship campaign, the most successful). In this respect, many of the Spanish aid campaigns bore comparison with the Jarrow March. The non-political march was tremendously successful in securing mainstream publicity, but in achieving this it had sacrificed its political message almost completely, to the extent of allowing Conservatives to become involved and even to emerge appearing as though they cared.[7] In both cases, Faust had done fairly badly on the deal.

While the Tyneside foodship campaign, at least, mobilised impressive numbers of people, and reached many others (in terms of a charity asking for help), it and certain other Spanish aid campaigns' contribution to 'antifascism' was more questionable. Certainly, a good deal of the rhetoric emerging from these campaigns was *not capable* of doing much to 'awaken public opinion to the ineffectiveness of the National Government's foreign policy, and to the implications of the spread of Fascism'.[8] Indeed, to a significant extent, the neutral humanitarian language of these campaigns served to detract from even a simple 'fascism against democracy' understanding of what was going on in Spain. Clearly, in the case of these Spanish aid campaigns, it was not, contrary to what Cripps told Northumberland miners in 1937, 'worth sacrificing everything to preserve unity in the face of united capitalism'.[9]

If these campaigns *were* the popular front in action, then it was not an honest policy: it deceived some of those who donated (admittedly probably very few) who genuinely thought that the aid went impartially to both sides. It also deceived those making these claims, in that they convinced themselves that their actions were having some form of significant political impact. As secretary of Ashington ILP branch Chas Cole said 'it was far better to do a little work honestly than an impressive looking amount of work and not be particular about its honesty'.[10]

Advocacy of the popular front within the labour movement also distracted many on the left from the Republic's cause. The popular frontist left used the situation of Spain as an example of where the labour movement was going wrong at that moment, and asserted that Spain could only be saved by a popular front. Thus, the popular frontist left did not particularly engage the Labour leadership *specifically* on the issue of Spain within the movement: it invariably became an argument about the popular front.

Somewhat ironically, when popular fronters got their labour movement debate on the popular front, they often did not seem to want it. Certainly, Cripps did not take his chance to debate the issue when defending himself at the 1939 Whitsun Labour conference.[11] Likewise, speaking at a Wansbeck CLP meeting, while in the process of being expelled from the Labour Party over the issue, C.P. Trevelyan complained to his wife that he could not keep the debate 'to the expulsion of Cripps. The debate would go on to the merits of the Popular Front'.[12] Presumably, on these occasions popular fronters knew that their cause was not actually that popular amongst the rank-and-file, and recognised that their arguments had been, and remained, unconvincing.

Associating the Republic's cause with the popular front project within the party played into the leadership's hands as the battleground shifted from the issue of Spain, where many rank-and-filers did want more action; to the popular front, which never had anything like a majority following within the constituencies. Due to the popular front's association with the CP, the leadership could easily play the anti-Communist card, neutralising most objections in an instant. The national leadership thus pointed to the association of some activities on Spain with popular fronters as an excuse not to act. Nevertheless, this *was* simply an excuse. The leadership knew that it had far more to fear from its own membership who were not popular fronters but who wanted more concerted action on Spain. For left popular fronters, the campaigns around Spain served to show how the cooperation they advocated might work in practice. But this was a mirage, and must have been recognised as such by Labour leaders, at least those at a regional level.

Alternatively, was the popular front a tactic for *political* campaigning; i.e. to build as broad-based a movement as possible around an issue? It was certainly viable for this, if only those on the popular frontist left had not insisted on rigidly applying the humanitarian message in many of the Spanish aid campaigns. True, any campaign with a clear pro-Republican message was unlikely to have attracted the patronage of figures like C.V.H.

Vincent, but surely, the Republic could do without friends like him. Any such campaign would have been based on a 'fascism against democracy' discourse and been able to employ only democratic methods, but it would still have been something akin to a popular front: i.e. a mass cross-party, cross-class alliance with a specific 'political' aim. However, with a handful of exceptional cases – some (a very few) of the Spanish aid campaigns that demonstrated about Non-Intervention to a limited extent – this popular front pro-Republican movement did not exist in the north-east.

Perhaps the popular front was best understood as a strategy for achieving parliamentary power by building a progressive alliance? If so, this would detract from the campaign for the Republic as it demanded the building of close links on a sufficient number of foreign and domestic issues in order to create a programme that could be put before the electorate. Ending Non-Intervention no longer became the sole issue around which to act; it was only one of very many that needed to be agreed on. Furthermore, it postponed the possibility of doing much about Non-Intervention until a general election had been held and won. Indeed, Labour popular fronters like G.D.H. Cole criticised Cripps' memorandum for weakening the popular front's case by depicting it as an electoral strategy rather than as a way of immediately mobilising public opinion against government foreign policy. This allowed the NEC to retort that Cripps was 'surrendering socialism'.[13] Thus, the short-term goal of saving Spain was likely to be lost from sight in the wrangling over agreeing a programme for the longer-term.

As a strategy for achieving parliamentary power, the popular front demanded an even more strictly constitutional approach; there could be no talk of industrial direct action and other unconstitutional action to force the government to lift Non-Intervention if the force making the demands was planning to take power constitutionally. In this respect, popular fronters and some non-popular fronters in the labour movement agreed. W.J. Stewart MP, for example, told a 'Spanish relief fund' meeting that there was 'no greater crime' than preventing the Spanish government from getting arms, and commented on the need to get people in the Commons who 'understand the workers' position'.[14] However, other Labour parliamentarians like Nye Bevan recognised 'There was only one way to bring Tories to reason – by trouble outside'.[15] Yet the popular front only allowed for certain kinds of 'trouble outside': the acceptable forms of protest such as demonstrations that the government could, and did, ignore (as in the well-publicised case of the Jarrow marchers).

Some popular fronters claimed that their cause was both an electoral alliance *and* a way of creating a mass movement against government support for Non-Intervention. But these were two quite distinct projects that demanded different types of language, institutional forms and levels of political understanding and commitment in order to work. In the event, popular fronters' efforts often fell between the two poles; they certainly did not achieve a campaigning movement for the Republic against Non-Intervention (due to the humanitarianism). The extent to which the popular front (in terms of Liberal-Labour cooperation) could have worked at a parliamentary election was a separate question. Even ILPer Fenner Brockway argued that the popular front was a useful temporary tactic for purely electoral purposes in countries like France and Spain with proportional second ballot voting systems.[16] In the north-east, certainly, a 'progressive' electoral alliance was highly unlikely. However, Martin Pugh has shown that in some constituencies local popular front pacts were likely in the event of a 1939 or 1940 general election.[17] But these fundamentally entailed cooperation between Labour and Liberals, the Communists were only an annoyance and generally regarded as a hindrance in electoral terms. Still, they undermine Fyrth's claim that the Spanish aid campaigns were the closest thing to a popular front in Britain. It seems a popular front as defined as a progressive electoral alliance of Labour and Liberal was viable in some localities. The Spanish aid campaigns were perhaps the closest that *the CP* came to involvement in a British popular front, which illustrated merely how politically isolated the party remained, in spite of all its post-1935 efforts.

Some subsequent commentators on the popular front have gone even further and claimed not only was it the right way to defeat fascism, but that it was also the correct strategy for achieving socialism.[18] This seems untenable. Certainly, the evidence suggests that very few were brought to a pro-Republican viewpoint by their involvement in the predominantly humanitarian Spanish aid campaigns. If they could not achieve even this limited form of consciousness, then to expect some to convert to Communism seems to be asking too much. Indeed, the popular front has taken on an almost mythic quality for some commentators who were active at the time. It is treated as a kind of political nirvana, a golden age when the CP had all the answers; it was apparently the 'most fruitful period in the history of the British left and of the Communist Party in particular'.[19]

Indeed, in much of this treatment the unhelpful reality that the Republic lost, and did so in large part because of the British government's foreign policy, seems almost forgotten. But lose the Republic did, and the extent to which the British left (and the British people) had, in Jim Atkinson's words, 'the blood of these [Franco's] victims on our own heads' as a result of the political choices made, was, and remains, an important matter for debate.[20]

Michael Foot wrote: 'Maybe the Popular Front was always a desperate, forlorn bid. But what other card in the Socialist hand was there left to play? Better this than the infuriating inertia of official Labour in the face of calamity'.[21] John Saville commented similarly.[22] Yet there *were* other choices between the 'unpopular front' and inertia.[23] Indeed, advocacy of the popular front actually helped to bolster that inertia, certainly when it came to the mainstream movement's role on Spain. The labour leadership certainly could have done a good deal more than it did. But poor, uninspired and short-sighted leadership was no excuse for failings on the part of much of the left, which was awestruck by the Soviet achievement and keen to support any policy that carried the international Communist movement's endorsement.

Clearly, a strong case could be made that the British labour movement leaders would never have supported strike action as in 1920 or 1926; or perhaps, that the British working-class was too conservative to have gone along with such a policy; or that it might have done, but not in 1936 when so much of the (minority organised) working-class was apathetic, its fighting spiriting crushed by defeat in 1926 and the depression and unemployment that followed.[24] Even in South Wales, Hywel Francis' work suggests that the miners were not in a position to challenge the government with a political strike, even had the CP encouraged them to try rather than scuppered their efforts. Yet much of the Labour left made little concerted effort to force the issue of what to do about Spain within the labour movement without accompanying it with calls for a popular front. At the same time a good degree of the popular fronters' efforts were dedicated not to forming grassroots alliances within the movement to push a call for radical action against Non-Intervention on Spain, but rather in attempting to build the illusive 'People's Front from below' by inspiring essentially humanitarian campaigns.[25] These collected, in some instances, impressive sums of money, but nothing like what the labour movement could raise if it put its mind to it. Furthermore, the energy spent and the political sacrifices made in no way justified the sums raised which could at best help to feed a starving population, or poorly armed soldiers, while the Republic succumbed to a far better armed and supported enemy.

As with the Spanish Republic, the popular front policy, as it applied to activism on Spain, did not do much for the CP in the north-east. The district party recruited during the period, but it remained in strictly numerical terms far weaker than it had been even in September 1927, when the majority of the miners' lockout recruits had come and gone. The calibre of north-east recruits to the party after July 1936 was unclear, though, unlike pre-1935 members, many were unlikely to have regarded the popular front as merely a temporary expedient to defeat fascism in the short-term. What was clear was the calibre of those the party had lost, both permanently and in the shorter-term, in Spain. Permanently, it lost two well-known activists and several other committed militants, all of whom were irreplaceable for a party of such scant means. But it also lost many more activists, especially from the NUWM, momentarily, and the decline of the NUWM in this period must have had a deep relationship with it losing many of its dedicated members.

Many of those who went to Spain had inspiring and life changing experiences. Many, of course, did not return. Of those who did, some then dedicated their lives to the CP. Others remained dedicated to the memory of what happened in Spain, but could not reconcile themselves to what the CP then did in the short-term (the Hitler-Stalin pact and then declaring the war with Germany an 'imperialist war' that was to be opposed) or the longer-term (Hungary 1956, Prague 1968, and so forth). Their families often suffered from losing loved ones, or having the main breadwinner return incapacitated. A handful within brigaders' families may have been politicised to a degree, but others were angered and alienated by their ordeals at the hands of complex and confused bureaucratic structures that often could not tell them for long periods of time if their loved ones were alive or dead.

At home, while the sacrifice was 'respected', it did not automatically translate into any kind of improved relations with Labour. Indeed, if anything the sacrifices that Communist activists were prepared to make in Spain merely served to underscore the vast differences in political outlook between them and many in the mainstream of the Labour Party. The party tried, as well, to engage Labour at home on solidarity efforts but these almost always came to nothing where there was not already a history of co-operation between the parties (in places like Blaydon). Indeed, the issue of solidarity work was as likely to cause division, especially when popular fronters attacked the official movement for doing very little on Spain. On occasion, these attacks appeared to stimulate official activity, but this was never with the 'aggressor' party. When it did happen, the CP had undermined its own case that labour would not act alone and that only a popular front could save the Spanish Republic. (C.P .Trevelyan performed a similar role in his Labour Party: his activism on the issue appeared to absolve many other activists from taking action on the issue).

If local labour wanted to act on Spain then this certainly did not lead it, ineluctably, into the arms either of the CP or of the popular front. In fact, much of the official movement was, and remained, hostile to cooperation with liberals (as were most north-east liberals hostile to cooperation as well) and in this sense the popular front policy was something of a millstone around the CP's neck in the region. It meant that, when the official labour movement was contemplating radical action on Spain in the summer of 1938, the CP was in no position to be able to channel and inform these discussions. It remained muted and sidelined as much of the regional movement momentarily occupied a political space where the CP might have been had it not had to tone down its rhetoric in order to appeal to liberals. At a time when the CP was devoting a great deal of energy to the 'non-political' humanitarian Spanish aid campaigns that yielded it so little, a policy openly calling for industrial direct action could have resonated through a significant section of the regional labour movement; in the same way its stance critical of the Durham miners' leadership in 1926 had chimed with many disenchanted miners.

It is difficult to determine if the CP at district, branch and individual activist levels regarded everything it did at grassroots as somehow in accordance with, and the furthering of, the popular front. If it did, then part of the way in which the popular front was applied was for Communists to become involved in, indeed to establish, many of the Spanish aid campaigns, but, at the same time, to attempt to blend into them, and to disappear. This was the result of a policy that demanded no party politics within these campaigns and, often, no kind of partisan campaigning message for the wider public. But it seemed a little perverse for the party to adopt a policy of activity but invisibility within these campaigns and then to complain when no one noticed them.[26] Like the Jarrow marchers, the northeast CP found the 'politics of self-effacement' brought scant reward.[27]

The popular front produced some bizarre scenes indeed. At a YCL dance in Sunderland in late April 1937, where there was a presentation to a 'comrade from Spain', Communists 'showed their loyalty to the English throne by having played the national anthem and standing to attention during the playing of this'.[28] This caused some confusion, too, for a correspondent to the *Sunderland Echo* who asked if Sunderland Communists were as loyal as their actions denoted; or were they merely being polite to guests at the dance other than themselves? 'It has always been understood by the writer that Communists were definitely anti-royalist'.[29]

Similarly, in June 1937, a well-known South Shields Communist wrote to his local newspaper in praise of the Catholic Church's housing of Basque refugees. A. Codling, the brother of an International Brigader, called on other groups to follow the Catholic Church's example and to widen the support given to the children to other organisations in the area. This opened up Codling to attack and in early July, 'Iconoclast' replied quoting the *Catholic Times* and other Catholic sources to argue that Catholics were solely involved in the campaign in order to stop the children getting into the hands of Communists.[30]

Yet, on the whole, CP activists appeared simply to get on with the new popular front policy, as if its truth was a given and did not need to be justified. However, the full implications of the policy took some time to filter through, broadly coinciding with the CP's change in emphasis from agitation on the united to popular fronts in later 1937 and early 1938. Thus, the direct action that did happen on Spain, such as the *Linaria* dispute, and other attempts by activists within the labour movement to gain support for the tactic came in early 1937. Even then, though, left-wingers were divided over the right course of action. Thus, when Blyth left-winger 'Janus', for example, attacked local Labour for inactivity on Spain in early January 1937, this did not accompany a call for industrial direct action, but rather for a greater degree 'of working-class unity' and for Blyth Labour simply to 'rouse' public opinion against Non-Intervention.[31]

In 1938, while some popular fronters ignored industrial direct action altogether, others made overt attempts at depicting the policy in a militant light. Some saw no contradiction, in public at least, between advocacy of the popular front and industrial direct action. Yet, the popular front served merely to muddy the waters and confuse the issues when talked about in association with industrial direct action: the success of the former would surely have precluded the deployment of the latter (and vice versa). It was also clear that left-wingers who were strong advocates of the Republic spent far less time over the course of the conflict talking about the use of direct action than they did agitating for a popular front. This must surely have been because they regarded the popular front as *the* way to aid the Republic. That this effectively meant abandoning the *possibility* of using 'undemocratic' tactics like industrial direct action was so unpalatable a truth that it was not even recognised as such, overtly at least, by some non-CP popular fronters.

In general, while the reaction in the official movement to Spain at grassroots was highly complex, there was a fairly clear institutional divide. As might be expected, most trade unions at district and branch level tended to act solely on industrial matters, letting the Labour Party do the campaigning on Spain. This contrasted strongly with the national picture, of course, where, as Buchanan has shown, the unions largely determined the movement's stance on the issue.[32] The miners (and especially the DMA), were a significant exception to this (in terms of numbers and consequent influence), using both their industrial and political institutions to further this and other causes. Other unions mostly chose to show solidarity in the form of donations to Spain causes.

There was also a good deal of diversity in the reaction of Labour Parties, too, over time, at separate institutional levels and in different localities. The local parties proved themselves to be, overall, the most dynamic and capable of donating and taking on a campaigning role before changes in national movement policy led the previously usually inactive constituency parties into (often short-lived) action. In 1936–7, many institutions on both wings of the movement appeared to consider making financial donations sufficient action on Spain. This changed in spring 1938. While most institutions continued to supply funds, many Labour Parties also began to accompany this with campaigning. Supplying funds alone after January 1938 did not appear to satisfy most parties, or the miners' unions, that they were doing enough.

The LLP (sometimes the ward party), miners' lodge and, occasionally, union branch were often the units in which the individual activist could best effect their political beliefs. They were capable of giving form to political expression, albeit largely enacted through the traditional and accepted channels of demonstrations and door-to-door collections. In some regards, being closest to the grassroots, these units were the most likely to make an impact in their local geographical communities. Again, however, the response from sub-constituency sections was by no means uniform. Indeed, each separate institution at all levels had its own individual way of reacting to the conflict. These reactions could vary even between meetings, depending on who was and was not present at any given moment.

Did Spain unite or divide the left? There was certainly a divide between much of the north-east rank-and-file and the national leadership, especially over the issue of a national conference in spring and summer

1938. However, this did not appear to have any long-term consequences; there was no measurable exodus from the movement and certainly not into the arms of popular fronters in the region.[33] Loyalty played its part in this, coupled with the realisation that the regional movement had nowhere else to go. In the early period, too, there was a degree of anger and disenchantment at the national movement's support for Non-Intervention and even the DCFLP wanted a firm stance taken for a while. But, again, this did not have serious consequences. Ultimately, that the national leadership could refuse to act on repeated calls from so much of the regional movement (along with those from elsewhere in the country) and not suffer overly as a consequence, was testament both to the strength of loyalty and the perceived lack of alternatives.

Other sections of the movement at grassroots level were satisfied at that time with fundraising activities, and in this albeit limited sense the movement had not completely vacated political space on the issue. Furthermore, institutions at grassroots level, and their interpenetration, often allowed those who wanted to become active on Spain to do so: if one institution they were involved in did nothing on Spain, there was often another that was active in some form. Thus, while some trades unions did, in different ways, constrain their members from working through them in meaningful ways, these individuals had other outlets, like trades councils or Labour Parties, through which to manifest their political concerns. Again, there was room to accommodate these aspirations within the structures of the official labour movement.

More militant activists in elements of the north-east labour movement did not need to create 'unofficial' rank-and-file movements in order to take action in the political sphere. The official machinery itself proved a perfectly adequate tool for the task, with the additional bonus, of course, of being 'official'. In this context, the DMA's stance was vital, and it actually performed a very similar institutional role on Spain to the supposedly far more militant and Communist inspired SWMF. In the north-east it donated more, and arguably campaigned more in some of the most significant ways than did any other north-east labour movement institution (though it did not endorse industrial direct action for Spain). Indeed, with a lack of internal lodge pressure from those aligned with International Brigaders (hardly any DMA members fought in Spain), the DMA's institutional response was in some senses more spontaneous than that of the South Wales miners. Certainly, if there was substance in Francis' concept of 'proletarian internationalism' in the SWMF, then the DMA had a good claim to have been actuated by it too, notwithstanding the relative lack of internationalism manifest before 1936.[34]

Official labour movement activists at local level were inhibited very little by nationally applied, supposed restrictions. They were only really constrained by their own politics, and their own view of the purpose of the institutions in which they operated. Thus, while the official movement was certainly divided as to what, if anything, to do on Spain before 1938, these divisions did not cause serious repercussions. Furthermore, the vast majority of north-east activists who wanted more action on Spain over time were never interested in the popular front and were not militant left-wingers. Thus, when the national leadership failed to organise a national conference in 1938 this was not a defeat for the left, but for 'moderate' grassroots activists who merely wanted their movement to act more concertedly on issues that concerned them. It was also, if the north-east was representative, another defeat for democracy in the labour movement; elements of which, at grassroots level, practised a form of representative democracy superior to that in operation in the main decision-making institutions of the national movement.

As Buchanan wrote, the national leader's vision 'was of an internationalism defined by and expressed through a small number of leaders; and certainly not an internationalism that could be used to mobilise and politicise the rank-and-file'.[35] As nationally, so regionally 'the labour movement was virtually unchanged in 1939 in terms of its structure and concept of political action'.[36] Yet the official, moderate and loyal north-east movement had revealed that at times its concept of political action could include considering transgressing normal constitutional boundaries, as had occurred in more propitious times.

One internal division that existed to differing degrees of intensity elsewhere in the country but not especially in the north-east was that engendered by the potential problems Spain bought for Catholic movement activists. This was due to the high degree of integration that they experienced in the region, in society generally and in the labour movement particularly. When, however, domestic issues that directly impinged on their lives emerged, Catholic activists in the regional movement did not hesitate to act in the defence of their interests. In fact, there were many factors including organisational (and therefore financial) weaknesses, apathy, deference to higher authorities within the movement (which were regarded occasionally as sufficiently active on the issue, or whose inactivity bred grassroots inactivity), other pressing charitable, local (and municipal), regional and international demands on time and resources within official institutions on both industrial and political wings that could all militate against solidarity support.

In Sheffield and Birmingham, relations between the trades council and Labour Party were strained by the conflict. In Newcastle, there was an insignificant issue about which institution would foot the bill for a Spain meeting, but the more moderate party did not seek to impede the more radical trades council's action on Spain; indeed, the party officially supported the trades council's Spain initiatives.[37] In the north-east, domestic issues and personalities, often working through the divisions in the movement between the industrial and political wings, for example, were more divisive than the issue of Spain. More divisive, too, were the explicit united and popular front campaigns themselves, but even then this division was manifest in only a handful of expulsions from one CLP (Bishop Auckland).

Spain had very little effect in uniting the Labour Party with the left parties outside it in the north-east. Thanks to the flexibility of their own institutions, many labour activists did not need to look outside to build cooperation on the issue. Most of those who did so were already favourable towards the CP and looking for an excuse for more joint work. While many of these activists also embraced explicit united and popular front projects, these links were not invariably made and there were cases of activists seemingly content to work with Communists on Spain who opposed all forms of formal unity with them and liberals.

Spain demanded action between erstwhile comrades or parties that had acted together against fascism before (such as between the Socialist League, ILP and the CP). However, Spain appeared more prone to dividing than uniting, as it was the issue that tainted relations between the ILP and the CP in the region after the parties' activists had worked together so effectively against home-grown fascism in the earlier 1930s. Spain also failed to prevent other divisions on the left, such as those between the Socialist League and ILP.

Noreen Branson wrote that 'It was clear that the anti-fascist cause in Spain was arousing more feeling among British working people than almost anything since the 1926 General strike'.[38] She employed the example of the well-attended September 1936 Spain meeting in Newcastle to support this claim. Yet this was to downplay the anti-fascist struggle against the BUF in the earlier 1930s. Similarly, James Jupp asserted that the conflict in Spain united the left as the Republic's struggle was 'more vital than the battles against the British Union of Fascists in the streets of London'.[39]

But the experiences of both forms of 'anti-fascism' suggests that this was not the case in the north-east. Indeed, it is clear that the potential local threat of fascism provoked a more dynamic working-class response, both at the spontaneous street level and within some labour movement institutions. It was also clear that the 'democracy against fascism' paradigm did not harness anything like the same forces that were at work in anti-fascism before 1935.

The reasons for this contrast were partly to do with the nature of the issue. Spain was an international cause and therefore solidarity was more inclined to be manifest through official institutional channels, at the grass-roots as well as nationally. It could not provoke the kind of spontaneous acts that a fascist presence on the streets facilitated in the earlier 1930s. The spontaneity that there was around Spain was evident in the creation of new institutions, but these still acted in some respect to limit and control, to channel energies often in essentially humanitarian directions. The response to some campaigns was often spontaneously generous, but that was it. Naturally, there remained room for more militant action, but the blacking of ships at an effective level had to be organised properly and as such was subject to the restricting influence of the trade unions, especially the NUS.

However, a strong and clear stance maintained by militants could have facilitated the discussions over and implementation of various kinds of industrial direct action and allowed for its development in a more concerted and longer-lasting way than that which occurred. Thus, while the nature of the cause meant that the response was very different from that to the BUF in the earlier 1930s, the popular front also helped to determine these contrasts. It acted to silence or confuse most talk of militant tactics in this context and it even served to eliminate to a great extent a simple (anti-fascist), pro-Republican message from many of the Spanish aid campaigns. Its effect was to make the Spain campaigns, in significant ways, far less vital than those many activists in the region had enjoyed in the earlier 1930s. This was most obvious in the activism of the left-wingers in the Labour Party, and the CP and ILP outside it. They were united and militant in opposing the BUF before 1935, but increasingly disunited and less militant as the later 1930s progressed.[40] It was no coincidence that the acceptance and dissemination of the popular front policy occurred in between times. In this respect, the BUF's ability to maintain street-level activity in Battersea throughout the late 1930s offers some explanation of why Spain was better able to help unite the wider labour movement there.[41]

Spain also radicalised the movement in Battersea, and it appeared to have this effect on sections of the official north-east movement too, albeit momentarily in 1938. Before 1935, north-east Labour leaders tended to endorse the national leadership attitude, arguing that the BUF should be ignored in order to deny it publicity and that 'socialism' would remedy the situation.[42] The CP's adoption of the popular front, combined with increasingly assertive and (potentially) militant sections of the official movement made for a good degree of role-reversal in the months after July 1936. Clearly, the north-east response to the BUF in the early 1930s was of little utility in predicting what would come after 1935.

Don Watson wrote of the reaction in the north-east to Spain that 'it is doubtful whether at any time before or since have so many of its people responded to an international cause'.[43] Certainly, as far as the late 1930s were concerned, the Spain campaigns were clearly the most 'popular' of the many international solidarity campaigns that emerged. However, this did not prevent Communist William Allan from condemning, in July 1938, the 'Public indifference in this country to the plight of the people of Spain', which was 'an indication that the claims of Englishmen to be lovers of fairplay were based upon a false legend'.[44] Yet, Allan was complaining here of the lack of financial support for solidarity funds and the attitudes of some of those who did donate (as if 'Spain' were a charity). In crucial respects, more important than the numbers involved were the *forms* this response took and their political effects.

Jim Fyrth speculated that it was possible that the TUC became involved in the Basque Children's Committee and foodships as the 'Aid Spain movement' had grown so large that the Labour leadership feared alienating too many activists.[45] He also claimed that the growing support for the Republic and the 'Aid Spain movement' meant that the government was not more openly pro-Franco.[46] This latter claim seems somewhat desperate: it is difficult to see how the government could have been more pro-Franco short of actually supporting his forces militarily. British support for Non-Intervention remained because, according to Bill Moore, 'the power of the appeasers was too strong in the absence of a really united working class ... It was a division that was fatal to any hope of mounting a campaign strong enough to move the government...'.[47] Yet this was unconvincing. Ultimately, the labour movement had the resources and power to tackle the government without the need for unity with the Communist Party, which only brought a few thousand activists and was, ultimately, more trouble than it was worth. The real division that mattered was most evident in the summer of 1938 when the left could have informed and furthered debates inside the labour movement about the use of direct action to save the Republic. Instead, in order to maintain 'the appeal to the middle classes inherent in the Popular Front strategy', it remained largely silent on this issue, and the leadership could knowingly use the popular front as a stick to beat any kind of dissent.[48] In some respects, Trevelyan was right to claim that 'people respond to those who believe in themselves'. Yet the very policy he advocated when uttering these words, the popular front, suggested that he believed far more in the dictates of the Comintern than he did in the possibilities within his own movement.[49]

However, in the 'external' 'Aid Spain' agitation, too, the popular front as applied by the CP and Labour left had problematic effects. Public opinion was clearly supportive of the Republic and activists harnessed this to some degree. The trouble was that they did so in ways that often did not particularly help the Republican cause, at least as far as undermining Non-Intervention was concerned. Indeed, the tactic of depoliticising many of the Spanish aid campaigns in order to achieve, supposedly, a popular front, helped to seriously blunt these campaign's political edge. In many respects the Tyneside foodship campaign was emblematic of all that was inspiring about the Spanish aid campaigns and all that was wrong with them. It demanded and received tremendous amounts of energy and sacrifice from many people, but it had a negligible impact in terms of politicising those it touched and it did not, for the most part, even propagate a critique of government foreign policy. Indeed, some of the messages associated with it around neutrality on Spain probably brought negative repercussions for the Republic's cause. This was due in no small part to the effects of the popular front on left-wingers who ordinarily might have been expected to provide a clear militant critique of Non-Intervention and ideas for ways in which it could be attacked, as they had done for the Means Test. The popular front, as it affected the politics, rhetoric and actions of left-wing activists in Labour and the Communist Parties, went some way to explaining why a coherent, militant, politically focussed, mass movement against Non-Intervention capable of challenging the Labour movement leadership and the government never emerged in Britain. Instead, a great deal of energy, time and personal sacrifice from many who were dedicated to the Republican cause was dissipated in activities that brought this cause very little return. The popular front as operated by the Labour left and CP in the Spanish aid campaigns at grassroots in the north-east was far from fruitful for itself or for the campaign against Non-

Intervention; it was also highly doubtful that it yielded much in terms of advances for Labour in the post-war world. But it was, however, a strangely appropriate policy for Auden's 'low dishonest decade'.[50]

NOTES AND REFERENCES

Introduction

1. See Paul Preston, *A Concise History of the Spanish Civil War* (2nd edition, 1996) and Gerald Brenan, *The Spanish Labyrinth* (Cambridge, 1976).
2. David Blaazer, *The Popular Front and the Progressive Tradition* (Cambridge, 1992).
3. George Orwell, *Homage to Catalonia* in *Orwell in Spain* (2001), p.170.
4. Gerald Howson, *Arms for Spain* (New York, 1998).
5. Will Lawther, 'Before the Labour Party Conference', *Labour Monthly*, 18 (October, 1936), p.599.
6. For a detailed introduction to this topic see Tom Buchanan, *The Spanish Civil War and the British Labour Movement* (Cambridge, 1991), pp.1–36.
7. Buchanan, *British Labour Movement*, pp.167–195.
8. Labour Party AR, 1936, pp.172–173.
9. Michael Foot, *Aneurin Bevan 1897–1945 Vol. One* (1962), p.230.
10. See Buchanan, *British Labour Movement*, pp.37–72.
11. *Sunderland Echo*, 8 May 1937; Buchanan, *British Labour Movement*, pp.74–75, 137, 159, 161–3; Jim Fyrth, *The Signal Was Spain* (1986), pp.220–240; Jim Fyrth, 'The Aid Spain Movement in Britain, 1936–39', *History Workshop Journal*, 35 (1993), p.156.
12. Fyrth, *Signal Was Spain*, p.21.
13. Richard Baxell, *British Volunteers in the Spanish Civil War* (2004), pp.18, 24.
14. Tom Buchanan, 'The Role of the British Labour Movement in the Origins and Work of the Basque Children's Committee 1937-9', *European History Quarterly*, 18:2 (1988), pp.155–174.
15. Hywel Francis, *Miners Against Fascism. Wales and the Spanish Civil War* (1984).
16. *Blaydon Courier*, 6; 13 May 1938; Buchanan, *British Labour Movement*, pp.123–4.
17. James Jupp, *The Radical Left in Britain, 1931–1941* (1982), pp.112, 116, 154; B. Pimlott, *Labour and the Left in the 1930s* (Cambridge, 1977), pp.106, 160.
18. Foot, *Bevan*, p.296.
19. Gidon Cohen, *The Failure of a Dream. The ILP From Disaffiliation to World War II* (2007).
20. George Orwell, 'Spilling the Spanish Beans' in *Orwell in Spain*, p.220.

21. Quoted in S. Orwell and I. Angus (eds.), *The Collected Essays, Journalism and Letters of George Orwell, Vol.1* (1968), p.305.

22. Blaazer, *Progressive Tradition, passim*.

23. Eric Hobsbawm (in 'Fifty Years of People's Fronts', in Jim Fyrth (ed.), *Britain, Fascism and the Popular Front* (1985), p.240), described the popular front in a similar fashion.

24. See Fenner Brockway, *The Workers' Front* (1938), pp.154–155, 238.

25. See Preston, *Concise History*, p.185. For an eyewitness account, see Orwell, *Homage to Catalonia* in *Orwell in Spain*, pp.103–127.

26. 'Objectivity and Liberal Scholarship' in Noam Chomsky, *American Power and the New Mandarins* (1971), pp.62–105.

27. Bill Alexander, *British Volunteers for Liberty. Spain, 1936–1939* (1982).

28. Francis, *Miners Against Fascism*; Hywel Francis, 'Welsh Miners and the Spanish Civil War', *Journal of Contemporary History*, 5:3 (1970), pp.177–191.

29. Peter D. Drake, 'Labour and Spain: British Labour's Response to the Spanish Civil War with Particular Reference to the Labour Movement in Birmingham', (Birmingham University, M.Litt., 1977).

30. For example, Win Albaya, John Baxter and Bill Moore, *Behind the Clenched Fist: Sheffield's 'Aid to Spain', 1936–1939* (Sheffield, 1986).

31. Angela Jackson, *British Women and the Spanish Civil War* (2002), p.189.

32. H. Beynon and T. Austrin, *Masters and Servants. Class and Patronage in the Making of a Labour Organisation. The Durham Miners and the English Political Tradition* (1994), p.4.

33. Francis, 'Welsh Miners', pp.180, 190.

34. Fyrth dealt with the popular front in *Britain, Fascism and the Popular Front*, p.6.

35. Buchanan, *British Labour Movement*, p.2.

36. Tom Buchanan, 'Britain's Popular Front?: Aid Spain and the British Labour Movement', *History Workshop Journal*, 31 (1991), pp.60–72; Fyrth, 'Aid Spain Movement', pp.153–164.

37. Rob Stradling, *Cardiff and the Spanish Civil War* (Cardiff, 1996); *Wales and the Spanish Civil War: The Dragon's Dearest Cause* (Cardiff, 2004).

38. J.K. Hopkins, *Into the Heart of the Fire. The British in the Spanish Civil War* (California, 1998), pp.37–38, 123, 125, 153, 298, 377.

39. Baxell, *British Volunteers*.

40. Jackson, *British Women*, p.154.

41. Mike Squires, *The Aid to Spain Movement in Battersea, 1936–1939* (1994).

42. Don Watson and John Corcoran, *An Inspiring Example: the North-east of England and the Spanish Civil War, 1936–1939* (1996); information from Don Watson.

43. Buchanan, *British Labour Movement*, p.5.

44. Stuart Macintyre, *Little Moscows. Communism and Working-class Militancy in Interwar Britain* (1980), p.17.

45. For example, Duncan Tanner, *Political Change and the Labour Party, 1900–1918* (Cambridge, 1990) and Mike Savage, *The Dynamics of Working-class Politics. The Labour Movement in Preston, 1880–1940* (Cambridge, 1987).

46. Francis, 'Welsh Miners', p.187.

47. As argued in chapter three, the north-east *may* have been exceptional regarding labour movement Catholics' attitudes.

48. Drake, 'Labour and Spain', pp.92, 135–137, 146, 156–157, 160–165.

49. D.M. Goodfellow, *Tyneside. The Social Facts* (Newcastle, 1941), p.77. Teesside has not been included.

50. D.J. Rowe, 'The North-east', in F.M.L. Thompson (ed.), *The Cambridge Social History of Britain 1750–1950, Volume One. Regions and Communities* (Cambridge, 1990), p.417.

51. *Blyth News*, 11; 18 July 1938; Rowe, 'North-east', p.417.

52. F.W.S. Craig, *British Parliamentary Election Results, 1918–1949* (1977), pp.136, 196, 201–204, 247, 254–255, 260, 263, 338–348, 440–442.

53. M.H. Gibb and M. Callcott, 'The Labour Party in the North-east Between the Wars', *Bulletin of the North-east Group for the Study of Labour History*, 8 (1974), pp.18–19.

54. John Stevenson and Chris Cook, *Britain in the Depression. Society and Politics, 1929–1939* (2nd. edition, 1994), p.124.

55. Stevenson and Cook, *Britain in the Depression*, pp.124–127.

56. *North Mail*, 6; 16 February 1937.

57. Maureen Callcott, 'The Making of a Labour Stronghold: Electoral Politics in County Durham Between the two World Wars', in Maureen Callcott and Ray Challinor, *Working-class Politics in North-east England* (Newcastle, 1983), p.68.

58. *Evening Chronicle*, 2 November 1933; 2 November 1934; 2 November 1935; *North Mail*, 2 November 1932; *Blyth News*, 5 November 1931.

59. *North Mail*, 17 March 1937; 6; 7 April 1937; 22 March 1938; 5 April 1938; 25 February 1939; 3 April 1939; *Durham Chronicle*, 19 February 1937; 19; 26 March 1937; *Heslop's Advertiser*, 13 April 1934.

60. *Shields Gazette*, 14 March 1938; *Sunderland Echo*, 11 April 1938.

61. DRO, D/X 1268/14 and /59, *The Socialist*, February 1937 (Seaham CLP) and *The Labour Sentinel*, January 1937 (Sedgefield CLP).

62. Lewis Mates, 'A "Most Fruitful Period"? The North-east District Communist Party and the Popular Front Period, 1935–9', *North-east History*, 36 (2004), p.58; Jupp, *Radical Left*, pp.112, 116, 154.

63. *Shields Evening News*, 6 February 1939.

64. Lewis Mates, 'Durham and South Wales Miners and the Spanish Civil War', *Twentieth Century British History*, 17:3 (2006), p.379.

65. GPL, L331.88, *Durham Mineworker*, 2, May 1934.

66. TWAS, 673/3, TGWU District Area Committee Minutes, 27 October 1936.

67. TWAS, 673/144, *The Record* (TGWU paper), February 1938.

68. See SSPL, LPM4, South Shields LP&TC Minutes, 20 February 1934.

69. J.F. Clarke and T.P. McDermott, *Newcastle and District Trades Council 1873–1973. Centenary History* (Newcastle, 1973), pp.34–36.

70. Beynon and Austrin, *Masters and Servants*, pp.340–341.

71. Manny Shinwell, *Lead With the Left* (1981), p.106.

72. DRO, D/DMA, Acc: 2157 (D), 194 (vol.), Seaham Lodge Minutes, 15; 22 November 1936; 17 March 1937.

73. *Sunderland Echo*, 23 July 1937.

74. *Sunderland Echo*, 29 July 1937.

75. Beynon and Austrin, *Masters and Servants*, p.xvi.

76. Beynon and Austrin, *Masters and Servants*, p.348.

77. Beynon and Austrin, *Masters and Servants*, pp.338, 348, 351, 354, 359–362.
78. DMOR DMA Minutes, Circulars etc., 16 June 1936; Dave Douglass, *Pit Life in County Durham. Rank and File Movements and Workers' Control* (Oxford, 1972), pp.76-78 and *The Miners of North Durham* (Doncaster, 1975), pp.29–30.
79. E. Shinwell, *Conflict Without Malice* (1955), p.127.
80. Thus, Ryhope lodge's total debt was £10,000. *North Mail*, 19 August 1939.
81. *North Mail*, 29 June 1937.
82. DRO, D/Sho 115/6, *Emmie Lawther – A Tribute* (1965); Mates, 'Most Fruitful Period?', pp.63-64.
83. *North Mail*, 11 April 1938.
84. P. Seyd, 'Factionalism Within the Labour Party. The Socialist League, 1932–37' in A. Briggs and J. Saville, *Essays In Labour History, 1918–1939, Vol.3* (1977), pp.208, 226.
85. TWAS, PO/SLI/1, Gateshead Socialist League Branch EC Minutes, 5 December 1935; 23 July 1936; M. Callcott and M. Espinasse, 'Ruth Dodds (1890–1976)' in J. Bellamy and J. Saville (eds.), *Dictionary of Labour Biography, Vol.VII* (1984), pp.63–67.
86. Archie Potts, *Zilliacus. A Life for Peace and Socialism* (2002), p.66.
87. Lewis Mates, 'From Revolutionary to Reactionary: The Life of Will Lawther' (Newcastle University, MA, 1996), pp.5, 10; A.W. Purdue, 'The ILP in the North-east', in D. James, T. Jowitt and K. Laybourn (eds.), *The Centennial History of the Independent Labour Party. A Collection of Essays* (Krumlin, 1992), pp.35–42; Callcott, 'Labour Stronghold', pp.63–75.
88. BLPES, COLLMISC702/6; /10 and /12; ILP3/24; ILP7/1/3; Undated report on the state of the party (January–May 1934); NAC Minutes, 10; 11 February 1934; 28 June 1935; 2 November 1935; 4; 5 July 1936; NAC financial report (February 1939); *Evening Chronicle*, 2 November 1934.
89. Len Edmondson Interview with Lewis Mates, 19 June 1998.
90. Len Edmondson Interview with Lewis Mates, 4 November 1994.
91. Such as the TJPC; see below. *Shields Gazette*, 7 December 1936.
92. Mates, 'Lawther', pp.1–14, 59–63. However, the region did produce Tom Brown, one of the most significant anarcho-syndicalists of the era. See *Tom Brown's Syndicalism* (1990).
93. Francis, *Miners Against Fascism*, p.33.
94. Jupp, *Radical Left*, p.178; Purdue, 'ILP in the North-east', *passim*.
95. Mates, 'Most Fruitful Period?', *passim*.
96. James Klugmann, *History of the Communist Party of Great Britain, Vol.2. The General Strike, 1925–26* (1969), p.162.
97. *Workers' Weekly*, 3 September 1926.
98. Klugmann, *Communist Party*, pp.345–349.
99. *Workers' Life*, 30 September 1927; Anthony Mason, *The General Strike in the North East* (Hull, 1970), p.102.
100. Stuart Howard, 'Dawdon in the Third Period: the Dawdon Dispute of 1929 and the Communist Party', *Bulletin of the North-east Group for the Study of Labour History*, 21 (1987), pp.3–16.

101. Mates, 'Durham and South Wales Miners', p.381; Andrew Thorpe, 'The Membership of the Communist Party of Great Britain, 1920–1945', *Historical Journal*, 43:3 (2000), p.792.
102. LHASC, CP Central Committee Minutes, 10 November 1936.
103. Francis, 'Welsh Miners', p.180.
104. Lewis H. Mates, 'The United Front and the Popular Front in the North East of England, 1936–1939', (Newcastle University, PhD, 2002), pp.61–64.
105. LHASC, CP/CENT/PERS/1/01, Tom Aisbitt biography by Horace Green. 'Crypto-Communist' here is defined as a paid-up CP member who hides this in order to remain active in the official movement.
106. Mates, 'Most Fruitful Period?', pp.74-84.
107. Mates, 'United Front', pp.31–32, 55.
108. LHASC, CP/IND/KLUG/11/02, Alex Robson autobiography; *Shields News*, 26 November 1936; 7 December 1936; 27 January 1937; *North Mail*, 24 February 1937; 18 January 1938; Nigel Todd, *In Excited Times* (Whitley Bay, 1995), p.48.
109. Mates, 'Durham and South Wales Miners', pp.385–386, 378–379.
110. Todd, *In Excited Times*, p.73.
111. Todd, *In Excited Times*, *passim*.
112. LHASC, CP Central Committee Minutes, 6 August 1937.
113. *Blyth News*, 27 March 1939.
114. Mates, 'United Front', pp.35–40, 51, 55, 116, 145, 174–175.
115. Martin Pugh, 'The Liberal Party and the Popular Front', *English Historical Review*, CXXI, 494 (2006), p.1331.
116. Mates, 'United Front', pp.47–50.
117. *Sunderland Echo*, 26 August 1938.
118. D.S. Birn, *The League of Nations Union, 1918–45* (Oxford, 1981), p.188.
119. See, for example, views – including pro-government foreign policy – at Lynemouth LNU branch annual dinner. *Morpeth Herald*, 24 February 1939.
120. *Blaydon Courier*, 31 October 1936.
121. Mates, 'United Front', pp.172, 244, 252.
122. L.H. Mates, 'The North-east and the Campaigns for a Popular Front, 1938–9', *Northern History*, XLIII (2) (2006), pp.294–298.
123. *Sunderland Echo*, 1 May 1937; *Durham Chronicle*, 25 November 1938.
124. For conditions in Jarrow, see Matt Perry, *The Jarrow Crusade: Protest and Legend* (Sunderland, 2005), pp.10, 108, 133.
125. *Newcastle Journal*, 22 March 1937.
126. Rowe, 'North-east', p.432.
127. Archie Potts, 'Forty Years On. The Labour Party in Sunderland 1900–1945', *Bulletin of the North-east Group for the Study of Labour History*, 24 (1990), p.14.
128. *Sunderland Echo*, 29 November 1937.
129. Shinwell, *Conflict Without Malice*, p.128.
130. *New Leader*, 29 January 1937.
131. For example, see comments in the *Sunderland Echo*, 7 June 1937.
132. Rowe, 'North-east', p.468.
133. Rowe, 'North-east', pp.435–436.
134. CCC, LSPC, 1/2/134, Blenkinsop to Pole, n.d. [June 1937?].

135. *Shields News*, 7 May 1937.
136. Todd, *In Excited Times*, pp.93–95.
137. *Evening Chronicle*, 23 April 1937; *Sunderland Echo*, 3 May 1937.
138. See, for example, *Evening Chronicle*, 4 May 1937.
139. Watson and Corcoran, *An Inspiring Example*, pp.74, 80.
140. *Blyth News*, 21 February 1938.
141. Fyrth, *Signal Was Spain*, p.276. Fyrth noted that there were Spaniards in Franco's army. (p.188).
142. Stradling, *Wales and the Spanish Civil War*, p.223.
143. Naturally, the term 'Republican' as employed in this study refers to the Spanish Republic only.
144. J. Klugmann, 'The Crisis of the Thirties: a View From the Left' in J. Clark, M. Heinemann, D. Margolies, and C. Snee, *Culture and Crisis in Britain in the 30s* (1979), p.19.
145. Jim Atkinson of Hexham risked his life when driving ambulances to Republican Spain as did Francis Gill, a 23 year-old, working-class Sunderland lad, who, in early 1937, agreed to work on the *Alice Marie*, a ship breaking Franco's blockade with food and medical supplies, because, according to his sister, 'he always wanted to help the underdog'. Mrs. Gill Interview with Lewis Mates, 31 October 1994; *Blyth News*, 13 March 1939.

Chapter One

1. Lewis Mates, 'Durham and South Wales Miners and the Spanish Civil War', *Twentieth Century British History*, 17:3 (2006), pp.373–395.
2. *Blaydon Courier*, 13 March 1937.
3. *Blaydon Courier*, 27 February 1937.
4. *North Mail*, 29 May 1937.
5. Clifford Lawther letter to Will Lawther, 3 February 1937 (in possession of the late Jack Lawther).
6. *Shields Gazette*, 8 February 1937.
7. *Sunday Sun*, 6 June 1937.
8. *Blyth News*, 1 July 1937.
9. *North Mail*, 24 July 1937.
10. *North Mail*, 24 July 1937.
11. *North Mail*, 24 July 1937.
12. *Shields Gazette*, 8 January 1938.
13. *Sunday Sun*, 29 May 1938.
14. *Shields Gazette*, 5 August 1938.
15. Angela Jackson, *British Women and the Spanish Civil War* (2002), pp.183–185.
16. *Shields Gazette*, 5 August 1938.
17. *Sunday Sun*, 6 June 1937.
18. *North Mail*, 2 April 1937.
19. See below.
20. J.K. Hopkins, *Into the Heart of the Fire. The British in the Spanish Civil War* (California, 1998), p.279.
21. *Blyth News*, 26 July 1937.
22. *Shields Gazette*, 12 December 1938.

23. *Shields Gazette*, 5 August 1938.
24. *Shields Gazette*, 27 December 1938.
25. Hopkins, *Heart of the Fire*, p.221.
26. Halliwell was an Englishman who had emigrated to Canada aged 13. He came to the north-east as a result of meeting north-easterner Cliff Lawther while in Spain. *Hexham Courant*, 31 December 1939.
27. *Hexham Courant*, 14 January 1939.
28. *Shields Gazette*, 19 February 1938.
29. *Blyth News*, 24 June 1937.
30. *Blyth News*, 15 March 1937.
31. MML, D7/A/2, International Brigade List with Party Affiliations.
32. *Shields Evening News*, 3 May 1938.
33. *Shields Evening News*, 3 May 1938.
34. *North Mail*, 26 February 1937.
35. A British anti-tank battery pay sheet for December 1937 (in the possession of Jim Carmody) suggests Genther's claimed figure was a little high, but not beyond the realms of possibility.
36. *North Mail*, 26 February 1937.
37. B. Alexander, *British Volunteers For Liberty. Spain, 1936–1939* (1982), p.81.
38. *Sunderland Echo*, 1 September 1937.
39. *Sunderland Echo*, 4 September 1937.
40. *North Mail*, 2 April 1937.
41. Jim Fyrth, *The Signal Was Spain* (1986), p.63; Don Watson and John Corcoran, *An Inspiring Example. The North-east of England and the Spanish Civil War, 1936–1939* (1996), p.42.
42. Tom Buchanan, *The Impact of the Spanish Civil War on Britain: War, Loss and Memory* (Eastbourne, 2007), p.58.
43. IWMSA, 11877/6, Frank Graham Interview; *Sunderland Echo*, 10 April 1937.
44. Watson and Corcoran, *An Inspiring Example*, p.66.
45. *Shields Gazette*, 16 August 1938.
46. MML, 39/D/35, Wounded Brigaders File.
47. *Sunday Sun*, 29 May 1938.
48. *Shields Gazette*, 20 January 1939.
49. *Blyth News*, 26 July 1937.
50. *North Mail*, 27 October 1938.
51. *North Mail*, 25; 26; 27; 31 October 1938; *Shields Gazette*, 22 July 1938; 26; 28 October 1938; *Blyth News*, 15 August 1938.
52. *North Mail*, 29 October 1938.
53. George Orwell, 'Looking Back on the Spanish War', in *Orwell in Spain* (2001), p.345.
54. *Sunderland Echo*, 6 October 1938.
55. *Shields Gazette*, 20 January 1939.
56. *Shields Gazette*, 20 January 1939.
57. Don Watson, 'Bobbie Qualie, 1909–1982', *North-east Labour History*, 30 (1996), pp.66–67.
58. *North Mail*, 6 April 1937; 25 June 1938; *Evening Chronicle*, 5 April 1937.

59. *Sunderland Echo*, 1 July 1938; 6 February 1939; Watson and Corcoran, *An Inspiring Example*, p.64.
60. *Evening Chronicle*, 22 March 1937.
61. Bill Reynolds Interview with Lewis Mates, 8 February 2006.
62. *North Mail*, 24 July 1937.
63. Watson and Corcoran, *An Inspiring Example*, p.27.
64. Watson and Corcoran, *An Inspiring Example*, pp.32–33; Alexander, *Volunteers for Liberty*, pp.82–83.
65. *North Mail*, 18 March 1937; 6 April 1937; *Evening Chronicle*, 5 April 1937.
66. Moira Tattam written testimony to Lewis Mates, 26 June 2006.
67. *Sunday Sun*, 6 June 1937; *Newcastle Journal*, 7 July 1937; *North Mail*, 7; 16; 30 July 1937; 21 July 1938; *Blaydon Courier*, 10 July 1937; *Daily Worker*, 19 August 1937; Watson and Corcoran, *An Inspiring Example*, p.34.
68. *North Mail*, 25 June 1938; 6 August 1938; 27; 31 October 1938; *Shields Gazette*, 3 May 1938 and *Sunderland Echo*, 1 July 1938.
69. *North Mail*, 26 October 1938.
70. *North Mail*, 1 July 1938; 16 September 1938; 25; 29 October 1938; *Sunderland Echo*, 6 October 1938; 6 February 1939.
71. These references also provide CP affiliations of those killed. MML, 21/B/3K, D7/A/2 and /3, Lists of International Brigaders; North-east International Brigade Memorial Programme, 15 January 1939 (in possession of the late Jack Lawther); International Brigade 'Debt of Honour week' 1939 Memorial Programme (in possession of Peter Rose); *Sunday Sun*, 29 May 1938; W. Rust, *Britons in Spain* (1939), pp.189–199; Alexander, *Volunteers for Liberty*, pp.263–276; Watson and Corcoran, *An Inspiring Example*, p.85. I am also grateful to Jim Carmody for supplying information.
72. *Blyth News*, 15 August 1938.
73. Watson and Corcoran, *An Inspiring Example*, p.35.
74. Jackson, *British Women*, p.187.
75. MML, 39/D/35, Wounded Brigaders File.
76. *Shields Gazette*, 27 December 1938.
77. *Shields Gazette*, 20 January 1939.
78. Watson and Corcoran, *An Inspiring Example*, p.61.
79. *Blyth News*, 26 July 1937.
80. *North Mail*, 9 September 1937.
81. Watson and Corcoran, *An Inspiring Example*, p.35.
82. Watson and Corcoran, *An Inspiring Example*, p.36; Jackson, *British Women*, pp.80–81.
83. *Shields Gazette*, 12; 19 August 1937; 1 October 1937; 2 November 1937; 26 July 1938; *North Mail*, 12 April 1938.
84. *Durham Chronicle*, 6 August 1937.
85. Rust, *Britons in Spain*, p.136.
86. *Blaydon Courier*, 1 July 1938.
87. *North Mail*, 9 September 1937; Watson and Corcoran, *An Inspiring Example*, pp.27, 36.
88. Bill Reynolds Interview with Lewis Mates, 8 February 2006.
89. Moira Tattam written testimony to Lewis Mates, 26 June 2006.

90. Brian Walsh written testimony, 5 January 2007.
91. LHASC, CP/CENT/PERS/7/07, Johnny Walsh autobiography.
92. Bill Reynolds Interview with Lewis Mates, 8 February 2006.
93. *Shields Gazette*, 19 March 1937.
94. LHASC, CP/IND/POLL/2/6, Frank Graham letter to Harry Pollitt, 16 April 1936 [presumably a mistake for 1937].
95. *Evening Chronicle*, 22 March 1937.
96. *Evening Chronicle*, 22 March 1937; Frank Graham, *The Battle of Jarama* (Newcastle, 1987), p.73.
97. *North Mail*, 12 April 1938; *Blaydon Courier*, 1 July 1938.
98. Bill Reynolds Interview with Lewis Mates, 8 February 2006.
99. Clifford Lawther letter to Will Lawther, 3 February 1937.
100. *Blaydon Courier*, 29 July 1938.
101. Elliott also intervened in domestic matters from the front, supporting the annual poor children's outing in July 1937. *Blyth News*, 26 July 1937.
102. *Shields Gazette*, 24 July 1937; 24 September 1937.
103. *Heslop's Advertiser*, 11 June 1937.
104. *Shields Gazette*, 8 February 1937.
105. *North Mail*, 2 April 1937; 30 July 1937; *Evening Chronicle*, 11 May 1937.
106. Alexander, *Volunteers for Liberty*, pp.138–139.
107. *Sunday Sun*, 23 May 1937.
108. *North Mail*, 2 April 1937; 24 July 1937; *Heslop's Advertiser*, 11 June 1937; *Sunderland Echo*, 19 June 1937.
109. *Shields Gazette*, 24 September 1937.
110. Graham, *Battle of Jarama*, p.27.
111. *Sunday Sun*, 18 July 1937.
112 *Shields Evening News*, 3 May 1938.
113. *North Mail*, 12 April 1937; *Sunderland Echo*, 17 April 1937.
114. *Blyth News*, 14; 26 July 1937; 3 August 1937; 13 September 1937.
115. *Blyth News*, 26 July 1937.
116. MML, Box B-4 M/7, Bill Advertising Sunderland Memorial Meeting, 31 March 1939; MML, Box B-4 M/5d and M/5e, newspaper articles; *Shields Gazette*, 26 November 1938; 31 December 1938; *North Mail*, 5 December 1938; 16 January 1939; *Newcastle Journal*, 16 January 1939; *Daily Worker*, 10 December 1938; Graham, *Battle of Jarama*, pp.36, 74–76.
117. *Newcastle Journal*, 16 January 1939; Graham, *Battle of Jarama*, pp.74–76.
118. Jackson deemed the process 'legendising'. H. Francis, *Miners Against Fascism. Wales and the Spanish Civil War* (1984), pp.248–250; Jackson, *British Women*, p.180.
119. *Shields Gazette*, 20 January 1939.
120. *Newcastle Journal*, 16 January 1939.
121. MML, Box A–6/C/3 and /8, Report on International Brigade convoy, 8 September 1939 and Newcastle Memorial Leaflet, 27 January 1939; *North Mail*, 26; 27 January 1939.
122. *North Mail*, 12; 22 July 1939; *Daily Worker* (final edition), 17 July 1939.
123. *Blyth News*, 1 July 1937; 3 August 1937.
124. *Shields Gazette*, 8 January 1938.

125. Graham, *Battle of Jarama*, p.73.
126. LHASC, CP/IND/POLL/2/6, Ernest Reynolds letter to Frank Graham, n.d.; *Sunday Sun*, 23 May 1937; 29 May 1938; *North Mail*, 29 December 1936; 26 February 1937; 12 March 1937; 30 July 1937; 30 August 1937 (country edition); *Blyth News*, 26 July 1937; Watson and Corcoran, *An Inspiring Example*, p.53.
127. *Shields Gazette*, 3 May 1938.
128. Alexander, *Volunteers for Liberty*, p.138; Francis, *Miners Against Fascism*, p.251.
129. *Blyth News*, 26 July 1937; 13 September 1937.
130. *North Mail*, 31 August 1937; TUC AR, 1938, p.367; Graham, *Battle of Jarama*, pp.74–76.
131. LHASC, CP/DUTT/05/11, Andy, Steve and Robert Lawther letter to Will Lawther, 4 November 1939.
132. *Shields Gazette*, 27 September 1937.
133. See chapter three.
134. *Blyth News*, 25 January 1937.
135. *Blyth News*, 13 September 1937.
136. *Blyth News*, 26 July 1937. This was one of very few occasions when Elliott's pronouncements were linked with calls for an end to Non-Intervention in the local press (see below).
137. *Blaydon Courier*, 20 March 1937.
138. *Blaydon Courier*, 12; 19 September 1936; 17 April 1937.
139. John Baxter, 'Arthur Newsum died in Spain', in W. Albaya, J. Baxter and B. Moore, *Behind the Clenched Fist: Sheffield's 'Aid to Spain', 1936–1939* (Sheffield, 1986), p.14.
140. Graham Holtham written testimony to Lewis Mates, 15 March 2006.
141. N. Green, *A Chronicle of Small Beer. The Memoirs of Nan Green* (Nottingham, 2004), p.99.
142. Francis, *Miners Against Fascism*, p.251.
143. Francis, *Miners Against Fascism*, p.253.
144. Alexander, *Volunteers for Liberty*, p.16.
145. *Shields Evening News*, 27 January 1939; *North Mail*, 31 January 1939.
146. *Shields Gazette*, 20 January 1939.
147. *Shields Gazette*, 1 November 1938.
148. *Shields Gazette*, 8 December 1938
149. *Shields Gazette*, 20 January 1939.
150. *Shields Gazette*, 20 January 1939.
151. *North Mail*, 6 August 1938.
152. *Shields Gazette*, 5 August 1938.
153. *Shields Gazette*, 20 December 1938.
154. *Shields Gazette*, 20 January 1939.
155. *Sunderland Echo*, 6 October 1938.
156. *Shields Gazette*, 6; 20; 30 December 1938. See chapters five and six.
157. Francis, *Miners Against Fascism*, p.252.
158. Alexander, *Volunteers for Liberty*, p.137.
159. *Shields Gazette*, 8 January 1938.

160. *Blaydon Courier*, 27 February 1937; *Sunderland Echo*, 10 April 1937; 19 June 1937; *Sunday Sun*, 6 June 1937; *Heslop's Advertiser*, 11 June 1937; Rust, *Britons in Spain*, p.129.

161. *Sunday Sun*, 23 May 1937.

162. *North Mail*, 12 April 1938; 26 July 1938; 6 August 1938; *Blyth News*, 5 May 1938; 28 July 1938 *Blaydon Courier*, 13 May 1938; *Sunday Sun*, 29 May 1938.

163. MML, Box A12/Gr/8, Frank Graham Notes for Speeches, n.d. [probably late October 1938].

164. *Shields Gazette*, 8 December 1938. See also *Shields Gazette*, 12 December 1938.

165. *Shields Gazette*, 31 December 1938.

166. *Hexham Courant*, 14 January 1939.

167. MML, Box A12/Gr/8, Frank Graham Notes for Speech in the Miners' Hall, Roker, 27 January 1939.

168. *Sunderland Echo*, 2 March 1939.

169. Bill Moore, '"Aid for Spain" in Sheffield', in Albaya et al., *Clenched Fist*, p.19.

170. Alexander, *Volunteers for Liberty*, p.135.

171. See chapter four.

172. Frank Graham Interview, 12 October 1994; LHASC, CP/IND/POLL/ 2/6, Frank Graham letter to Harry Pollitt, 16 April 1937; IWMSA, 11877/6, Frank Graham Interview; *North Mail*, 10 April 1937; *Durham Chronicle*, 7 May 1937; Graham, *Battle of Jarama*, p.27.

173. MML, Box B-4M/6 and Box A12/Gr/8, Bill advertising 'Save Spain rally', 27 January 1939 and Frank Graham Speeches; Graham, *Battle of Jarama*, p.39.

174. NRO, 527/A/3, Wansbeck CLP Minutes, 16 April 1938; LHASC, CP/ CENT/PERS/2/01, George Coyle autobiography, MML, D7/A/2, List of International Brigaders, n.d.; *North Mail*, 18 January 1937; 2 May 1938; *Blaydon Courier*, 6; 13 May 1938; *Shields Gazette*, 2 May 1938; *Blyth News*, 5 May 1938; *Durham Chronicle*, 3; 10 June 1938; *Sunderland Echo*, 6 June 1938.

175. NRO, 759/68, NMA EC Minutes, 11 April 1938; *North Mail*, 16 May 1938.

176. *Gateshead Labour Herald*, April 1937.

177. *Gateshead Labour Herald*, March 1937; *North Mail*, 12 April 1937; 26 July 1937; 10; 13 September 1937; *Blaydon Courier*, 20 March 1937; 17 April 1937; *Blyth News*, 26 July 1937; 3 August 1937; 13 September 1937; 14 July 1938; *Tribune*, 16 July 1937; *Daily Worker*, 3 September 1937.

178. MML, Box B-4 M/5d and M/5e, newspaper articles; MML, Box B-4 M/7, Bill advertising memorial meeting, 31 March 1939; DMOR, DMA Minutes, Circulars etc., 21 November 1938; DMA EC Minutes, 9 January 1939; *North Mail*, 5 December 1938; 16 January 1939; *Shields Gazette*, 31 December 1938; *Daily Worker*, 10 December 1938; Graham, *Battle of Jarama*, p.36.

179. MML, Box B-4 M/5a, North-east International Brigade Memorial Meeting Leaflet, *Newcastle Journal*, 16 January 1939; Graham, *Battle of Jarama*, pp.74–6.

180. *Daily Worker*, 17 July 1939. See chapter two.

181. TWAS, 608/Box 1252, Newcastle City Labour Party Delegate Meeting Minutes, 10 January 1939. See chapter four.

182. In 1935, Henderson was still an ILP member (and local election candidate) in Gateshead. He had joined the Socialist League by July 1936. BLPES, COLL-MISC 702/10, ILP NAC Minutes, 28 June 1935.

183. *Daily Worker*, 3 September 1937.
184. *North Mail*, 24 August 1937; *Blyth News*, 30 September 1937. See chapter four.
185. *Blyth News*, 5 May 1938.
186. See, for example, the report on Communist Tom Dolan's memorial meeting that recorded Graham's CP membership. *Sunderland Echo*, 17 April 1937.
187. See chapters two and four.
188. The NMA had already donated £10 to IBDWAC. NRO, 759/68, NMA EC Minutes, 16 February 1938.
189. See chapters two and six.
190. *Blyth News*, 26 July 1937.
191. *North Mail*, 17; 20 September 1937.
192. See reference 71 relating to total numbers killed.
193. *Blaydon Courier*, 17 April 1937.
194. *Daily Worker*, 3 September 1937.
195. *Blyth News*, 26 July 1937.
196. *Blyth News*, 9 December 1937.
197. Bill Reynolds Interview with Lewis Mates, 8 February 2006.
198. WMRC, 292/946/34 and MML, D7/A/2, Lists of International Brigaders; *Sunday Sun*, 6 June 1937.
199. Graham, *Battle of Jarama*, p.72.
200. Graham, *Battle of Jarama*, p.73.
201. *Shields Gazette*, 23 September 1936; 25 September 1936.
202. *Shields Gazette*, 31 July 1937.
203. MML, Box B-4/M/1, Charlie Woods letter to Jim Fyrth, 18 February 1985.
204. Watson and Corcoran, *An Inspiring Example*, p.37.
205. LHASC, CP/IND/KETT/05/04, George Short Interview, n.d.
206. Bert Ward written testimony to Lewis Mates, 22 February 2006.
207. John McIlroy, Barry McLoughlin, Alan Campbell and John Halstead, 'Forging the Faithful: the British at the International Lenin School', *Labour History Review*, 68:1 (2003), pp.122–3.
208. Francis, *Miners Against Fascism*, p.251.
209. Douglas Hyde, *I Believed* (1952), p.60.
210. Alexander, *Volunteers for Liberty*, p.105.
211. A. Durgan, 'Freedom Fighters or Comintern Army? The International Brigades in Spain', *International Socialism*, 86 (1999), p.127.
212. Hywel Francis, 'Welsh Miners and the Spanish Civil War', *Journal of Contemporary History*, 5:3 (1970), p.189.
213. Francis, *Miners Against Fascism*, p.251.
214. See chapter four.
215. TWAS, TUASW2/1/2, Gateshead No.1 ASW Branch Minutes, 25 April 1932; 2 August 1932; 15 August 1932; 16 October 1932; McIlroy et al., 'Forging the Faithful', p.206. See chapter two.
216. *North Mail*, 24 September 1936; 9 October 1936; P. Kingsford, *The Hunger Marchers in Britain 1920–1940* (1982), pp.63, 138, 184–185, 225.
217. *Shields Gazette*, 23 January 1937; 23 July 1937; *North Mail*, 26 January 1937; 22 August 1939; *Heslop's Advertiser*, 19 February 1937; *Durham Chronicle*, 16 September 1938.

218. LHASC, CP Central Committee Minutes, 8 December 1937.
219. Richard Croucher, *We Refuse to Starve in Silence. A History of the National Unemployed Workers Movement, 1920–46* (1987), p.188.
220. LHASC, CP Central Committee Minutes, 8 December 1937.
221. *Blyth News*, 3 August 1937; 9 August 1937; 16 August 1937.
222. *Blyth News*, 15 November 1937; 17 October 1938.
223. Hopkins, *Heart of the Fire*, p.264.
224. *Shields Gazette*, 20 January 1939.
225. *Shields Gazette*, 7 February 1939.
226. *Shields Evening News*, 4 January 1939. (My thanks to Don Watson for this reference). For the *Jeanie Stewart*, see chapter six.
227. MML, Box 39, A/54, *Sunday Despatch* article, 19 December 1939.
228. Francis, *Miners Against Fascism*, p.251.
229. Watson, 'Bobbie Qualie', pp.66–67.
230. IWMSA, 10357/3, George Aitken Interview with Judith Cook.
231. McIlroy et al., 'Forging the Faithful', pp.120–1; Judith Cook, *Apprentices of Freedom* (1979), p.28.
232. Watson and Corcoran, *An Inspiring Example*, pp.54–61.
233. Watson and Corcoran, *An Inspiring Example*, p.61.
234. I am grateful to Don Watson for this information.
235. McIlroy et al., 'Forging the Faithful', pp.113, 121.
236. Watson and Corcoran, *An Inspiring Example*, pp.63, 65.
237. *Sunderland Echo*, 6 October 1938.
238. *North Mail*, 26 January 1939; 12 July 1939.
239. *Sunderland Echo*, 10 April 1937.
240. *Sunderland Echo*, 6 October 1938.
241. Frank Graham, *The Spanish Civil War. Battles of Brunete and the Aragon* (Newcastle, 1999), pp.63-65.
242. Frank Graham Interview, 12 October 1994; Jackson, *British Women*, pp.193–6.
243. Francis, *Miners Against Fascism*, p.222.
244. Hopkins, *Heart of the Fire*, p.136.
245. Hopkins, *Heart of the Fire*, p.137.
246. *North Mail*, 12 January 1937.
247. *Sunday Sun*, 23 May 1937.
248. *Sunderland Echo*, 10 April 1937.
249. Watson and Corcoran, *An Inspiring Example*, p.53.
250. Hyde, *I Believed*, pp.56–57.
251. Hopkins, *Heart of the Fire*, p.138.
252. See Durgan, 'Comintern Army?', p.122.
253. *Sunday Sun*, 18 July 1937.
254. Hyde, *I Believed*, p.59.
255. *Blyth News*, 17 August 1936.
256. *Shields Gazette*, 22 July 1938. My emphasis.
257. *Sunderland Echo*, 23 December 1938.
258. *Sunderland Echo*, 3 December 1938.
259. Hopkins, *Heart of the Fire*, p.137.
260. *Blyth News*, 1 July 1937.

261. Tim Rees, 'Battleground of the Revolutionaries: the Republic and Civil War in Spain, 1931-39', in Moira Donald and Tim Rees, *Reinterpreting Revolution in Twentieth Century Europe* (2001), p.133.
262. Noreen Branson, *History of the Communist Party of Great Britain 1927–1941* (1985), p.237.
263. *Shields News*, 23 November 1936.
264. *Morpeth Herald*, 22 April 1938.

Chapter Two

1. MML, Box B-4/M/1, Charlie Woods letter to Jim Fyrth, 18 February 1985.
2. Frank Graham Interview with Lewis Mates, 12 October 1994.
3. Jim Fyrth quoted Woods verbatim in *The Signal Was Spain* (1986), p.281.
4. Tom Buchanan, *The Spanish Civil War and the British Labour Movement* (Cambridge, 1991), pp.137–138.
5. Don Watson and John Corcoran, *An Inspiring Example: the North-east of England and the Spanish Civil War, 1936–1939* (1996), p.11.
6. See Lewis Mates, 'Durham and South Wales Miners and the Spanish Civil War', *Twentieth Century British History*, 17:3 (2006), pp.373–395.
7. NRO, 759/68, NMA EC Minutes, 21 September 1936; 15 January 1937; 30 March 1937; 16 February 1938; 25 March 1938; 17 May 1938; 31 May 1938; 24 December 1938; 7 June 1939; *Morpeth Herald*, 23 July 1937; TUC AR, 1938, pp.64–66.
8. TWAS, 673/3 and /4, TGWU Area Committee Minutes, 27 October 1936 and 31 January 1939.
9. TWAS, 1280/15, ASW Tyne and Blyth District Minutes, 22 October 1936.
10. TWAS, TU/UPM/1/1/5, United Patternmakers Newcastle East Branch Minutes, 5 July 1937; 28 February 1938; 23 April 1938; 15 August 1938.
11. Those showing no signs of support were: Newcastle and District Typographical Association, United Patternmakers Newcastle East, Sunderland NUS, Gateshead NALGO and North Shields Bank Officers' Guild branches; the latter two were not TUC-affiliated in 1936.
12. NRO, 527/B/3, Newburn and District LLP Minutes, 2 September 1936; 2 June 1937; 4 January 1938; 2 March 1938; 5 May 1938; 12 October 1938; 1 February 1939.
13. SSPL, LPM5 and LPM6, South Shields LP&TC Minutes, 31 July 1936; 4 August 1936; 7 December 1937; 29 March 1938; 9 September 1938; 13 September 1938; 16 December 1938; 20 December 1938.
14. NRO, 1587/10, Newbiggin and North Seaton LLP Minutes, 14 December 1938.
15. DRO, D/SHO/93/2, Durham CLP Minutes, 18 March 1939; NRO, 527/A/3, Wansbeck CLP Minutes, 22 May 1937.
16. DRO, D/SHO/99, Houghton-le-Spring CLP AR 1937.
17. TWAS, 608/Box 1252, Newcastle City Labour Party EC Minutes, 6 April 1937; 2; 7 November 1937; 4 January 1938; 24 February 1938.
18. NRO, 527/C/2, Tyneside Federation of Labour Parties Statement for 1937.
19. DRO, D/Sho 131/5, DCFLP Agenda for Annual Meetings, 4 June 1937 and 18 June 1938.

20. *Sunderland Echo*, 15 February 1937.
21. *Shields Gazette*, 31 August 1936; 21 May 1937; 4 June 1938.
22. NRO, 3793/30, Cambois Lodge Minutes, 3 July 1938; 20 October 1938; 11 December 1938.
23. *Blyth News*, 13 March 1939.
24. SSPL, LPM6, South Shields LP&TC Minutes, 23 September 1938; 7 October 1938; NRO, 527/B/3, Newburn and District LLP Minutes, 6 January 1937.
25. Sunderland NUJ branch's opposition is discussed below.
26. DRO, D/DMA/334/11, Eden Lodge Minutes, 20; 28 August 1936; 4 February 1937; 24 March 1937; 6 May 1937; 22 December 1938. See chapter three.
27. Buchanan, *British Labour Movement*, p.155.
28. The vote was more than double that against the proposal nationally. TWAS, TUASW2/1/2, ASW Gateshead No.1 Branch Minutes, 23 January 1939.
29. See Mates, 'Durham and South Wales Miners', pp.373–395.
30. Boldon sent at least two, Ryhope at least one (March 1938). *Shields Gazette*, 2 November 1937; 28 February 1938; *Sunderland Echo*, 28 March 1938.
31. *Shields Gazette*, 17 August 1936; 31 August 1936; 12 October 1936.
32. *Shields Gazette*, 2 March 1937. See chapter four.
33. *Daily Worker*, 26 January 1937.
34. NRO, 759/68, NMA EC Minutes, 14 March 1938; 18 October 1938; 19 November 1938; *North Mail*, 12 April 1938.
35. NRO, 3793/30, Cambois Lodge Minutes, 4 June 1938; 2; 20 October 1938; 22 January 1939; NRO, 759/68, NMA EC Minutes, 25 March 1938.
36. NRO, 1331/7, Ellington Lodge Minutes, 16 March 1938; 20 March 1938; 9 November 1938; 7 December 1938; 21 December 1938.
37. NRO, 4222/1/5, Pegswood Lodge Minutes, 30 December 1936; TWAS, 1691/1/3, Burradon Lodge Minutes, 9; 22 December 1937.
38. WMRC, 78/ASW/4/1/17, ASW Journal and Reports, July 1937, p.488; *Daily Worker*, 26 January 1937.
39. Mates, 'Durham and South Wales Miners', pp.375–386.
40. Lewis Mates, 'A "Most Fruitful Period"? The North-east District Communist Party and the Popular Front Period, 1935–9', *North-east History*, 36 (2004), pp.74–81.
41. *North Mail*, 28 December 1937; *Heslop's Advertiser*, 17 February 1939.
42. DMOR, DMA EC Minutes, 11; 31 August 1936; 25; 28 January 1937; *Sunderland Echo*, 7 June 1937; *North Mail*, 23 June 1937. See chapter five.
43. Mates, 'Durham and South Wales Miners', pp.382, 387–389.
44. WMRC, 175/6/BR/31, NUS North Shields Branch Minutes, 7 October 1937; 28 July 1938; 29 September 1938; *Shields Gazette* 29 July 1938.
45. H. Francis, *Miners Against Fascism. Wales and the Spanish Civil War* (1984), pp.29–39.
46. *Blaydon Courier*, 19 December 1936.
47. DRO, D/EBF92/26, MFGB AR, 1937, p.295; *Blyth News*, 21 January 1937;
48. DRO, D/DMA 119, 120, 123, 125, 126, Ascertainments, Return Sheets, etc., 3 October 1931; 8 March 1932; 30 June 1932; 28 December 1933; 13 October 1934; 27 June 1935.

49. *Blaydon Courier*, 4 February 1938.
50. DRO, D/DMA/124, DMA Council Meeting, 24 March 1934.
51. DRO, D/DMA 126, Ascertainments, Return Sheets, etc., 27 June 1935.
52. DRO, D/DMA, Acc: 2157 (D) 194 (vol), Seaham Lodge Minutes, 7 October 1936; 9 December 1936; 18 March 1937; 31 March 1937.
53. *Blyth News*, 23 January 1939.
54. *Blyth News*, 5 January 1939.
55. *North Mail*, 15 August 1936.
56. TWAS, TU.TA1/1/11, Typographical Association Newcastle and District Branch Minutes, 31 October 1936; 20 February 1937; 25 September 1937; 30 October 1937; 27 November 1937; 18 December 1937; 19 February 1938; 30 April 1938; 28 May 1938; 27 August 1938; 29 October 1938.
57. TUC AR, 1938, p.367.
58. Mates, 'Durham and South Wales Miners', pp.394–395.
59. Francis, *Miners Against Fascism*, pp.143, 160; Mates, 'Durham and South Wales Miners', pp.393–394.
60. See Horner's and Lawther's comments in *Blyth News*, 11; 18 July 1938.
61. TWAS, 673/2, TGWU Area Committee Minutes, 26 April 1933; 30 January 1934.
62. Buchanan, *British Labour Movement*, p.10.
63. TWAS, 673/3, TGWU Area Committee Minutes, 27 October 1936.
64. WMRC, 175/6/BR/31, NUS North Shields Branch Minutes, 13 November 1935; 12 May 1936; 24 November 1936; 27 January 1937.
65. TWAS, TU/NUJ1/1/2, NUJ Sunderland, Shields and Hartlepool Branch Minutes, 26 February 1937; 10 March 1939; 9 December 1938.
66. TWAS, TU.TA1/1/11, Typographical Association Newcastle and District Branch Minutes, 22; 29 May 1937; 26 June 1937; 30 April 1938.
67. In many localities, when local Labour Parties emerged they were attached to the already existing trades council and they operated as joint bodies, though their relationships and ways of functioning varied considerably. The 1927 Trades Disputes Act 'made joint electoral and industrial bodies less common', and certainly had the effect of dividing the Sunderland trades council and Labour Party. However, in localities like Jarrow and Gateshead, the institutions retained their 'Labour Party and trades council' name and continued to operate in the public sphere as one organisation. In places like Newcastle, on the other hand, the City Party and trades council were separate entities that behaved publicly, and operated privately, in distinct ways. A. Clinton, *The Trade Union Rank and File. Trades Councils in Britain, 1900–40* (Manchester, 1977), p.183; DRO, D/X 1208/41, *Adventure into the Past. A History of the Sunderland Borough Labour Party* (1954), p.9.
68. *Newcastle Journal*, 9 September 1936. See chapters four and five.
69. LHASC, CP/CENT/PERS/1/01, Tom Aisbitt biography.
70. Lewis H. Mates, 'The United Front and the Popular Front in the North East of England, 1936–1939', (Newcastle University, PhD, 2002), pp.31–32.
71. TWAS, 608/Box 1252, Newcastle City Labour Party EC Minutes, 1 September 1936; SSPL, LPM5, South Shields LP&TC Minutes, 5 January 1937.
72. Labour Party AR, 1936, pp.172–173.

73. *Shields Gazette*, 17 July 1937; 19 July 1937; 21 July 1937.
74. CCC, LSPC, 1/2/99, Jas. Hutchinson letter to Pole, 19 May 1937; *Gateshead Labour Herald*, December 1936; *Evening Chronicle*, 19 April 1937.
75. For details on these, see chapters four and five.
76. *Sunderland Echo*, 31 May 1937; 30 August 1937; *Blyth News,* 25; 28 January 1937; 3 May 1937; *Morpeth Herald*, 7 May 1937; 18 June 1937; *Newcastle Journal*, 28 May 1937; *North Mail*, 27 August 1937.
77. DRO, D/Sho 131/5, DCFLP Meeting Agenda, 10 December 1936.
78. DRO, D/Sho 131/5, DCFLP Meeting Minutes, 6 March 1937; Agenda, 13 August 1937.
79. TWAS, 608/Box 1252, Newcastle City Labour Party EC Minutes, 3 May 1938; 7 June 1938; 5 July 1938; 6 December 1938; 2 January 1939.
80. *Sunderland Echo*, 31 January 1938; 4; 11 April 1938; 16 May 1938; 6 June 1938.
81. *North Mail*, 29 November 1937; 2 December 1937; 2 May 1938; *Shields Gazette*, 17 December 1937; 18 February 1938; 16; 26 March 1938.
82. *Blaydon Courier*, 4 February 1938; 8; 15 April 1938; 6 May 1938; 10; 17 June 1938; 4 November 1938; 17; 24 February 1939; *North Mail*, 13 June 1938.
83. SSPL, LPM5 and LPM6, South Shields LP&TC Minutes, 8; 12 April 1938; 6 May 1938; 3 June 1938; 1; 19 July 1938; 9 September 1938; 16 December 1938; 28 February 1939.
84. NRO, 1587/10, Newbiggin and North Seaton LLP Minutes, 18 January 1939.
85. DRO, D/SHO/93/2, Durham CLP Minutes, 28 May 1938; *Sunderland Echo*, 20 December 1937; 14 March 1938; 23 May 1938; 6 June 1938.
86. *North Mail*, 31 January 1938.
87. NRO, 527/A/3, Wansbeck CLP Minutes, 16 April 1938; 1 October 1938.
88. *Morpeth Herald*, 18 March 1938; 25 March 1938.
89. SSPL, LPM6, South Shields LP&TC Minutes, 12; 24 April 1938; 6 May 1938; 3 June 1938; 5; 15 July 1938; *Shields Gazette* 11 May 1938.
90. NEC Minutes, 5 May 1938; DRO, D/Sho 131/5, DCFLP AGM Agenda, 18 June 1938; DRO, D/SHO/93/2, Durham CLP Minutes, 28 May 1938; NRO, 527/A/3, Wansbeck CLP Minutes, 19 March 1938; *Durham Chronicle*, 24 June 1938; *Sunderland Echo*, 4; 11 April 1938.
91. Mates, 'Durham and South Wales Miners', pp.390–391.
92. NRO, 759/68, NMA EC Minutes, 14 March 1938; 5 April 1938.
93. *North Mail*, 20 June 1938.
94. TWAS, 608/Box 1252, Newcastle City Labour Party EC Minutes, 3 May 1938; Delegate Meeting Minutes, 10 May 1938.
95. *Shields Gazette*, 3 January 1938.
96. *North Mail*, 15; 31 January 1938; *Shields Gazette*, 21 January 1938.
97. *Sunderland Echo*, 31 January 1938.
98. WMRC, 292/946/18B, SMAC Bulletin, May 1938.
99. NRO, 759/68, NMA EC Minutes, 14 March 1938; *Morpeth Herald*, 18 March 1938; Mates, 'Durham and South Wales Miners', pp.390–391.
100. *Sunderland Echo*, 23 May 1938.
101. DRO, D/SHO/93/2, Durham CLP Minutes, 18 February 1939.
102. Buchanan, *British Labour Movement*, pp.152–153.
103. Mates, 'Durham and South Wales Miners', p.387–390.

104. NRO, 527/A/3, Wansbeck CLP Minutes, 17 October 1936.

105. NRO, 1331/6, Ellington Lodge Minutes, 17 August 1938.

106. DRO, D/X 1099/1, Durham County Teachers' Labour Group Minutes, 24 October 1936.

107. SSPL, LPM6, South Shields LP&TC Minutes, 16 December 1938; 28 February 1939; See chapter four.

108. See for example comments of the Wansbeck CLP secretary in response to an invitation to organise attendance at a local conference organised by the left-wing paper *Tribune*. NRO, 527/A/3, Wansbeck CLP Minutes, 13 November 1937.

109. *Morpeth Herald*, 6 May 1938.

110. The Bishop Auckland EC Minutes (in possession of the late Walter Nunn) record only four meetings (two of which were 'special') during the period the war was on. Ben Pimlott concluded that this was the sum total of EC meetings of the party. This was unclear as there were no mentions, for example, of two occasions on which the party expelled dissidents. B. Pimlott, *Hugh Dalton* (1986), pp.176–7.

111. DRO, D/SHO/99, Houghton-le-Spring CLP AR 1937.

112. TWAS, TU.TA1/1/11, Typographical Association Newcastle and District Branch Minutes, 26 February 1938.

113. TWAS, 608/Box 1252, Newcastle City Labour Party EC Minutes, 13 September 1936; 2 March 1937; 2 November 1937; 7 June 1938; 4 November 1938; 6 December 1938; 2 January 1939; 7 February 1939; 7 March 1939.

114. Ibid. 2 January 1939.

115. Peter D. Drake, 'Labour and Spain: British Labour's Response to the Spanish Civil War With Particular Reference to the Labour Movement in Birmingham', (Birmingham University, M.Litt., 1977), p.123.

116. TWAS, 608/Box 1252, Newcastle City Labour Party EC Minutes, 18 September 1936.

117. NRO, 527/A/3, Wansbeck CLP Minutes, 17 October 1936.

118. Buchanan, *British Labour Movement*, p.11.

119. TWAS, 608/Box 1252, Newcastle City Labour Party EC Minutes, 16 January 1937; *Blyth News*, 26 April 1937; 24 February 1938; 16 May 1938.

120. Mates, 'United Front', pp.65–78.

121. Drake, 'Labour and Spain', pp.135–137.

122. DRO, D/SHO/99, Houghton-le-Spring CLP AR, 1937.

123. *Blyth News*, 15 February 1937.

124. *North Mail*, 20 June 1938. Curiously, this conference seemed more interested in industrial direct action: see chapter four.

125. NRO, 527/A/3, Wansbeck CLP Minutes, 9 January 1937. See introduction.

126. NRO, 4222/1/5, Pegswood Lodge Minutes, 13 January 1937.

127. NRO, 527/A/3, Wansbeck CLP Minutes, 20 March 1937.

128. CCC, LSPC, 1/2/134, Blenkinsop letter to Pole (LSC), n.d. [post 18 July 1937].

129. CCC, LSPC 1/2/47, Blenkinsop letter to Pole, n.d. [pre-11 April 1937].

130. CCC, LSPC, 1/2/53, Blenkinsop letter to Pole, 11 April 1937; *Newcastle Journal*, 5 April 1937; 28 May 1937; 31 May 1937.

131. *Shields Gazette*, 14 November 1936; 16 November 1936; 22 February 1937; 26 February 1937; *North Mail*, 25 July 1938.

132. *Morpeth Herald*, 23 April 1937.

133. NRO, 1286/3, Ashington Miners Federation Minutes, 21 March 1937.

134. *Morpeth Herald*, 22 April 1938. See chapter six.

135. *Morpeth Herald*, 22 April 1938.

136. *Morpeth Herald*, 1 July 1938.

137. *Blyth News*, 12 September 1938.

138. NRO, 3793/44, Woodhorn Lodge Minutes, 30 June 1937.

139. NRO, 3793/44, Woodhorn Lodge Minutes, 30 June 1937. There was also a question here of how attractive the kinds of activities the SMAC could offer were to movement activists: see chapters five and six.

140. Buchanan, *British Labour Movement*, p.31.

141. *Blaydon Courier*, 21 January 1938; 4; 25 February 1938; 8 April 1938; 17 June 1938; 30 September 1938; *North Mail*, 15; 31 January 1938; 21 February 1938; *Shields Gazette*, 25 January 1938; *Blyth News*, 21 February 1938.

142. *Shields Gazette*, 2; 11 December 1937; *North Mail*, 13 December 1937.

143. Mates, 'United Front', p.68. See chapter five.

144. Paul Corthorn, *In the Shadow of the Dictators. The British Left in the 1930s* (2006).

145. Mates, 'Most Fruitful Period', p.63.

146. David Blaazer, *The Popular Front and the Progressive Tradition* (Cambridge, 1992), pp.163–5.

147. David Blaazer made a case for the Labour left arriving independently at positions on fascism that coalesced with the CP in the 1930s. Blaazer, *Progressive Tradition, passim.*

148. Mates, 'United Front', pp.88–89, 112–113, 119, 163–164, 181, 199–201.

149. See chapters four and six.

150. Buchanan, *British Labour Movement*, pp.47, 137.

151. LHASC, CP Central Committee Minutes, 10 November 1936.

152. NRL, CPT 182/21, Text for Speech on Spain and Czechoslovakia, 30 May 1937.

153. See chapters four and six.

154. Mike Squires, *The Aid to Spain Movement in Battersea, 1936–1939* (1994), pp.26–28; Bill Moore, '"Aid for Spain" in Sheffield', in W. Albaya, J. Baxter and B. Moore, *Behind the Clenched Fist: Sheffield's 'Aid to Spain', 1936–1939* (Sheffield, 1986), p.15; Buchanan, 'Britain's Popular Front?', p.65.

155. *Blaydon Courier*, 22 August 1936.

156. A.J.A. Morris, *C.P. Trevelyan, 1870–1958. Portrait of a Radical* (Belfast, 1977), p.191.

157. Mates, 'United Front', pp.37–38. See chapter six.

Chapter Three

1.   Tom Buchanan, *The Spanish Civil War and the British Labour Movement* (Cambridge, 1991), p.168.

2.   Pauline Lynn, 'The Impact of Women. The Shaping of Political Allegiance in County Durham 1918–1945', *The Local Historian*, 23 (1998), p.167.

3.   *Catholic Herald* (Tyneside), 18 September 1936; *Universe* (Northern Edition), 25 September 1936; Lewis H. Mates, 'The United Front and the Popular Front in the North-east of England, 1936–1939', (Newcastle University, PhD, 2002), pp.79–80.
4.   *Newcastle Journal*, 9 September 1936.
5.   *Evening Chronicle*, 9 October 1936.
6.   *North Mail*, 12 October 1936.
7.   *Evening Chronicle*, 18 November 1936; *Sunday Sun*, 25 October 1936.
8.   *Sunday Sun*, 18 October 1936.
9.   *Sunday Sun*, 25 October 1936.
10. Tom Buchanan, 'Divided Loyalties: the Impact of the Spanish Civil War on Britain's Civil Service Unions 1936–1939', *Historical Research*, 65 (1992), p.104.
11. *Universe* (Northern Edition), 4 September 1936.
12. There was no separate north-east Catholic press after the *Tyneside Catholic News* was incorporated with the *Catholic Herald* in July 1934.
13. *Catholic Herald* (Tyneside), 22 January 1937; 12 March 1937; 6 August 1937.
14. *Sunday Sun*, 8; 15; 22 November 1936; 13; 20; 27 December 1936.
15. *Sunday Sun*, 10 January 1937.
16. LHASC, CP Central Committee Minutes, 10 November 1936.
17. See, for example, letters in *Evening Chronicle*, 5 August 1936.
18. *Evening Chronicle*, 24 September 1936.
19. *Shields News*, 24; 26 November 1936.
20. For examples see *North Mail*, 8; 13 August 1936; 2 September 1936.
21. See, for examples, letters in *Sunderland Echo*, 31 December 1936; 11; 27 January 1937; 29 April 1937; 8 October 1937; 26 November 1937; 22 February 1938.
22. *Blaydon Courier*, 5 September 1936.
23. *Blaydon Courier*, 12; 19 September 1936.
24. *Blaydon Courier*, 29 August 1936.
25. Buchanan, *British Labour Movement*, p.184.
26. Buchanan, *British Labour Movement*, p.184.
27. *Sunderland Echo*, 1 April 1939.
28. Buchanan, *British Labour Movement*, pp.175, 191–192; Peter D. Drake, 'Labour and Spain: British Labour's Response to the Spanish Civil War With Particular Reference to the Labour Movement in Birmingham', (Birmingham University, M.Litt., 1977), p.191.
29. *Universe* (Northern Edition), 26 February 1937. See chapter two.
30. *Sunderland Echo*, 15 February 1937.
31. *Catholic Herald* (Tyneside), 11 June 1937.
32. DRO, D/DMA/334/11, Eden Lodge Minutes, 17 December 1936; 21 October 1937.
33. *Sunderland Echo*, 24 May 1938.
34. *Sunderland Echo*, 26 May 1938.
35. LHASC, CP Central Committee Minutes, 10 November 1936.
36. MML, Box B-4/M/1, Charlie Woods letter to Jim Fyrth, 18 February 1985.
37. SSPL, LPM6, South Shields LP&TC Minutes, 12; 19; 27 April 1938; 16 December 1938.

38. David Clark, *We do not Want the Earth– History of the South Shields Labour Party* (Newcastle, 1992), pp.86–87.
39. SSPL, LPM6, South Shields LP&TC Minutes, 5 July 1938.
40. *Shields Gazette*, 29 October 1937. See chapter two.
41. NRO, 1286/3, Ashington Miners Federation Minutes, 19 June 1938.
42. LHASC, CP/CENT/PERS/1/01, Tom Aisbitt biography by Horace Green.
43. See chapter four.
44. Ellen Wilkinson, *The Town That Was Murdered* (1939), pp.101–2, 244; H.A. Mess, *Industrial Tyneside. A Social Survey* (1928), pp.35, 135; F. Ennis, 'The Jarrow March of 1936: The Symbolic Expression of the Protest', (Durham University, MA, 1982), pp.85–86; D.M. Jackson, '"Garibaldi or the Pope!" Newcastle's Irish Riot of 1866', *North-east History*, 34 (2001), p.58.
45. *Shields Gazette*, 8 September 1936.
46. *Evening Chronicle*, 17 August 1936; 12 September 1936.
47. *Shields Gazette*, 13 December 1937.
48. *Shields Gazette*, 17 December 1937.
49. *North Mail*, 15; 23 December 1937.
50. *Shields Gazette*, 13 December 1937.
51. See Mates, 'United Front', pp.72–76.
52. *North Mail*, 13 January 1937.
53. *Shields Gazette*, 31 December 1936.
54. GPL, L908.9, Newspaper Cuttings, pp.92, 121 (n.d.s); F.W.D. Manders, *A History of Gateshead* (Gateshead, 1973), pp.277–285; T.P. MacDermott, 'Irish Workers on Tyneside in the 19th Century', in Norman McCord (ed.), *Essays in Tyneside Labour History* (Newcastle, 1977), p.159; Archie Potts, '"Bevin to Beat the Bankers": Ernest Bevin's Gateshead Campaign of 1931', *Bulletin of the North-east Group for the Study of Labour History*, 11 (1977), p.31.
55. *Sunday Sun*, 13 June 1937; *North Mail*, 14; 15 June 1937.
56. GPL, L908.9, Newspaper Cuttings, 1931–33, 1 June 1931, p.129; S. Fielding, *Class and Ethnicity. Irish Catholics in England, 1880–1939* (Buckingham, 1993), p.119; Neil Riddell, 'The Catholic Church and the Labour Party, 1918–1931', *Twentieth Century British History*, 8 (1997), pp.179–182; J.E. Keating, 'Roman Catholics, Christian Democracy and the British Labour Movement 1910–1960' (Manchester University, PhD, 1992), p.108.
57. Fielding, *Class and Ethnicity*, pp.109–110.
58. B.E. Naylor, 'Ramsay Macdonald and Seaham Labour Politics', *Bulletin of the North-east Group for the Study of Labour History*, 15 (1981), p.20; Lynn, 'Impact of Women', p.167.
59. MacDermott, 'Irish Workers on Tyneside', p.159; Riddell, 'Catholic Church', p.187; Keating, 'Roman Catholics', pp.217–218; Archie Potts, 'Forty Years On. The Labour Party in Sunderland 1900–1945', *Bulletin of the North-east Group for the Study of Labour History*, 24 (1990), pp.12–17.
60. *Sunderland Echo*, 25 April 1938.
61. *North Mail*, 13 December 1937; Woods letter to Fyrth, 18 February 1985.
62. *Shields Gazette*, 24 January 1939. See chapter five.
63. *Daily Worker*, 15 September 1936.
64. Buchanan, *British Labour Movement*, pp.188–190.

65. LHASC, SCW/12/1i, F. O'Hanlan letter, 15 January 1938.
66. LHASC, SCW/12/2i, F. O'Hanlan letter to James Middleton (Labour Party Secretary), 6 February 1938.
67. LHASC, SCW/12/3, F. O'Hanlan's draft of the letter with signatures on it.
68. *North Mail*, 23 January 1939; *Newcastle Journal*, 23 January 1939; MML, Box B-7B/30 and Box B-4M/5a, newspaper articles (nds).
69. *North Mail*, 4 August 1938; *Durham Chronicle*, 5 August 1938.
70. *Durham Chronicle*, 9 December 1938.
71. *Sunday Sun*, 18 October 1936; 1; 29 November 1936; 6; 13 December 1936; 1 August 1937; *North Mail*, 2; 6 March 1937.
72. See for example, WMRC, 78/ASW/4/1/19, ASW Journal, May 1939, p.391.
73. This was not a wholly isolated occurrence. Almost two years later, J.H. Ashington withdrew his children from an unnamed Roman Catholic school because prayers were 'being offered up daily for the success of Franco'. *North Mail*, 5 July 1938.
74. *North Mail*, 17 September 1936.
75. *Evening Chronicle*, 21 September 1936.
76. *Shields Gazette*, 11 September 1936.
77. *Sunday Sun*, 13 December 1936.
78. *Sunday Sun*, 3 January 1937.
79. *Catholic Herald* (East), 28 January 1938; Mates, 'United Front', pp.96–7; T. Buchanan and M. Conway, *Political Catholicism in Europe, 1918–1965* (Oxford, 1996), pp.265–266.
80. Buchanan, *British Labour Movement*, p.172.
81. Buchanan, *British Labour Movement*, p.186.
82. Buchanan, *British Labour Movement*, p.169.
83. *Catholic Herald* (Tyneside), 11 June 1937.
84. *Catholic Herald* (Tyneside), 9 April 1937.
85. *Catholic Herald* (Tyneside), 6 November 1936.
86. *Evening Chronicle*, 2 November 1935; 3 November 1936; 2 November 1937; 2 November 1938.
87. Ibid. North ward was not contested in 1937 and 1938.
88. *Gateshead Municipal News*, October 1936; November 1936.
89. *Gateshead Labour Herald*, December 1936.
90. Drake, 'Labour and Spain', pp.104–105, 137, 156, 202.
91. *Sunderland Echo*, 22 February 1937; Mates, 'United Front', p.67.
92. *Sunderland Echo*, 30 October 1936.
93. *Sunderland Echo*, 1 November 1937.
94. Mates, 'United Front', p.103.
95. D. Byrne, 'Immigrants and the Formation of the North-eastern Industrial Working Class', *Bulletin of the North-east Group for the Study of Labour History*, 30 (1996), pp.31, 35; R.J. Cooter, 'The Irish in County Durham and Newcastle', (Durham University, MA, 1972), pp.60–61; MacDermott, 'Irish Workers on Tyneside', p.163.
96. A. Archer, *The Two Catholic Churches. A Study in Oppression* (1986), pp.20, 53–54; Keating, 'Roman Catholics', p.314.

97. J. Keating, *Irish Heroes in the War* (1917), p.21, quoted in Byrne, 'Immigrants', p.31. See also Norman McCord, 'Some aspects of north-east England in the nineteenth century, *Northern History*, 8 (1972), pp.85–86; Jackson, 'Newcastle's Irish Riot', pp.49–82; Caroline Scott, 'A Comparative Re-examination of Anglo-Irish Relations in Nineteenth Century Manchester, Liverpool and Newcastle-upon-Tyne' (Durham University, PhD, 1998).

98. Cooter, 'Irish in County Durham', pp.239, 266, 269–270.

99. Archer, *Two Catholic Churches*, p.54; Jackson, 'Newcastle's Irish Riot', p.68; MacDermott, 'Irish Workers on Tyneside', pp.170–173; T. MacDermott, 'The Irish in Nineteenth Century Tyneside', *Bulletin of the North-east Group for the Study of Labour History*, 16 (1982), p.46.

100. *Catholic Herald* (Tyneside), 7 May 1937.

101. *Catholic Herald* (Tyneside), 30 April 1937; *Sunderland Echo*, 3 May 1937.

102. *Universe* (Northern Edition), 25 September 1936.

103. *Catholic Herald* (Tyneside), 30 October 1936.

104. *Universe* (Northern Edition), 25 September 1936; Kester Aspden, *Fortress Church. The English Roman Catholic Bishops and the Catholic Church* (Leominster, 2002), pp.210–11.

105. Mates, 'United Front', *passim*.

106. *Catholic Herald* (Tyneside), 11 June 1937.

107. Frank Graham, *The Battle of Jarama* (Newcastle, 1987), p.27.

108. Aspden, *Fortress Church*, p.218.

109. *Catholic Herald* (Tyneside), 18; 25 June 1937; Don Watson, 'Politics and Humanitarian Aid: Basque Refugees in the North-east and Cumbria During the Spanish Civil War', *North-east History*, 36 (2005), p.23.

110. *Evening Chronicle*, 26 June 1937; 7; 12; July 1937; *Newcastle Journal*, 7 July 1937. It also appeared to act as a disincentive for some groups to act. Morpeth LNU, for example, did not initially begin to raise money for Basque children as 'the R.C. are taking responsibility for these …' NRO, 1566/3, Morpeth LNU Branch Minutes, 28 June 1937.

111. Municipal Workers' Journal, August 1938; Mates, 'United Front', p.73. Whether other Catholic activists in Jarrow LP&TC endorsed the institution's more formal support for cooperation with Communists and the popular front is unclear: see chapter four.

112. M. Alpert, 'Humanitarianism and Politics in the British Response to the Spanish Civil War, 1936–9', *European History Quarterly*, 14:4 (1984), pp.429.

113. Tom Buchanan, *Britain and the Spanish Civil War* (Cambridge, 1997), p.183.

114. Len Edmondson Interview with Lewis Mates, 11 November 1994.

115. Buchanan, *Britain and the Spanish Civil War*, p.178.

116. Keating, 'Roman Catholics', pp.314–315, 387–388; J.M. Cleary, *Catholic Social Action in Britain 1909–1959* (Oxford, 1961), pp.137–138.

117. *Catholic Herald* (Tyneside), 11 June 1937.

118. *Catholic Herald* (Tyneside), 26 February 1937.

119. *Catholic Herald* (Tyneside), 6 August 1937.

120. *Sunderland Echo*, 21 June 1937.

121. Riddell, 'Catholic Church', p.176; T.O. Hughes, *Winds of Change the Roman Catholic Church and Society in Wales, 1918–1962* (Cardiff, 1999), pp.6–10, 63–78.

122. A. Flinn, "'Prospects for Socialism". The Character and Implantation of Working-class Activism in the Manchester Area, 1933–1941' (Manchester University, PhD, 1999).
123. Drake, 'Labour and Spain', p.100.

Chapter Four

1. Noreen Branson, *History of the Communist Party of Great Britain 1927–1941* (1985), p.225.
2. LHASC, CP Central Committee Minutes, 10 November 1936. See chapter six.
3. The extent to which a de facto popular front emerged over activity on Spain and the role of the CP in instigating joint activities are discussed chapter six.
4. *Daily Worker*, 18 August 1936.
5. *Daily Worker*, 15 September 1936; *Newcastle Journal*, 14 September 1936; *New Leader*, 18 September 1936.
6. Lewis Mates, 'A "Most Fruitful Period"? The North East District Communist Party and the Popular Front Period, 1935–9', *North-east History*, 36 (2004), pp.65–66.
7. Blaydon CLP supported Cripps. Mates, 'Most Fruitful Period?', pp.62–4.
8. Jarrow CLP opposed Cripps. Mates, 'Most Fruitful Period?', pp.57–8, 60–1.
9. DMOR, DMA Minutes, Circulars etc., 11 June 1938; NRO, 3793/30, Cambois Lodge Minutes, 19 May 1938; *North Mail*, 28 March 1938.
10. WMRC, 292/78/44, NEFTC Minutes, 8 February 1936; 28 March 1936; *Blaydon Courier*, 8 August 1936.
11. Mates, 'Most Fruitful Period?', pp.57–8, 60–4.
12. *New Leader*, 14 February 1937; *Gateshead Labour Herald*, January 1937.
13. *Gateshead Labour Herald*, March 1937; *New Leader*, 19 March 1937; *Shields Gazette*, 15 March 1937; Nigel Todd, *In Excited Times. The People Against the Blackshirts* (Whitley Bay, 1995).
14. *New Leader*, 9 September 1938; Len Edmondson Interview with Lewis Mates, 19 June 1998; H. Francis, *Miners Against Fascism. Wales and the Spanish Civil War* (1984), p.114.
15. *Gateshead Labour Herald*, January 1938; February 1938.
16. Lewis H. Mates, 'The United Front and the Popular Front in the North East of England, 1936–1939', (Newcastle University, PhD, 2002), pp.140–1.
17. *Northern Echo*, 25 February 1939; Mates, 'Most Fruitful Period?', pp.67–8.
18. TWAS, 608/Box 1262, Newcastle City Labour Party Delegate Meeting Minutes, 18 September 1936; 12 January 1937; 11 May 1937; 11 January 1938; 10 May 1938; 13 September 1938; 14 February 1939; 9 May 1939; TWAS, 608/Box 1252, Newcastle City Labour Party EC Minutes, 1 September 1936; 2 March 1937; 6 July 1937; 30 September 1937; 4 January 1938; 1 March 1938; 5 April 1938; 6 September 1938; 6 December 1938; 7 February 1939; 7 March 1939; 14 March 1939; 4 April 1939; 11 April 1939; 2 May 1939; Mates, 'United Front', pp.141, 196–8.
19. WMRC, 292/79S/37, South Shields LP&TC AR, 1934; WMRC, 292/777.1/15, South Shields LP&TC letter to TUC, 19 January 1935; SSPL, LPM4, South Shields LP&TC Minutes, 10 November 1933; 23 January 1934;

LPM5, 4 August 1936; LPM6, 20 May 1938; 31 January 1939; 11 April 1939; *Shields Gazette*, 23 January 1937; 23 July 1937; 4 May 1938; Mates, 'United Front', pp.43, 125–6, 130, 142, 167–8, 201–2.

20. *Blyth News*, 20 December 1937.
21. *Blyth News*, 23 July 1936; 10; 13; 17 August 1936; 21; 25; 28 January 1937; 1 February 1937; 27; 30 September 1937; 21 March 1938; 9 May 1938; 28 July 1938; *Morpeth Herald*, 29 July 1938; Mates, 'United Front', pp.30–1, 40, 44–5, 55, 62, 124–7, 134–5, 162, 202–5.
22. L.H. Mates, 'The North-east and the Campaigns for a Popular Front, 1938–9', *Northern History*, XLIII (2), 2006, pp.290, 295–6.
23. Mates, 'United Front', pp.24–9, 34, 49–50, 117, 150–1, 159–161, 177–8, 193–6.
24. DRO, D/DMA/326/9, Brancepeth No.2 Lodge Minutes, 19 May 1938; DRO, D/DMA/310, Murton Lodge Minutes, 16 February 1939; 2 March 1939.
25. DRO, D/EBF92/26, MFGB AR, 1937, p.295.
26. Mates, 'Most Fruitful Period?', p.70.
27. See chapter two.
28. *Shields Evening News*, 6 February 1939; Mates, 'United Front', pp.31, 32, 36, 40–47, 62, 92, 93, 125, 202, 204, 208, 219.
29. *North Mail*, 3 April 1939; Mates, 'North-east Campaigns', p.284.
30. *Daily Worker*, 15 September 1936.
31. *New Leader*, 23 October 1936.
32. Mates, 'Most Fruitful Period?', pp.68–9, 71; Archie Potts, *Zilliacus. A Life for Peace and Socialism* (2002), p.116.
33. *Sunderland Echo*, 25 April 1938; Mates, 'United Front', p.24.
34. *Northern Echo*, 27 February 1939; Mates, 'North-east Campaigns', pp.280–284.
35. DRO, D/Sho 131/5, DCFLP circular letter, 3 May 1938.
36. Mates, 'United Front', pp.109–221.
37. Mates, 'North-east Campaigns', pp.277–8.
38. TWAS, 608/Box 1252, Newcastle City Labour Party Delegate Meeting Minutes, 4 August 1936; 11 May 1937; 7 June 1938; 13 December 1938; 10 January 1939; 14 February 1939; 4; 11 April 1939; TWAS, 608/Box 1252, Newcastle City Labour Party EC Minutes, 1 September 1936; 1 December 1936; 2 March 1937; 7 June 1938; 6 December 1938; 2 January 1939; *North Mail*, 29 October 1937; *Sunday Sun*, 31 October 1937; *Daily Worker*, 26 January 1937; *Tribune*, 10 February 1939.
39. Mates, 'United Front', pp.112–3, 164–5, 185.
40. WMRC, 292/946/18B, SMAC Bulletin, May 1938.
41. Mates, 'Most Fruitful Period?', p.71.
42. Mates, 'United Front', pp.69–70, 78.
43. *Shields Gazette*, 22 February 1937; 26 February 1937.
44. Quoted in Tom Buchanan, *The Spanish Civil War and the British Labour Movement* (Cambridge, 1991), p.153.
45. Branson, *Communist Party*, p.225.
46. DRO, D/Sho 131/4, 'Now for Local Elections, 1937'.
47. Mates, 'United Front', pp.118, 198.

48. Buchanan, *British Labour Movement*, p.35.
49. Mates, 'United Front', p.61.
50. Buchanan, *British Labour Movement*, p.12–13.
51. DRO, D/Sho 131/5, DCFLP circular letter, 3 May 1938.
52. See Mates, 'North-east Campaigns', pp.285–294.
53. *Blaydon Courier*, 10 June 1938; 17 June 1938.
54. *Newcastle Journal*, 30 May 1938; *Blaydon Courier*, 3 June 1938.
55. *North Mail*, 31 August 1937.
56. *Durham Chronicle*, 4 June 1937.
57. See chapter six.
58. LHASC, CP Central Committee Minutes, 30 October 1937; 19 March 1939.
59. NRL, CPTEX133, C.P. Trevelyan letter to wife, 6 February 1939.
60. Buchanan, *British Labour Movement*, p.31.
61. NEC Minutes, 5 May 1938.
62. Buchanan, *British Labour Movement*, p.35.
63. Francis, *Miners Against Fascism*, p.108–118, 132.
64. Francis, *Miners Against Fascism*, p.112.
65. P.D. Drake, 'Labour and Spain: British Labour's Response to the Spanish Civil War With Particular Reference to the Labour Movement in Birmingham' (Birmingham University, M.Litt, 1977), p.156.
66. Drake, 'Labour and Spain', pp.96–168, 271.
67. Mike Squires, *The Aid to Spain Movement in Battersea, 1936–1939* (1994), p.43.
68. Buchanan, *British Labour Movement*, pp.9, 110–1, 117.
69. *Durham Chronicle*, 4 November 1938.
70. A.J.A. Morris, *C.P. Trevelyan, 1870–1958. Portrait of a Radical* (Belfast, 1977), p.191.
71. TUC AR, 1935, pp.353–354.
72. WMRC, 292/78/44, NEFTC AGM Minutes, 13 June 1936.
73. DRO, D/DMA/128, DMA EC Circular to Lodges, 28 February 1936.
74. *Evening Chronicle*, 17 May 1937; *Newcastle Journal*, 17 May 1937.
75. *Durham Chronicle*, 9 October 1936.
76. *Sunderland Echo*, 17 May 1937; 24 November 1937; 6; 13 December; 21 March 1938.
77. *Sunderland Echo*, 30 May 1938.
78. DRO, D/DMA Acc: 2157 (D) 236 (vol), Hamsteels Lodge Minutes, 1 April 1937; DRO, D/DMA Acc: 2157 (D) 194 (vol), Seaham Lodge Minutes, 24 March 1937; 16 April 1937; DRO, D/DMA/334/11, Eden Lodge Minutes, 4 February 1937; *Evening Chronicle*, 19 April 1937.
79. DRO, D/DMA/122 and 126, Ascertainments, Return Sheets, etc., 22 April 1933; 27 April 1935.
80. *North Mail*, 19 August 1936.
81. *North Mail*, 17 August 1936.
82. *Shields Gazette*, 19 August 1936.
83. *Shields Gazette*, 17 November 1936.
84. Don Watson, 'Politics and Humanitarian Aid: Basque Refugees in the North-east and Cumbria During the Spanish Civil War', *North-east History*, 36 (2005),

p.14; Don Watson and John Corcoran, *An Inspiring Example. The North-east of England and the Spanish Civil War, 1936–1939* (1996), p.11.

85. *North Mail*, 7 April 1938.

86. *Evening Chronicle*, 15 April 1937; 24 June 1937; *Morpeth Herald*, 10 March 1939; *Sunderland Echo*, 7 January 1939; *Blyth News*, 30 January 1939; 13 March 1939; *North Mail*, 2 August 1938; 27 January 1939.

87. José Peirats, *The CNT in the Spanish Revolution, Vol.2* (Sussex, 2005), p.25.

88. WMRC, 159/5/3/202, Newcastle trades council circular, 23 January 1937; Buchanan, *British Labour Movement*, pp.82–83.

89. WMRC, 159/3/C/6/3, Jim Henson letter to Edo Fimmen (International Transport Workers' Federation).

90. See Buchanan, *British Labour Movement*, pp.210–15; Watson and Corcoran, *An Inspiring Example*, pp.15–23.

91. *North Mail*, 24 February 1937; A. Robson, *Spike: Alec 'Spike' Robson 1895–1979: Class Fighter* (North Shields, 1987).

92. *Shields Gazette*, 22; 25 February 1937; *North Mail*, 22; 24 February 1937.

93. *North Mail*, 4 May 1937; 5 May 1937; 7 June 1937.

94. *Shieldsman*, 22 April 1937. Quoted in Buchanan, *British Labour Movement*, p.210.

95. The *Blyth News* (25 February 1937) reported that the crew signed on in Blyth in November 1936.

96. *North Mail*, 16 March 1937.

97. Lewis Mates, 'Durham and South Wales Miners and the Spanish Civil War', *Twentieth Century British History*, 17:3 (2006), pp.382, 392.

98. *North Mail*, 20 June 1938. My emphasis.

99. Buchanan, *British Labour Movement*, p.220. See chapter two.

100. WMRC, 127NU/1/1/26, NUR Quarterly Meeting, June 1938, pp.191–2.

101. WMRC, 127NU/1/1/26, NUR Quarterly Meeting, June 1938, pp.191–2.

102. Mates, 'Durham and South Wales Miners', pp.391–392.

103. NRO, 1331/6, Ellington Lodge Minutes, 16; 20 March 1938. It is unclear why Ellington did not go through official channels starting with the NMA.

104. NRO, 759/68, NMA EC Minutes, 15 May 1937; 25 March 1938.

105. Buchanan, *British Labour Movement*, p.122.

106. Buchanan, *British Labour Movement*, p.198.

107. DRO, D/EBF92/26, MFGB AR, 1937, p.295.

108. *Shields Gazette*, 25 July 1938.

109. *North Mail*, 2 November 1936.

110. *Evening Chronicle*, 18 November 1936; *North Mail*, 22 February 1937.

111. DRO, D/Sho 97, Blaydon CLP AR, 1936.

112. *Blaydon Courier*, 6 May 1938. My emphasis.

113. *Blaydon Courier*, 6 May 1938.

114. *Blaydon Courier*, 13 May 1938.

115. LHASC, CP/DUTT/05/11, Andy, Steve and Robert Lawther letter to Will Lawther, 4 November 1939.

116. Fenner Brockway, *The Workers' Front* (1938), p.183.

117. *Blyth News*, 20 July 1936.

118. Mates, 'United Front', pp.146–7.

119. *Sunderland Echo*, 17 August 1936.

120. Francis, *Miners Against Fascism*, p.261.
121. GPL, L331.88, DMA *Monthly Journal*, 12, March 1939.
122. *Tribune*, 17 February 1939.
123. Francis, *Miners Against Fascism*, pp.146, 150–2, 199–201; Mates, 'Durham and South Wales Miners', pp.378, 393–4.
124. Rob Stradling, *Wales and the Spanish Civil War: The Dragon's Dearest Cause* (Cardiff, 2004), p.108.
125. Mates, 'Durham and South Wales Miners', pp.391–2.
126. NRO, 1331/6, Ellington Lodge Minutes, 9 November 1938.
127. See Buchanan, *British Labour Movement*, p.107-136.
128. Buchanan, *British Labour Movement*, p.126.
129. Buchanan, *British Labour Movement*, p.127.
130. See for example: NRL, CPT 182, Text for Speech, 30 May 1937.
131. NRL, CPT 183, Text for Speech, 23 October 1938.
132. CCC, LSPC, 1/6/74, Blenkinsop letter to Pole, 19 October 1938.
133. NRL, CPT EX 133, Trevelyan to wife, 6 February 1939.
134. *Morpeth Herald*, 10 March 1939.
135. George Orwell, *Homage to Catalonia* in *Orwell in Spain* (2001), p.188.
136. *Shields Gazette*, 17 November 1936.

Chapter Five

1.   Some of these committees adopted different names, sometimes not including 'medical' in their titles, for example (and titles changed). They are deemed SMACs here because the all took inspiration from the national committee, which did have 'medical' in its title.
2.   There was a Willington SMAC (County Durham) operating in April 1939, but there was curiously no evidence of its existence before this time. DRO, D/DMA/326/9, Brancepeth No.2 Lodge Minutes, 20 April 1939.
3.   Nancy Newbigin letter to Mrs. [Irene] Walker, 23 February 1942 (in possession of Marleen Sidaway).
4.   *Evening Chronicle*, 13 May 1937; 6 July 1937.
5.   NRO, 759/A1/36, Jim Smith letter to NMA, 4 January 1937; A.G. Furness circular, 26 April 1937 (Marleen Sidaway); *Newcastle Journal*, 4; 14 December 1936; *North Mail*, 15 January 1937; 18 September 1937; 17 February 1938; *Shields Gazette*, 22 November 1938; 5; 17 December 1938.
6.   *North Mail*, 6; 8; 16; 24 March 1937; *Shields Gazette*, 20 March 1937.
7.   *North Mail*, 16 March 1937.
8.   *North Mail*, 5 May 1937; *Shields Gazette*, 13 March 1937; 19; 27 April 1937.
9.   See, for example, NRO, 3793/44, Woodhorn Lodge Minutes, 5 May 1937.
10. See chapter one for details of brigader's activities and chapter six for more discussion on official and unofficial in this context.
11. *North Mail*, 29 June 1937; 7; 30; 31 July 1937; 3; 4; 10 August 1937; 9 October 1937; 10 December 1937; *Shields Gazette*, 21 June 1937; 10 February 1938; *Evening Chronicle*, 31 May 1937; *Sunderland Echo*, 10 November 1937; Don Watson, 'Politics and Humanitarian Aid: Basque Refugees in the North-east and Cumbria During the Spanish Civil War', *North-east History*, 36 (2005), pp.14,

33; Don Watson and John Corcoran, *An Inspiring Example: the North-east of England and the Spanish Civil War, 1936–1939* (1996), pp.73–84.

12. *Sunday Sun*, 30 October 1938.
13. *Morpeth Herald*, 13 January 1939.
14. *Shields Evening News*, 30 January 1939.
15. *North Mail*, 23 January 1939; Jim Fyrth, 'The Aid Spain Movement in Britain, 1936–39', *History Workshop Journal*, 35 (1993), p.156.
16. Lewis Mates, 'Britain's De Facto Popular Front? The Case of the Tyneside Foodship Campaign, 1938–1939', *Labour History Review*, 69:1 (2004), pp.323–345.
17. *Blyth News*, 9 January 1939; Mates, 'Tyneside foodship', p.37.
18. *Northern Echo*, 21 January 1939.
19. WMRC, 259/1/2/73, AEU EC Minutes, 18 November 1938.
20. Tom Buchanan, *The Spanish Civil War and the British Labour Movement* (Cambridge, 1991), p.156.
21. MML, Box B-7 B/6, *Spanish Relief*, March 1939.
22. LHASC, CP/CENT/PERS/5/05, Tom O'Byrne autobiography; *Daily Worker*, 15 September 1936; *Sunday Sun*, 11 July 1937.
23. *North Mail*, 29 September 1936; *Chester-le-Street Chronicle*, 16 July 1937.
24. *North Mail*, 5 May 1937; 2 June 1937; *Evening Chronicle*, 2; 6 July 1937; *Newcastle Journal*, 3 July 1937; *Sunday Sun*, 11 July 1937.
25. *Sunday Sun*, 25 July 1937.
26. *Sunderland Echo*, 2 February 1937; 29 March 1937; *Evening Chronicle*, 31 May 1937.
27. *Durham Chronicle*, 26 March 1937.
28. *Shields News*, 13; 24 October 1936.
29. *Sunderland Echo*, 3 May 1937.
30. *Durham Chronicle*, 11 June 1937.
31. *Durham Chronicle*, 30 July 1937.
32. DMOR, DMA EC Minutes, 7 November 1938.
33. *Blaydon Courier*, 16 January 1937; 17 April 1937; 8 April 1938.
34. *Shields Gazette*, 23; 25 September 1936; 22; 26 February 1937.
35. *North Mail*, 23 June 1937.
36. *North Mail*, 6 February 1937; 6 April 1937; 5 July 1937; *Heslop's Advertiser*, 16 April 1937; 17 September 1937; *Morpeth Herald*, 23 April 1937; 7 May 1937; *Gateshead Labour Herald*, December 1936.
37. *North Mail*, 26 January 1937; *Durham Chronicle*, 29 January 1937; 19 March 1937.
38. *Heslop's Advertiser*, 14 May 1937.
39. *Morpeth Herald*, 23 April 1937.
40. NRO, 1286/3, Ashington Miners Federation Minutes, 30 January 1938.
41. W. Albaya, 'A Sheffield Volunteer in Spain, 1936–1937', in W. Albaya, J. Baxter, and B. Moore, *Behind the Clenched Fist: Sheffield's 'Aid to Spain', 1936–1939* (Sheffield, 1986), p.9.
42. H. Francis, *Miners Against Fascism. Wales and the Spanish Civil War* (1984), p.120.
43. Watson and Corcoran, *An Inspiring Example*, p.9.

44. NRO, 1566/3, Morpeth LNU Branch Minutes, 8 September 1937; *Morpeth Herald*, 8 October 1937; *North Mail*, 17 February 1938.
45. *New Leader*, 12; 19 March 1937; 2 April 1937.
46. *Shields Evening News*, 1 February 1939.
47. LHASC, CP/CENT/PERS/5/05, Tom O'Byrne autobiography; *Shields Gazette*, 13 March 1937; 19; 27 April 1937; *North Mail*, 19 April 1937.
48. Buchanan, *British Labour Movement*, p.164.
49. See chapter four.
50. *Shields Gazette*, 21 June 1937; 8 December 1937; *North Mail*, 3 August 1937; 11 December 1937; *Gateshead Labour Herald*, August 1937.
51. *North Mail*, 29 June 1937; 7 July 1937; 9 October 1937; 10 December 1937; Watson and Corcoran, *An Inspiring Example*, pp.77–78; Watson, 'Humanitarian Aid', p.14.
52. *Morpeth Herald*, 28 May 1937; 16 July 1937.
53. Len Edmondson Interview with Lewis Mates, 19 June 1998.
54. *Shields Gazette*, 12; 19 August 1937; 1 October 1937; 2 November 1937.
55. *Sunday Sun*, 21 May 1939; *Chester-le-Street Chronicle*, 26 May 1939.
56. *Evening Chronicle*, 13 May 1937.
57. *North Mail*, 17 March 1939.
58. Watson, 'Humanitarian Aid', p.16.
59. DMOR, DMA EC Minutes, 26 June 1939; 31 July 1939.
60. NRO, 4222/1/5, Pegswood Lodge Minutes, 23 May 1937.
61. NRO, 1331/7, Ellington Lodge Minutes, 7; 21 December 1938.
62. *Blyth News*, 17 March 1938; *North Mail*, 6 July 1937; 6 March 1939; Watson, 'Humanitarian Aid', p.14.
63. *Durham Chronicle*, 3 June 1938; 10 June 1938.
64. *Blaydon Courier*, 4 May 1939.
65. *Shields Gazette*, 13 January 1939.
66. *Sunderland Echo*, 13; 17; 19 December 1938; 11 January 1939; *Blyth News*, 15 December 1938; 26 January 1939; Mates, 'Tyneside foodship', pp.38–39.
67. *Northern Echo*, 20; 24; 27 February 1939; Jack Coward, *Back From the Dead* (Liverpool, 1985), n.p.n.
68. Mates, 'United Front', pp.41–43, 129–133, 274.
69. North-east International Brigade Memorial Programme, 15 January 1939 (in possession of the late Jack Lawther).
70. *Blaydon Courier*, 16 January 1937.
71. *Shields Gazette*, 26 February 1937.
72. *Shields Gazette*, 25 April 1938.
73. *Durham Chronicle*, 1 June 1937.
74. *Durham Chronicle*, 16 July 1937.
75. *Durham Chronicle*, 16 July 1937. Fred Peart echoed this. *Durham Chronicle*, 23 July 1937. See also *Durham Chronicle*, 11 June 1937; 16; 30 July 1937.
76. *Durham Chronicle*, 1 January 1937; 11 June 1937.
77. *Evening Chronicle*, 2 February 1937.
78. *Durham Chronicle*, 26 March 1937.
79. *Durham Chronicle*, 26 March 1937.
80. *Morpeth Herald*, 10 September 1937.

81. *Gateshead Labour Herald*, February 1937.
82. *Gateshead Labour Herald*, February 1937.
83. For examples, see comments in *North Mail*, 19 April 1937; 10 May 1937; *Newcastle Journal*, 14 April 1937; *Gateshead Labour Herald*, October 1937.
84. *Gateshead Labour Herald*, March 1937.
85. *Morpeth Herald*, 7 May 1937.
86. NRO, 1286/3, Ashington Miners' Federation Minutes, 13 June 1937. See also NRO, 3793/44, Woodhorn Lodge Minutes, 2 June 1937; 29 September 1937; 17 November 1937.
87. *Sunderland Echo*, 3 May 1937.
88. *Shields News*, 13 October 1936.
89. *Evening Chronicle*, 27 October 1936.
90. *Evening Chronicle*, 26 November 1936.
91. *Sunday Sun*, 25 July 1937.
92. TWAS, 608/Box 1252, Newcastle City Labour Party EC minutes, 18 September 1936.
93. *North Mail*, 29 September 1936; *Evening Chronicle*, 27 October 1936.
94. WMRC, 292/946/18B, NJCSR Bulletin No.3, 5 May 1937.
95. *North Mail*, 2 November 1936; 18 January 1937; 5 May 1937; 12; 13 July 1937; 25 April 1938; *Sunday Sun*, 11; 18; 25 July 1937; *Newcastle Journal*, 18 January 1937; 9; 12 July 1937. *Daily Worker*, 15 September 1936.
96. *Gateshead Labour Herald*, January; February; April 1937; *North Mail*, 19 April 1937.
97. *North Mail*, 24 March 1937.
98. *North Mail*, 5 July 1937; *Morpeth Herald*, 9 July 1937; *Blyth News*, 28 July 1938.
99. *Morpeth Herald*, 3 December 1937.
100. *Sunderland Echo*, 25 March 1937.
101. Notwithstanding, of course, some brigaders' evident desire to temper their speeches depending on the campaign and the audience (see chapter one).
102. *Newcastle Journal*, 4 December 1936.
103. *Newcastle Journal*, 14 December 1936.
104. They collected over a ton of food and £7. *North Mail*, 17 December 1936.
105. *Newcastle Journal*, 14 December 1936.
106. *North Mail*, 17 February 1938.
107. *Shields Gazette*, 17 November 1938; 17 December 1938.
108. *Shields Gazette*, 13 March 1937.
109. *Shields Gazette*, 19 April 1937.
110. *Shields News*, 19 April 1937.
111. *Shieldsman*, 22 April 1937. Quoted in Buchanan, *British Labour Movement*, p.210.
112. NRO, 3793/44, Woodhorn Lodge Minutes, 5 May 1937.
113. *Shields Gazette*, 19 August 1937.
114. Watson, 'Humanitarian Aid', p.28.
115. Watson, 'Humanitarian Aid', p.35.
116. *Blyth News*, 17 March 1938.
117. Such as 'Thankful' in the *Evening Chronicle* (18 June 1937).
118. *Shields Gazette*, 8 December 1937.
119. *North Mail*, 5 April 1938.

120. Francis, *Miners Against Fascism*, p.125.
121. Watson, 'Humanitarian Aid', p.36.
122. This served to confuse the issue for practising Catholics too: see chapter three.
123. NRO, 4222/1/5, Pegswood Lodge Minutes, 27 January 1937.
124. NRO, 1331/7, Ellington Lodge Minutes, 12 October 1938.
125. *North Mail*, 26 July 1938.
126. *Shields Gazette*, 3 January 1939.
127. *Blyth News*, 3; 9 January 1939; *Morpeth Herald*, 13; 27 January 1939.
128. *Shields Evening News*, 30 January 1939.
129. *Shields Evening News*, 27 January 1939; *Blyth News*, 26 January 1939.
130. For examples, the letters pages in *Sunderland Echo*, 3; 5 January 1939.
131. *Shields Gazette*, 20 December 1938.
132. *Sunderland Echo*, 31 January 1939.
133. *Shields Evening News*, 7 February 1939.
134. Mates, 'Tyneside foodship', pp.39–41.
135. Francis, *Miners Against Fascism*, p.120.
136. Francis, *Miners Against Fascism*, pp.96–132.
137. *Sunderland Echo*, 1 January 1937; *Newcastle Journal*, 2 January 1937.
138. *Sunderland Echo*, 23 January 1937.
139. Buchanan, *British Labour Movement*, pp.163–164.
140. *Morpeth Herald*, 16 July 1937.
141. Watson, 'Humanitarian Aid', p.15.
142. A. Jackson, *British Women and the Spanish Civil War* (2002), p.52.
143. Jim Fyrth, *The Signal Was Spain* (1986), p.276.
144. *Sunderland Echo*, 9 December 1936.
145. Buchanan, *British Labour Movement*, p.156.
146. *North Mail*, 18 January 1937.
147. *Evening Chronicle*, 7 May 1937.
148. *Blyth News*, 4 February 1937.
149. *Blyth News*, 10 December 1936.
150. *Blyth News*, 17 December 1936.
151. *Blyth News*, 28 January 1937.
152. Watson, 'Humanitarian Aid', p.15.
153. *Morpeth Herald*, 23 April 1937.
154. Francis, *Miners Against Fascism*, p.127.
155. *Evening Chronicle*, 6 July 1937.
156. Watson, 'Humanitarian Aid', p.28.
157. For example, T.T. Anderson in *Shields Gazette*, 6 February 1939.
158. *Morpeth Herald*, 27 January 1939.
159. Fyrth, *Signal Was Spain*, p.53.
160. José Peirats, *The CNT in the Spanish Revolution*, *Vol.2* (Sussex, 2005), p.105.
161. H. Francis, 'Welsh Miners and the Spanish Civil War', *Journal of Contemporary History*, 5:3 (1970), p.188.
162. The main figurehead of the foodship campaign, T.T. Anderson, was a likely humanitarian. See chapter six for further discussion on this.
163. *Gateshead Labour Herald*, February 1937.

164. *North Mail*, 7 July 1937; Eric Walker Testament, 2002 (Marleen Sidaway).
165. Watson, 'Humanitarian Aid', p.37.
166. NRO, 759/68, NMA EC Minutes, 18 November 1938; *North Mail*, 6 December 1938; *Shields Gazette*, 12 December 1938; *Blyth News*, 9 January 1939; *Morpeth Herald*, 13 January 1939; *Shields Evening News*, 30 January 1939.
167. *Morpeth Herald*, 13 January 1939; 10 February 1939.
168. *Morpeth Herald*, 13 January 1939.
169. See, for example, the T.T. Anderson letter in *North Mail*, 19 January 1939.
170. *Blyth News*, 5; 9; 26 January 1939.
171. There was some 'overlapping' of efforts in a Newcastle ward. TWAS, 608/ Box 1252, Newcastle City Labour Party EC Minutes, 2 January 1939.
172. The *Sunderland Echo* called it the 'Tyneside and Wearside foodship' on occasion. *Sunderland Echo*, 3; 31 January 1939.
173. *North Mail*, 29 September 1936; *Gateshead Labour Herald*, July 1937.
174. See chapter three.
175. *Gateshead Labour Herald*, July 1937.
176. Watson, 'Humanitarian Aid', p.19; Fyrth, *Signal Was Spain*, p.234.
177. This was Eden lodge (DMA); see chapter three.
178. *Newcastle Journal*, 22 March 1937; 16; 23 January 1939; 6 February 1939.
179. *North Mail*, 13 December 1937.
180. NRO, 527/C/2, Dan Dawson letter to Citrine, 20 July 1938; TWAS, 608/ Box 1252, Newcastle City Labour Party EC Minutes, 24 February 1938; *Daily Worker*, 15 September 1936; *North Mail*, 13 July 1937; *Sunday Sun*, 25 July 1937.
181. *Shields News*, 19 April 1937; *Shields Gazette*, 13 March; 19; 27 April 1937.
182. *Daily Worker*, 18 August 1936; 15 September 1936; *North Mail*, 18 January 1937.
183. *Blaydon Courier*, 6 February 1937; *Evening Chronicle*, 15 April 1937.
184. *Sunday Sun*, 18 July 1937.
185. *Sunday Sun*, 25 July 1937.
186. CCC, LSPC, 1/2/134, Blenkinsop letter to Pole, n.d. [post 18 July 1937].
187. NRO, 1331/7, Ellington Lodge Minutes, 21 December 1938.
188. *Blaydon Courier*, 6 February 1937.
189. *Morpeth Herald*, 16 July 1937.
190. *Sunderland Echo*, 25 June 1937.
191. *Morpeth Herald*, 22 April 1938.
192. *Morpeth Herald*, 3 February 1939.
193. *Shields Evening News*, 27 January 1939; 7 February 1939.
194. *Sunday Sun*, 18 July 1937.
195. *Sunday Sun*, 25 July 1937.
196. *North Mail*, 13 July 1937; *Sunday Sun*, 25 July 1937.
197. *Sunday Sun*, 30 October 1938; *North Mail*, 31 October 1938.
198. *North Mail*, 1 June 1937.
199. *Blyth News*, 5; 26 January 1939.
200. *Morpeth Herald*, 3 February 1939.
201. *Shields Evening News*, 7 February 1939.
202. *Morpeth Herald*, 13 January 1939.

203. *Northern Echo,* 21 January 1939.

204. *Morpeth Herald,* 10 February 1939.

205. Bill Moore, '"Aid for Spain" in Sheffield', in Albaya et al., *Clenched Fist,* p.17.

206. *Morpeth Herald,* 16 July 1937; See chapter two.

207. See chapter two.

208. *Blyth News,* 30 January 1939.

209. *Shields Evening News,* 3 February 1939.

210. *Blyth News,* 20 October 1938.

211. *Morpeth Herald,* 29 July 1938.

212. *Sunderland Echo,* 25 June 1937.

213. *Evening Chronicle,* 21; 24 June 1937; 2; 12 July 1937; *Sunderland Echo,* 1; 3; 8 June 1937; 14; 19 February 1938; *Newcastle Journal,* 5 July 1937.

214. *Shields Gazette,* 24; 28 December 1938.

215. George Orwell, *Homage to Catalonia* in *Orwell in Spain* (2001), p.188.

216. It sent only £5, the same as the DMA. NRO, 759/68, NMA EC Minutes, 18 November 1938; DMOR, DMA, EC Minutes, 5 December 1938.

217. In June 1937, an average Durham miners' wage of £2 10s. a week left 3s. 'pocket money' and 'a football match or the films knocks the stuffing out of that'. *Sunday Sun,* 13 June 1937.

218. Quoted in Jackson, *British Women,* p.49.

219. See for examples *Evening Chronicle,* 19 May 1937; 2; 6 July 1937.

220. *Evening Chronicle,* 15 April 1937; *Blyth News,* 15 December 1938.

221. *Evening Chronicle,* 15 April 1937.

222. *Sunderland Echo,* 25 June 1937; *Evening Chronicle,* 2 July 1937.

223. Fyrth, *Signal Was Spain,* p.259.

224. *Gateshead Labour Herald,* December 1938.

225. *Shields Gazette,* 13 December 1937.

226. *Morpeth Herald,* 7 May 1937.

227. *Evening Chronicle,* 24 June 1937.

228. *Blyth News,* 9 January 1939.

229. *North Mail,* 23 January 1939.

230. *Sunderland Echo,* 31 January 1939.

231. Moore, '"Aid for Spain" in Sheffield', p.18.

232. Len Edmondson Interview, 11 November 1994.

233. Jack Lawther Interview with Lewis Mates, 30 July 1996. Dave Goodman and Frank Graham made similar claims. Dave Goodman written testimony to Lewis Mates, 27 October 1994; for Graham see chapter two.

234. *Morpeth Herald,* 10 March 1939.

235. *Evening Chronicle,* 7 July 1937.

236. *Morpeth Herald,* 13 January 1939.

237. *North Mail,* 6 July 1937.

238. *Morpeth Herald,* 3 December 1937.

239. Moore, '"Aid for Spain" in Sheffield', p.17; D. Hyde, *I Believed* (1952), pp.58–59.

240. *Morpeth Herald,* 10 March 1939.

241. See chapter six for examples.

242. *Heslop's Advertiser,* 11 June 1937; 13 August 1937; 17 February 1939.

243. *North Mail*, 10 January 1939.
244. *Sunderland Echo*, 8 June 1937.
245. Moira Tattam written testimony to Lewis Mates, 26 June 2006
246. Francis, *Miners Against Fascism*, p.96.

Chapter Six

1. M. Alpert, 'Humanitarianism and Politics in the British Response to the Spanish Civil War, 1936–9', *European History Quarterly*, 14:4 (1984), p.437.
2. A. Jackson, *British Women and the Spanish Civil War* (2002), p.55.
3. Don Watson, 'Politics and Humanitarian Aid: Basque Refugees in the Northeast and Cumbria During the Spanish Civil War', *North-east History*, 36 (2005), p.14.
4. *Sunderland Echo*, 2 February 1937; 2 May 1937; *North Mail*, 7 July 1937; Frank Graham, *The Battle of Jarama* (Newcastle, 1987), p.34.
5. See chapter five.
6. Lewis Mates, 'Britain's De Facto Popular Front? The Case of the Tyneside Foodship Campaign, 1938–1939', *Labour History Review*, 69:1 (2004), pp.38, 41–2.
7. *Evening Chronicle*, 6 July 1937; *Newcastle Journal*, 7 July 1937. See chapter five.
8. *Shields Gazette*, 6 January 1939; 22 February 1939.
9. Jackson, *British Women*, p.55.
10. Joyce Hall Interview with Lewis Mates, 9 March 2006.
11. Watson, 'Humanitarian Aid', p.36.
12. Watson, 'Humanitarian Aid', p.37.
13. Watson, 'Humanitarian Aid', p.37.
14. Tom Buchanan, *Britain and the Spanish Civil War* (Cambridge, 1997), p.101.
15. Jackson, *British Women*, p.55.
16. Jim Fyrth, 'The Aid Spain Movement in Britain, 1936–39', *History Workshop Journal*, 35 (1993), pp.162–163.
17. Mates, 'Tyneside foodship', pp.43–44.
18. Fyrth, 'Aid Spain Movement', pp.162–163.
19. *North Mail*, 19 January 1939.
20. Fyrth, 'Aid Spain Movement', p.162.
21. H. Thomas, *The Spanish Civil War* (1977), pp.875–6; C. Fleay and M.L. Sanders, 'The Labour Spain Committee: Labour Party Policy and the Spanish Civil War', *Historical Journal*, 28:1 (1985), p.195.
22. MML, Box B-4/M/1, Charlie Woods letter to Jim Fyrth, 18 May 1985.
23. Don Watson and John Corcoran, *An Inspiring Example: the North-east of England and the Spanish Civil War, 1936–1939* (1996), p.82.
24. Fyrth, 'Aid Spain Movement', pp.162–163.
25. Mates, 'Tyneside foodship', p.41. See below.
26. Tom Buchanan, 'Britain's Popular Front?: Aid Spain and the British Labour Movement', *History Workshop Journal*, 31 (1991), p.70.
27. See Lewis H. Mates, 'Practical anti-fascism? The Spanish Aid Campaigns in North-east England, 1936–1939', in N. Copsey and D. Renton (eds), *British Fascism, the Labour Movement and the State* (2005), pp.134–137.

28. Hywel Francis, *Miners Against Fascism. Wales and the Spanish Civil War* (1984), p.115; Douglas Hyde, *I Believed* (1952), p.63.
29. Jim Fyrth, *The Signal Was Spain* (1986), p.22.
30. Even evidence of involvement in pro-Republic institutions like the Labour Party did not necessarily mean that a given individual had a pro-Republican perspective: see the discussion on Mayor Summerbell below.
31. Lewis H. Mates, 'The United Front and the Popular Front in the North East of England, 1936–1939', (Newcastle University, PhD, 2002), pp.35–38.
32. *Sunday Sun*, 25 July 1937.
33. While Mayor Summerbell was involved in both, Sunderland SMAC did not emerge from the SDPC: both operated separately in supporting the Basques.
34. *Sunderland Echo*, 2 May 1937.
35. *Sunderland Echo*, 2 May 1937.
36. *Sunderland Echo*, 1 October 1938.
37. *Sunderland Echo*, 16 May 1939.
38. *Sunderland Echo*, 2 May 1937.
39. Tom Buchanan, 'The Role of the British Labour Movement in the Origins and Work of the Basque Children's Committee 1937–9', *European History Quarterly*, 18:2 (1988), p.156.
40. Watson, 'Humanitarian Aid', p.36; Woods to Fyrth, 18 February 1985.
41. Mates, 'United Front', pp.244–245.
42. *Morpeth Herald*, 20 January 1939.
43. *Blyth News*, 14 November 1938; *Morpeth Herald*, 13 January 1939.
44. NRO, 1566/3, Morpeth LNU Branch Minutes, 8 September 1937; 25 February 1938; *Morpeth Herald*, 28 May 1937; 16; 23 July 1937; 19 November 1937; 4 March 1938.
45. *Morpeth Herald*, 14 October 1938.
46. *Morpeth Herald*, 27 January 1939.
47. *Morpeth Herald*, 27 January 1939.
48 *Tribune*, 27 January 1939.
49. Fyrth, 'Aid Spain Movement', p.161. See below.
50. Fyrth, 'Aid Spain Movement', p.160. Buchanan wrote that the national leadership was not 'greatly discomforted' at local cross-party Spanish aid activity. Buchanan, 'Britain's Popular Front?', p.71.
51. Peter D. Drake, 'Labour and Spain: British Labour's Response to the Spanish Civil War With Particular Reference to the Labour Movement in Birmingham' (Birmingham University, M.Litt., 1977), p.156.
52. L.H. Mates, 'The North-east and the Campaigns for a Popular Front, 1938–9', *Northern History*, XLIII (2) (2006), p287.
53. See chapter four.
54. Mates, 'North-east Campaigns', pp.294–300.
55. Len Edmondson Interview, 4 May 1999; Woods to Fyrth, 18 February 1985.
56. Frank Graham Interview with Lewis Mates, 12 October 1994.
57. Tom Buchanan, *The Spanish Civil War and the British Labour Movement* (Cambridge, 1991), p.139.
58. Fyrth, 'Aid Spain Movement', p.161.
59. Fyrth, 'Aid Spain Movement', p.161.

60. Drake, 'Labour and Spain', p.167.
61. Hywel Francis, 'Welsh Miners and the Spanish Civil War', *Journal of Contemporary History*, 5:3 (1970), p.179.
62. Francis, *Miners Against Fascism*, p.112.
63. Fyrth's claim was not valid: see the conclusion.
64. NPL, L329.4, 'The North East Marches On' (North-east District Committee CP, n.d. [1938?]).
65. *Morpeth Herald*, 8 April 1938.
66. *Blaydon Courier*, 3 March 1939.
67. *Morpeth Herald*, 23 October 1936.
68. Buchanan, 'Britain's Popular Front?', p.67.
69. Jackson, *British Women*, p.52.
70. LHASC, CP Central Committee Minutes, 10 November 1936.
71. *Shields Gazette*, 28 July 1936.
72. *Daily Worker*, 18 August 1936.
73. Drake, 'Labour and Spain', pp.253–257; Mike Squires, *The Aid to Spain Movement in Battersea, 1936–1939* (1994), pp.8–12.
74. The *New Leader* claimed joint involvement; the *Daily Worker* and Noreen Branson claimed the meeting was the CP's child. *New Leader*, 18 September 1936; *Daily Worker*, 15 September 1936; N. Branson, *History of the Communist Party of Great Britain 1927–1941* (1985), p.225.
75. LHASC, CP Central Committee Minutes, 10 November 1936.
76. Buchanan, *British Labour Movement*, p.35.
77. *Sunday Sun*, 1 August 1937.
78. See chapters two and four.
79. *Blyth News*, 25; 28 January 1937.
80. The rivalry between the populations of Newcastle and Gateshead was manifest in an ongoing demarcation dispute between the trades councils over the affiliation of Newcastle NUR branches that began in 1928. Mates, 'United Front', p.68.
81. MML, Box B-4/M/1, Charlie Woods letter to Jim Fyrth, 18 February 1985.
82. *Morpeth Herald*, 18 March 1938.
83. *Durham Chronicle*, 11 June 1937; 30 July 1937.
84. *Sunderland Echo*, 4 October 1937.
85. *Sunday Sun*, 9 April 1939.
86. Drake, 'Labour and Spain', pp.274–276.
87. Don Watson, 'To the Head Through the Heart: The Newcastle Left Book Club Theatre Guild, 1937–1939', *Bulletin of the North-east Group for the Study of Labour History*, 23 (1989), pp.3–21.
88. Watson and Corcoran, *An Inspiring Example* , pp.10–11.
89. *Shields Gazette*, 28 July 1936; Francis, *Miners Against Fascism*, p.108.
90. *Shields Gazette*, 25 August 1936.
91. *Shields Gazette*, 31 August 1936; 4; 29 September 1936; 16 November 1936; 7 December 1936; 15 March 1937; 12; 19 August 1937; 1 October 1937; 2 November 1937; 29 March 1938; 24 May 1938; 21 June 1938.
92. Drake, 'Labour and Spain', p.ii.
93. Squires, Aid to Spain Movement, p.10.

94. *Blyth News*, 30 November 1936.
95. See chapter one.
96. MML, Box B-4/M/2, Wilf Jobling Memorial Leaflet produced by Blaydon Spanish Aid Committee; *Shields News*, 13 October 1936; *North Mail*, 18 January 1937.
97. Francis, 'Welsh Miners', p.188.
98. In the earlier 1930s, the CP cell produced *The Gun* propaganda paper. TWAS, D/VA/67, *The Gun*; *Daily Worker*, 8 September 1936.
99. *Morpeth Herald*, 3 February 1939.
100. Fyrth, 'Aid Spain Movement', p.160.
101. *Sunday Sun*, 25 July 1937.
102. Squires, *Aid to Spain Movement*, p.28.
103. Fyrth claimed that the Labour leadership feared its members working with CP activists in the Spanish aid campaigns as this would make Communists 'respectable'. Fyrth, 'Aid Spain Movement', p160.
104. MML, Box B-4/M/2, Wilf Jobling Memorial Leaflet.
105. *Newcastle Journal*, 14 September 1936.
106. *Evening Chronicle*, 27 October 1936.
107. Watson, 'Humanitarian Aid', p.21.
108. LHASC, CP Central Committee Minutes, 19 March 1939.
109. LHASC, CP Central Committee Minutes, 19 March 1939.
110. LHASC, CP Central Committee Minutes, 19 March 1939.
111. *North Mail*, 29 August 1938; LHASC, CP Central Committee 15th Congress Report, 1938, pp.26, 30; A. Thorpe, 'The Membership of the Communist Party of Great Britain, 1920–1945', *Historical Journal*, 43:3 (2000), pp.783, 790.
112. Drake, 'Labour and Spain', pp.96, 168.
113. Len Edmondson Interview with Lewis Mates, 19 September 1998.
114. Buchanan, *British Labour Movement*, p.138.
115. Buchanan, *British Labour Movement*, p.138.
116. MML, Box B-4/M/1, Charlie Woods letter to Jim Fyrth, 18 February 1985.
117. TWAS, 608/Box 1252, Newcastle City Labour Party EC Minutes, 18 September 1936.
118. SSPL, LPM5, South Shields LP&TC Minutes, 5 January 1937.
119. Lewis Mates, 'Durham and South Wales Miners and the Spanish Civil War', *Twentieth Century British History*, 17:3 (2006), pp.386–389.
120. TWAS, 673/4, TGWU Area Committee Minutes, 31 January 1939.
121. NRO, 1286/3, Ashington Miners Federation Minutes, 7 February 1937.
122. See chapter two.
123. Buchanan, *British Labour Movement*, p.164.
124. *Sunderland Echo*, 7 June 1937.
125. *Evening Chronicle*, 24; 26 June 1937.
126. NRO, 3793/44, Woodhorn Lodge Minutes, 17 November 1937.
127. Mates, 'Durham and South Wales Miners', p.387.
128. Buchanan, *British Labour Movement*, p.161.
129. WMRC, 292/946/41, Robert McDarmont (Boldon Labour Party men's section secretary) letter to Citrine, 15 September 1936.

130. *Sunderland Echo*, 20; 24; 30 January 1939; *Durham Chronicle*, 6; 13 January 1939; *Blyth News*, 13 February 1939..

131. *Shields Evening News*, 6; 7 February 1939.

132. TWAS, 608/Box 1252, Newcastle City Labour Party EC Minutes, 6 December 1938; 2 January 1939; Delegate Meeting Minutes, 13 December 1938.

133. Buchanan, *British Labour Movement*, p.138.

134. Buchanan, *British Labour Movement*, p.139.

135. Buchanan, *British Labour Movement*, p.139.

136. MML, Box B-4/M/1, Charlie Woods letter to Jim Fyrth, 18 February 1985.

137. NRL, CPT 184, Text for Speech, 12 March 1939.

138. Fyrth, 'Aid Spain Movement', p.157.

139. Buchanan, *British Labour Movement*, p.140.

Conclusion

1. Tom Buchanan, *The Spanish Civil War and the British Labour Movement* (Cambridge, 1991), p.136.

2. José Peirats, *The CNT in the Spanish Revolution, Vol.2* (Sussex, 2005), p.25.

3. *Sunderland Echo*, 9 January 1939.

4. *North Mail*, 15 March 1937.

5. MML, Box A-12/Gr/8, Frank Graham Notes for Speech in the Miners' Hall, Roker, 27 January 1939.

6. *Durham Chronicle*, 6 May 1938.

7. See Lewis Mates, 'Debunking Myths', review essay of Matt Perry, *The Jarrow Crusade: Protest and Legend*, in *North-East History*, 38 (2006), pp.171–179.

8. James Jupp, *The Radical Left in Britain, 1931–1941* (1982), p.123.

9. *Morpeth Herald*, 23 July 1937.

10. *Morpeth Herald*, 8 April 1938.

11. Lewis Mates, 'The North-east and the Campaigns for a Popular Front, 1938–39', *Northern History*, XLIII (2) (2006), p.286.

12. NRL, CPTEX133, C.P. Trevelyan letter to wife, 20 March 1939.

13. G.D.H. Cole, *A History of the Labour Party from 1914* (New York, 1969), p.358. see also G.D.H. Cole, *The People's Front* (1937).

14. *Sunderland Echo*, 6 June 1938.

15. Michael Foot, *Aneurin Bevan 1897–1945 Vol. One* (1962), p.239.

16. Fenner Brockway, *The Workers' Front* (1938), pp.154–155, 238.

17. Martin Pugh, 'The Liberal Party and the Popular Front', *English Historical Review*, CXXI, 494 (2006), pp.1349–1350.

18. N. Branson, 'Myths from Right and Left' in J. Fyrth (ed.), *Britain, Fascism and the Popular Front* (1985), p.127. See also E. Hobsbawm, 'Fifty Years of People's Fronts', pp.235–250.

19. J. Fyrth, 'Introduction: In the Thirties', in Fyrth (ed.), *Britain, Fascism*, p.15.

20. *Morpeth Herald*, 10 March 1939.

21. Foot, *Bevan*, p.280.

22. John Saville, *The Labour Movement in Britain: a Commentary* (1988), p.78.

23. See letter from J. Henderson in *Blaydon Courier*, 13 May 1938.

24. See Ben Pimlott, *Labour and the Left in the 1930s* (Cambridge, 1977), pp.2–5.

25. Jim Fyrth, 'The Aid Spain Movement in Britain, 1936–39', *History Workshop Journal*, 35 (1993), p.161.
26. LHASC, CP Central Committee Minutes, 19 March 1939.
27. Richard Croucher, *We Refuse to Starve in Silence. A History of the National Unemployed Workers Movement, 1920–46* (1987), p.181.
28. *Sunderland Echo*, 8 May 1937.
29. *Sunderland Echo*, 8 May 1937.
30. *Shields Gazette*, 18 June 1937; 3 July 1937.
31. *Blyth News*, 25 January 1937.
32. Buchanan, *British Labour Movement*, p.16.
33. Tom Buchanan, 'Britain's Popular Front?': Aid Spain and the British Labour Movement', *History Workshop Journal*, 31 (1991), p.71.
34. H. Francis, *Miners Against Fascism. Wales and the Spanish Civil War* (1984), pp.29; 39.
35. Buchanan, 'Britain's Popular Front?', p.68.
36. Buchanan, *British Labour Movement*, p.222.
37. Bill Moore, '"Aid for Spain" in Sheffield', in W. Albaya, J. Baxter, and B. Moore, *Behind the Clenched Fist: Sheffield's 'Aid to Spain', 1936–1939* (Sheffield, 1986), pp.15–19; Peter D. Drake, 'Labour and Spain: British Labour's Response to the Spanish Civil War with Particular Reference to the Labour Movement in Birmingham' (Birmingham University, M.Litt., 1977), pp.137–157.
38. Noreen Branson, *History of the Communist Party of Great Britain 1927–1941* (1985), p.225.
39. Jupp, *Radical Left in Britain*, p.87.
40. N. Todd, *In Excited Times. The People Against the Blackshirts* (Whitley Bay, 1995), pp.11, 13, 23, 36.
41. M. Squires, *The Aid to Spain Movement in Battersea 1936–1939* (1994), p.36.
42. Todd, *In Excited Times*, p.40.
43. Don Watson and John Corcoran, *An Inspiring Example: the North-east of England and the Spanish Civil War, 1936–1939* (1996), p.13.
44. *Morpeth Herald*, 29 July 1938.
45. Fyrth, 'Aid Spain Movement', p.163.
46. Fyrth, 'Aid Spain Movement', p.163.
47. Bill Moore, '"Aid for Spain" in Sheffield', in Albaya et al., *Behind the Clenched Fist*, p.16.
48. Buchanan, *British Labour Movement*, p.122.
49. NRL, CPT 183, Notes for Speech at LSC Conference, 23 October 1938.
50. W.H. Auden, 'September 1, 1939'.

BIBLIOGRAPHY

Primary Sources

Party and Organisational Papers

Labour Party Subject Files and annual reports (LHASC).

Labour Spain Committee papers (CCC).

Bishop Auckland CLP EC minutes (in possession of the late Walter Nunn).

Bishop Auckland LLP minutes (DRO).

Blaydon CLP annual report 1936 (DRO).

Durham CLP minutes and annual reports (DRO).

Houghton-le-Spring CLP annual reports (DRO).

Newbiggin and North Seaton LLP records (NRO).

Newburn and District LLP minutes (NRO).

Newcastle City Labour Party EC and delegate meetings minutes and annual reports (TWAS).

NTFLP correspondence (NRO).

Seaham CLP: *The Socialist* (newssheet).

Sedgefield CLP: *The Labour Sentinel* (newssheet).

South Shields LP&TC minutes (SSPL).

Spennymoor CLP AGM 1937 agenda (DRO).

Wansbeck CLP minutes and miscellaneous papers (NRO).

Socialist League, Gateshead branch EC minutes (TWAS).

ILP printed material including annual reports; National Administrative Council minutes and documents; material on branches; branch members' papers (BLPES).

CP Central Committee minutes and records (microform); files on individual members; subject files; papers and correspondence of national party figures (LHASC).

The Gun (newsheet of Communist Engineers at Vickers Works, Elswick, Newcastle) (TWAS).

The Steel Point (Newsheet of South Durham Communist Iron and Steel Workers) (WMRC).

CP (North-east District) Pamphlets: *United Tyneside* (1937) (NRO) and *The North-east Marches On* (n.d., probably 1938) (NPL).

International Brigade Association Records (MML).

Newcastle Liberal Club records (TWAS).

LNU Morpeth branch minutes (NRO).

Woodcraft Folk, North-east Area minutes and other material (BLPES).

National Peace Council, minutes, reports etc., (BLPES).

Trades Union Congress subject files and annual reports (WMRC).

Trades Council annual conference reports (WMRC).

AEU reports; EC minutes (WMRC).

AEU Sunderland No.7 branch minutes (TWAS).

Amalgamated Society of Locomotive Engineers and Firemen, reports (WMRC).

ASW reports; General Council minutes (WMRC).

ASW Felling branch minutes, Gateshead No.1 branch minutes and Tyne and Blyth District minutes (TWAS).

Bank Officers Guild North Shields branch minutes (TWAS).

DMA Minutes, Circulars, etc., and Council Programmes (DMOR).

DMA Ascertainments, Return Sheets etc., and EC minutes (DRO).

DMA lodges minutes: Brancepeth No.2; Eden; Hamsteels; Lambton; Murton; North Bitchburn; Seaham; Ushworth and Vane Tempest (DRO).

Electrical Trades Union Gateshead branch minutes (TWAS).

MFGB annual reports (DMOR).

NALGO North-east Provincial Council agendas and minutes, Gateshead branch minutes and Sunderland branch letter book (TWAS)

Northumberland Colliery Mechanics Association EC minutes; Delegate and Council meetings minutes (NRO).

NMA correspondence with lodges; annual reports (NRO)

NMA lodges minutes: Cambois; Ellington; Pegswood; West Wylam; Woodhorn (NRO); Burradon (TWAS) and Ashington Miners Federation Minutes (NRO).

National Union of Foundry Workers journal and reports (WMRC).

NUJ Sunderland, Shields and Hartlepool branch minutes (TWAS).

National Union of Railwaymen annual reports (WMRC).
NUS Newcastle branch minutes, North Shields branch minutes and Sunderland branch minutes (WMRC).
Pressed Glassmakers' Association half yearly reports (TWAS).
TGWU Area Committee minutes and general correspondence (TWAS).
Typographical Association reports of delegate meetings; Newcastle branch minutes (TWAS).
United Patternmakers' Association Jarrow branch minutes and Newcastle East branch minutes (TWAS).

Personal Papers

G.D.H. Cole Papers (Nuffield College Oxford).
Walter Citrine Papers (BLPES).
Stafford Cripps Papers (Nuffield College Oxford).
Hugh Dalton Papers (BLPES).
Chuter Ede Papers (Surrey County Record Office).
Francis Johnson (ILP General Secretary) Correspondence (BLPES).
F.W. Jowett (ILP) Papers (BLPES).
Jack Lawson Papers (Durham University Library).
J.S. Middleton Papers (LHASC).
Herbert Morrison papers (BLPES).
D.N. Pritt Papers (BLPES).
Emmanuel Shinwell Papers (BLPES).
C.P. Trevelyan Papers (Newcastle University Robinson Library).

Newspapers and Journals

National

AEU Monthly Journal, ASW Journal, Catholic Herald, Controversy, Daily Worker, DMA Monthly Journal, Labour Monthly, New Leader, New Statesman, Labour Woman, Left Book News, NUGMW Journal, Railway Review (NUR), *Record* (TGWU), *Socialist, Socialist Leaguer, Spain and the World, Times, Tribune, Typographical Circular* (Typographical Association), *Universe, Worker, Worker's Weekly.*

Regional

Blaydon Courier, Blyth News, Chester-le-Street Chronicle, Consett Guardian, Durham Chronicle, Durham County Advertiser, Evening Chronicle, Gateshead Labour Herald, Gateshead Municipal News, Gateshead Weekly Pictorial Post, Heslop's Local Advertiser, Hexham Courant, Newcastle Journal, Newcastle Weekly Chronicle,

North Mail, Northern Echo, Shields Gazette, Shields (Evening) News, Shieldsman, Sunday Sun, Sunderland Echo, Tynedale Mirror.

Written Testimony

Written testimonies (normally responses to a questionnaire) from Dave Goodman (27 October 1994); Graham Holtham (15 March 2006), Moira Tattam (27 June 2006). Brian Walsh (5 January 2007) and Bert Ward (22 February 2006)

Oral History

Tape-recorded interviews conducted by Lewis Mates with Dave Atkinson (with Don Watson, 21 February 2006), Harry Clarke (5 February 1999), Len Edmondson (4 November 1994, 19 June 1998 and 4 May 1999), Mrs. Gill (13 October 1994), Frank Graham (12 October 1994), Joyce Hall (9 March 2006), Tommy Kerr (14 October 1994), Jack Lawther (24 October 1994, 20 November 1995 and 30 July 1996) and Bill Reynolds (8 February 2006).

Tape-recorded interviews conducted by Raymond Challinor with Tom Brown, Len Edmondson and Jack Parks.

Tape-recorded interviews conducted by Judith Cook with George Aitken and Frank Graham (IWMSA).

Transcripts of interviews with Tom Brown (GPL), Margaret Gibb (NRO), Andy Lawther (GPL) and Will Lawther (NRO).

Contemporary Writing
(Place of publication is London unless otherwise stated)

The Communist Solar System (Labour Party Publication, 1933).

What Spanish Democracy is Fighting For (Labour Party Publication, 1936).

British Labour and Communism (Labour Party Publication, 1938).

The Labour Party and the Popular Front (Labour Party Publication, 1938).

Unity, True or Sham? (Labour Party Publication, 1939).

Duchess of Atholl, *Searchlight on Spain* (1938).

Beynon H. and Hutchinson C. (ed.s), *Jack Common's Revolt Against an Age of Plenty* (Newcastle, 1980).

Brockway, F. *The Workers' Front* (1938).

Brown, T. *Tom Brown's Syndicalism* (1990).

Cole, G.D.H. *The People's Front* (1937).

———. 'The British People's Front. Why, and How?', *Political Quarterly*, 7:4 (October–December 1936), pp.490–498.

Common, J. *Freedom of the Streets* (1988).

———. (ed.), *Seven Shifts* (1938).

Dalton, H., 'The Popular Front', *Political Quarterly*, 7:4 (October–December 1936), pp.481-489.

Dutt, R. P., *World Politics, 1918–1936* (1936).

Gannes H. and Repard T., *Spain in Revolt* (1936).

Goodfellow, D.M., *Tyneside. The Social Facts* (Newcastle, 1941).

Hannington, W., *The Problem of the Distressed Areas* (1937).

Horner, A., *Towards a Popular Front*, (CP Pamphlet, c.1937).

Mess, H.A., *Industrial Tyneside. A Social Survey* (1928).

Orwell, G., *Orwell in Spain* (2001).

Orwell S. and Angus I. (eds.), *The Collected Essays, Journalism and Letters of George Orwell, Vol.1. An Age Like This, 1920–1940* (1971).

A Socialist, 'Working Class Unity and a Popular Front', *Political Quarterly*, 7:4 (October–December 1936), pp.499–508.

Thorez, M., *France Today and the People's Front* (1936).

Wilkinson, E., *The Town That Was Murdered* (1939).

Memoirs, Diaries and Interviews

Adamson, J., 'A Comment by James Stephenson of Winlaton', *Bulletin of the North-east Group for the Study of Labour History*, 4 (1970), pp.25–32.

Armstrong K. and Beynon H. (eds.), *Hello Are You Working? Memories of the Thirties in the North-east of England* (Whitley Bay, 1977).

Beavis, D., *What Price Happiness? My Life From Coal Hewer to Shop Steward. Life in Dean and Chapter Pit 1929–1966* (Whitley Bay, 1980).

Brockway, F., *Inside the Left. Thirty Years of Platform, Press, Prison and Parliament* (1942).

———. *Towards Tomorrow* (St.Albans, 1977).

Brown, T., Edmondson, L. and Hardy, G., 'The Struggle Against Fascism in the Thirties', *Bulletin of the North-east Group for the Study of Labour History*, 18 (1984), pp.20–23.

Callaghan, T., *Those Were the Days* (Newcastle, 1992).

Callcott, M., (ed.), *A Pilgrimage of Grace. The Diaries of Ruth Dodds, 1905–1974* (Whitley Bay, 1995).

Challinor, R., 'Jack Parks, Memories of a Militant', *Bulletin of the North-east Group for the Study of Labour History*, 9 (1975), pp.34–42.

Clark, B., *No Boots to My Feet. Experiences of a Britisher in Spain, 1937–8* (Stoke, 1984).

Clarke, J.F., 'An Interview with Sir William Lawther', *Bulletin of the Society For the Study of Labour History*, 18 (1969), pp.27–33.

Copeman, F., *Reason in Revolt* (1948).

Coward, J., *Back From the Dead* (Liverpool, 1985).

Goodman, D., *From the Tees to the Ebro* (Middlesborough CP Publication, Middlesborough, n.d.).

Green, N., *A Chronicle of Small Beer. The Memoirs of Nan Green* (Nottingham, 2004).

Gregory, W., *The Shallow Grave. A Memoir of the Spanish Civil War* (1986).

Gurney, J., *Crusade in Spain* (1974).

Hyde, D., *I Believed* (1952).

Paynter, W., *My Generation* (1972).

Pimlott, B. (ed.), *The Political Diary of Hugh Dalton 1918–1940, 1945–60* (1986).

Robson, A., *Spike. Alec 'Spike' Robson 1895–1979. Class Fighter* (North Tyneside TUC, North Shields, 1987).

Shinwell, E., *Conflict Without Malice* (1955).

——. *I've Lived Through it All* (1973).

——. *Lead With the Left. My First Ninety Six Years* (1981).

Watson, J., *The Freedom Tree* (1978).

Secondary Sources

Published Works

Albaya, W., Baxter, J. and Moore, B., *Behind the Clenched Fist: Sheffield's 'Aid to Spain', 1936–1939* (Sheffield, 1986).

Alexander, B., *British Volunteers For Liberty. Spain, 1936–1939* (1982).

Alexander M. and Graham, H. (eds), *The French and Spanish Popular Fronts. Comparative Perspectives* (Cambridge, 1989).

Alpert, M., *A New International History of the Spanish Civil War* (Basingstoke, 1994).

——. 'Humanitarianism and Politics in the British Response to the Spanish Civil War, 1936–9', *European History Quarterly*, 14:4 (1984), pp.423–439.

Andrews, G., Fishman, N. and Morgan, K., *Opening the Books. Essays on the Social and Cultural History of the British Communist Party* (1995).

Archer, A., *The Two Catholic Churches. A Study in Oppression* (1986).

Aspden, K., *Fortress Church. The English Roman Catholic Bishops and the Catholic Church* (Leominster, 2002).

Bateman, D., et al., *The Spanish Civil War. The View From the Left* (1992).

Baxell, R., *British Volunteers in the Spanish Civil War* (2004).

Bean, D., *Armstrong's Men. The Story of the Shop Stewards' Movement in the Tyneside Works* (Newcastle, 1967).

Bellamy, J. and Saville, J. (eds.), *Dictionary of Labour Biography, Vol.VII* (1984)

Beynon, H. and Austrin, T., *Masters and Servants. Class and Patronage in the Making of a Labour Organisation. The Durham Miners and the English Political Tradition* (1994).

Birn, D.S., *The League of Nations Union, 1918–45* (Oxford, 1981).

Blaazer, D., *The Popular Front and the Progressive Tradition* (Cambridge, 1992).

Bolloten, B., et al., *The May Days. Barcelona, 1937* (1987).

Branson, N., *History of the Communist Party of Great Britain, 1927–1941* (1985).

——. and Heinemann, M., *Britain in the Nineteen Thirties* (St. Albans, 1973).

Brenan, G., *The Spanish Labyrinth* (Cambridge, 1976).

Briggs, A. and Saville, J., *Essays In Labour History, 1918–1939, Vol.3* (1977).

Buchanan, T., 'The Role of the British Labour Movement in the Origins and Work of the Basque Children's Committee 1937–9', *European History Quarterly*, 18:2 (1988), pp.155–174.

——. *The Spanish Civil War and the British Labour Movement* (Cambridge, 1991).

——. 'Britain's Popular Front?: Aid Spain and the British Labour Movement', *History Workshop Journal*, 31 (1991), pp.60–72.

——. 'Divided Loyalties: the Impact of the Spanish Civil War on Britain's Civil Service Unions 1936–1939', *Historical Research*, 65:156 (1992), pp.90–107.

——. and Conway, M., *Political Catholicism in Europe, 1918–1965* (Oxford, 1996).

——. *Britain and the Spanish Civil War* (Cambridge, 1997).

——. 'The Politics of Internationalism: the Amalgamated Engineering Union and the Spanish Civil War', *Bulletin of the Society for the Study of Labour History*, 53:3 (1998), pp.47–55.

——. *The Impact of the Spanish Civil War on Britain: War, Loss and Memory* (Eastbourne, 2007).

Byrne, D., 'Immigrants and the Formation of the North-eastern Industrial Working Class', *Bulletin of the North-east Group for the Study of Labour History*, 30 (1996), pp.29–36.

Callaghan, J., *The Far Left in British Politics* (Blackwell, Oxford, 1987)

Callcott, M., 'The Nature and Extent of Political Change in the Inter-war Years: the Example of County Durham, *Northern History*, 16 (1980), pp.215–237.

——. and Challinor, R., *Working Class Politics in North-east England* (Newcastle, 1983).

Campbell, A., Fishman, N. and Howell, D. (eds.), *Miners, Unions and Politics, 1910–1947* (Aldershot, 1996).

Challinor, R., 'Jimmy Stewart and his Revolting Children', *Bulletin of the North-east Group for the Study of Labour History*, 17 (1983), pp.6–10.

Challinor, R., *The Struggle for Hearts and Minds* (Whitley Bay, 1995).

Chomsky, N., *American Power and the New Mandarins* (1971).

Clark, D., *We do not Want the Earth. History of the South Shields Labour Party* (Whitley Bay, 1992).

Clark, J., Heinemann, M., Margolies, D. and Snee, C., *Culture and Crisis in Britain in the 30s* (1979).

Clarke, J.F. and McDermott, T.P., *Newcastle and District Trades Council, 1873–1973. Centenary History* (Newcastle, 1973).

Cleary, J.M., *Catholic Social Action in Britain 1909–1959. A History of the Catholic Social Guild* (Oxford, 1961).

Clinton, A., *The Trade Union Rank and File. Trades Councils in Britain, 1900–40* (Manchester, 1977).

Cohen, G., *The Failure of a Dream. The ILP From Disaffiliation to World War II* (2007).

Cole, G.D.H., *A History of the Labour Party from 1914* (New York, 1969).

Cook, J., *Apprentices of Freedom* (1979).

Copsey, N., *Anti-Fascism in Britain* (2000).

Copsey, N. and Renton, D. (eds), *British Fascism, the Labour Movement and the State* (2005).

Corthorn, P., *In the Shadow of the Dictators. The British Left in the 1930s* (2006).

Croucher, R., *We Refuse to Starve in Silence. A History of the National Unemployed Workers Movement, 1920–46* (1987).

Donald, M. and Rees, T., *Reinterpreting Revolution in Twentieth Century Europe* (2001).

Douglass, D., *The Miners of North Durham* (Doncaster, 1975).

——. *Pit Life in County Durham. Rank and File Movements and Workers' Control* (Oxford, 1972).

Durgan, A., 'Freedom Fighters or Comintern Army? The International Brigades in Spain', *International Socialism*, 86 (1999), pp.109–132.

Durham Strong Words Collective, *But the World Goes on the Same. Changing Times in Durham Pit Villages* (Whitley Bay, 1979).

Eaton, G., *Neath and the Spanish Civil War* (Neath, 1980).

Edwards, J., *The British Government and the Spanish Civil War, 1936–1939* (1979).

Fielding, S., *Class and Ethnicity. Irish Catholics in England, 1880–1939* (Buckingham, 1993).

Fishman, N., *The British Communist Party and the Trade Unions, 1933–1945* (Aldershot, 1995).

Fleay, C. and Sanders, M.L., 'The Labour Spain Committee: Labour Party Policy and the Spanish Civil War', *Historical Journal*, 28:1 (1985), pp.187–197.

Foot, M., *Aneurin Bevan, 1897–1945, Vol.1* (1982).

Francis, H., 'Welsh Miners and the Spanish Civil War', *Journal of Contemporary History*, 5:3 (1970), pp.177–191.

——. *Miners Against Fascism. Wales and the Spanish Civil War* (1984).

——. '"Say Nothing and Leave in the Middle of the Night": The Spanish Civil War Revisited', *History Workshop Journal*, 32 (1991), pp.69–76.

——. and Smith, D., *The Fed. A History of the South Wales Miners in the Twentieth Century* (Cardiff, 1998).

Fyrth, J., (ed.), *Britain, Fascism and the Popular Front* (1985).

——. *The Signal Was Spain* (1986).

——. 'The Aid Spain Movement in Britain, 1936–39', *History Workshop Journal*, 35 (1993), pp.153–164.

Garside, W.R., *The Durham Miners, 1919–1960* (1971).

Gibb, M.H. and Callcott, M., 'The Labour Party in the North-east Between the Wars', *Bulletin of the North-east Group for the Study of Labour History*, 8 (1974), pp.9–19.

Graham, F., *The Battle of Jarama* (Newcastle, 1987).

——. *The Spanish Civil War. Battles of Brunete and the Aragon* (Newcastle, 1999).

Graham, H. and Preston, P. (eds.), *The Popular Front in Europe* (1987).

Hall, C., *Disciplina Camaradas. Four English Volunteers in Spain, 1936–39* (Pontefract, 1994).

Hopkins, J.K., *Into the Heart of the Fire. The British in the Spanish Civil War* (Stanford, California, 1998).

Howard, S., 'Dawdon in the Third Period: the Dawdon Dispute of 1929 and the Communist Party', *Bulletin of the North-east Group for the Study of Labour History*, 21 (1987), pp.3–16.

Howson, G., *Arms for Spain* (New York, 1998).

Hughes, T.O., *Winds of Change the Roman Catholic Church and Society in Wales, 1918–1962* (Cardiff, 1999).

Jackson, A., *British Women and the Spanish Civil War* (2002).

Jackson, D.M., "'Garibaldi or the Pope!" Newcastle's Irish Riot of 1866', *North-east History*, 34 (2001), pp.49–82.

Jupp, J., *The Radical Left in Britain, 1931–1941* (1982).

Keating, J., 'The Making of the Catholic Labour Activist: the Catholic Social Guild and the Catholic Worker's College, 1909–1939?', *Labour History Review*, 59:3 (1994), pp.44–56.

Kingsford, P., *The Hunger Marchers in Britain 1920–1940* (1982).

Klugmann, J., *History of the Communist Party of Great Britain, Vol.2. The General Strike, 1925–26* (1969).

Lewis, J., *The Left Book Club. An Historical Record* (Gollancz, 1970).

Lynn, P., 'The Influence of Class and Gender: Female Political Organisations in County Durham During the Inter War Years', *Bulletin of the North-east Group for the Study of Labour History*, 31 (1997), pp.43–64.

——. 'The Impact of Women. The Shaping of Political Allegiance in County Durham, 1918–1945', *The Local Historian*, 23:3 (1998), pp.159–175.

MacDermott, T., 'The Irish in Nineteenth Century Tyneside', *Bulletin of the North-east Group for the Study of Labour History*, 16 (1982), pp.43–46.

Macintyre, S., *Little Moscows. Communism and Working Class Militancy in Inter-war Britain* (1980).

Manders, F.W.D., *A History of Gateshead* (Gateshead, 1973).

Mason, A., *The General Strike in the North-east* (Hull, 1970).

Mates, L., 'Britain's De Facto Popular Front? The Case of the Tyneside Foodship Campaign, 1938–1939', *Labour History Review*, 69:1 (2004), pp.323–345.

——. 'A "Most Fruitful Period"? The North-east District Communist Party and the Popular Front Period, 1935–9', *North-east History*, 36 (2004), pp.54–98.

——. 'Durham and South Wales Miners and the Spanish Civil War', *Twentieth Century British History*, 17:3 (2006), pp.373–395.

——. 'The North-east and the Campaigns for a Popular Front, 1938–9', *Northern History*, XLIII (2) (2006), pp.273–301.

McCord, N., 'Some aspects of north-east England in the nineteenth century, *Northern History*, 8 (1972), pp.73–88.

——. (ed.), *Essays in Tyneside Labour History* (Newcastle, 1977).

McIlroy, J., Morgan, K. and Campbell, A., (eds), *Party People, Communist Lives: Explorations in Biography* (2001).

——., McLoughlin, B., Campbell, A. and Halstead, J., "Forging the Faithful: the British at the International Lenin School", *Labour History Review*, 68:1 (2003), pp.99–128.

Moore, R., *Pitmen, Preachers and Politics* (Cambridge, 1974).

Morgan, K., *Against Fascism and War. Ruptures and Continuities in British Communist Politics, 1935–1941* (Manchester, 1989).

——. *Harry Pollitt* (Manchester, 1993).

Morris, A.J.A., *C.P. Trevelyan, 1870–1958. Portrait of a Radical* (Belfast, 1977).

Mowat, C.L., *Britain Between the Wars, 1918–1940* (1987).

Naylor, B.E., 'Ramsay Macdonald and Seaham Labour Politics', *Bulletin of the North-east Group for the Study of Labour History*, 15 (1981), pp.3–47.

Peirats, J., *The CNT in the Spanish Revolution Vol.2* (Sussex, 2005).

Perry, M., *The Jarrow Crusade: Protest and Legend* (Sunderland, 2005).

Pickard, T., *Jarrow March* (1982).

Pimlott, B., *Labour and the Left in the 1930s* (Cambridge, 1977).

——. *Hugh Dalton* (1986).

Potts, A. and Wade, E., *Stand True. NCMA–NUM, 1875–1975* (Blyth, 1975).

——. '"Bevin to Beat the Bankers": Ernest Bevin's Gateshead Campaign of 1931', *Bulletin of the North-east Group for the Study of Labour History*, 11 (1977), pp.28–39.

——. 'Forty Years On. The Labour Party in Sunderland 1900–1945', *Bulletin of the North-east Group for the Study of Labour History*, 24 (1990), pp.12–18.

——. *Zilliacus. A Life for Peace and Socialism* (2002).

Preston, P., *A Concise History of the Spanish Civil War* (2nd edition, 1996).

Pugh, M., 'The Liberal Party and the Popular Front', *English Historical Review*, CXXI, 494 (2006), pp.1327–1350.

——. *"Hurrah for the Blackshirts!" Fascists and Fascism in Britain between the Wars* (2006).

Riddell, N., 'The Catholic Church and the Labour Party, 1918–1931', *Twentieth Century British History*, 8:2 (1997), pp.165–193.

Royle, E. (ed.), *Issues of Regional Identity* (Manchester, 1998).

Rust, W., *Britons in Spain* (1939).

Samuel, R. (ed.), *Miners, Quarrymen and Slate Workers* (1977).

Savage, M., *The Dynamics of Working Class Politics. The Labour Movement in Preston, 1880–1940* (Cambridge, 1987).

Saville, J., *The Labour Movement in Britain. A Commentary* (1988).

Slowe, P., *Manny Shinwell. An Authorised Biography* (1993).

Spence, J., 'William Parlett, the man who nearly got away', *North-east History*, 36 (2005), pp.42–48.

Squires, M., *The Aid to Spain Movement in Battersea, 1936–1939* (1994).

Stevenson, J. and Cook, C., *Britain in the Depression. Society and Politics, 1929–1939* (2nd. edition, 1994).

Stradling, R., *Cardiff and the Spanish Civil War* (Cardiff, 1996).

——. *Wales and the Spanish Civil War: The Dragon's Dearest Cause* (Cardiff, 2004).

Thomas, H., *The Spanish Civil War* (3rd edition, 1977).

Thompson, F.M.L. (ed.), *The Cambridge Social History of Britain 1750–1950, Volume One. Regions and Communities* (Cambridge, 1990).

Thorpe, A. (ed.), *The Failure of Political Extremism in Interwar Britain* (Exeter, 1988).

——. *The British General Election of 1931* (Oxford, 1991).

——. *Britain in the 1930s. The Deceptive Decade* (Oxford, 1992).

——. *A History of the British Labour Party* (1997).

——. 'Stalinism and British Politics', *Historical Journal*, 83:272 (1998), pp.608–627.

——. 'Comintern "Control" of the Communist Party of Great Britain, 1920–1943', *English Historical Review*, 63:452 (1998), pp.637–662.

——. 'The Membership of the Communist Party of Great Britain, 1920–1945', *Historical Journal*, 43:3 (2000), pp.777–800.

Todd, N., *In Excited Times. The People Against the Blackshirts* (Whitley Bay, 1995).

Vernon, B.D., *Ellen Wilkinson, 1891–1947* (1982).

Vilar, P., *La Guerra Civil Española* (Barcelona, 2000).

Watkins, K.W., *Britain Divided. The Effect of the Spanish Civil War on British Political Opinion* (1963).

Watson, D., 'To the Head Through the Heart: The Newcastle Left Book Club Theatre Guild, 1937–1939', *Bulletin of the North-east Group for the Study of Labour History*, 23 (1989), pp.3–21.

——. and Corcoran, J., *An Inspiring Example. The North-east of England and the Spanish Civil War, 1936–1939* (1996).

——. 'Bobbie Qualie, 1909–1982', *North-east Labour History*, 30 (1996), pp.66–67.

——. 'Politics and Humanitarian Aid: Basque Refugees in the North-east and Cumbria During the Spanish Civil War', *North-east History*, 36 (2005), pp.9–41.

Williams, C., Alexander, B. and Gorman, J., *Memorials of the Spanish Civil War* (Stroud, 1996).

Worley, M., *Class Against Class: The Communist Party in Britain Between the Wars* (2000).

Unpublished Theses

Baxell, R., 'The British Battalion of the International Brigades in the Spanish Civil War, 1936–9' (LSE, PhD, 2002).

Cooter, R.J., 'The Irish in County Durham and Newcastle', (Durham University, MA, 1972).

Drake, P.D., 'Labour and Spain: British Labour's Response to the Spanish Civil War With Particular Reference to the Labour Movement in Birmingham' (Birmingham University, M.Litt, 1977).

Ennis, F., 'The Jarrow March of 1936: The Symbolic Expression of the Protest', (Durham University, MA, 1982).

Flinn, A., '"Prospects for Socialism". The Character and Implantation of Working-class Activism in the Manchester Area, 1933–1941' (Manchester University, PhD, 1999).

Francis, D.H., 'The South Wales Miners and the Spanish Civil War: A Study in Internationalism' (University of Swansea, PhD, 1978).

Keating, J.E., 'Roman Catholics, Christian Democracy and the British Labour Movement 1910–1960' (Manchester University, PhD, 1992).

Mates, L.H., 'The United Front and the Popular Front in the North-east of England, 1936–1939' (Newcastle University, PhD, 2002).

——. 'From Revolutionary to Reactionary: The Life of Will Lawther' (Newcastle University, MA, 1996).

McDermott, M., 'Irish Catholics and the British Labour Movement: A Study with Particular Reference to London 1918–1970' (Kent University, MA, 1978).

Scott, C., 'A Comparative Re–examination of Anglo-Irish Relations in Nineteenth Century Manchester, Liverpool and Newcastle-upon-Tyne' (Durham University, PhD, 1998).

INDEX